Contents

PART I

Enhancing the Quality of Working Life

PART II

Defining and Measuring the Quality of Working Life

PART III

Changing the Quality of Working Life

PART IV

Technology and Quality of Working Life

THE  QUALITY OF WORKING LIFE

VOLUME ONE

Problems, Prospects and the State of the Art

LOUIS E. DAVIS
ALBERT B. CHERNS
AND ASSOCIATES

 THE FREE PRESS
A Division of Macmillan Publishing Co., Inc.
NEW YORK

Collier Macmillan Publishers
LONDON

To E.K.D. and B.S.C.

The Free Press
A Division of Macmillan Publishing Co., Inc.
866 Third Avenue, New York, N.Y. 10022

Collier Macmillan Canada, Ltd.

Library of Congress Catalog Card Number: 74-24369

Printed in the United States of America

printing number
4 5 6 7 8 9 10

Library of Congress Cataloging in Publication Data
Main entry under title:

The quality of working life.

    Includes bibliographical references and index.
    CONTENTS: v. 1. Problems, prospects, and state of the art.--v. 2. Cases and commentary.
    1. Industrial sociology--Congresses. 2. Job satisfaction--Congresses. 3. Psychology, Industrial--Congresses. 4. Industrial organization--Congresses. I. Davis, Louis E. II. Cherns, Albert.
HD6955.Q3   301.5'5   74-24369
ISBN 0-02-907390-1 (v.1)
ISBN 0-02-907380-4 pbk. (v.1)

THE QUALITY OF WORKING LIFE

PART V

Quality of Working Life—The Context of Change

PART VI

Quality of Working Life—The Context of Bargaining

PART VII

Quality of Working Life—A Central Issue in Industrial Relations

Contributors

Louis E. Davis is Professor of Organizational Sciences, Graduate School of Management, and Chairman, Center for Quality of Working Life, Institute of Industrial Relations, University of California, Los Angeles. He was Visiting Fellow, Tavistock Institute of Human Relations, London; Professor of Industrial Engineering and Director, Human Factors in Technology Program, University of California, Berkeley; Lucas Professor, University of Birmingham, United Kingdom; and Senior Staff Advisor, O.E.E.C., Paris.

Albert B. Cherns is Professor and Head, Department of Social Sciences, Loughborough University. He was Secretary of Social Science Research Council and Head of Human Science Division, Science Research Council (formerly DSIR) of Great Britain; Chief Research Officer, Training Command, RAF; Senior Psychologist, Air Ministry. He is a governor of Ashorne Hill College (for management), and a member of Council of Tavistock Institute, and Research Council of International Sociological Association.

Judith B. Agassi is Senior Lecturer, Ruppin Institute for Kibbutz Management, Israel. She holds a Ph.D. in Sociology from University of London, and has taught at Emmanuel College, Boston College, Hebrew University, Haifa and Tel Aviv Universities.

Hans Berglind is Associate Professor of Sociology, University of Stockholm. He is currently doing research on problems of the labor market, employment possibilities for the "hard-to-employ," and the Swedish welfare system.

Alfred W. Clark is Professor of Sociology, La Trobe University, Melbourne. He was a Senior Social Scientist at Tavistock Institute of Human Relations, London, taught social psychology, and has been a consultant to industry and government. He is managing editor of *Human Relations* and with N. R. Yeomans, he is co-author of *Fraser House: Theory, Practice and Evaluation of a Therapeutic Community* (1969). Recently he edited *Experiences in Action Research* (1975).

Peter A. Clark is a lecturer in Organizational Sociology, Management Centre, Bradford University, England. He is developing a framework of organizational structures which incorporates social definitions of time. He is author of *Organizational Design: Theory and Practice* (1972) and *Action Research and Organizational Change* (1972).

Yves P. Delamotte is presently Directeur de l'Agence Nationale pour l'Amélioration des Conditions de Travail, Paris, and Directeur du Centre de Recherches en Sciences Sociales du Travail (Université Paris Sud). He is author of books and articles related to quality of working life and to industrial relations.

Henry Douard is Research Manager, Institute for Research and Development on Enterprise and Personnel, Paris, studying working conditions, work structuring, etc. He was a consulting industrial psychologist and is a member of the French Psychology Society and French Professional Relations Studies Association.

Robert Dubin is Professor of Sociology and Administration, University of California, Irvine. He is author and co-author of eight books and more than fifty articles on sociological theory, organizational and interpersonal behavior and industrial relations, work as a central life interest, and the sources of attachment to work.

James S. Dyer is Associate Professor of Operations Research, Graduate School of Management, University of California, Los Angeles. He was associated with Rand Corporation and Jet Propulsion Laboratory, and his papers have appeared in *Management Science, Operations Research,* and *Socio-Economic Planning Sciences.*

William A. Faunce is Professor of Sociology, Michigan State University. His primary professional interest is the sociology of work, and he is concerned with the way in which work-related values enter into status assignment and self-esteem maintenance processes.

Karl-O. Faxen is head of the Research Department of the Swedish Employers' Confederation since 1965. He is also Assistant Professor of Economics, University of Stockholm, since 1957.

Bertil Gardell is Associate Professor of Work Psychology, Psychological Laboratories, University of Stockholm. He was Head, Research Group on Social Psychology of Working Life, and worked in the Swedish Council for Social Science Research. Publications include *Effects of Technology on Alienation and Mental Health and Participation.* His present research is on occupational stress and work-leisure relationships.

Eli Ginzberg is chairman of the National Commission for Manpower Policy, Chairman of the Board of the Manpower Demonstration Research Corporation, and consultant to government, voluntary and private organizations. He is author of more than forty books primarily in the field of human resources and manpower, including *The Manpower Connection: Education and Work* (in press, Harvard).

James G. Goodale is Associate Professor, Faculty of Administrative Studies, York University, Toronto. He holds a Ph.D. in Industrial Psychology and concentrates his research on measurement of worker attitudes and behavior. Co-authors D. T. Hall, R. J. Burke, and R. C. Joyner are members of the Faculty of Administrative Studies, York University, Toronto.

Reine Hansson is Senior Research Fellow, Swedish Council for Personnel Administration, Stockholm, and Secretary for Research of the Development Council for Cooperative Questions (on Industrial Democracy) jointly established by the employers and trades unions confederations.

Phillip G. Herbst is Research Director. Work Research Institutes, Oslo. He holds a Ph.D. in Sociology from Oslo University and a D.Litt. from Melbourne for autonomous group functioning. He did research on the family at Melbourne and Pennsylvania Universities. While on the staff of the Tàvistock Institute he did research on sociotechnical systems.

Neal Q. Herrick is Senior Fellow, Academy for Contemporary Problems, Columbus, Ohio. He initiated the U.S. Department of Labor's triennial survey of working conditions and headed the Labor/HEW Task Force which drafted the Occupational Safety and Health Act first submitted to the Congress in 1968.

Marvin Hoffenberg is Professor and Director of Master of Public Administration Program, Department of Political Science, University of California, Los Angeles. He worked as an economist in U.S. Bureau of Labor Statistics, Rand Corporation, and Committee for Economic Development among others. His current research is on public organizations and public policy.

Edward E. Lawler, III is Professor of Psychology and Program Director, the Institute for Social Research, University of Michigan. He taught at Yale University. His books include *Behavior in Organizations* (1975), *Motivation and Work Organizations* (1970) and *Pay and Organizational Effectiveness* (1971).

Michael Maccoby is Director of the Harvard Project on Technology, Work and Character, a Fellow, Institute for Policy Studies, Washington, D.C., and is in private practice of psychoanalysis. He holds a Ph.D. from Harvard and is a graduate of the Mexican Psychoanalytic Institute.

John J. McDonough is Associate Professor, Graduate School of Management, University of California, Los Angeles. He is currently investigating the influence of structure as an organizing force in a variety of contemporary organizations ranging from accounting firms to community organizations.

Rudolf Meidner is an economist at Swedish Trade Union Confederation (LO) for special projects. He holds a Ph.D., was Head of Research Department, LO (1945–66), and Director, Swedish Institute for Labor Studies, University of Stockholm (1966–71).

Joseph Mire is an independent labor researcher who holds a Doctor of Law from University of Vienna and served in the Vienna Chamber of Labor (1930s). He taught at Ruskin College, Oxford, and taught and researched at University of Wisconsin, American Federation of State, County, and Municipal Employees, and School of International Service, the American University, Washington, D.C.

Michael J. Piore is Associate Professor of Economics, Massachusetts Institute of Technology. He holds a Ph.D. from Harvard University. His research has centered on manpower and industrial relations issues, particularly technological change, race, poverty and immigration, and he is currently comparing the structure of low wage labor markets in the United States and western Europe.

Jean-Daniel Reynaud is Professor, Conservatoire National des Arts et Métiers, Paris, and President elect, International Industrial Relations Association. He is author of *Les Syndicat en France* (1974), and *Tendances et volonté de la société francaise* (1966).

Stanley E. Seashore is Professor of Psychology, University of Michigan, and Program Director, Institute for Social Research. Since 1950 his research has been concerned with the social and psychological factors that optimize working conditions and organizational effectiveness.

Harold L. Sheppard is Staff Social Scientist, Upjohn Institute for Employment Research, Washington, D.C. He is author of several studies in problems of work and employment, including *Where Have All the Robots Gone?; The Job Hunt; Economic Failure, Extremism, and Alienation; and Poverty and Wealth in America.* He taught at Wayne State University (1947–59), was an Assistant Administrator of the Area Redevelopment Administration (1961–63), and a Staff Director of the U.S. Senate Committee on Aging (1959–61).

Gerald I. Susman is Associate Professor of Organizational Behavior, College of Business Administration, Pennsylvania State University. He holds a Ph.D. from University of California, Los Angeles, and is now engaged in coal mining organization and job experiments.

Shin-ichi Takezawa is Professor of Industrial Relations, Rikkyo University, Tokyo, and Chairman of the Japan Quality of Working Life Committee. He has written extensively on behavioral aspects of personnel and industrial relations, including *The Other Worker* (with A. M. Whitehill, Jr., 1968) and a number of articles in English.

James C. Taylor is Assistant Professor of Sociotechnical Systems, Graduate School of Management, University of California, Los Angeles, since 1972. From 1964–69 he was involved in organizational action research at Institute for Social Research, University of Michigan, and in 1970–71 at Center for Utilization for Social Science Research, Loughborough University, England.

Einar Thorsrud is Research Director, Work Research Institutes, Oslo. He was Program Director of the Norwegian Industrial Democracy Program (1962–72), Associate Professor of Psychology, Technical University, Trondheim, and Director of the Institute for Industrial Social Research, Trondheim (1958–65). He graduated from the University of Oslo, 1948, and worked in industry for five years.

Eric Trist is Professor of Organizational Behavior and Ecology, Wharton School, University of Pennsylvania, and Chairman of the University's Management and Behavioral Science Center. He was Chairman of the Human Resources Center of the Tavistock Institute of Human Relations, London.

Kenneth F. Walker is Professor of Industrial Relations, European Institute of Business Administration (INSEAD), Fontainbleu, France. He was Director of the International Institute for Labor Studies since 1972, Senior Staff Associate of the International Institute for Labor Studies (1966–71), Professor of Psychology, University of Western Australia (1952–65), and staff member, Australian Department of Labor (1942–51).

Richard E. Walton is Edsel Bryant Ford Professor and Director of Research, Harvard Graduate School of Business Administration, and a member of the International Council for the Quality of Working Life. He has helped design a number of quality of work life innovations in manufacturing plants.

Preface

THE structure and contents of this volume were first proposed by the Planning Committee for the International Conference on the Quality of Working Life, 1972. With the exception of selection 1, "Assessment," the contributions were written as background papers for the conference where they served that purpose well. The reports of the task forces were the only written product of the conference.

Since the conference, September 24–29, 1972, each of the selections has been rewritten a number of times and we are thankful to each one of the authors for their patience and support. To our editor Felicitas Hinman, and to our dedicated staff Beverly McDonald, Edith Jacobson, Debbie Judkiewicz, and Ann Tanner, we owe a debt of gratitude greater than we can express. We are thankful for the advice provided by Professor Arthur N. Turner in his review, and for the overview and chapter summaries provided by John Damm.

Finally, we deeply appreciate the advice and support of Basil Whiting whose keen interest and high standards have contributed immeasurably to the outcome.

Los Angeles   L. E. D. and A. B. C.

Prologue
Workers' Attitude—A Key to
the Quality of Working Life?

Kenneth F. Walker

THE worker's attitudes play a critical role in the acceptance of any changes that are intended to improve the quality of his working life. In his attitudes he voices his concern with the procedures by which various aspects of his working life are determined, and he wants to make his own decision as to his participation. However, "what the worker wants" is not an infallible guide to quality of working life. There must be multilateral consensus by all parties concerned, for an enterprise is a *coalition* of individuals who may have competing interests.

Attitudes, moreover, are dynamic; they are affected by the forces of information and persuasion and the subtle interplay of changes in conditions at the workplace or outside of it. Thus it is difficult, but perhaps not essential, to determine the degree of their rationality. A more fruitful approach in this context is posing the questions: What are the conditions which influence a worker's attitudes and behavior? And to what extent can workers' attitudes be inferred from available evidence?

This prologue is based on the author's paper, by the same title, presented at the International Conference on Quality of Working Life, September 1972.

1

We need to know both what workers say and what they do, not only under conditions of deliberate intervention, but what they say and do freely as well. Overt behavior, however, is difficult to interpret because different workers may act in the same manner for different reasons. Likewise, similar attitudes may be expressed in different behaviors by different workers. And there is the possibility of conflict of values and of interest in the quality of working life among different individuals and groups of workers, making it even harder to generalize from limited samples.

Because an individual's total life situation affects his attitude toward his working life, two questions are foremost in our mind: To what extent is working a central life interest? How does his working life affect a worker's outside life, and vice versa?

The elements of relevance to the worker's quality of working life involve the task, the physical work environment and the social environment within the plant, the administrative system of the enterprise, and the relationship between life on and off the job. The factors bearing upon the relative importance attached to these elements include demographic considerations, socioeconomic status, culture and personality, politics and ideology, and the "situation," which is concerned with technology and size of the plant.

Any effective approach to the enhancement of the quality of working life, therefore, must explore the weight of these factors on the worker's attitudes toward all the elements that make up his working life.

PART
I

Enhancing
the Quality of
Working Life

Growing Crisis

THE present cultural, social, and technological period—the industrial era, which began about 1800—is slowly waning, impelled by changes in social values and developments in technology. The relationship between work in its conventional form and economic production is growing tenuous and, as a result, the meaning both of work and of man's relationship to society is called into question. Also called into question is the widely accepted belief that a dehumanized work life is the inevitable cost of acquiring material rewards above subsistence levels. Growing numbers of people refuse to accept the inevitability of the kind of working life that is prevalent in most of the Western industrialized nations.

Society's response to these large-scale changes displays considerable confusion, as may be expected, given both their pervasiveness and newness. The disarray is captured by the following quotations, which focus on the work environment against the background of social and environmental pollution at a time when many needs are being given voice.

> Even in Sweden, the amount of attention given to conservation of the natural environment when compared to that given to the working environment is absurd; there may be storms of agitation about a few square kilometers of national parkland in far northern Lapland but silence about the obvious deficiencies in the working environment. Certain features of Nature which in Sweden can be enjoyed by just a few people during the short summer, attract public opinion to a far greater extent than do problems concerning the environment in which millions of people have to spend the principal part of their productive lives.[1]

> I read with some interest a news article describing your project "designs to improve the quality of working life in the United States." I note with some amusement and a great deal of skepticism that you hope to get results by calling in scholars and management experts.
> Why don't you call in the people who are doing the work and who are unhappy with their situations because of management's stupidity or indifference.
> After all, I've been at it for 30 years—and not only could I tell them how to make it more pleasant but could save them a ton of money. The real problem is that as long as they make the money, what do they care if the workers are uncomfortable, or unhappy.[2]

4

The capability of technology to provide abundantly for our material needs has supported the very large shift to services both private and public. At present, almost 60 percent of the U.S. work force is in the service sector, but service institutions seem to be using industrial models for their organizations and jobs. As a result, there may now be even more dehumanized jobs than there were a generation ago. This appears to indicate that the dominant influence on organizational form is not technology, but the values of society and its managers.

Over the past twenty-five years it has not been fashionable in the United States to raise any questions about the quality of working life. Instead, we have been preoccupied with the mirage of leisure and the bogey of technology. Fortunately or unfortunately, the problems confronting society do not follow intellectual fashion. Confronting us is the need to accept, as a national goal, both public and private responsibility for the quality of working life in all of productive society, particularly in facing the transition into the postindustrial era, if we are to develop useful social policy and devise workable responses to problems.

Five Salient Issues of the 1970s

The socioeconomic values that evolved in the United States over the last hundred years have carried within them the seeds of issues now coming to the forefront.

1. The pervasive acceptance of alienation as a cost of having more jobs and/or more income is now seen as a burden that, in the United States, only the older white middle class is willing to bear. Significant numbers are telling us they are not prepared to participate in productive society under these conditions. This issue raises the value question which sees men as spare parts in dead-end, locked-in jobs or as "operating units," to be adjusted and used for the needs of society. Also, the effects of dehumanized work life on other aspects of social life must be considered.

2. As noted above, industrial culture is spreading to the service sector, encroaching on personal services and professional jobs with negative consequences for workers as well as clients. But there may yet be opportunities to demonstrate that humane jobs and organizations can be developed for mass service organizations.

3. The spreading of advanced technology is absorbing routine activities, giving rise to fears over availability of jobs since men are still seen as competing with, rather than as being complementary to, machines. Changes in social priorities can open new functions previously unseen, and much work needs to be done in designing appropriate avenues for all who work to learn and relearn as job content changes.

4. Accelerating change in technology raises questions of how to develop flexible people and organizations, and how to absorb change as a continuing part of working life. New social inventions are called for to satisfy the needs of working society without imposing costly rigidities.

5. To build a basis for an orderly transition into the postindustrial era, particular attention must be given to providing the means by which the disadvantaged and powerless can progress into the mainstream of society; simply providing entry will not do.

Some Needed Responses

Western industrial societies have tried in a variety of pragmatic and ideological ways to achieve congruence between the quality of organizational life and the quality of social and political life. These attempts have taken many forms—from localized participation of employees on production committees and works councils to representative participation on boards of directors. In the United States, unions have sought economic and institutional social justice through collective bargaining. Management has tried, through various devices and managerial styles, to encourage participation and commitment of organization members. An enduring notion of the early 1900s, "industrial democracy," is seen today in Norway and Sweden as democratizing the workplace, meaning that all jobs in an organization should permit the qualities of democratic society to be maintained.

In short, there has been significant but isolated research on organizations and jobs directed at enhancing the quality of working life, and experience to date provides reasonably adequate indications that humanization of work, far from imposing economic costs, yields societal, personal, and economic gains. *Thus a body of knowledge and techniques common to, and usable by, the institutions and organizations centrally concerned with solving the problems of transition into the postindustrial era is partially available. Filling this gap is seen as crucial for the 1970s.*

Creating the Enabling Conditions

It is of critical importance to extend and sustain a systematic, comprehensive national inquiry (associated with similar inquiries in other countries) into the quality of working life and the prospect and need for revitalization of work. Both the content and the structure of high-quality employment and employing organizations must be developed, capable of coping in the evolving era of sophisticated, rapidly changing technology.

Managements will have to be concerned with the best use of the talents available in the organization, providing challenge and learning opportunities to members, and with developing appropriate jobs and organizational forms to suit the new technology. Organized labor will have to be concerned with the growth as well as the decline of tasks, learning and adaptability, rewards and satisfactions, and future structures of formal relationships with management. Government officials will have to be concerned with the effects of alienation on citizen behavior and with education, employment, and manpower programs which are also concerned with enhancing the quality of working life.

Each of these constituencies has particular concerns over, and is subject to, different risks and pressures in regard to the revitalization of work. Enhancement of the quality of working life can occur most effectively if both the technological and social systems of organizations are considered. The needs, concerns, and interests of everyone involved in work organizations must therefore be represented.

The Present Environment

A number of U.S. and Western European organizations, some in association with university researchers, have undertaken experiments that have changed conditions and relationships and led to enhanced satisfactions, more qualified people, and greater commitment at work. *The problem now is to determine how these pioneering changes can be generalized, built upon, and extended, in the face of the following:*

1. The diffusion of the research developments is exceedingly limited and has not spread very far among jobs at the lower levels of organizations. At higher levels, however, some developments are spreading in almost all institutions—a case of the privileged becoming more privileged.

2. The changes introduced reflect a number of different organizational intervention strategies associated with different researchers, who come from different disciplines, refer to different theories, and have different values. Largely, researchers and interveners are talking past each other, perhaps having in common only the objective of enhancing the quality of working life.

3. A deterrent to confronting institutional leaders with quality of working life issues is the apparent paucity of information and data about the various attempts undertaken in that direction. These difficulties apply equally to research and to practice, creating a curious situation in which occasional books on the subject are treated as prophetic pronouncements, and professional articles as reports of idiosyncratic happenings. These treatments indeed may be the consequence of the lack of generally available background information and knowledge of specific undertakings. But, within

schools concerned with the training of professionals, the same knowledge gap contributes to the continued transmission of prescriptions based on industrial-era concepts that have become as far removed from reality as old wives' tales.

4. Organizations that have gone farthest in changing their structures, job content, and relationships are by various social and economic indicators the better ones. As they continue these developments, the quality of working life in the best organizations becomes even better and that in poor organizations becomes relatively worse.

5. Organizational leaders, looking for objective results and conceptual guidance from researchers, are confused by the welter of disjointed and sometimes conflicting information on quality of work life measures and approaches that is placed before them.

The Opportunity

The key opportunity before us lies in formulating a coherent body of theory and practice on how to create the conditions for a humane working life in its relevant social environments. Researchers and practitioners must learn how to define the situation, how to study ongoing social systems, how to intervene in such situations with enhanced probability of success, how to identify and measure a successful outcome, how to develop conceptual bases within institutions that will support the diffusion of outcomes, and how to assure that continued adaptation will take place.

When properly understood, advanced technology is capable of providing a richness of alternatives for designing social systems. Far from having to subordinate jobs and organizations to the "technological imperative," greater opportunities are becoming available to humanize working life, since man no longer has to be either a slave or an appendage to the machine. There are a substantial and increasing number of instances in which the richness of alternatives do permit the design of technology to suit the needs of humane social organization and jobs.

The complexity of the issues and local problems, in addition to the magnitude of the changes that will have to be made, calls for approaches centered on research, experimentation, testing, and evaluation in ongoing institutions. Researchers and practitioners from different disciplines will need to join with members of cooperating private and public organizations to develop changes growing out of generalized concepts and theory. However, the first needs to be met are these: (1) bring together the knowledge and experience acquired so far, as well as the results achieved; (2) assess experiences to date; (3) examine and strengthen conceptual, theoretical, and value bases; and (4) generalize from the experimental learnings. The contents of these volumes provide a beginning.

The Sharing of Knowledge

In response to the first requirement, a group of scholars from the United States and England met late in December 1971 to discuss the need for and contents of what was to be the first worldwide review of knowledge on the quality of working life. Two similar meetings, largely of European scholars, followed shortly. Briefly, both the American and European scholars agreed that the tide of events in Western societies was such that the issues and problems surrounding the quality of working life must be made visible in view of mounting public concern. This shared belief was the basis for examining present knowledge about the determinants of the quality of working life, the consequences for individuals, organizations, and larger society when that quality is low and when it is high, what is known about enhancing it and what can be done about it. It was decided to bring together researchers and professionals with experience in this area, addressing themselves to issues and developments which are now salient and providing for other researchers, managers, union leaders, government executives, and policy makers a review of the state of knowledge and further action and research needs.

Papers and case reports on issues the planners decided were central were requested from experts on the study or change of the quality of working life. Many came from Western Europe, where both concern and experience have long existed in a number of countries. An international conference on quality of working life was convened on September 25–29, 1972, at Arden House, Harriman, New York. Here, in addition to exchange of ideas, major needs and approaches to them were to be developed by task forces, using the papers and cases as references. A number of questions formulated were considered foremost in affecting the quality of working life:

1. How can one define, evaluate, and measure the quality of working life in order to take appropriate action and establish policy in the public interest?
2. What is known about the aspects of work organization, jobs, careers, and so on, that affect the quality of working life?
3. What is known about enhancing the quality of working life that can be agreed upon and recommended?
4. What have been the consequences of enhancing quality of working life for individuals, organizations, and society in general?
5. What values and attitudes exist toward working life among workers, unions, management, and the public?
6. What are the special considerations of labor unions in relation to a high quality of working life?

7.   What are the effects of societal arrangements such as labor markets, legislation, and collective bargaining on quality of working life?

8.   What are the effects of relationships of workers to work organizations and the structure of organizations on quality of working life?

9.   How does technology affect quality of working life and what can be done in application of technology?

10. What has been learned from those changes deliberately undertaken to enhance quality of working life and how is one change to be compared with another?

11. What causes the slow diffusion of knowledge of effects on and means for enhancing quality of working life in Western societies?

These questions and others were thoroughly reviewed and task forces were established on these subjects:

a.   Substantive knowledge about quality of working life
b.   Evaluation
c.   Comparability
d.   Diffusion
e.   Institution building
f.   Intervention
g.   Measurement

The reader will share with the conference participants the review of issues, problems, work in progress, and current status of quality of working life, as seen from the perspective of a variety of disciplines. Although the conference was multidisciplinary, some papers still reflected a single disciplinary view in the face of complexity, indicating a future need that has to be met—the development of well-grounded multidiscipline-based researchers, professionals, and organization leaders. Those concerned with technology, its impact on quality of working life, and its design will find papers upsetting existing conceptions, pointing out that the design of technology includes, in part, social system design, and that design alternatives are available that have been neither conceived nor used before, permitting enhanced quality of working life to be developed, given acceptance of the need to do so.

The reader will gain some insights into new structural forms, new theories, and innovative roles required to aid organizations in changing themselves so as to enhance their members' quality of working life. These discussions begin to reveal the complexity of organizational change efforts, eschewing the overenthusiasm that most often pervades one-dimensional, and therefore simplistic, panaceas such as participative management or organization development. The various perspectives from which quality of working life must be viewed are discussed, beginning with the individual's values, attitudes, and choices of investment of self in work and nonwork life. The context of labor market, its policy and operation, is reviewed, showing the imperfections even in its most dedicated and extended form, as the one now existing in Sweden.

Union attitudes and concerns are examined, revealing the difficulties that will have to be surmounted when unions expand their areas of concern toward comprehensive quality of working life goals for members. Those who learn, through the study of cases, the effects on organizations and individuals of changes enhancing quality of working life will find comprehensive treatment of recent organizational and job changes as well as summary reports and abstracts.

The four selections which, together with this introduction, make up Part I variously examine what is meant by "enhancing the quality of working life." In Selection 1, Cherns and Davis review current developments in Western Europe and the United States and examine future needs for institution building, training, experimentation, and sharing of information. The potential contributions and limitations of the relevant major disciplines are examined. A new concept of "sociotechnical assessment" is introduced as a necessity if the means are to be developed for the humane (and socially appropriate) use of technology in both advanced and developing countries. Examined are the effects on enhancing the quality of working life of the structural situation of unions, social accounting, and such design approaches as sociotechnical systems.

Goals relating to the enhancement of the quality of life at the workplace are broadly discussed by Cherns and Davis in Selection 2, while Herrick and Maccoby, in Selection 3, focus on the need to humanize work as a major goal for the 1970s. Both selections emphasize the twin themes of individual autonomy and noncoercive modes of managing interdependence. Additionally, Herrick and Maccoby emphasize the issues of security and equity for the worker and tend to look primarily to government for developing the needed changes in the legal and economic structures under which employing organizations operate.

In the final selection of Part I, Eric Trist draws on recent experience in Peru to illustrate the crucial relevance of the quality of working life concerns to economic planning decisions, particularly in a developing economy.

NOTES

1. H. Berglind, "Working Conditions, Employment, and Labor Market Policy," selection 26.

2. Personal correspondence, April 1973, in response to the article appearing in many U.S. newspapers reporting the Quality of Working Life Program, Graduate School of Management, University of California, Los Angeles.

1

Assessment of the State of the Art

Albert B. Cherns and Louis E. Davis

QUALITY of working life is characterized as an area of emerging interest and significant impact on advanced societies during the next twenty-five years. The nature and size of the crisis is to be significant—including the related but diverse elements of alienation, growing disillusion in the service sector, perceived scarcity of jobs, as well as the problems of absorbing rapid technical and social changes, on the one hand, and including and incorporating the disenfranchised worker, on the other.

The foremost need at this time is knowledge—more information and techniques common to and usable by institutions centrally involved with solving the problems of enhancing the quality of working life. An important part of this body of knowledge is sociotechnical design, which can be relevant to multiple audiences.

The present environment for quality of working life is described as a welter of industrial and organizational experiments with the problem of how to generalize the findings therefrom. Although many problems are seen in this context (not the least of which is a factional division among social scientists along disciplinary lines, and the rigidities of a belief in technological determinism), clearly there exists the opportunity to share knowledge, and to begin to formulate a coherent theory and practice on how to create the conditions

12

for a humane working life. The International Conference on the Quality of Working Life in 1972 is cited as an initial attempt to realize these opportunities. The papers in the present volume represent the sharing of knowledge from this conference. Significant events since that conference are also noted.

Interest in the United States is growing, as it is in the rest of advanced Western industrial society. Quality of working life as an issue in developing countries is discussed, and is considered increasingly relevant. Sociotechnological assessment is recommended as a necessity for industrial development. The U.S. initiative at this time is recommended to be the development of institutes for training in sociotechnical job and organization design, action research, and diffusion.

Some political and economic implications are discussed, as are significant issues for research and development. Of central importance is the view that we are just commencing on the quest for systematic theory and practice—that training and the sharing of knowledge must enhance competence, but must also anticipate value changes and the options of organizational choice. Enhancing quality of working life will require different programs and training to suit different needs as well as an interdisciplinary thrust.

> The study of man at work is exposed to dangerous
> errors if it does not rest on the study of work itself, on
> the principles of the unity of its several aspects, and
> their reciprocal relationship.[1]

The Present State of Affairs

Since the convening of the international conference on the quality of working life, there has been a large upsurge in Western Europe as well as in the United States in public discussion and publications. Almost daily articles, books, and critiques have appeared. Unfortunately, this has not diminished the confusion and apprehension about (or, for so many, the poverty of) the quality of working life. In the United States we are witness to petty conflicts over who are the true defenders of quality of working life—union leaders, managers, or academics—without visible consequence for those being defended. Confusion continues because of the profusion of simplistic and frequently utopian panaceas as well as the suspect credentials of some of the advocates. The United States government, for example, becoming fearful over productivity, created a National Commission on Productivity. All was well until the quiescent commission, for individually if not institutionally sound reasons, took up the cudgel of improving productivity by enhancing the "quality of work," reinforcing latent union suspicions. There is concern among union leaders that improving quality of work to increase productivity is another underhanded means of weakening the benefits they have won on behalf of their members. Doctrinaire followers are joining sides, one set protecting the past—all is well at work and people are only in it for money—and the other proclaiming disaster is at hand of low job satisfaction.

The altogether extraordinary emphasis on job satisfaction in the current popular and professional press appears to be adding to the confusion and apprehension while not clarifying the fundamental issue—whether to retain or change the existing form of work organization and jobs, that is whether to change the means by which society gets its work done. Measuring job satisfaction takes the existing forms of organization of work as a given. Assuming there exists a phenomenon known as job satisfaction that can be measured reliably, four issues are fundamental to interpreting and using the measures as a basis for action. Two, widespread throughout industrial society, are fundamental to understanding the position of those who accept existing work organizations and jobs: First, work organizations of all kinds are confused with natural biological entities rather than seen as our inventions; even the oldest such invention, the family, having seen a change in its relationship to work, is being questioned. Second, the present dominant forms of work organizations and their jobs are seen as the only effective ones for achieving the goals of society and its members. Flowing from these issues is the position that the existing system should be changed only in response to massive poor outcomes such as high aggregate percentages of job dissatisfaction.

The remaining two issues are concerned with how and what job satisfaction does and does not measure about life in the workplace.[2] Although many technical factors are involved in how it is measured, the third issue is that, fundamentally, job satisfaction measures attitudinal responses to the present job without regard to past, to future, or to other choices. (It does not ask whether you are satisfied with your job relative to what else you think is available to you.) The fourth issue is that job satisfaction as an assessment technique completely overlooks the phenomenon of human adaptability. Most of us learn to adapt to work organizations in which we find ourselves, albeit with varying personal and social costs. Those who cannot adapt leave and are not there to be measured. Still fewer can neither adapt nor leave, becoming the casualties we see raging against the system or themselves.

The virulence of the attacks upon those who have come to see that enhancing the quality of working life will call for new forms of work organization and jobs can well be understood, for this position represents a fundamental challenge to the *status quo ante*. Having left utopian proposals in favor of experimentation with new forms of doing work, both the evidence and the proponents are under attack. There is growing evidence, unfortunately drawn from the few experiments possible to date, that different organizational forms, distribution of power, and job structures provide not only a richer and more rewarding life in the workplace but greater organizational effectiveness as well. Buried by the job satisfaction controversy is the fact that there are other means of structuring work organizations and jobs which possess opportunities for satisfying society's goals and individuals' needs.

Significant Developments in the United States

Perhaps the most significant development in this country since convening the international conference has been the growing attention to the issue of quality of working life; it is very slowly becoming possible for workers to question life in the workplace without being castigated as misfits. Some reactions to the growing discussion have been indicated above. Additionally, there are sharply increased visits by managers, union leaders, and government officials to firms in the United States and Western Europe experimenting with new forms or organization and jobs. Matching the popular press is the flow of articles in technical and professional journals.

1. *Government.* Government reaction, for the most part, is cautious indeed, with some government agencies and officials supporting and others opposing action or research on quality of working life. The strongest response has been to a widely circulated and officially rejected report, *Work in America,*[3] commissioned by the Secretary of Health, Education, and Welfare, which appeared at the end of 1972. The report was based on a series of commissioned[4] papers on various aspects of working life and a review of experimental changes in the workplace as well as some modest recommendations for government action.[5]

Turning now to government as a work organization, there are some attempts in one federal agency at experimentation with organizational structure and jobs inside the government bureaucracy itself. Local governments, too, beset by financial problems and union and citizen demands, are searching for new organization and job designs.

2. *Managements and unions.* A substantial number, but relatively few, organizations are engaged in experiments with organizational structure and job design. The motives behind the experiments range, at one extreme, from deep perceptions that the environments and people who work in organizations have changed in such ways as to call for more democratic, less coercive, and more

fully rewarding work settings. At the other extreme they are seen as a means for enhancing productivity. The purity of the motives may turn out to be irrelevant to the knowledge gained and the demonstration provided for other organizations.

The experiments, however, are giving rise to situations which may develop new areas of conflict between unions and management, in which the loser may be the worker whose interest both purport to be concerned with. All of the known experiments have been management initiated, with very few involving unions in their planning. Thus the reaction of union leaders is one of rising suspicion and, in a few instances, outright hostility.[6] Most needed now is union leadership that will differentiate the methods used in experiments from the potential good for workers, demanding a role in their guidance and further development. There are a few—very few—bright spots coming to the fore among the major unions.

The most encouraging development to date is embodied in the new contracts (1974) between the United Automobile Workers and General Motors, Ford, and Chrysler. These call for the creation of national level joint union-management committees to improve the quality of working life, whose responsibility is to (1) review and evaluate management programs directed at improving the work environment; (2) develop experiments and projects aimed at improved quality of working life; (3) report experimental results and evaluations to the corporation and the union; (4) jointly provide for the cost of outside counsel felt to be necessary and desirable; and (5) urge management and union to encourage their members and representatives to cooperate in experiments and projects.

3. *Researchers and professionals.* Presently, few research groups are involved in the quality of working life. However, a few groups and a substantial number of individual researchers have been concerned with certain aspects of the problem (usually job satisfaction) from the perspective of psychology. Some important sociological studies, such as those of Walker and Guest, Chinoy and others,[7] have focused on automobile assembly workers—the workers perhaps most stringently affected by the ultimate industrial era organization and technology. A growing number of researchers are breaking the mold, becoming concerned with the quality of life in the workplace in its growing complexity.[8]

Professional associations—particularly management-oriented ones such as the Conference Board, American Management Association, and the personnel branch of the American Psychological Association—are devoting meetings and publications to quality of working life aspects, again concentrating largely on job satisfaction and even reporting some "experiments" undertaken in firms.[9]

On the whole, the situation is reflected in the treatment of the problem by the popular press: commentators, authors, and artists are expressing deep concern over the impoverished quality of working life in this, the latter part of the twentieth century. Although researchers are largely locked into their disciplinary molds, there is the beginning of an awareness among professionals both as to the problems and the possible solutions.

Needed Initiative in the United States

Presently, the development of activities and programs in the United States to enhance the quality of working life may be divided into four categories: university-centered research efforts, which almost always follow disciplinary lines and predilections; action efforts undertaken for various motives by managements to improve one or many aspects of the worker's life at the workplace; associated with managerial interests and goals, the very extensive activities of consultants whose approaches range from nostrums to serious change programs for increasing job satisfaction and improving productivity; and, lastly, continuing union efforts to secure for members social justice at work, relief from coercion, higher wages, shorter hours, and better working conditions.[10]

Not mentioned in this review of the existing state of affairs is the relatively small effort of the Quality of Working Life Program at the Graduate School of Management, University of California, Los Angeles, which is proceeding on a national front but with limited resources to engage in action research on organizational and job changes, design of new organizations, research, training, and development of case reports, and information dissemination.

If reasonable progress is to be made in enhancing quality of working life the initiative in the United States must include action research, and training, and therefore must address the problems and requirements of managements, unions, research disciplines, professional practice, and government policy. Satisfaction of any or all of these needs at this time, with any expectation of truly enhancing quality of working life, calls for development of *institutions* rather than *programs*, since the crucial missing elements are focus, credibility, and competence.

It is important to note that focus in the case of a central societal issue can be provided only through the creation of institutions bringing together the relevant strands, and in so doing developing a new ground from which to proceed. The long history of activities and research on quality of working life without a specific focus has resulted in disjointed and disparate pieces of knowledge, programs, and policy, making it difficult if not impossible to answer in operational and evaluative terms the central questions concerning this subject. The situation is not likely to be remedied by more programs or greater support and funding of existing undertakings; rather, a focus must be built and directed at enhancing quality of working life, primarily by fusing action, research, policy study, training, and information dissemination, permitting close interchange and growth and so pushing ahead the state of the art. Secondarily, an institution providing focus will, through interaction with existing compartmentalized professional activities and research fragmented among the disciplines, begin to develop a reconceptualization that will create a new ground or base from which to move. This applies to technology, its design and operation, and its effects on quality of working life as well as to the organization, management, and control of enterprises and their work-places and the representation of workers by unions. The potency of the prospective contributions made through focused approaches is already visible in the activities of a few institutions.[11]

The size, complexity, and dispersion of the United States as well as its high regard for decentralization indicates that, if possible, more than one institution should be focusing its energies and competence on change, research, and teaching directed to enhancing the quality of working life. Too few now exist. This state of affairs intensifies the need to form additional institutes and centers as soon as possible, specifically designed to include the following characteristics:

1. an organization based on a network mode of operation to link it with other endeavors;
2. an organization in a boundary position of a major university to support the need to validate knowledge, provide training, and renew itself through the intake of young professionals and researchers;
3. an organization scrupulously neutral in attitude so that it can build credibility and trust with unions, managements, and academics.

Without the establishment of a number of interconnected action research institutes, developments in the United States will continue to be fragmented, focusing on short-term endeavors and subject to whims and suspicions.

Developments in Western Europe

Western Europe has shown far more interest and action, the industrial democracy project in Norway being the pioneer development. It was begun by the Work Research Institutes in 1961 under joint sponsorship of the Confederation of Trade Unions and Confederation of Employers. In seeking to enhance the quality of working life, it examined and recommended against representative democracy at the board level of firms, that is, some workers having membership upon boards of directors as a viable means of enhancing life in the workplace. Instead, it recommended democratizing the workplace and went on to experiment in five firms in important sectors of the economy, each selected jointly by the national confederations. These experiments are continuing and have expanded to other sectors, notably the Norwegian merchant marine.

A substantial part of our knowledge has come from the Norwegian experiments. The assistance of the Tavistock Institute, London, was sought early on, and the continuing association of the two institutes helped create a network of researchers and action research centers in many Western European countries—Holland, Sweden, Denmark, France, and Ireland, in addition to England and Norway. With the exception of Sweden, however, all the other efforts in Western Europe should be seen as single innovative cases of developing new forms of work organization, albeit in many instances having great impact. Holland is a case in point; considerable innovative efforts to enhance many aspects of quality of working life have been undertaken, but not coalesced into any integrated national commitment or program. Experiments in other countries have not gone that far, but may still be seen as innovative beginnings.

Sweden must be considered an important special development, for it has made a *national* commitment to enhance the quality of working life by means of democratization of the workplace, a commitment supported by the unions, employers, and dominant political party[12]—all under the notion of "industrial democracy." Spurred by many events, including the industrial democracy project in Norway and the dislocations caused by the importation of large contingents of foreign laborers, particularly from southern Europe, Sweden has turned to democratizing the workplace which it sees as the remaining frontier in an evolving social democratic society. Under an umbrella industrial democracy joint council, a large number of "experiments" are under way to find new forms of work organization, new roles, relationships, and distribution of power for workers, new relations for unions, and new methods of management—all directed at increasing democratic behavior in the workplace by means of shifting power and regulating and controlling work activities. It is too early to assess the outcome of these efforts in terms of organizational and job forms, management and union goals, as well as quality of working life. But, at the very least, life in the workplace will never again be the same.[13]

In England, aside from the early pioneering work of the Tavistock Institute, the development has been overly leisurely. A significant recent development is the issuance of a report *On the Quality of Working Life*,[14] sponsored by the Department of Employment, followed by the creation of a tripartite steering group of representatives of government, the Trade Unions Congress, and the Confederation of British Industries to plan, monitor, and evaluate a coordinated program of experiments aimed at enhancing quality of working life and diffusing an understanding of the outcomes.

On the whole, developments in Western Europe, while uneven, promise to provide substantial learning experiences for the reorganization and redesign of the various aspects of working life in order to enhance its quality.

International Council on Quality of Working Life

While institutes and research groups, which may be considered as "nodes" in a network, can be expected to emerge on the continent of North America in response to the clamant needs finding expression there, the situation else-where is less clear. Without the wholehearted support of governments, the prospects even in European countries are hard to judge. National govern-ments dispose of the overwhelming proportion of funds available for research; unless they are convinced of the need and the importance of satisfying it, the help of other sources, foundations, and so on, is inadequate to maintain the activities beyond initiation and early development.

Thus governments *must* be convinced; and that is most easily and effective-ly accomplished by the example of other governments, by international spon-sorship, and by the interest of groups which they perceive as "hardheaded" in their own countries. The strategy, then, is to encourage and support existing "nodes" in whatever country they now exist, utilize their resources as fully as possible in nurturing nascent nodes in nearby countries, and underwrite as much international activity as can be sustained without damage to the activi-ties of the individual nodes.

But there is a real danger: researchers drawn off into an international forum may be lost to real research without compensatory gains; the young researcher reaching the height of his power may realistically recognize that his most effective contribution for some years to come lies within his own institution, directed to problems within his own society. Without his active participation, however, an international forum is likely to become a talking shop of people who have passed the days of their creative contributions.

The balance between an international network and the national centers or nodes of which it is composed is bound to be delicate. On the one hand, the thrust of national activities will be toward problems of special national interest, and their impetus must be maintained. On the other, some problems cannot be tackled at all with the limited resources of individual national centers.

What kind of international network will best fill the need? It should be one firmly based on its nodes and numbering among its priorities the support and strengthening of its nodes. It should help new nodes to form where none now exist. It can best advance this task by facilitating the exchange of ex-perience and the sharing of resources.

Developments so far have been essentially international in character. Be-ginning with the studies in Britain and in India by members of the Tavistock Institute, ideas and methods have spread to Holland, Norway, Sweden, the United States, and Australia, carried by a handful of people who learned of one another's work and borrowed one another's expertise—working together, visiting, advising and participating in one another's projects, creating in the pro-cess nodal points around which gathered the few enthusiasts whose efforts have made the impact.

This has been but one—although the most significant—of the trends which have contributed to the present state of knowledge and practice, because of its blend of advancing theory and developing practice. The other trends have been diffused through more traditional, more separated channels. The theory of work groups, job satisfaction, work alienation, and so on has been developed mainly within behavioral science-oriented schools of management. What has spread in practice, largely through the agency of management consultants, has drawn on this theory, sold to management on the basis of a technique for aligning workers with managerial goals.[15]

We do not mean to imply that, heretofore, sociotechnical systems thinking has been adequately ecumenical or that it alone has provided a framework of ideas wide enough to encompass all the requirements set out in the last paragraph. But it has taken two strides in the right direction: the first, theoretical, the development of ways of taking account of the external environment of work organizations; and the second, practical, the introduction of multiple sanctioning of action research.

Open sociotechnical systems approaches, then, have been simultaneously the most significant of recent developments and entirely international in their basis and practice. As we have shown, their growth and spreading have been nourished, indeed made possible, by their roots in the international interest of a small group of researchers. To sustain that international activity, only the most rudimentary and informal network of association was required. All knew each other, all had the experience of working together and could call upon one another for help and advice. If the time has now come when these informal arrangements can no longer serve present and future needs, their replacement with all the formal paraphernalia of international organizations could represent an irreparable loss. The challenge is to evolve a real network, not a centralized and centralizing organ, and models are not abundant.

Thus, to repeat, the first charge on the international network is to sustain and help develop secure "nodes." The second is to facilitate the exchange of experience and knowledge. The third is to concern itself with the supply of people capable of meeting the demands for research and action. With good fortune the nodes will themselves undertake this responsibility in and for their own countries; some will certainly need help to do this.

The fourth charge is to keep the nodes abreast of new ideas and new knowledge. This is not simply a question of exchange of information—of cases or of published reports. Those have their place and are to a considerable extent already provided by the existing publications and media. But ideas develop to a major degree through discussions among colleagues; often the most fruitful discussion is not with one's closest colleague, but with one from an adjacent field of work or within the same field but from another institution. There appears to be an optimal "distance" for stimulating interaction of this kind. At intervals there is need also to undertake a review of the state of knowledge and the capacity of the membership; a coming together, a "flocking" conference of the kind represented by the International Conference on Quality of Working Life at Arden House.

Fifth comes the task of assembling a critical mass of effort beyond the capacity of any one of the nodes or of any pair working together. A major effort which would serve as a demonstration of how to replace the assembly line, for example, or of how to design clerical jobs in the face of computerization could be mounted only by a number of nodes acting in concert. Two centers can work together effectively on the basis of their own devoted commitment; beyond two, some organization of at least a temporary nature is required.

Last but not least is the role of pushing forward the leading edges of knowledge and practice, assessing and foreseeing trends, sensing what is developing, and exchanging impressions.

These requirements were set out in the report of the Task Force on Institution Building of the International Conference on Quality of Working Life. Since then a planning committee did its work and an interim International Council on the Quality of Working Life was formed in August 1973. The generous support of the Ford Foundation has again provided both the means and much of the inspiration. By the time this book appears, the first group of study grants will have been awarded and the first international summer schools held by the international council to provide the exchange of experience and assist in the development of competent contributors to action research programs advancing the quality of working life.

Developing Countries

The agenda of issues facing developing countries is so formidable that questions of quality of working life may appear very small indeed if not hopelessly idealistic. Poor countries need desperately to create employment. For their people to have work at all—any kind of working life—is the overriding aim; the quality of working life appears no more than a frill, to be introduced when luxuries can be afforded, if that happy day ever arrives.

This generally held notion is, however, a misreading based on false historicism. Because industrialization was accompanied in the past by a widespread decline in the quality of working life, it has become accepted that the price of industrialization is alienation as well as dense urbanization. Yet neither of these consequences is an inevitable concomitant of industrialization. Furthermore, the currently present symptoms of dissatisfaction in advanced countries appear to be largely associated with, and more than partially the outcome of, steps taken to advance the efficiency of work organizations. Again the ills are seen as part of the cost of efficient operation. Costs they are, but paradoxically uncosted: necessary costs they are not. Newly industrializing countries need no more follow the road of "scientific management" than they need begin their industrialization with the James Watt steam engine.

Indeed, the principles of scientific management and organizations based upon them stand in the way of rational industrial development, demanding a labor force trained in alienation, imposing social costs on a social infra-structure unadapted to provide them. Such organizations imply a particular kind of family structure, organized around the daily absent wage earner whose schooling provided by a particular kind of educational system equipped him with the skills of compartmentalizing work from nonwork, work from play, work from social life, work skills from social skills. Industrial countries are paying the price for this in the problems which beset virtually every social institution.

Many of these problems have been self-inflicted by the choice of industrial technology. In the case of the Western industrialized countries, choice was available, but this was not recognized; we did not know that there were other paths that could have been followed; we did not realize that what was brilliantly successful and profitable in the short run might pile up enormous costs and diseconomies in the not-so-long run. Have developing countries, then, a choice in the matter? In principle, certainly: there may indeed be only one way open once the technological decisions have been made, but there is not just one way of industrializing, one way of organizing work, one way of achieving a technological objective. There are many options open before the technological decisions have been made. This is in principle only, because the knowledge and skills needed to generate and evaluate these options are scarce and the appreciation that they are required is equally scarce.

Most planners at national or regional levels are not technologists; for their technological decisions they depend on specialists, most trained in a cultural context which has evolved together with the technology it embodies. Their solutions to these problems are based on the unvoiced assumptions of a society already geared to the use of advanced technologies with their attendant values, advantages, and dysfunctional aspects. But most of these features are not problematic for the planner; his options are limited in advance in ways of which he is at best only dimly aware. The technologist trained in an advanced country—this includes most technologists in policy-making roles—applying in developing countries the scientific values and technological solutions of the advanced countries is, of course, made daily aware of the limitations hindering his work. He adapts so far as he can to the social and political climate; he learns new ways of doing things; he may enlist the aid of anthropologists and sociologists to assess the acceptability of his proposals or even examine their likely effects on the life of the people concerned. And in small-scale projects he may be influenced in the choice of technology by their advice. While anthropologists' advice about small-scale community projects may be precise and relevant, social science recommendations on large-scale matters tend to be vague and general and of very little use to the planner or technological adviser, who needs something tangible to put into even the crudest cost-benefit analysis. On the other side, the sociologist has little or no grasp of technological considerations and will be unable to propose alternative solutions or indeed to realize that there are technologically feasible alternatives.

Is there a way out? We believe there is and that it lies along the lines of what we may call "sociotechnical assessment." Coining a new phrase solves no problems. Much work is required before this concept can be realized in action. What we mean is this: Every objective needs to be seen in sociotechnical terms, to become a sociotechnical objective. In most of Western society, premature fragmenting into social and technical objectives is encouraged by the separation of political systems from technical organization. In this model the social objectives are set by the political system; the means of attaining them is handed over to the technocrats. Unfortunately, the quality of life in such a society is determined more by the means characteristically adopted for achieving ends than by the choice of the ends themselves. If we choose technically dominated modes of solving social problems or attaining social objectives, we inevitably acquire a society in which the machine dominates the man. Paradoxically, by subordinating the technical to the political, we subordinate man to the machine.

If, on the other hand, we take into account technical considerations in determining social objectives, we are still importing with these considerations a whole raft of assumptions and valuations that go with the technology. We must begin by rigorously analyzing the social assumptions underlying the structure of societies and the images we have of these structures. We will then perceive that our societies are sociotechnical systems with sociotechnical objectives. Fully to recognize the costs and benefits of sociotechnical options requires a new form of sociotechnical assessment, based on the skills of people who have acquired the capacities to understand both the social and the technical characteristics of these systems.

Without this sociotechnical assessment the developing countries are importing the quality of working life of their people along with imported technology. When a country imports a steel mill or a textile factory or an oil refinery, it imports a number of jobs designed by the engineers of steel mill, textile factory, or oil refinery. One of the problems arising from this has long been recognized: the industrial skills needed to cope with these jobs may be lacking. Solutions have included the temporary appointment of expatriate staff, more minute division of labor, or the proposal to utilize "intermediate technologies" based on the availability of existing skills and on the assumptions of a plentiful and cheap but low-skilled supply of labor.

Thus there is an opportunity to design new technologies in which the desired quality of working life can be a major factor. Where else can industry serve so many social objectives? The development of the social as well as the industrial skills of the people should be one objective for design. If workers in developing countries persistently absent themselves for family, social, and personal reasons, we do not have to go the way of training them in a "disciplined" way of life to the exclusion of the spontaneity we at other times and in other contexts admire. Nor will it avail to condemn as evidence of irresponsibility what may be the acceptance of responsibilities seen within their culture as being truly personal. Indeed, we could argue that our culture places what should be the community's responsibility—to get society's work done—on the individual, while placing what should be the individual's responsibility —to make himself available for other people who need him—on impersonal community organizations. Perhaps some way of contracting for jobs with local communities could form the basis of a more appropriate relationship of work organization to community. This would have wide implications for all aspects of the organization, not least on the way in which its tasks are combined with jobs.

But there would be equally far-reaching implications for community development. The objectives of community development can be attained only by the judicious employment of appropriate technologies. Whatever the goal, some means must be employed. And if the means selected are themselves a part of the goal, a hopeful spiral of development can occur. A technology chosen by a community not only to provide it with industry and employment, but also to build its members' social and occupational skills and capacity for group decision making simultaneously advances community development and the development of the industrialization. The means, then, advance the ends and simultaneously promote the emergence of further motives and means directed toward those ends. The dynamics of community development can be coupled with industrial development through the choice of a sociotechnology directed toward the creation of jobs which enhance the quality of working life. Also, by choosing technology and work organization which depend upon and advance "self-training," we can bring about the amplification of learning within the work force, each cadre helping the next to learn, without resort to locking up scarce skills in formal training schemes which possess the traditional demerit of leading toward hierarchical systems of organization and occupational structure.

This is the merest sketch of what sociotechnological assessment might mean for developing countries. In principle, of course, it could be a beneficent factor in selecting new developments for advanced countries, incorporating simultaneously ecological considerations of two kinds, environmental and social. Aid-giving institutions could use sociotechnological criteria for disbursing aid, thus encouraging the development of a sociotechnical assessment capability in the developing countries themselves. Ultimately, such capabilities should be associated with member institutions in the quality of working life network; meanwhile, the latter will need help to form and grow.[16] Eric Trist in selection 4 describes the planning development in Peru which, if adopted, will provide the appropriate climate and setting for sociotechnological assessment, choice of technology, and design of organizations and jobs.

Some Political and Economic Implications

Although most Western countries have political structures which express a political philosophy that appears to be broadly the same, their histories and cultures differ significantly: each has been affected strongly by some event or events which brought the modern version of the nation into being. On the face of it, therefore, the political assumptions and legal structures of these countries should be eminently favorable to the enhancement of the quality of working life of their peoples. Laws, however intended in their origins to protect certain functions and rights, operate in unexpected ways to impair the realization of newer functions and rights.

It would seem, for example, appropriate that an organization designing a new plant should be able to consult with the union likely to organize it about the planning of members' jobs. While this would be encouraged, even applauded, in some countries and facilitated by the laws regulating union-management relations, in the United States it would be considered in restraint of free collective bargaining under the law. Nor is it only the United States in which laws regulating trade and monopoly practices could hinder the free cooperation of firms in exchanging information and experiences.[17] In Britain the reluctance of unions to cooperate too closely with government, especially a conservative one, makes government's role more difficult and more hesitant. These are matters of political traditions as well as political structure and legal regulation that may come in the way of a total commitment to enhance the quality of working life.[18]

What are the economic implications of quality of working life? If happy workers always worked more productively, the economic implications would look universally favorable. But they might not be. Quality of working life means more than better designed jobs making workers more satisfied. If workers learn to participate in decisions concerning their work, they also learn to participate in decisions affecting the security of their jobs; they may work better, but they may also require better compensation for jobs lost; indeed, they may impede the economically motivated policies which threaten to render their jobs redundant.

From a narrow microeconomic viewpoint, the effects may appear negative, but a broader view would likely show a different picture. Today firms can profit from the pursuit of policies paid for by the community at large; a case in point is that of atmospheric pollution, in which macroeconomic and socioeconomic considerations have reasserted themselves. The cost to the community of badly designed jobs, of unhappy unsatisfied workers, of under-utilized skills, of human beings treated as parts rather than as people has not been quantified economically, for the very good reason that no one societal entity has had to pay for it (except the inarticulate individual affected). Thus, in a real sense, the economic implications of quality of working life policies are not known:[19] Western thinking has adhered too firmly to a view of life which separates economic from social considerations. In Eastern Europe it has been far easier to adopt policies giving economic weight to any desired objective, although in fact quality of working life does not appear to have been assigned any focal significance.

The impact of improving the quality of working life and of the steps taken to realize this goal will be felt on a wide range of social institutions—family, schools, universities, voluntary and welfare societies, community organizations of all kinds. We cannot trace all of these; it is salutary, however, to examine the impact on the school. During the century and a half when on an increasing scale industry was the dominant institution in society, schools evolved to prepare the future worker for his role. The virtues of obedience, of perseverance with intrinsically unrewarding tasks, of punctuality and meticulousness were inculcated by them. If this enumeration is not descriptive of the schools of today, it is not least so because society places less value than heretofore on such industrial virtues. Whether change in social values has preceded or has been the consequence of change in industry's needs and industry's supremacy is an interesting theoretical as well as empirical question. For our purpose, it is sufficient to recognize the circular relation involved.

In most of Western society the world of education is presently in considerable flux (if crisis is too strong a word). The balance for students of values of self-expression and ecological concern may be crucial to the evolution of man as a responsible member of the earth's living complement; the impact on industry cannot be apprehended. But the fact that these values could have developed is in turn due to the productive success of industry in satisfying basic needs and instigating imaginary ones—and its consequent threat to our environment. The interactive and systemic nature of change in social institutions links work and education.

Availability of Expertise

No inventory or register exists of people with skills and expertise in enhancing quality of working life; indeed, almost any definition of "appropriate skills and experience" would probably prove too restrictive. As with all new disciplines or interdisciplines, we are still in the state of development in which most of the main contributors to knowledge have come into the field from outside, from the more traditional fields of psychology, sociology, engineering, and economics. It is only now that we are in a position to undertake the professional training of new researchers and practitioners. Thus, for some time to come, we shall be obliged to rely upon sources of recruitment similar to those used in the past for the bulk of our strength.

But where are they to be found? Of the existing leaders in the field, some are in independent research institutes; some are in universities, in the graduate schools of psychology, sociology, management, and education; some are in research and development centers attached to government institutions or to employers' associations or unions; some are consultants; and a few are in staff capacities in firms.

We are now at a crossroads. More organization and coordination of effort will have to come, yet we risk the loss of spontaneity and innovation if we move toward bureaucratization, certification, and other restrictive practices associated with growth and formalization. For these reasons the successful development of the network concept is vital; the network would link persons of different intellectual backgrounds and experience, in different institutions and engaged in different ways, with problems of quality of working life, serving to advance knowledge and experience in quality of working life as a whole.

Social Accounting

Quality of working life brings sharply into focus the issues involved in attempts to develop social accounting frameworks, of which social indicators are one manifestation. One reason for the decline of quality of working life is the fact that it has not figured in economic measures of well-being, such as GNP, GNI per caput, and so on. The weakness of these measures even as indices of prosperity has now become apparent; we are discovering that the costs of creating undesirable outcomes and of clearing them up again both boost GNP while their avoidance does not, unless money is paid for that purpose. Furthermore, even in terms of material welfare, what is measured is by no means consistent nor does it correlate as highly as would be anticipated with measures of consumer welfare such as telephones, radios, vehicles, and refrigerators. For the purposes of international comparison a more effective index can be developed from such basic data.[20]

Turning now to more intangible elements in the quality of life such as freedom from noise, clean air, and safe streets, the defects of economic measures become even more salient; it is probable that there is a negative correlation between GNI per caput and these precious possessions. The quality of working life is, on the one hand, a part of the quality of life as a whole, and like the whole unrelated or negatively related to measures of prosperity; on the other hand, it is largely a product of the mode of organizing work in the name of efficiency and profitability, measurements of which are as partial and limited as GNP.

The search for social indicators is a response to the recognition that traditional measures are dangerously misleading—dangerous because they encourage the wasteful narrow or blinkered approach whose consequences we are now suffering. This search is in its early stages, but it is already clear that measures of quality of working life do not receive very prominent consideration. For example, in the social indicators program of the Organization for Economic Cooperation and Development they represent a "sub-sub-concern." While this is doubtless fair enough in that even the most ardent advocate of enhancing quality of working life would give higher priority to reduction of infant mortality, for example, there is another respect in which the low priority this represents is unsatisfactory. From the point of view of its contribution to potential social unrest and the consequent diminution in society's capabilities to achieve other more eleemosynarily attractive objectives, low quality of working life is a danger signal.

The link between action research devoted to improving quality of working life and the development of social indicators is at present weak; its strengthening requires intimate collaboration among individuals whose main interests and concerns, not to mention methodological approach, have until now been widely separated. One measure of the adequacy of the networks that are now being formed will be their ability to bring about this cooperation. We have assembled a fomidable shopping list of things that need to be done, problems to be tackled, issues to be clarified and confronted. Some will need national, some international, effort. We may adopt as a reasonable guiding principle the view that what should be done internationally should be confined to what cannot be done nationally. The difficulty with this principle is that hitherto most significant developments have involved cross-national collaboration, albeit of an unorganized nature. Partly, this has been a function of the paucity of qualified people, but it also has been due to the limited number of available opportunities; whenever these have opened up, they have been able to attract the most interested and experienced persons of a given country.

As opportunities grow in each country, the tendency to concentrate on development in one's own country will grow too, and thus will be a mixed blessing. The stimulus of experience in another culture leads one to question one's own cultural assumptions. Nevertheless, a tendency may develop for workers in the field of quality of working life to look inward as the opportunities increase in their own countries, as the need to train a new generation begins to make itself felt and absorb effort, and as governments and public authorities urge national action. If this view is correct, international activities will need considerable assistance; detaching effort from national activities will not be easy.

Existing international organizations will in time come to play a significant role both in sustaining international cooperation and in clearing the intergovernmental ground. We have already referred to the activities of the Organization for Economic Cooperation and Development in respect of social indicators. It is also exploring the "internal environment" of work organizations, bringing this topic to the attention of "experts" and government representatives. It plans to widen the scope of intergovernmental action and conventions, already developed with regard to the physical aspects of organizations' internal environments. Its industrial relations division is concerning itself with intergovernmental action on humanizing work, bringing in unions and employers' associations as well as governments and social scientists.

The European Economic Community (European common market) with its recent call for action to end assembly-line work indicates the kind of leadership multinational organizations may try to provide, setting the pace with longer term objectives, concentrating attention—wisely or unwisely—on what appears to be an easily understood salient issue. Even a defensive treaty organization such as NATO has identified problems of work motivation and satisfaction as one of the "challenges of modern society." At its suggestion, the Department of Employment of Great Britain sponsored the study *On the Quality of Working Life* reported in 1973.[21]

The International Labor Organization's interest in the quality of working life is demonstrated by the program of its International Institute of Labor Studies.[22]

> The Institute's interest in problems concerned with the quality of working life arose from its international comparative research project on workers' participation in management. This project, now in its final stages, involved studies of the functioning of the systems of workers' participation in management in twelve countries (carried out by scholars and research institutes in those countries according to a common framework developed by the Institute). During the course of the project it became apparent that interest in workers' participation in management stems from three basic problems of work organizations:
>
> a. power-sharing between managers and those whom they manage;
> b. encouragement of effective cooperation between managers and workers and the reduction of conflict between them;
> c. the personal involvement of workers in their tasks and work situation.
>
> While the various forms of workers' participation in management are concerned with all three problems, arrangements which give the worker greater control over his own task and his own work situation have an important part to play, particularly in connection with the third problem. For this reason the Institute's research project has included a review of developments of this type, and a member of the staff concerned with this project accepted the invitation to participate in the Arden House Conference, and to join in the development of an International Council on the Quality of Working Life.
>
> There is an obvious and urgent need for intensified and more extensive research on the issues concerned with the quality of working life. It is, however, equally vital that information on such research and on the various issues arising from attempts to improve the quality of working life, be made available to all those concerned, so that they may engage in thorough and informed discussion of the issues which affect them. There can be no doubt that the attempts to improve the quality of working life raise issues which can involve conflicts of interests. These need to be brought out into the open and worked through in informed dialogue between those concerned. Unless this is done developments in this field, which appear to be of growing importance in industrialized societies, will be set back by the opposition of various groups who feel themselves threatened by the innovations involved. Such groups include not only workers and their organizations and representatives, who may fear that attempts to improve the quality of working life are merely a new variety of exploitation, but also managers at various levels, technical specialists in various fields, experts in financial management and control, specialists in organization and methods, including systems analysts, production and design engineers, and those engaged in engineering and management education. All these groups need to have objective information on the

implications of attempts to improve the quality of working life for their present ways of thinking and procedures. They need means whereby they can confront these implications and discuss them, before having to take up a policy position and make practical decisions.

The Institute hopes to make a significant contribution to the above needs. It is well placed to do so because of the tripartite character of its parent organization (the International Labor Organization) and its experience in working as a bridge between the world of academics and specialists on the one hand and that of practitioners in the labor and social field on the other. It hopes to obtain resources to establish an International Information Exchange on the Quality of Working Life. The Exchange will include specially prepared documents presenting the issues of concern to each of the various groups in terminology familiar to them. Such documents will need to be made available in several languages. They will report on experiments and developments in the field and will focus on the points that concern the various groups. The Exchange will also involve meetings of various types where the groups concerned can obtain practical information and discuss the issues involved. A third element in the Exchange may be the organization of study tours and visits, so far as these may be practicable.

In accordance with its constitution and functions, the Institute will seek to promote, through the proposed Exchange, the expression of the full range of views on all the issues involved. The controversial character of some of the developments in this field is fully recognized, and this makes it all the more necessary that all those concerned have an adequate opportunity to inform themselves and to exchange views in frank but uncommitted discussion.

As it gains momentum, a role will emerge for other international agencies, such as GATT and UNCTAD, concerned with the international economic scene. This is predictable from the trends, already discussed, which point to a broadening, however slowly, of the concepts of economic well-being and success. International organizations serve not only to urge and prod governments to actions thought desirable or in the common interest; they can also help clear the barriers and facilitate positive action by governments which may be restricted by international agreement or convention—that is, to prevent one earlier recognized good from hindering the attainment of a newer one.

Significant Issues for Research and Development

Looking back on the International Conference on Quality of Working Life, Arden House, we may come to view it as a watershed dividing individual efforts in this field which preceded it from the more conscious participation in a network of collaborative action and research. Today, however, it represents more a signpost, pointing in the directions we need to go and indicating the distances we have yet to travel. From the reports of the task forces containing a long research agenda we have selected those issues which, in the light of the conference, seem to warrant immediate attention and cooperative action on a considerable scale.

The issue of comparability is very important indeed. The best of the available case studies offer some degree of controlled comparison of events before and after an experimental or deliberately induced change, but none actually compares, say, job enrichment with the introduction of autonomous group working. Nor can we expect such comparison. But if we are to answer questions such as "When and in which situations is X likely to achieve better results than Y?", techniques for comparison must be developed that are far more sophisticated than any presently known. This can be done only on a basis of cooperation, demanding far better developed network relationships than now exist.

There are serious gaps in the knowledge that must underlie comparison. Studying a given case, we are likely to find many leaps of intuition on the part of the researcher, who followed what at the time appeared to be a promising approach. And in the outcome a number of changes occurred. But what actually *caused* what? True, the notions of linear causation and single-factor determination are simplistic and may even be misleading. But the gap remains; we cannot advance very far without identifying the causal sequences involved.

"White-Collar Woes"

Events since the conference have confirmed an impression which emerged strongly at that meeting—that we are moving rapidly toward the time when disaffection with the nature of their jobs will be as widespread among white-collar workers as it has been among blue-collar workers. The reasons are not difficult to find. Income differentials have become eroded, the greater security of white-collar employment is neither so marked as it was in the past nor so vital since social security benefits ward off the direct effects of unemployment for most. But, above all, factors intrinsic to the jobs themselves have been undergoing change. In the interests of "productivity" and "efficiency" principles derived from "scientific management," work study, systems analysis, operations research, and other techniques have been applied to white-collar jobs. More recently the invasion of the computer has been accepted in the spirit of technological determinism; systems analysts and computer programmars have designed the jobs of the white-collar employees without their experienced counterparts in manufacturing, the industrial engineers, but with similar outcomes. Many offices have undergone "improvements" which have reproduced the atmosphere of an assembly line.

Of course, no one wishes to recreate the Dickensian clerk on his office stool at a tall desk in a dimly lit counting house, any more than one wishes to revert to the barbarities of the nineteenth-century mill. This is not the issue. In many a modern office, however, the clerk has *less* control over his work and over the way his job is organized and evaluated than did his Dickensian counterpart. And, as the array of white-collar jobs grows while the blue-collar labor force diminishes, we observe the growth of the former's alienation. In Britain, for example, the recent pay "freeze" (a limit on pay awards) brought a burst of militancy from white-collar workers—teachers, nurses, civil servants—and workers in the public sector—hospital auxiliaries, gas workers—where public service motivation could traditionally be relied upon to preclude strike action. At the same time white-collar unionism is growing rapidly, often at the expense of "staff associations" or other "professional" groups. White-collar workers see themselves on the opposite side of the fence to "management" in an unprecedented way and to an unprecedented degree.

All the factors mentioned above contribute to these phenomena, of course, but it is precisely in those jobs whose discretionary element has been eroded by importing forms of managerial control from manufacturing industry and in those occupations where the criterion of service has been replaced by criteria of *efficiency* and *productivity* that the pressure is now greatest. Again, in Britain, among the most militant groups are now the railway motormen, whose jobs have steadily become less discretionary and increasingly more dominated by cost-conscious changes in routes, practices, and manning ratios.

In the United States and Great Britain we are witness to the phenomenon of government bureaucracies as white-collar factories not noticeably distinguishable from the automobile assembly lines. The whole field of redesign of white-collar organizations and jobs is an urgent topic for research and development.

"Blue-Collar Blues"

Enough has been said and written on this topic, both in this volume and elsewhere. From the standpoint of research and development the problem is clear enough, but some obstinate issues will have to be cleared up before *consistent* advance is possible. Here we shall mention three of the most obvious ones.

The Notion of Satisfaction

This issue involves the interpretation of the circular relationship between job design and organization design, on the one hand, and measure of attitudes and job satisfaction, on the other. Inevitably, "satisfaction" is based on comparison: "I am satisfied with what I have if it is up to my expectations. My expectations change if I see something better than I had previously known about or if you who belong to my reference group gets something better."

Predictably, then, there is a steady rate of expression of satisfaction representing a form of adaptation. Researchers become cynical about measures of satisfaction and suspect that quite radical changes will bring only short-term changes in levels of satisfaction. Certainly, other behavioral observations do and will show changes which are simply not reflected in measures of attitude. Yet these observations lack firm, agreed-upon criteria, comparability in time or space. In a word, we need something as flexible and readily available, as measurable and as comparable as attitudes, but something which will have real meaning.

THE STRUCTURAL SITUATION OF THE UNIONS

It is clear that improving the quality of working life poses problems for employers, too. They are conscious that a process of this kind, once begun, is hard to control, that the appetite grows on what it feeds. But they may also reap a potentially high return. If the alternatives are a reluctant labor force, high turnover and absenteeism, continued industrial strife and organizational rigidities brought about by resistance to change, the farsighted employer may hasten to embrace a policy which may not only avoid these grave problems, but would offer the bonus of social acclaim and the genuine excitement and satisfaction of helping to pioneer a socially desirable program.

For the unions, however, the situation is even more hazardous, with much to lose and comparatively little to gain. Over many years the unions have painfully earned the rights to consultation and negotiation with management. Inevitably, union discipline has meant the acquisition or the attempt to acquire the sole right to bargain and negotiate on behalf of its members, even extending to the denial of the individual's right to negotiate or bargain on his own behalf. The notions of democracy at the workplace with sharing of power, autonomous work groups, and so on, involving the worker in decisions about his own work, can appear as devices for undermining the loyalties of union members. Yet the whole concept of enhancing quality of working life is doomed if it is opposed by unions or confined to nonunion organizations. The problem to be solved here is to bring quality of working life into union-employer negotiation, across the bargaining table, and adopt a joint problem-solving mode of introducing improvements.

The support of the unions must be sought with the realization that they will not accept new proposals, however idealistic or well founded, which may undermine their position as the workers' champion. We believe the goodwill is there. In Norway the unions now cooperate on a national scale in efforts to enhance the quality of working life. In other countries, however, fragmented union organizations and employee associations make for greater mistrust between organized labor, government, and employers. Furthermore, while employers can comparatively easily cope with the organizational demands of change to enhance quality of working life, organized labor can do so only at a pace that can be followed by its constituents. Social scientists will have to work with labor unions through the phases of adaptation needed to precede their substantial commitment to that goal.

BLUE-COLLAR CAREERS

Is the notion of career purely a middle-class concept applying only to professions? Our values which emphasize deferred gratification, working today toward a more affluent, more prestigious future, certainly presuppose the assurance of stability and control over one's fate and the possession of marketable skills, knowledge, and experience. All these are assumptions of middle-class life, but are no part of the facts of life of the semiskilled and the unskilled. Indeed, our ideas about development, growth, and technological change *demand* the existence of a reservoir of workers whose skills are not too specialized and who expect, as part of their life experience, to change jobs and firms and industries. What can be the meaning of a progressive career under these circumstances? [23]

But if we cannot yet visualize how a progressive blue-collar career can be evolved, we can no longer accept or cope with the social disturbance which is the outcome of our present arrangements. When security of employment, compensation for redundancy, annual wage increases, shorter work weeks (not to be worked, but to serve as basis for overtime calculations), all become subject to relentless bargaining, the costs of technological change, both benign and malign, become increasingly hazardous.

Two concepts offer some prospects as to possible resolutions: one is the "horizontal career"; the other is "continuing education." The first suggests that continuity of employment can be combined with a variety and broadening of experience without the onerous requirement of greater responsibility or a higher skill. For some workers, horizontal moves would alternate frequently with vertical ones; for others, very few vertical moves would be possible or even desired. But for most workers moves could be accompanied by new learning experiences, partly in work organizations, partly in educational institutions with more or less formality. Plans for achieving these aims would be assessed by the amount of opportunity they provide for individual choice. Both call into question the employment boundaries between organizations and the relations between employers, unions, and government.

Future Research Agenda

Few employers foresaw that their employees would demand more from work than more money, better physical working conditions, and improved fringe benefits. Nor was there much warning from social scientists on what was to come. Those who did speak out could offer no more than the plausible but unsupported prediction that better education would render workers less willing to accept authoritarian supervision or monotonous jobs. Where was the evidence that values were changing?

The evidence of change in the dominant social values of our societies has been all around us for at least a decade—for much longer if we include the convulsions in the world of art. We know a fair amount about the interrelationships of value systems and about the processes of diffusion in society, but we do not know enough to make more than vague predictions, and we honestly know next to nothing about the time scales involved. If we had a reliable and consistent system of social indicators, which take a long time to develop, they would necessarily include indicators of attitudes and values as well as of their tangible consequences. We could then monitor value changes and, with experience, predict them. Meanwhile deeper probes are needed and concentrated studies in one or two areas, institutions, and work organizations could give us better ideas of the channels and rates of diffusion of values. These should be supplemented by systematic scanning for developments in sectors of society which signal value change: entertainment, media, art, education.

If we fail to anticipate changes in values, attitudes, and expectations, we run the risk of painfully evolving solutions to yesterday's problems. It goes without saying that these must be transnational studies; values are quickly transmitted from one society to another, and every material good exported carries with it value assumptions about its use. Additionally, the multinational corporation acts as a channel for diffusion of values about work and work organization.

Quality of Working Life and Technology Assessment

We hear a great deal these days about technological assessment. Broadly, as we understand it, this requires a cost-benefit analysis of every proposed technological innovation, in which full weight is given to the costs and benefits to society as a whole and to local communities in particular. Doubtless, ways will also have to be found of including ecological considerations of conservation of natural resources as well as of potential pollution. The task is formidable and any proposal to complicate it further would not be welcome. Nevertheless, two points need to be made.

First, technological assessment, to be effective at all, requires that at least two alternative ways of doing something be provided by the technology designers. Only in the process of *deciding between alternatives*, rather than deciding whether to do something at all, is there an assessment of costs and benefits. Second, every technological development should rightly be seen as a *socio*technological development—any technology proposed to perform a task requires people to operate and maintain it. The characteristics of their working life must be a prominent factor in the choice of technology, which should optimize the social values of achieving community objectives at lowest community cost, involving the quality of working life of those employed in achieving them. Earlier, we discussed this issue in connection with developing countries. It is equally cogent in this context. High on any agenda for research should be the evolution of methods of sociotechnological assessment, which should be as rigorous as our present limited knowledge allows.

Among the early stimuli to research on the quality of working life were the discoveries by the researchers in the Tavistock Institute that (1) the selection of a particular technological system for performing a task did not preclude a choice of organizational forms to manage that system, and (2) under certain circumstances at least, work groups which combined individual autonomy with group interdependence (autonomous work groups) were more effective and provided greater satisfaction to members. A further discovery was that technological systems could be modified to take account of the needs of the people who manned them; more knowledge of the latter could and should be a factor in the selection and design of the former. But we need to know much more about the relationship of organizational forms to quality of working life.

A serious limitation on these studies is set by the absence of a rigorous means of measuring quality of working life. The report of the Task Force on Measurement[24] is a research agenda in its own right. Here we may point to one or two critical issues. Elsewhere,[25] some unease has been voiced concerning the use of measures of job satisfaction: as Seashore[26] pointed out, the proportion of workers expressing satisfaction with their jobs is both high and steady, apparently uninfluenced by those factors which from other evidence is known to be relevant to quality of working life. Furthermore, their relationship to measures of productivity are low and variable, which may indeed have as much to do with the defects of our concept of productivity as with the frailties of our measures of job satisfaction. Finally, as Faunce and Dubin[27] suggest, the worker whose self-investment in work is low may be highly satisfied with a job which meets his economic requirements only.

At this point we stand on the brink of the argument as to whether low self-investment in work is intrinsically a good or a bad thing: whether it is a response to a situation in which more self-investment in work is likely to lead to frustration and would change under more favorable circumstances. So far the argument has been conducted on the basis of whether low self-investment is psychologically crippling and associated with a similar attitude toward all activities, or whether it is psychologically releasing and associated with high self-investment in activities outside of work. The evidence is ambiguous. What is certain is that many jobs do not deserve any degree of self-investment, and we would probably all agree that it would be best to eliminate or change such jobs. What priority should be given would depend upon our position with regard to the self-investment controversy, whose resolution must be on our agenda for research.

In selection 2 on goals we point to the need for new accounting and legal practices which would force work organizations to evaluate the cost to the community of their labor practices. We believe that if they had to pay for a decreasing quality of working life and were rewarded for increases in quality, they would more quickly and effectively search for, find, and adopt means of enhancing the quality of working life of their work force. New accounting practices or new legal forms will remain mere happy thoughts unless research in this direction is undertaken and pressed with vigor. Without the cooperation of professionals and researchers in these and other disciplines, our research, however well and scholarly devised, is doomed to futility.

Design

The design of new organizations and jobs, and therefore the design of technological systems, has been vastly undervalued and underutilized as a means of providing the enabling conditions for enhanced quality of working life. This may be one explanation why new designs or demonstration "experiments" are so eagerly sought after. The same may be said of redesign of existing organizations and their technologies, necessitated by changes in products, markets, or processes. The failure to understand and grasp the opportunities existing in design has led to a split in integrated design, placing technical system design firmly with engineers and technologists and social system design with managers and "organization specialists."

This split has permitted technical system design to dominate and foreclose, for reasons discussed below, options in design of organizations and jobs that enhance quality of working life, and to maintain virtually unchallenged values and dogmas of the industrial era that developed about 150 years ago. Organization and job design, as a consequence, has been reactive to technical system design for the past hundred years, and at best has been a marginal activity combining bureaucratic concepts with those that will support the previously designed technical systems. This state of affairs is visible in the meager knowledge base of social system design evidenced in texts and handbooks on organization now in common usage, largely concerned with platitudes and dogmas having neither a scientific base nor supportive experimental evidence.

The separation has been maintained by the encapsulation (failure to diffuse) of that potent fundamental concept coming from sociotechnical systems —the concept of *joint* optimization of technical and social systems. It is based on the reality that work organizations accomplish their objectives through both technical and social systems and that these are interactive. Further, these systems are independent in the sense that they derive, respectively, from theories and experiences in the physical sciences for technology and in the social sciences for organizations and jobs. Outcomes depending upon the interactions between independent systems require that they be optimized jointly, which can, in practice, be done only at design or redesign stages. No matter how perfect or optimal the design of a technical system, fitting a social system to it subsequently produces only a suboptimal outcome for work organization, and vice versa.

Examining the process of designing technical systems in work organizations, the uninitiated will find some surprises (see Davis and Taylor, selecton 15). In addition to optimizing technical systems by narrow and increasingly inappropriate criteria, engineers and technologists approach technical system design as synonymous with or including organization design. They see both as their proper and inherited domain of competence and responsibility. Therefore, in examining the application of technology to work organizations in the design phase, that is, before organizational and social arrangements and encrustations exist, we find that not only does technology design influence social system design and behavior—a belated learning of social scientists which they wish us all to know about—but that technological system design *includes* social system design. Unfortunately for society at large, the inclusion of social system design is implicit, seldom if ever explicit, and is passed on to the outsiders as a requirement of the technical system not to be questioned if the promised outcomes are to be realized. An unfortunate corollary is that attempts to modify technological systems after work organizations have been designed almost always involves fiddling on the margin or away from the central transformations of the organization, leaving "change makers" to the bravely impossible task of improving their effectiveness by concentrating on social relationships. Perhaps this may explain why so many reports of organizational changes made to improve life in the workplace, that is, to make it less coerced, more autonomous or self-controlled, reveal minor or innocuous modifications, sadly leading to the conclusion that little can be done with technical systems and contributing to the fallacious vicious circle that technology is a given and we had best leave it alone.

Do engineers and technologists know they are designing social systems when they design technical systems? There is no question that they do. They consider such design to be in their purview, as first implicitly stated by Taylor in 1911, in his scientific management system,[28] and recently openly stated by Williamson, an eminent British engineer, in a most insightful paper to the Royal Society of Great Britain in 1972.[29] In his review of the engineering of production systems, he discusses the responsibility of engineers for social system design, castigating them for poor designs in the name of productivity. Given the position and actions of engineers, two conclusions should therefore be apparent: first, that technological determinism is a nonsense useful to doomsayers for frightening the uninformed or for supporting preexisting ideological positions of engineers, managers, and even social scientists; second, that the design of technical systems has to be viewed as making choices from among *sets of opportunities* available in the technology to permit the creation of jointly optimal sociotechnical systems. The availability of such sets becomes very visible when the design process is one of jointly designing the technical and social systems. This process, when contrasted with monosystems or dominant technical systems design, not only reveals a large number of available options in the technical system but generates a large number of social system alternatives.

An examination of the design process of social systems, undertaken independently of technical systems design, reveals a number of glaring inadequacies which in most cases point to the futility of such independent design. Many of the inadequacies stem from the fact that virtually all knowledge about organizations and jobs accumulated by the social sciences has come from studies of existing organizations. Most such knowledge is descriptive and not predictive. The understandings and experiences have general nonspecific utility in design situations which demand data and knowledge useful for making predictions about future relations and performances of organizations not yet in being. The consequences are that the social sciences have lacked power comparable to that brought by technologists to the design process.

The history of the evolution of the social sciences based on study of existing institutions has shaped the development of concepts and the analysis and synthesis methodology whose applicability to design and modification of organizations is questionable. Their applicability to the process of design with its creation of alternatives, examining of contingencies assessing costs and gains, and predicting outcomes suitable to later verification, would seem very limited and at best sufficiently unknown because untested.

Participation in the process of joint sociotechnical systems design of organizations and jobs requires a new role to be undertaken by social scientists. However, there is presently a lack of capability to deal realistically with technical as well as social system variables. In all of the United States and Western Europe, there were probably not more than fifteen or twenty social scientists in 1973 with the requisite competence and experience to engage profoundly and responsibly in this process—a glaring need that will have to be remedied before extensive efforts to enhance the quality of working life can be undertaken through designing organizations and jobs.

Competence in design raises the prospect of satisfying another urgent need —that of technology or technical systems assessment now virtually never undertaken. As discussed earlier in relation to developing countries, it is now possible to assess technical systems, existing or proposed, to determine what requirements and constraints are being imposed on social systems preventing their design and development as effective, humane organizations and jobs. The processes and competences need for technical systems assessment are taken from those of design. Again, this activity, intended to prevent design of organizations and jobs leading to low quality of working life, cannot now be undertaken except in a few isolated cases because of lack of competence and experience. We appear doomed to a cycle of seeing poor organizations and jobs designed and then struggling to modify some after they have come into being. At best this is a losing endeavor; at worst it is hopeless.

In the few instances of comprehensive joint technical and social systems design, new learning has emerged as to the prospects for achieving high levels of quality of working life. The joint systems design process has shown that technical systems constraints can be modified, if not removed, and that a substantial number of technical systems alternatives can be generated providing more choices in social systems design (again pointing to the need for criteria by which to make these choices). It has also become evident that social systems criteria can be specified and incorporated as requirements of technical systems design.

Sociotechnical variance analysis[30] identifying constraints in the technical system and critical actions to be taken by social systems to provide a viable, self-maintaining social organization and satisfy the needs of its members has proved an even more potent analytic method than originally conceived. Such analysis has made it possible to assess technological processes, machinery, instrumentation, and control systems (including computers) to assure that inhibiting or harmful technical systems constraints are not imposed on social systems. It is very important to note that this analytic methodology makes sense to technologists and engineers, since its use generates objective data, given acceptance of criteria, and has been adopted by them after very short experience in those few instances mentioned previously. The potential contribution to enhancing the quality of working life through the process of design is enormous and as yet untapped.

Training Needs for Enhancing Quality of Working Life

The training needs in relation to quality of working life of all Western countries are about the same as to kind, if not intensity. The kinds of training, of course, depend on specific requirements of the intended recipients. In terms of reconceptualizing man's work role in an industrial society, we are all the recipients. If the quality of working life is to be enhanced in that context, then specific role holders in our societies who can sanction, make, or accelerate needed changes will have to be the recipients of general and specific training.

What Kind of Training for Whom?

To reach the largest numbers and expecting to aid future developments, a key group to reach are teachers for all levels of students including the universities. The needs here are for "training of trainers" and for text materials to raise the issues and examine the consequences of enhancing quality of working life, reconceptualizing man's work role and its relationship to the functioning of society. Such training can then be passed on to the classroom teachers through summer schools, using teaching methods compatible with the concepts of enhanced quality of working life, and outcomes will depend on the potency of the teaching materials which have been developed.

Without support from those who set policy and standards in all the institutions of a society, the outcomes of such training may create unfulfilled expectations. Managers and union leaders as well as policy makers of public and private organizations exercise two roles that require training in the context considered here. First, they develop institutional policy and standards which set the basis for work roles and quality of working life at all levels. Second, they are the instigators of change and as such are central to those activities aimed at enhancing quality of working life within their own organizations. Through seminars these individuals can be aided in reconceptualizing man's relationships to work organizations and the latter to society at large and in examining the positive consequences of enhanced quality of working life, including means of assessing them, existing social and economic misconceptions, and requirements and processes of introducing needed changes. In addition, because their roles often transcend individual organizations, union leaders and officials of public agencies need to obtain an understanding of the societal effects, the required systems of social accounts and public policy needed to support high quality of working life. It has been suggested that lawyers be included so that they can provide assistance in public policy formation as well as dealing with existing or needed laws that may aid in enhancing the quality of working life.

Again, we see here that to be effective policies and programs need the support of those who carry on the technical aspects of management—the consultants, accountants, personnel and industrial relations officials, and, in manufacturing and science-based firms, the engineers. In addition to more general conceptual training, these persons will require training tailored to their roles as the planners, evaluators, and developers of criteria of organizational and individual effectiveness, whose decisions determine day-to-day life in the workplace. Also, they influence policy through the methods they use, the effects they choose to measure or ignore, and the advice they give. Training directed to these purposes has been provided in a few instances; with adaptations it could be made more widely available.

Training for engineers—both practicing and student engineers—is a matter of special concern. Engineers serve as managers in science-based organizations engaged in complex manufacturing processes as well as in the application of science research. Additionally, as designers, they play a central role in determining the technology of work organizations, in which their impact on social systems and on the jobs of all our organizations is immense.

Recent sociotechnical developments and the joint technical-social systems design activities undertaken in a few instances reveal a vast potential for enhancing quality of working life through design and redesign of technology. These experiences seem to overturn our conventional view of technology as an unmodifiable cause of poor quality of working life. Instead we find that, with appropriate analysis of the interaction between technical and social systems, numerous technical systems alternatives become available which can be designed to permit high quality of working life. Practicing engineers have applied the new analytic and design methods successfully, and the methods can be taught through on-the-job training as well as in schools. The new approaches supported by the concepts of man-at-work discussed in this volume also seem to have aided in developing changes in organization and jobs of engineers themselves, enhancing their own quality of working life.

Thus the central role of engineers in technologically advanced societies requires particular concern. Our earlier discussion of prospective new forms of assessment for technological choices in less advanced societies indicates how the engineer's role can be enhanced in this context as well.

Organizations of all kinds seeking to enhance quality of working life will need assistance from trained advisers to help plan, guide, and carry through the mechanisms for changing organizations and jobs, particularly in ways compatible with this goal. Most such advisers work on behalf of management, instituting changes conceived at the top. Thus they must learn to assist the top levels of both unions and managements as well as lower levels of supervision such as foremen and shop stewards. They may also have to learn that they are not the change makers, but the helpers of managers, supervisors, and union officials who plan and introduce new and better working lives.

Those engaged in aiding the change processes may also contribute to a more general knowledge of planning and evaluating changes. In this context some preparation in concepts and methods of action research is especially helpful. A reference to the report of the Task Force on Comparability in *The Quality of Working Life: Cases and Commentary*, selection 4 indicates how our learning from planned changes may be enhanced.

A particular category of training needs concerns middle managers, supervisors, and workers in organizations who will be called upon to participate centrally or cooperatively in changing their organizations and jobs. Such training has been given many times and is best accomplished within organizations, for to be effective it requires focusing on specific problems.

Finally, we need to concern ourselves with researchers, largely university based, including economists, sociologists, psychologists, and engineers. Seminars have to be developed to focus on new appreciations, reconceptualizations, and research compatible with our goal: the enhancement of quality of working life. Such seminars, to be acceptable, can probably be conducted only by institutes with established research reputations or affiliated with major universities.

Meeting the Needs

To meet these various training needs, two kinds of resources will be required: (1) courses and programs, and (2) instructional materials and curricula. The former have already been initiated by one center, but their growth and diversification could best be supported by universities both in their regular and extension teaching. Universities can develop competent staff to carry on training tailored to the variety of needs; union schools also may take on this role for their members. Institutes or research centers attempting to engage in extensive training, however, will find that they become diverted from their action research roles. (They do have to engage in training to test programs and, where needed, to support action research efforts.)

A major undertaking of institutes, particularly in the United States, is the development of suitable teaching materials—instruction guidelines, cases, and curricula—for training programs at all levels of instruction, particularly at that of the university and its professional schools of business administration, engineering, law, and education. In the United States only independent institutes with reputable staffs can hope to undertake such curricular development.

The Disciplines and a New Interdiscipline

The Biases of the Disciplines

It has become commonplace to claim that the division of knowledge into "subjects" or "disciplines" fails to match the requirements of the use of knowledge in tackling practical issues. We need not rehearse those arguments here. Nor shall we expound the need for multidisciplinary research, especially when action research methods are required. Rather, we wish to concentrate on identifying the specific orientations of the relevant social science disciplines, not for the purpose of attacking them, but to identify the areas of particular need for multidisciplinary research.

The disciplines relevant to enhancing the quality of working life are economics, psychology, sociology, industrial relations, and engineering and systems theory, which is not to say that insights into the nature of work and work organizations have not been provided by social anthropology, political science, and economic history. But these insights have been of a more general contextual kind.

ECONOMICS

The approach of economists to the nature of work has essentially assumed that work is done in exchange for appropriate, largely monetary, rewards, and that the imposed constraints on behavior will be accepted if the price is right. So long as the value of the marginal increment of wages exceeds the value of the marginal increment of leisure required to secure it, work will be preferred. In a sense, the theory that the nature of work is defined by its exchange value is tautologous, but so long as the curves of marginal value slope in the predicted direction there is no reason to query its utility. Labor market economists have been conscious of the constraints needed in order to make these assumptions valid, the market for labor being highly imperfect.

To the topic of work organization, economic theory has contributed mainly through its influence on doctrines of management and through its use in accounting. The theory of the firm is a microeconomic approach, treating organizational structure as rationally determined by the needs of accountability for use of the firm's resources. This theory originated in the days of the entrepreneurs and required modification to assimilate the advent of the joint stock company. Entrepreneurial behavior was perceived as economically rational and managerial behavior was essentially entrepreneurial. Burnham's

"Managerial Revolution" [31] was an attempt to expose this bias in economic and political thought and to correct for it.

Economics has been most succinctly defined as "the science of the allocation of scarce resources." From the early days of industrialization the "scarce" resources were *capital,* not labor, *entrepreneurial,* not physical (worker) skills. A scientific system of allocating resources paid attention to those which were scarce, taking the abundant ones for granted or considering their replacement as a no-cost item. The economic theory of the firm and the organizational doctrines based upon it were appropriate to this situation. They have run into trouble, however, as resources formerly regarded as no-cost items, like clean air and water, have become replaceable only at considerable cost. Human resources are only the latest of a series to display characteristics of high-cost replaceability. This change will take time to become assimilated into the economic theory of the firm and, indeed, its importance may impose modifications so large as to make the theory unwieldy or unbalanced. Current theories of organization are predominantly based on theories of human behavior; economic concepts and measures may become secondary unless it can be shown, as it has not so far, that they possess the best potentiality for representing the most significant features of the human resource. Economists are not the last to become aware of these trends; recent developments in social accounting, social indicators, and human resources accounting are illustrations of attempts to generalize economic method to areas outside its traditional scope. Certainly, attempts to introduce any rigor into the measurement of quality of working life will not get far without a major contribution from economics and its applied branches.

Psychology

The approach of psychologists to the problem of quality of working life has suffered from a certain ambiguity. On the one hand, psychologists have tended to accept the goals of organizations as "givens," outside the scope of their inquiry. Likewise, they have tended to accept the technology of an organization as given. On the other hand, they have tended to treat motivation and behavior as a dependent variable: if your goals and technology are given, you can only intervene to affect motivation and behavior by changing people's attitudes.

The contribution of psychology to organizational theory has been mainly in the area of relationships within peer groups and between superiors and subordinates. Major questions of organizational design were ignored. The recent introduction of sociotechnical systems thinking helped to reinstate motivation— if not as an independent variable, at least as a variable contingent upon factors outside as well as inside the organization. Thus possibilities were opened up of meeting goals and operating technology with alternative forms of organization based on motivational as well as technological requirements. More recently still, some psychologists in the sociotechnical systems trend of thought, particularly those with adequate preparation in technology, have begun to challenge the assumptions underlying the choice of technology itself, breaking out of the constraints previously accepted. This exposes the inter-active nature of organizational structure and motivation and the permeability of both to environmental pressures. Even the choice of organizational goals has become problematic.

In the field of measurement the contribution of psychology has been least satisfactory. While psychometric measurement has grown in sophistication, the choice of variables measured has become more and more assailable. For example, now that we have highly developed measures of "intelligence," the concept of intelligence itself has become an issue which exposes the relation-ships of theory to ideology, the dependence of the concept upon assumptions about the structure and nature of society. In the field of organizational be-havior, the key concept which psychologists have measured is "job satisfaction." The history of this concept is a long one; it has now achieved such prominence that it is treated as a surrogate for behavior itself. It is used as a base measure in change experiments as well as for every kind of psychologically based and nonpsychologically based organizational activity. It is used for cross-sectional, transorganizational, even international comparisons.

Job satisfaction measures the degree to which a job satisfies man's needs. In a static, snapshot way these are perfectly legitimate assumptions. Diachron-ically, they are weak if not false. Needs and expectations emerge in the job situation: we expect our jobs to satisfy needs to which our experience in our jobs has given rise. If I have been challenged by a job to develop a need for mastery, I may now judge jobs by whether they offer me an opportunity to exercise and satisfy this need. If, on the other hand, my experience of jobs excludes such a challenge, I may never develop the "need" or suffer from the lack of its satisfaction. In other words, our satisfaction with our jobs depends upon what we look for, and what we look for is partly an outcome of what we have been given. This argument is developed by Thorsrud in a review given at the international conference[32] of the Faunce and Dubin selection (20).

The full contribution of psychology to quality of working life will come when psychologists succeed in freeing themselves from the constraints of *regarding* organization as given. When one remembers that psychologists working within organizations have essentially been management-oriented, one sees that this freedom may come only when psychologists are able to operate under more universal or more neutral auspices.

SOCIOLOGY

Sociologists have been accused of taking organizational goals for granted and of adopting a managerial perspective in describing organizational life. The derogatory appellation, "plant sociology," has been applied to this orientation. On the other hand, far more than either economists or psychologists, socio-logists have identified themselves with the worker's perspective, notably in Europe, where the Marxist tradition has been more influential in sociological thinking than in America. Sociologists have tended to concern themselves with large organizations, especially bureaucratic ones. More than the psychologists, they have seen life within the organization in relation to life outside and have related the organization to its community environment. From this sociological perspective, the state of the labor market, the cycle of family responsibilities, class attitudes and values, and conflicts of interest all contribute to workers' orientation toward work and attitudes toward their jobs. Long on theory and on detailed reporting, sociologists have been short on prediction and prescription. They have tended to take the view that it is the business of sociology to describe, to understand, and to criticize—not to solve problems.

Nevertheless, sociologists have provided indicative data. By explaining the relationship of technology to organizational structure and its effects upon industrial relations, they have given management a yardstick against which to assess their own organizational structure and relations with their workers. By tracing the relationship between environmental uncertainty and change and organizational modes of functioning, they have likewise provided management with useful insights. But, by and large, sociologists have found it more difficult, perhaps more at odds with their traditions and perspectives, to engage in action research in industry than have social psychologists.

It is worth mentioning here that microsociological approaches used by social anthropologists, or borrowed from them, have illuminated the nature of rationality in organizational life. For example, behavior which restricts output —apparently thereby reducing the rewards to the workers themselves—has been shown to be explicable as attempts to optimize rewards in the face of uncertainty, given the worker's appreciation of the payment system, and requiring no recourse to semimystical notions of an "informal organization."

Industrial Relations

Industrial relations is itself an interdisciplinary subject, drawing on labor history, labor and industrial economics, and, to a lesser extent, political science and sociology. Its major contribution to the issues of quality of working life is to set them in the context of labor market realities and the system of collective bargaining. These are also to some extent its limitations. The study of industrial relations tends to see issues as between management and union, related to formal structures of negotiation and representation. As a constant reminder that these issues exist, that formal structures cannot be ignored or bypassed without peril, this approach is invaluable. But students of industrial relations have conducted their analyses on the basis that understanding is most advanced by treating the motivation of workers as instrumental and calculative. The fact that deductions reached on this basis may not be false does not, of course, substantiate the correctness of the assumption. And indeed, as we have said, most methods of organizing work have left scant opportunity for other forms of motivation to operate. The present trends in the study of industrial relations show few signs of breaking out of this circle.

Systems Theory

Systems theory, the borrowing and elaboration of analytical models and theorems from biology, anatomy, and engineering, has strongly influenced all the disciplines we have discussed. It has proved especially assimilable to structural functional sociology. Social psychology, too, has adopted a systems model for treating role relationships in organizations; its weakness has been the imputation of homeostatic models of organizational functioning. Systems theory worked most effectively within a closed system framework, more recently it has advanced beyond this. Open system theory, however, tends to import evolutionary and teleological models which are helpful in some respects, but not in others. In particular, its treatment of endemic conflict of aims, of metastable coalitions of interest is sketchy and unsatisfactory. Nevertheless, through its contribution to the open sociotechnical systems approach to organizational analysis, it has given us a tool without which we would be hard put to identify the variances in organizations and thus the key points of entry and leverage to job design.

INDUSTRIAL (PRODUCTION) ENGINEERING

The contributions of the disciplines cannot be concluded without reference to industrial (production) engineering, which is influential in practice if not in theory. This branch of engineering sees itself as the inheritor and propagator of the philosophy and practices of Frederick W. Taylor—or scientific management. The United States branch is presently engaged, even if not wholeheartedly, in a protective campaign[33] to keep others from encroaching on what it believes is its preserve, the design of organization and jobs—especially at the shop floor level. This is but the current response in a long line of such defenses which began with the United States Senate's hearings on the Taylor System in 1912.[34] Over the last sixty years, the attacks and defenses have led to the incorporation of some concepts from other disciplines when these could be accommodated to the machine theory of organizations (organizations as clockworks), and to continuing the unyielding basic position of men as machine-like elements in a production system.

For those few aspects of quality of working life whose understanding is aided by seeing men as special machines or as machine-like elements, such as workplace arrangement, some contributions to knowledge have been made. Well-founded research in this field has turned almost completely to ergonomics (human factors) and operations research. Sadly, however, after sixty years of intimate association with work systems design and measurement, few if any theoretical or operational contributions to understanding or enhancing quality of working life are forthcoming today. This is particularly troublesome since any attempt to enhance quality of working life would be aided by the industrial engineer's assistance or made more difficult by his resistance, for he is seen in many firms, whether accurately or not, as the protector of production efficiency and as the rearguard fighting to protect the values and practices of the waning industrial era.

Where social scientists have become involved in action research on design problems within organizations, engineers, for example, after an initial hesitancy, have shown interest in the possibility that the sociotechnical approach could add a new capability to their armory. Thus a collaborative approach has proved possible with mutual benefits to both engineering and social science.[35]

From the foregoing sketchy review of the varying perspectives of the disciplines, it is clear that each has imputed value assumptions, usually unconsciously held, and always unanalyzed. The new interdiscipline or multidiscipline required for tackling the problems of further enhancing quality of working life will have to utilize the insights, methods, and frames of reference of all of them. But clearly it has its own set of values and assumptions. It is based on a special view of man which can be argued over but not, in the present state of knowledge, proved or disproved. Its adoption leads to creative forms of organization and to a critical view of the relationships between organizations and society—between man at work and man alive.

Commencement

The assessment of the state of the art in enhancing the quality of working life indicates a number of anomalies and shortcomings. Among the anomalies are great differences in advanced Western countries as to readiness for and changes made in the quality of life in the workplace. In the United States, attraction to the purpose and concept—in keeping with some of its most positive societal values—is coupled with considerable unease over the implications for management and unions, and with the tendency to characterize the concern over the quality of working life as wooliheadedness and do-goodism. In this pragmatic and action-oriented society, the anomaly of the attraction of purpose and concept to leaders in business, unions, and government and to younger people is coupled with aversion because of complexity and multidimensionality, seen as obfuscation, intellectualizing, and putting off. The implication is that there must be a nice, clean, simple answer being concealed. Related to this feeling is the expressed frustration over the lack of "final proof" either that the quality of working life is absolutely terrible or that its poor quality is having visibly disastrous consequences requiring urgent remedial action. That both may be so and not visible contributes to the unease and frustration, for the quality of working life issue challenges the core relationship of how society uses its members to get its work done.

The public concern in the United States is rapidly rising over the many restrictive, dysfunctional, and inequitable features of life in the workplace and over the rigidities of organizations, their managements and unions, in failing to accommodate to the evolving needs of society and its members, including entry and advancement of women and minorities.

This recognition is reflected in the extensive recommendations of the 43rd American Assembly, November 1–4, 1973, a national convocation, as contained in its *Report*, "The Changing World of Work." Private and public organizations, unions, government, and foundations are urged to support and engage in experiments with new forms of organization and jobs, with removing constraints in law and practice, and with providing methods and means permitting all who work to have a rewarding, economically viable, equitable, and satisfying working life—one which enhances the individual and builds more adaptive and effective organizations.

Affecting all the developments currently under way, however, are a number of anomalies which impede the dissemination of learnings and the diffusion of practice. Among these is the noncomparability of case reports of innovations, each written to suit what the author believed was significant. The need for comparability in this field is a newly recognized requirement, as is the need to provide reports in such form that readers can develop insights and understandings in order both to relate a case study to their own experiences and to help them build upon what they already know. In this way each case becomes an accretion to knowledge. As it is now, each case remains a unique or single instance. Although a considerable number of organizational and job innovations are known to be taking place, only some of these are reported and the reports are widely scattered, making for great difficulty both in ascertaining the state of development and in having one organization learn from another. Lastly, the understandable slowness of the diffusion of learnings and practice is being taken as evidence in support of two widely different positions: first, that the issues addressed either are inconsequential or the proposals offered in the case studies are insignificant; second, that achieving the outcomes reported are so time-consuming or costly as not to be worth the effort in the face of the large number of changes needed.

The shortcomings confronting developmental efforts are numerous. They include the lack of a common language among researchers and practitioners, which is disturbing to those not intimately acquainted with the research literature. Adding to this confusion is the fact that none of the different languages used is easily understood, thus requiring a number of nonexistent dictionaries. Further, the reports of most studies done in the past and the current understandings are based on unidimensional or, at best, on single-discipline perspectives.

The position papers prepared for the International Conference on the Quality of Working Life, invited for the purpose of sharing accumulated knowledge and assessing the state of the art, reveal these shortcomings. They also display the complexity of the issues both in their multidimensionality and in the variety of interrelationships. The papers realistically indicate that we should hold only modest hopes for rapid spread of understanding and replication of experience. They point strongly to the difficulties that lie ahead, but contribute to our recognition of the problems and to our insights.

Before turning to the first ever assemblage of papers involving almost all aspects of the quality of working life, excepting the interrelationships with formal education and community life, we should briefly review the international conference, held at Arden House, Harriman, New York, September 24–29, 1972, which was the stimulus for this collection.

The structure of the conference was composed of a series of introductory review plenary sessions, followed by general discussion of related sets of invited papers and case studies previously read by the conferees. Most of the conference time was spent in continuous participation in the intensive work sessions of the task forces. The papers and cases and general discussions were intended as background support for the work to be done by the task forces. These were structured by the conference planning committees to create working parties focused on topics crucial to advancing the state of knowledge of quality of working life and of its application. The conferees were assigned to task forces on the bases of their special competences and interests.

The task forces assessed substantive knowledge on the quality of working life that could be reported, requirements for changing organizations and jobs, for diffusion of knowledge and practice, for measuring and evaluating what has occurred, for comparability among case reports, and for building institutions that carry forward simultaneously the acquisition of data and change experiments to enhance life in the workplace. The reports of the task forces on comparability and evaluation appear in the volume, *The Quality of Working Life: Cases and Commentary.*

The majority of the conference participants have large experience in research and action research on the quality of working life, including those who have made the historically significant breakthroughs. A significant outcome emerging from group discussions was that the pace was quickening in advanced societies for modifying traditional work arrangements. There was a widely shared concern that in some instances time was running out, leading to turbulence rather than orderly transition. To meet these strongly felt societal needs in a responsive rather than an *ad hoc* fashion, one of the major conclusions reached was that the relevant disciplines will have to be pulled together into a multidisciplinary field and that research and education have to be organized around it. Institutional and programmatic needs were thus seen as having priority over developing more individual projects (which should go on in any event). These assessments are not contained in the papers, all prepared prior to the conference.

The conference chairman, Louis E. Davis, noted at the conclusion of the meetings that once again, as in other events in a dynamic process, the conclusion is the commencement. The conference, an international sharing of knowledge and experience, is a significant turning point in revealing the commonality and similarity of working life problems that beset advanced industrialized nations. It also demonstrated the support of the international research community for prospective engagement with working life problems in the United States.

Specific beginnings would have to be made and, for the United States in particular, the needs are to develop the institutional and programmatic responses to achieve the goal of enhancing the quality of working life. Required are simultaneous increases in the scientific, professional, and institutional resources available and increasing the awareness of all who work. In lesser degrees, this is the case in all advanced countries.

Three different sets of needs were defined for the United States: First is the establishment of at least one, and hopefully more than one, institute of high competence and impartial professional position whose services would be available to unions, management, and government in developing needed changes and, as a part of this endeavor, conducting and disseminating research on both how and why the outcomes were achieved. Second, through such institutes by means of training, conferences, and so on, the scientific, professional, managerial, union, and teaching resources available in the United States would be increased to meet the growing needs in various organizations. Such institutes would aid in bringing about curricular changes in the relevant disciplines and professions. Third, to increase the awareness of all who work, an "Association for the Advancement of the Quality of Working Life" is needed, which would draw together through meetings and journals all who are interested—professionals, researchers, and those committed to that goal.

On a worldwide basis, to support each national endeavor, an International Council for the Quality of Working Life was agreed to draw together institutes and groups in each country, aid in the formation of new centers as requested, and exchange knowledge, experience, and staff; an interim international council has come into being through the endeavors of many present at the conference.

The selections in this volume contain the most comprehensive examination to date of the issues and problems confronting the enhancement of the quality of working life. This collection and the authors' interpretation of the movement is a commencement—a beginning in addressing one of the central needs of advanced societies as they move into the last twenty-five years of the twentieth century.

NOTES

1. A. Touraine, *L'evolution du Travail Ouvrier aux Usines Renault* (Paris: Centre National de la Recherche Scientifique, 1955).

2. L. E. Davis, "Job Satisfaction Research: The Post-Industrial View," *Industrial Relations*, 10, no. 2 (May 1971), 176–193.

3. *Work in America* (Cambridge: M.I.T. Press, 1973).

4. James O'Toole (ed.), *Work and The Quality of Life: Resource Papers for "Work in America"* (Cambridge: MIT Press, 1974).

5. Preceding the report was the establishment by the U.S. Department of Labor of the triannual survey of working conditions which has been conducted by the Survey Research Center, University of Michigan. For the 1969–1970 survey report see S. E. Seashore and J. T. Barnowe, "Behind the Averages: A Closer Look at America's Lower-Middle Income Workers," *IRRA Proceedings, 24th Winter Meetings*, December 27–28, 1971, pp. 358–376. For 1973 survey report see R. P. Quinn, T. W. Mangione, M. S. Baldi De Mandilovitch, "Evaluating Working Conditions in America," *Monthly Labor Review*, November 1973.

The U.S. Department of Labor also supported the research for the *Annotated Bibliography on Quality of Working Life 1957–72*, Quality of Working Life Program, Graduate School of Management, UCLA, 1973. Additionally, the National Commission on Productivity's Quality of Work Project is supporting a few research attempts having some promise.

6. Only some of this is related to the perception that unions and their leaders will be required to face changes when workplaces become more democratic. The difficulties arising in such changes in Europe are discussed by Delamotte in selection 27, by Douard and Reynaud in selection 26, and by Mire in selection 28.

7. C. R. Walker and R. H. Guest, *The Man on the Assembly Line* (Cambridge: Havard University Press, 1952), and E. Chinoy, *Automobile Workers and the American Dream* (Garden City, N.Y.: Doubleday, 1955).

8. H. L. Sheppard and N. Q. Herrick, *Where Have All the Robots Gone?* (New York: Free Press, 1972).

9. H. M. F. Rush, *Job Design for Motivation*, Report no. 55 (New York: Conference Board, 1971).

10. At present unions seem somewhat beleaguered, given that they represent a minority of workers in the United States, by the growing popular attention to additional dimensions of life in the workplace. Only some grant the need and others see this as an unwelcome intrusion, retarding the development of joint endeavors.

11. An example is to be found in the work of the Quality of Working Life Program, Graduate School of Management, UCLA, where new alternative opportunities for design of organizations and jobs have been developed through new conceptual bases of technology. The same holds for redesign.

12. A Myrdal, *Towards Equality* (Stockholm: Prisma Press, 1971).

13. D. Jenkins, *Job Power* (Garden City, N.Y.: Doubleday, 1973).

14. N. A. B. Wilson, *On the Quality of Working Life*, Manpower Papers no. 7 (London: Department of Employment, 1973).

15. "Organizational development," "job enrichment," and similar methods have made a contribution to present knowledge and practice. However, their potentiality for further development depends on their future association with more sociologically oriented and less management dominated approaches, given the rapidly changing social and ethical climate within which work is being viewed.

16. Regional institutions are likely to be more viable than national ones in underdeveloped countries, particularly because of the scarcity of trained researchers and the growing viability of regional undertakings.

17. Should cooperative union-management relations be legally specified as in codetermination (*mitbestimmung*), for example, it is too early to say whether they would aid or create difficulties for developments more specifically concerned with quality of working life.

18. Indications are that different political colorations and structures require different strategies both for research and development of quality of working life. The long spells of social democratic government in Norway and Sweden have favored the open cooperative means in the progress toward better quality of working life.

19. Changes in accounting procedures and perhaps legal regulations will be required to enable economic implications and social costs to be accurately known. Likely collaboration between accountants, economists, lawyers, and social scientists will be called for. See also Cherns and Davis, selection 2.

20. D. V. McGranahan, "Analysis of Socio-economic Development through a System of Indicators," *The Annals*, 393, (January 1971), 63–81.

21. Wilson, *op. cit.*

22. K. E. Walker, Director, IILS, Statement to OECD Joint Working Party on Internal (Organization) Environment, Paris, May 10, 1973.

23. These have been the assumptions and experience of all Western industrializing nations. Only Japan both industrialized and evolved the equivalent of a blue-collar career. While achieving industrial peace it was paid for in concealed overmanning. Older blue-collar workers accepted careers as lifetime employment but not progressive in any other respect than pay. Young workers are less and less inclined to accept the negative aspects of such careers.

24. Report of Task Force on Evaluation, selection 5 in *The Quality of Working Life: Cases and Commentary.*

25. See sections on Research and Development plus the Disciplines and a New Interdiscipline of this selection.

26. S. E. Seashore, "Defining and Measuring the Quality of Working Life," selection 6.

27. W. A. Faunce and R. Dubin, "Individual Investment in Working and Living," selection 19.

28. F. W. Taylor, *Scientific Management* and *Shop Management* (New York: Harper, 1911).

29. D. T. N. Williamson, "The Anachronistic Factory," *Proceedings Royal Society,* A. 331 (London, 1972) 139–160.

30. P. H. Englestad, "Socio-Technical Approach to Problems of Process Control," chap. 23, in L. E. Davis and J. C. Taylor (eds.), *Design of Jobs* (London: Penguin Books, 1972), pp. 328–356.

31. J. Burnham, *The Managerial Revolution* (Bloomington: Indiana University Press, 1960).

32. Thorsrud disagrees with Faunce and Dubin who favor the compensatory model that "individuals can and do find different kinds of compensation for a poor fit between requirements of personality and work." Granting that compensatory mechanisms are needed in deprived work situations, Thorsrud cautions that the basic data used by social scientists to build theories about working life derive from psychopathological studies. Evidence from Norweigian studies indicates that the spillover from fractionated work life into family life causes some grave maladjustments and low levels of self-esteem in nonwork situations. People given elbow room in their work situations tend to generate and protect values that do not lead to a one-dimensional society emphasizing consumerism.

It is true that working-class and lower-class youth begin early to develop self-investment in areas other than work because they do not anticipate a large payoff from work. It does not necessarily follow that importance of work will decline in American society. A diminishing return from investment in work may lead, as Faunce and Dubin look at it, not to a withdrawal of self-investment, but rather to a dispersion of self-investment into new areas in which anticipated returns may be greater. If opportunities for self-investment in nonwork areas is reduced, the situation may become serious.

33. M. Fern, "The Myth of Job Enrichment," *The Humanist,* 33, no. 5 (September 1973), 30–32.

34. U.S. Congress, House of Representatives, 63rd, 2nd sess. Special Committee to Investigate Taylor and Other Systems of Shop Management, under authority of H.R. 90 (1912).

35. An example is given in P. A. Clark, *Organizational Design in Theory and Practice* (London: Tavistock, 1972).

2

Goal for Enhancing the Quality of Working Life

Albert B. Cherns and Louis E. Davis

THERE has been an important societal shift in the value placed on the benefits of industrialization, leading to reckoning its costs in what we call the quality of working life.

Quality of working life permits a focus on a key problem of great significance—the dysfunction in the individual experience between work and the rest of life. This concept also implies a problem for which social sciences may have developed a viable change methodology.

Needed are reliable, comparable indicators of quality of working life supporting the emerging central theme of the individual's development and life experience. This theme is intended to penetrate the more fractionated national foci such as education, production, and the like. The first attempt at such indicators should include the values of autonomy, responsibility, and interdependence. These in turn require that they be jointly optimized among themselves, and be optimized in turn, jointly, with other social values.

In creating these new indicators it is not enough to recognize that different social planners base their plans on different goals, but that social scientists cannot tell them what their goals should be. The study of quality of working life as a social issue can advance only as collaboration occurs among scholars of all types and between scholars and "practical people."

Because of its immediate relevance to the practical, quality of working life is not served by a continuation of the use of physical science models of investigation. Action research, which challenges the distinction between a system of science and a system of application, is advanced as a more effective paradigm in molding the many concerns and viewpoints of those involved in the further study and change to improve the quality of working life.

In starting this new field of study and action, four elements are considered necessary:

1. The emergence and acceptance of knowledge concepts concerning quality of working life. This is the principal agenda of the conference reported in this volume.

2. The institutional framework for the generation, diffusion, and validation of the knowledge concepts.

3. The diffusion of change processes—emergence of a "learning society perspective."

4. Transcending quality of working life—preparing the way to push the frontiers out as required.

The first International Conference on the Quality of Working Life is the background to developing a scenario which features the first coming to grips with a new and immensely important shift in social values. For decades we have bewailed the "world we have lost" romantically regretting the disappearance of the simple pleasures of the manly dignity of toil in preindustrial society. We have contrasted these losses with the manifold benefits of industrialization, perceiving the latter as a tradeoff for the former. Today's mood has changed. We now doubt the value of these benefits; increasingly, we reckon their cost; and many succumb to a deep pessimism about the future of our society—indeed, about the future of human life on our planet.

As social scientists we have contributed to this pessimism. Social engineering solutions to social problems for the price of increased support for the social sciences have been exposed as failures, but much of the disappointment derives from the inadequacies of the social engineering model as the paradigm of social science utilization. We are, then, pursuing two objectives: to seek a model of a new industrial society which does not trade off dubious benefits against real losses of dignity and self-development; and to seek ways of utilizing our knowledge, our concepts, and our present models to help bring about that new society.

The key concept is the quality of working life. First, we claim that it permits a focus on a key problem of great significance for the future of developed societies because of its multiplier effect. And we claim, further, that this is one problem for which the social sciences may have developed viable problem-solving means.

Both these claims call for justification. We have already indicated that a good deal of the unanticipated dissatisfactions, disharmonies, and dysfunctions of industrial society have pivoted on the developments in the nature of how work is required to be done. The division of work from nonwork has emphasized the penal aspects of the former and the trivial aspects of the latter, thereby creating serious dysfunctions in the individual experience as a result of work arrangement and job organization; between education and employment, learning and earning; and between the behavior expected of the individual as producer and as consumer. But the responsible citizen demands responsibility, the learning experience leads to further learning, development implies further development. The multiplier effect is clear, and it creates the need to reconstruct the jobs.

Our second claim is concerned with change. Change is not brought about by sudden revelations, repentance, or a change of heart; nor does it follow from the report of a scientific investigation. A change, like the problem itself, has multiple ownership. It can be brought about by the collaboration of all concerned—employer, worker, union, and social scientist; even government is involved. In contrast, the engineering model, calling for "experts" to adopt and apply a new development, has failed us every time.

Asserting that certain experiments have been successful is insufficient. We must know why and under what conditions success is probable. Nor is success an all-or-none matter; measures are needed of the degree of success obtained. Our emphasis on careful learning about evaluation experiments derives not only from the need to convince the doubters; it derives even more strongly from the scientific requirements for validation and generalization of knowledge.

Suppose we know how to enhance the quality of working life; that in itself will not necessarily make other people want to do it. The goal is not just a better functioning work organization and, therefore, is not a matter for employers and employees (and unions) alone. The goal is a better society, which will not come about through isolated experiments. Enhanced quality of working life is a public goal, and the expression of public goals is through the plural political processes of our society—through legislators, administrators, pressure groups.

Demanding a "better" quality of working life is meaningless if we cannot compare what we have with something else—what somebody else has, for example. We need reliable, comparable indicators of quality of working life. New indicators can make headway only if misleading indicators can be replaced. We need the reverse of Gresham's Law.

In neutral terms, borrowed from the engineering concept of efficiency, productivity is a ratio of output to input. Labor productivity is a ratio of increment to output (value added) divided by unit of work input (man-hours). The classic paradigm treats this ratio as a closed system; that is, it closes off a consideration of anything other than the specific outputs and inputs. To make the classic paradigm useful, we are required to accept that the only cost to society as a whole and each of us individually of the value-added increment is the cost of man-hours directly used in achieving the units of output. We are required, therefore, to carry the welfare decrements or increments in some other system: for example, improved capacity through training to the individual, impaired health, mental health, burden on social security system of displaced workers, impaired organizational capacity to cope with long-term future, and so on, are all treated as inputs (positive or negative) to some other system.

Likewise, *increased* industrial output (value added) obtained at the cost of loss of amenities of life or decrements to health, mental health, capacity to enjoy life, skills, and social skills may figure in conventional accounting as a productivity increase only by excluding these costs. Calculated on a wider system basis, the changes concerned may represent an increment of output at the cost of a greater proportional increment of input from other systems (*loss* to other systems—community, etc.).

It is through penetrating the existing foci of national concern that the issue of quality of working life will become salient. So long as the individual is seen as the "product" of one (educational) system to be "consumed" by the other (industrial), our attention is diverted from the central theme, the individual's development and life experience, which his schooling and his work should both be designed to enhance. If, then, we can only maximize that which can be comparatively assessed or measured, a key task is to develop such measures on the lines of social indicators.

Our first attempt to define the concept of quality of working life has been to emphasize the component values of individual and group autonomy, individual responsibility, and interpersonal interdependence. One simple indicator is unlikely to represent adequately all four of these. Indeed, we may find that the simultaneous maximization of all four values is not possible, or if it is, that it conflicts with other social values of equal importance. Two requirements follow: first, examine means of jointly optimizing the values identified as components of a high quality of working life; second, attend to the wider problem of jointly optimizing these and other social values. The provision of such indicators is essential if we are to present politicians, administrators, engineers, economists, lawyers, and accountants with targets to which their special skills can be mobilized and aimed.

It is not enough to recognize that engineers design jobs on the basis of technological considerations, not of social and personal values; that accountants evaluate individual operations on the basis of conventional principles which omit personal and social gains and losses; that politicians seek "prosperity" for their constituencies on the basis of a narrow concept of prosperity. We can make progress not by attacking, but by working with these specialists to devise new bases on which we can advance together; we as social scientists cannot *tell* them what their goals should be.

In addition to scholarly collaboration there must be collaboration with the manager, administrator, union official, technical specialist, and political leader, who is rightly and necessarily sensitive to his constituency. His perspective, too, may need to broaden, but through persistent programs of mutual learning and collaboration. The Norwegian exponents of such programs emphasized the tentative nature of what has been learned by their experiments. The development of a new technology of cooperation between social scientists and other specialists and managers and administrators—"practical men"—is required here, a technology of "action research."

The assumptions of the physical science model in the social sciences are that the generation of our knowledge, its transmission, and its validation are the functions of the system of science; and its wider diffusion and translation into practical application are the functions of the system of practice. The action research paradigm challenges these distinctions, claiming not only that the generation of new knowledge can take place in a mode in which many traditional scientific constraints are inapplicable and inappropriate, but also that certain kinds of knowledge are inaccessible to the methods of scientific inquiry which emphasize objectivity and replicability. And it denies the necessity of the distinction between generation and diffusion of knowledge, asserting that forms of knowledge are generated within the diffusion process itself. Lastly, it claims that the validation of knowledge can take place within the action context and is not subject to the traditional validation criteria of the scientific method insofar as these represent the hypothetico-deductive, controlled experiment paradigm.

There is no doubt that much of our knowledge of the methods of enhancing quality of working life derives from the action research paradigm, and that issues of the utmost scientific importance are involved. The methods have corresponding consequences for the institutional framework, which will need to emerge to handle these issues. Some aspects of the traditional university (whose mores and value systems reflect the conventional scientific paradigm of the processes of generating, transmitting, and validating knowledge, protected by its models of the legitimate relationships between sponsors, clients, and researchers) may pose problems for the collaborative relationship of action research and for the action researcher's exchange model of the transaction-based generation of knowledge. Yet certain kinds of intellectual activity, which may be essential to the goals of our program, can proceed only within the university framework and with the attendant protections for worker and researcher alike. For some features of the program, however, new institutional frameworks may be essential.

So we are trying to start a new field of study and action. But what? Our scenario must contain these elements: (1) a way in which knowledge concepts emerge and obtain acceptance; (2) the institutional frameworks for the generation, diffusion, and validation of these increments to knowledge; (3) the diffusion of change processes in society which will promote the under-standing, acceptance, and centrality of the quality of working life concept, and develop the thrust to bring about these changes; (4) the promotion of other conceptual frameworks, institutional developments, and diffusion processes transcending the concentration on quality of working life which someday will doubtless be seen as limited, culture-bound, and institutionally circumscribed, as we now perceive its predecessors.

The Emergence and Acceptance of Knowledge Concepts Concerning Quality of Working Life

That is, of course, the principal agenda of this quality of working life con-ference, representing the first getting together of diverse approaches under the umbrella concept of quality of working life: multidisciplinary, multinational, theory- and problem-oriented reports and evaluations of experimental ap-proaches and analyses of action research projects. In our scenario, they are given a new coherence, focus, and challenge by their mutual confrontation; a new interdiscipline emerges seeking its own rigorous criteria.

The Institutional Frameworks

We are already engaged in institutional building. From the outset, we have perceived the vital role of a network system—one network for the generation and validation of knowledge and another for its diffusion. The first is our network of researchers, its form, criteria for membership, mode of operation. While collegial values are indispensable, they imply the mutual respect and trust, egalitarian attitudes, communitarian resolution of differences, tolerance of divergence, and ready personal access which characterizes small enduring communities of scholars. Their generalization and inevitable mod-ification to suit a network basis of communication and operation has yet to be worked out. Models of various kinds exist. (One word of warning is in order: institutions exist to allocate resources; without resources, we have nothing to share. Of course, these resources include ourselves and our time, knowledge, experience, and commitment. These our network freely commits. But the main-tenance of institutional linkages and frameworks are continuing tasks which must be paid for.)

Networks for diffusion are more problematical because models are scarcer and less obviously appropriate. There are models of organizations based on perceived mutual interests or trust. They may express these interests or their response to threat in terms of "OK" values like "free enterprise," "fair practices," and so on. Models are scarcer of organizations perceiving themselves as primarily in conflict with one another, which can collaborate freely on the basis of some overriding value accepted by all. In the face of extreme threat— war, famine, revolution—such collaboration becomes possible, but it seldom outlasts the threat. Our venture in institution building must aim to bring together, *in cooperative endeavor,* organizations with many conflicting objectives which are yet able to subscribe to the relatively abstract value of enhancing quality of working life. Our success will depend to a great extent on our inventiveness in tackling this task.

The Diffusion of Change Processes

This topic is too vast to be sketched in more than one salient feature. Running right through our approach has been the implied criticism that the "ownership" of problems is a hindrance to their solution. It is not just a matter of groups and individuals having vested interests in the problem for which they are responsible. The real problem is the rigidity of the complex arrangements for the division of labor in society. That many of the revolts against these rigidities have their pathetic, if not absurd, side should not divert our attention from the reality of the dysfunctions. If engineers "own" the problem of designing jobs, economists, the problem of assessing the true prosperity of enterprises, and lawyers, the problem of deciding what ethical principles of former days mean in modern society, then each narrowly conceived problem will be resolved at the expense of shifting the dyseconomies onto the problem area of someone else. Even the ownership of problems by trained experts is a function of the systems of higher education which often faithfully reflect the adaptive solutions of former times. Institutions and organizations faced with turbulent environments have evolved model devices—none, of course, perfect. The matrix organization, for example, combines the functional discipline-based division of labor with the problem-oriented multidisciplinary team organization, an arrangement virtually prohibited in our system of higher education at graduate school level, and the employment market both faithfully reflects and reinforces that orientation. Our scenario must then call for both a new division of labor and a new graduate school design to stimulate and reinforce this new pattern.

Transcending Quality of Working Life

Who could have predicted one hundred years ago the travails of the birth of the postindustrial society? Who, then, can foretell today how long the problems of quality of working life will remain with us? If we focus our attention on a concept as important and central as quality of working life, are we not in danger of developing solutions which can be as dysfunctional for future problems as the doctrine of work rationalization has been for us?

Already we speak of the "learning society," a concept of generality and potential applicability reaching far beyond our focus on quality of working life. In our attack on the problem of enhancing the quality of working life, we must avoid temptations to seal off options, to reduce the capability of societal institutions, and to tackle new and so far unforseen problems. The most sketchy of all our attempts at a scenario is this: the institutional-building model we adopt—the conceptualization of our problems and our activities —must incorporate the learning society perspective. The selections, discussions, and case studies that follow indicate the kind of modest start we have made.

3

Humanizing Work: A Priority Goal of the 1970s

Neal Q. Herrick and Michael Maccoby

To optimize the worker's well-being and correspondingly that of society, four principles of humanization of work are presented: security, equity, individuation, and workplace democracy. Obstacles to humanization of work are discussed, as are the positive effects on economic and human outcomes. The role of public policy should be extended and strengthened beyond existing efforts to enhance security to include equity issues within firms and between individuals. Individuation and democracy should be stimulated by public funding to support experimental and demonstration projects, retraining of engineers, altering of university curricula, and research projects. Legislation may be needed to reward firms that humanize work and prescribe and limit institutional practices which are unhealthy for workers and society.

The views expressed by the authors are not intended to reflect the positions of the Academy for Contemporary Problems, Harvard University, or the Institute for Policy Studies.

Four Principles for the Humanization of Work

What can the American worker rightfully expect from work? Growing evidence shows that the organization and nature of work are key elements in determining a worker's physical and mental health and his behavior as a citizen. Certainly, then, he should have the right to expect a work environment that is not detrimental to his health, and that encourages the practice of responsible citizenship. A central goal of our society, therefore, should be the development of institutions of work that stimulate the creative abilities of workers: activeness, cooperativeness, interest in learning, and self-development—all of which will encourage positive attitudes of citizenship and spark the hope necessary to build a more just and humane society.

We have formulated four basic principles which together underlie the humanization of work: security, equity, individuation (i.e., craftsmanship, autonomy, and learning), and democracy at the workplace. We will discuss these principles as well as their effect upon the restructuring of the workplace. Then we analyze the factors that have stood in the way of achieving that goal, and describe developments that could work for its support. Finally, we outline the role of public policy as it could contribute to the humanization of work.

The Principle of Security

Security at the workplace implies the worker's need to be free from fear and anxiety concerning his health and safety, income, and future employment. One cannot regard work as "humanized" when physical conditions are dangerous or the air is polluted, and when insecurity and economic want provoke fear and anger.

What is a measure of security? Since the enactment of the Fair Labor Standards Act in 1938 providing for a minimum hourly wage, much has changed in our society: our notions of acceptable standards of living have increased; changes in the consumer credit structure have made an annual income rather than an hourly wage the measure of security; many employers have become larger and richer and better able to insure the worker's security, and the family as a social institution no longer provides insurance against economic hardship—individuals must turn elsewhere for help in time of need. Thus, a worker in fear of losing his income lacks the security necessary to develop his present skills and ideas. He also needs to be secure about his long-range future. Besides Social Security, he needs protection of his retirement benefits, that is, immediate vesting and/or portability so these benefits are not lost if he wants to change his job.

The Principle of Equity

Equity implies that workers should be compensated commensurately with their contribution to the value of a service or product. Lack of equity (e.g., large differences in income between managers and workers and lack of sharing in profits) causes resentment and hostility. In practice, equity requires searching for methods of evaluating individual contributions considered just by all involved. Although collective bargaining has contributed toward equity in many industries, adopting the principle of equity leads to increased responsibility and concern for fairness in both work and other relationships.

The principle of equity also includes the concept of profit sharing. Workers should be assured contractually a specified percentage of the profits divided among work groups, taking into account the contribution of each group toward increased productivity. While this may be difficult to ascertain, once the principle is accepted many companies have developed equitable profit-sharing plans with good effects on both the attitudes of the worker and the economic health of the industry.

A final element of equity is the concept of paying a worker not for a particular task, but on the basis of skills and knowledge developed with respect to other jobs in the establishment—paying him for what he knows and can do rather than for his specific job (in contrast to payment according to credentials). This idea makes sense, particularly when other aspects of work are humanized; for example, when work is structured around democratic teams rather than authoritarian hierarchies. In sum, all experience indicates that the principle of equity results in greater productivity on the part of the worker.

The Principle of Individuation (Craftsmanship, Autonomy, and Learning)

Work should stimulate the development of unique abilities, craftsmanship, and the capacity for continued learning. The principle of individuation, once adopted, can lead to a nonbureaucratic work environment in which workers are encouraged to develop themselves and learn as much as they wish about the organization as a whole. Individuation also involves bringing back the concept of craftsmanship, which means that workers have maximum autonomy in determining the rhythm of their work and in planning how it should be done.

The desire for craftsmanship is deeply imbedded in the American character. For example, recent studies of workers' attitudes have clearly revealed their desire that jobs be more interesting, provide more autonomy, and allow them to develop abilities, factors concerning them more after they have reached a certain level of income. These studies indicate that the workers have a sense of what is important to their mental health, indeed, to their sanity. As Erich Fromm has written recently, both psychological and physiological studies show a direct relationship between boredom and destructiveness in people.[1] The health of both the worker and the society we live in depends on putting into practice the principle of individuation at the workplace.

The Principle of Democracy

Degrees of democracy at the workplace range from participatory management, where workers' views are heard and considered in decision making, to systems of worker control, where a structure is created in which workers' authority and responsibility are institutionalized. The principle of democracy, like that of individuation, is opposed to making the worker into a passive object, part of a machine. Wherever feasible, workers should manage themselves; authoritarian, hierarchical control should be replaced by cooperative, self-managed groups. Where supervisors are necessary, they should be elected directly by workers.

The concept of democracy also includes the right to citizenship, including free speech within the workplace as well as outside; it requires great activeness and responsibility on the part of all participants. In its most fully developed form, democracy in the workplace means that workers also take responsibility for what is produced, how money is invested, and for the social consequences of production.

These four principles—security, equity, individuation (craftsmanship, autonomy, and learning), and democracy—together describe a system that is constructed to optimize the worker's well-being and, correspondingly, that of society. Such a system would develop in the worker a sense of hope, activeness, and productiveness, alleviating symptoms of discontent, mental illness, and despair. It must be noted here that many attempts for change have been based on the erroneous belief that certain symptoms have a single cause. This kind of thinking does not take into account that individuals live in social systems in which every factor is related to every other factor. Changing one principle without paying attention to others may lead to results very different from the ones desired (i.e., healthy and productive workers). For example, a system of democratic decision making, which requires responsibility and achievements in the absence of security or equity, becomes exploitative as workers are asked to give more of themselves without proper guarantees and rewards. Even forms of security, democracy, and equity without individuation may be experienced as unsatisfying, as reported in some Yugoslavian worker-managed industries, since the work remains boring for many workers and they have no chance to develop themselves or to understand the total process.

Obstacles to the Humanization of Work

Although there have been some moves toward implementing the principles of humanized work, as a society we are still far from achieving this goal. This is true even though experiments have shown both greater productivity and increased worker well-being. Many managers and large stockholders still believe the only purpose of business is to make as large a profit as possible, that the profits will trickle down and the goods produced will be useful to all people. They do not realize that more income and consumer goods cannot compensate for wasted lives. A society based on greed, mechanization, and compulsive consumption will not be a healthy, just, or even strong society. Furthermore, the mechanistic concept of "efficiency," based on the idea that the workplace resembles a machine in which the worker is an interchangeable part, is self-defeating in a society in which people are not willing to be dehumanized or docile. Yet some managers still hold on to the old ideas, although they no longer fit reality. Even the machinery of work is often designed in terms of this mistaken and mechanistic view of efficiency.

Another obstacle to the humanization of work is the difficulty of translating needs and principles into actions. Even though workers suffer because of the organization of their work, often they see no real alternatives. They ask for improvements in the areas of security and equity, but cannot envisage how these could be put into practice. Most unions, too, limit their attempts to humanize work to issues of security and equity, mainly because of the difficulty of translating principles into specific bargaining items, but also because of the conviction that they can best maintain their power by sticking to the traditional issues of higher wages, early retirement, and more time off from work. True, for some jobs humanization may be only partially obtainable, but workers and industrial engineers have to put their minds to conceiving new ways of organizing and designing work by studying models already developed in this country and abroad.

Factors Supporting the Humanization of Work

Despite inertia and opposition to change from many managers and union officials, a number of factors support the possibility of humanizing work at this time. First is the pressure of international competition. The cost per unit production in the United States increased 22 percent between 1965–1970 as compared to only 3 percent in Japan. Thus, industry in America has to search for more productive ways of organizing work, reexamining assumptions about the productivity of the old mechanized system. The need for higher productivity also encourages greater automation, requiring better educated workers who must understand machines and be alert to problems before they develop. Increasingly, therefore, industry will need a more qualified and versatile workforce, one which is less likely to accept the dehumanization of the workplace.

Growing worker dissatisfaction is another development that may promote the humanization of work.[2] To maintain productiveness, industry and office alike must reckon with new attitudes developing in the work force. The

Triennial Working Conditions Survey, conducted by the U.S. Department of Labor, shows workers' deep concern that their work is not interesting, that it does not give them the opportunity to develop special abilities, and that it does not allow sufficient autonomy (freedom to decide how they will do the job). Young workers, the group expressing the most dissatisfaction, valued these positive dimensions of work even more than did their elders. The challenge to arbitrary and illegitimate authority, which accelerated with the civil rights movement of the early 1960s, has resulted in a general demand by most Americans that society be based on rational principles and that institutions serve people rather than people serve institutions.

Another related symptom is the increase of strikes.

Days Lost Due to Work Stoppages (in millions)

1965	1966	1967	1968	1969	1970	1971*
23	25	42	49	43	66	47

Source: Analysis of Work Stoppages, BLS, U.S. Department of Labor, 1970.
* Unpublished data.

Furthermore, the Bureau of Labor Statistics reports that, on a nationwide basis, the average daily rate of absenteeism has risen 35 percent since 1961. These statistics suggest that the mechanized concept of efficiency does not meet the needs of the workers nor those of the economy.[3]

A third factor is the changing character of the manager, especially the professional manager, who is himself a worker in a bureaucracy and suffers from conditions that do not allow his full human development. Intelligent and farsighted new managers have seen that individuals interested in their work can change the whole atmosphere at the workplace. While at present not many managers have been innovative in humanizing work, those who have are becoming well known and are considered as models for the best young students of industrial engineering and management.

Since the question of whether humanizing work can bring about increased productivity is so crucial, three experiments in work humanization —and their economic consequences—are described below. While we do not claim that every effort will succeed, the three very different examples show that such projects—even though they may only approximate the four principles discussed earlier—*can* have highly favorable economic and human results.

Norsk Hydro.[4] The Norsk Hydro (Norway) fertilizer company was facing increasingly stronger competition; profits were decreasing and cooperation between labor and management was considered by management to be unsatisfactory. In response to this situation, the company selected a fertilizer processing plant with about fifty employees for experimentation. The following organization changes were made:

The shifts were organized in flexible subgroups, responsible for production in assigned work areas. (Individual workers were not given specific jobs.)

The organization was built up without "first hands" (i.e., supervisors).

Each worker was given the opportunity to learn all the tasks within his subgroup through job rotation and mutual aid.

It was left to the worker to decide how quickly and how much he wanted to increase his competence, thus leaving little chance for too much or too little variation in a job.

The idea behind the organization was that every man should be able to get help from others when his own abilities were not sufficient, and vice versa.

A bonus system was installed which paid the workers according to factors they themselves could influence, such as quantity produced, cost, loss of materials, and working hours. The bonus was paid to all workers in the fifty-man plant in order to stimulate cooperation.

Basic wages were paid according to the number of jobs in the plant which a worker was able to do rather than the actual work he did.

The human outcomes of reconstructing the work arrangements to bring workers into participation in decision making were measured by asking the workers before and after the experiment whether their jobs were satisfying or not satisfying in general, and with regard to variety, learning, responsibility, and security. The percentage of workers expressing satisfaction increased from 58 to 100 on general view, from 45 to 85 on variety, from 33 to 96 on learning, from 42 to 96 on responsibility, and from 39 to 73 on security. The economic result was decreased production costs per ton of about 30 percent during the first six months of the project; absenteeism in the experimental factory was 4 percent against 7 percent for the controlled factory.

Norsk Hydo has since extended this participative management experiment throughout the company. Top management sums up its reaction: "It is not only the production that matters, human values become more central."

General Foods (GF).[5] Lyman Ketchum, a GF plant manager, experimented with participative management and became convinced that if work were humanized, high productivity would follow naturally. An operations manager for the Pet Foods Division, he designed a new plant in Topeka, Kansas, based on sociotechnical principles which were translated into these kinds of techniques:

All personnel are on a monthly payroll and share the same general conditions of work.

Compensation is made according to the number of jobs a worker can do rather than the specific job he happens to be doing at any given time.

Autonomous work groups are collectively responsible for all tasks involved in accomplishing specified processes (e.g., processing, testing, packaging).

Work roles within each group are interchangeable.

The human outcomes of this experiment are suggested by Richard Walton, of the Harvard Business School, who writes that the Topeka workers "have been unusually active in civic affairs—apparently more active than is typical of other plants of the same corporation or other plants in the same community." [6]

The basic economic result is a saving of $810,000 during the first year of operations, based on the estimate that 248 people would have been required to man the plant under traditional work structures while only 182 are needed to do the job at Topeka. Much of the difference resulted from a decreased need for operating managerial staff. In addition, there has been a steady increase in the level of quality control.

Texas Instruments (TI). [7] In 1967 TI's principal location in Dallas contracted for its cleaning and janitorial services. TI's facility engineers evaluated the location as being only 65 percent clean, and the contractor's ability to do the job was aggravated by a quarterly turnover rate of 100 percent. Preceded by careful planning and training, the following actions were taken in a test site involving 120 maintenance personnel:

Cleaning service teams of nineteen people each were organized and given a voice in planning, problem solving, and goal setting.

Each team was held accountable for its overall job; the means of getting the job done were left to the team. It was the team's responsibility to act independently to devise its own strategies, plans, and schedules to meet the objective.

Workers were taught how to measure their own performance and given the freedom to do so, both as individuals and as teams.

While here only economic results were directly measured, human outcomes can be inferred from the drop in the turnover rate:

The cleanliness level rating improved from 65 percent to 85 percent.

Personnel required for cleaning dropped from 120 to 71.

Quarterly turnover dropped from 100 percent to 9.8 percent.

From the fourth quarter of 1967 until the fourth quarter of 1969, cost savings for the entire site averaged $103,000 per year.

Although the humanization of work may prove both productive and humanly satisfying, there is no guarantee that it will be adopted as policy. Authoritarian managers will be fearful of losing their power; middle management may feel their jobs are threatened as workers take on more responsibility; and top managers might prefer tightening discipline to eliminate worker discontent rather than undergoing the painful task of reorganizing the workplace and taking the personal risks involved. In the Lordstown strike,* for example, the first responses to workers' unwillingness to accept speedup

* Personal communications with UAW.

and ultramechanization were mass firings and disciplinary actions. Most of all, the system itself causes a powerful inertia; systemic restructuring requires far more commitment than merely assenting to a need for change. If industry and labor ignore the possibilities of humanizing work, however, a cycle of strikes and even of sabotage and more policing will lead to disintegration in this country, both material and spiritual, the outcome of which cannot be predicted.

How will the process of humanizing work in the United States get under way?

So far most of the models, particularly in the United States, have been unilaterally developed by corporations. While this is understandable, future progress requires that organized labor take a leading role. Otherwise, unions will remain suspicious that these projects have the goal of undermining their hard-won gains of security and equity for workers. In fact, joint union-management initiative can assure that all new projects have built-in provisions for workers' rights and protect union members from exploitative practices.

The Role of Public Policy

Although public policy can and should encourage the humanization of work, that goal can really be achieved only through the combined efforts of trade unions, industry, and the government, as awareness grows of the human and economic costs of dehumanized work.[8] The point most appropriate for public intervention is the specific role of legislation and executive action in providing security, equity, craftsmanship, and democracy in the workplace.

In fact, public policy has helped to provide employment security for at least thirty-seven years, since the Social Security Act of 1935, followed by the Employment Act of 1946. But workers have not yet achieved a guaranteed income, and the existence of a public employment service, modest unemployment insurance payments, and limited federal training programs have neither guaranteed employment security nor brought unemployment rates into line with those of other developed countries.

The Occupational Safety and Health Act of 1970 was an important step toward achieving security from physical harm, but it does little to promote or protect the mental health of workers. In terms of equity, the federal income tax law acts as a force to redistribute income, but only when compared to other types of taxation which take equally from the rich and the poor. While basic tax reform would increase equity, public policy should also be considered to regulate the equity of incomes within organizations.

Public policy has indeed a necessary role in humanizing work, and this is a propitious time to develop specific programs because of the need for increased productivity brought about by international competition, new technology, and the need for educated people to man it, and changes in the demands of workers, due, in part, to the progressive development of the

American character. While the goals embodied in the four principles of security, equity, individuation, and democracy are not new, the approaches, procedures, and mechanics of achieving them have in many cases never been considered or debated by and before the American people. There is no intent here to present worked-out solutions, but rather possibilities are suggested for consideration and debate, both in the congress and in other forums, so that a feasible legislative program can begin to evolve.

To assure employment (security) for workers in relatively large firms, legislation analogous to the present Fair Labor Standards Act may be considered; that is, such firms would have to guarantee their employees—after a short probationary period—fifty 30-hour weeks of employment each year at a stated minimum wage.[9] If a firm could not comply with this requirement because of economic reasons, there could be provisions for a federally insured loan or federal assumption of responsibility for backing the guarantee by other employment or training. A supplementary approach—geared toward workers in smaller firms—might be the adoption of a major continuing education program, such as the one proposed by Dean Striner of American University in March 1972.[10] It would provide an opportunity to learn skills and develop individual abilities, but if industry does not allow individuation, such programs may be useless.

Another possibility is, of course, employment guaranteed by the federal government through states and municipalities, which would eliminate unemployment except among those unable to work. However, the possibility of further government employment must be considered in the light of the quality of work. Government work also should be constructed according to the principles of security, equity, individuation, and democracy.

Continued employment in the same firm (particularly one which initiates the other three principles) is the most desirable and economically productive form of security since it encourages productive behavior by reducing psychological as well as economic fears. However, security cannot, in a market economy, be solely an employer responsibility. A guaranteed minimum income financed through the tax system would provide a necessary backup element.

Proposals to eliminate unemployment must be discussed in detail as well as in principle. Questions such as the roles of public employment offices in a zero unemployment situation need to be aired and made explicit. Cost-benefit analyses, for example, of the cost of guaranteed public service employment vs. the present cost of unemployment insurance need to be made and widely discussed. The public cannot form its opinion on these concepts until it knows what they imply in specific basic situations.[11]

The tax reform approach to the redistribution of income—the goal of (equity)—is presently before the public, but there are societal values that must be considered involving appropriate compensation differentials.

First, there is need for national maximum wage guidelines to remedy a situation that came to light at the recent General Motors stockholders' meeting.[12] We believe that the present gap between the lowest paid members of the employed labor force and the highest paid members cannot be defended as equitable. Nonbinding maximum wage concepts as explicit statements of societal value should be considered by the congress, the executive branch, trade unions, and other institutions of our society, the maximum wage being expressed as the appropriate ratio between the highest and lowest salaries in an establishment. It could apply to the professional managerial class, but not to entrepreneurs, and could recognize the effect of the size of the corporation upon appropriate maximum salaries.[13]

A second approach to a more equitable distribution of income, profit sharing, also has potential for increasing the amount of income available to distribute; it has been a factor in simultaneously increasing individual income and profits in many firms.[14] Profit sharing means first, that profits based on increased productivity be shared among all the workers in an organization, and second, that these profits be shared equitably according to special contributions made by individuals or groups. Profit sharing could be encouraged by providing tax relief to corporations and companies to set aside a minimum percentage of annual net profits for distribution among their employees on a basis which decreases income gaps.[15] Such tax relief would take the form of partial tax credits for monies set aside. Wage increases bargained apart from a consideration of profits are usually passed on to the consumer—who is also the worker. Increases in income, bargained as a pre-agreed share of profits, are tied to productivity and therefore noninflationary; they mean real income gains for workers. When these increases are paid in the form of stock ownership, they are of increased economic as well as psychological benefit.

Federal standards would be needed to assure sound profit-sharing arrangements:[16]

1. *Make profit sharing clearly an addition to wage and fringe benefits.* Where this is not the case, profit sharing is exploitative: a substitute for wage and fringe increases which, because it is more complicated than these increases, is more subject to manipulation by the employer and can easily become a new form of piecework compensation.

2. *Provide payments that reflect the real contribution of each worker or of small groups of workers.* The implementation of this principle requires a redefinition of productivity to account for indirect costs, such as turnover, absenteeism, and other costly symptoms of the "work withdrawal" syndome, along with the development of sound techniques for measuring small group productivity: group discussions of individual participation and group awarding of bonuses to those who contribute most.

3. *Make the plan a contractual arrangement.* Arrangements which can be arbitrarily rescinded are paternalistic and unsuited to the current and future labor force.

4. *Open the books to the union and workers.* Failure to maintain open books leads to suspicion, distrust, and possibility of manipulation.

The principles of (*individuation*) and (*democracy*) at the workplace alter the work environment and the conditions of employment to provide people with the maximum opportunity for individual achievement and cooperation— as producers and as human beings. Most techniques which focus on the actual work environment attempt to achieve this goal through providing autonomy, encouraging learning through job interchangeability,[17] and stimulating cooperation through democratic decision making. Growth outside the immediate work environment is approached by means such as continuing education and training.

Because of the dynamics of the present business system, individuation and democracy are most in need of societal intervention. Short of legislation or an exercise of destructive worker power, there is little hope for effective decentralization of decision-making power from management to work groups. Proposed below are experimental changes which will perhaps be immediately acceptable, and long-run systemic changes which require much debate and refinement.

Federally funded experimental and demonstration projects in the public and private sectors to discover and refine those forms of work structure most conducive to both productivity and human values.

Programs to retrain the tens of thousands of industrial engineers brought up with the "efficiency expert" concepts of Frederick W. Taylor. While our existing institutions of higher education should primarily deal with this problem jointly with employers and employer associations, the government should give financial support.

Stimulus grants to institutions of higher learning assisting them in altering their undergraduate curricula to include and emphasize modern concepts of efficiency and the humanization of work.

Research projects addressing the problems of physical assembly lines and undesirable entry-level jobs. Manpower Development and Training Authority funds could be allocated in both the private and public sectors with the aim of improving entry-level jobs and thus reducing frictional unemployment. This research would be aimed at discovering solutions of general applicability to some of the economy's worst jobs (e.g., garbage collection).[18]

Concerning long-run changes, congressional hearings are suggested on means to institutionalize workers' rights to conditions of security, equity, individuation, and democracy, focusing on the viability of legislation based on the concept that human and economic goals can be achieved through workers' sharing in both the responsibilities of production and the profits earned. The agreement and conditions of sharing cannot be left to collective bargaining, *after the fact*, because this removes the motivational aspects of agreeing in advance that increased profits will be shared in a specified manner. Second, there is no built-in guarantee against inflationary settlements which—in the long run—hurt everyone.

We have already discussed profit sharing and the possibility of achieving it through tax-oriented legislation. It is also important that such legislation include provisions for responsibility sharing. It might provide a tax advantage to firms operating under contractual arrangements with their workers which include both of these mutually supportive elements:

Provisions meeting the profit-sharing standards already set forth.

Decentralization of decision-making power to workers. Federal standards could provide for different acceptable mixes of autonomy and interdependence designed to fit various business situations. Contracts would be submitted to the government for tax credit approval.

A classification of the degrees of decentralized decision making in experimental Norwegian plants is described below:

Gulowsen's Levels of Work Group Decision Making[19]

A. The group members decide their individual production methods.

B. 1. The group decides the internal distribution of tasks.

    2. The group decides on questions of recruitment.

    3. The group decides questions regarding internal leadership.

C. 1. The group decides what additional tasks to take on.

    2. The group decides when it will work.

    3. The group decides questions regarding the production method.

D. 1. The group has influence upon its quantitative goals.

    2. The group decides questions regarding external leadership.

E. The group has influence upon its qualitative goals.

This type of decision making is different from but not incompatible with representative industrial democracy. Rather, it refers to participatory or group democracy, the making of decisions cooperatively by small groups of people engaged in a common endeavor. These standards of shared decision making would give workers rights such as: electing their supervisor; deciding who is to fill a vacancy from among the prospective applicants; deciding who among them will do what tasks; and making their voices heard on matters of economic and financial policy. Small companies would no doubt qualify for a tax advantage without such a formal plan: it would perhaps be unreasonable to expect employers or entrepreneurs with very small numbers of employees to adopt formal profit- and responsibility-sharing contracts with their workers.

To conclude, the role of public policy in the humanization of work should first of all be to reward companies that develop programs based on the principles of security, equity, individuation, and democracy. Second, the federal government can also play a role in supporting these efforts (e.g., with federal insurance) and in speeding efforts to humanize the federal bureaucracy. Finally, it may be necessary to proscribe and limit institutional practices which are unhealthy for workers and, in the long run, for society. The process of humanizing work is in its infancy, and further development of policy will depend on experimentation with new models, supported by both unions and management.

NOTES

1. Erich Fromm, *The Anatomy of Human Aggressiveness and Destructiveness* (New York: Holt, Rinehart, & Winston, 1973).

2. The Gallup Poll job satisfaction index, which had remained about constant from 1963 to 1969, dropped 7 points, from 88 to 81 percent, in the number of satisfied respondents in 1971. Opinion Research Corporation, studying over 25,000 employees working for ninety companies, found that since 1966 employees have rated their companies lower than they did from 1955–1966 in three critical areas: basic working conditions, personnel practices, and communications. A 1968 survey for the John D. Rockefeller, 3rd, Foundation showed that 56 percent of a national sampling of students would not mind being bossed around on the job; by 1971 this figure had decreased to 36 percent.

3. It might be noted here that at a time when people are demanding more autonomy, the possibilities for autonomous work are decreasing. While many Americans still maintain the illusion that this is a nation of the self-employed, the statistics demonstrate a very different reality. The last frontier of self-employment is rapidly disappearing, at a rate of about 4.5 percent each decade. In 1950, 16 percent of the work force was self-employed; in 1960 it was 12.2 percent; in 1970 it was 8.1 percent. This decrease in possibilities for autonomy through self-employment makes it even more important to humanize the institutional workplace.

4. A. Bregard, J. Gulowsen et al., "Norsk Hydro—Experiment in the Fertilizer Factories," unpublished paper, January, 1968.

5. Louis E. Davis and Eric L. Trist, *Approaches to Improving the Quality of Working Life*, June 1972. Unpublished paper written for the U.S. Department of Health, Education, and Welfare's Work in America project.

6. Richard E. Walton, *Work Place Alienation and the Need for Major Innovation*, May 1972. Unpublished paper written for the U.S. Department of Health, Education, and Welfare's Work in America project.

7. Harold M. F. Rush, *Job Design for Motivation*, Conference Board, 1971, pp. 39–45.

8. In our society as a whole, lack of equity has its costs. The 1972 Report of the Presidential Committee on Population Growth on the American Future predicts that average real family income will rise from $12,000 to $20,000 per year over the next twenty years, and that there will be no decrease in the percentage of U.S. citizens living in poverty. It is in our real interest as a society to make sure this does not happen. The costs of inequity are staggering: they include the costs of crimes committed by the underemployed and the devastating psychological effects of underemployment—both on the men and women involved and on their children.

9. This approach has been shown to be workable by such firms as the Lincoln Electric Company of Cleveland, Ohio. According to the March 1967 issue of *Assembly Engineering*, Lincoln Electric was selling its welding equipment and electric motors at generally the same or lower prices than in 1937.

10. Herbert E. Striner, *Continuing Education as a National Capital Investment*. W. E. Upjohn Institute for Employment Research (Washington, D.C.: 1972). This type of program would also address the principle of individuation.

11. Dean Striner pointed out, when considering the cost of alternative approaches, we must keep in mind that over $4 billion were paid in unemployment insurance benefits during 1970, and that (as of June 30, 1970) there were over $12 billion in state unemployment insurance reserves.

12. At a stockholders' meeting in Detroit on May 19, 1972, the General Motors chairman was voted a 1971 salary and bonus of $825,000. The sixty-two other principal officers and directors received salaries, bonuses, and stock options totaling $17,952,561. UAW Vice President Irving Bluestone expressed doubt that the chairman contributed ninety times as much to the industrial process as did the man on-the-line. He suggested that, if corporation officers were entitled to profit sharing in the form of stock options and bonuses, so were workers.

13. For example, the difference between the lowest paid person and the highest paid person at the General Motors Corporation might reasonably be a multiple of twenty. The difference between the lowest paid and the highest paid worker in a smaller firm might more reasonably be a multiple of six or seven. A maximum wage based on an acceptable ratio between the salaries of the highest and lowest paid employees in an establishment would have two major values: establish a principle of equity, and provide a built-in self-interest motive for management to increase worker compensation.

14. B. L. Metzger and J. A. Colletti, *Does Profit Sharing Pay?*, 1971. The study says, "The group of companies with employee profit sharing programs performed in a superior fashion on all financial measures."

15. Present federal income tax law encourages deferred profit-sharing plans by devices such as exempting contributions and fund earnings from current taxation. However, because it is designed for deferred payment plans and because it lacks provisions for responsibility sharing, the present law does not have strong motivational implications and is only indirectly associated with the humanization of work. It acts principally to encourage a specific means of funding pension arrangements.

16. The same legislation would incorporate standards on guidelines for responsibility-sharing arrangements. Responsibilty sharing is the *quid pro quo* of profit sharing, required in order to promote increased productivity and humanized work. Responsibility-sharing guidelines are discussed below.

17. The Polaroid Corporation's programs to promote learning about many jobs in the company and to encourage scientific and cultural learning were a more advanced example of learning stimulation. Unfortunately, these programs were discontinued.

18. The practicality of this approach is illustrated by the application of existing technology to sanitation worker jobs in Venice, Florida. Trash and garbage collection in Venice was a major municipal problem. People were reluctant to take the job and, when they did, they were often absent, ill, or in search of other jobs; garbage was sometimes uncollected. Desperate, the city administrator bought six Cushman scooters with dumping mechanisms and gave one to each garbage/trash man. These scooters went up and down side streets and driveways, loading the main dump trucks. There is now a waiting list for sanitation jobs in Venice, the garbage is collected regularly, and the city is saving $65,000 per year.

19. Jon Gulowsen, Central Institute for Industrial Research, Oslo, Norway, used these levels to discuss several experimenting Norwegian establishments in an unpublished paper written in 1971. See J. Gulowsen, "A Measure of Work-Group Autonomy," Chapter 25, in L. E. Davis and J. C. Taylor, eds., *Design of Jobs* (London: Penguin Books, Ltd., 1972). He found establishments ranging from level A, where participation was limited to decisions on individual production methods, to level D, where participation included all the elements listed except an influence on qualitative goals. Level B firms were found to include level A as well as level B characteristics and so on.

4

Planning the First Steps toward Quality of Working Life in a Developing Country

Eric Trist

IN a developing country the quality of working life can become both ends and means. It is an end in itself because it is a highly significant component in the quality of life—the goal of all development. It is a means because the experiences of participation in decision making at the workplace and of progressive learning help workers acquire the civic competences and skills on which a country developing in the social democratic mode must rely. In principle, such countries have a choice of technology, the correct one being that which develops its own people as well as their material goods. The wrong choice would purchase economic advancement at the cost of binding the country to the skills, technology, and investment capital of an advanced nation. A form of sociotechnical assessment, as suggested by Cherns and Davis (selection 1), and development is suggested in Peru; an approach to planning is described which, if adopted, will provide the proper climate and setting for development of high quality of working life.

It would be tragic if in industrializing the less developed countries adopt the authoritarian management styles from which the advanced countries are beginning to break loose. It would retard development of their productivity, increase their comparative economic disadvantage, and all too rapidly create alienated workers likely to cause severe political problems. Their best strategy would be to "century skip"—to ignore nineteenth-century models of industrial organization and the dehumanizing values embodied in them—and experiment in ways suitable to the conditions of the Third World, with new forms of organization that give first importance to the quality of life in the workplace.

The author recently examined some of these problems in Peru, where he advised the Ministry of Industry on the development of industrial democracy in the newly established Industrial Communities, described below.

Recent Political Developments

The population of Peru, the pivotal country of the Andean region, is largely Indian. Of the country's 13 million people, 40 percent live in traditional Indian communities in the highlands, while another 35 percent, also Indian but known as "cholos," have moved into the *barriadas* surrounding the industrial cities of the coastal plain. Apart from a small group of Negroes in the north and a Japanese colony, the remaining 20 percent are "whites by definition"; they include mestizos as well as persons of pure Spanish and other European descent. Since the conquest and continuing after independence, this minority has comprised *the* society, and a privileged few among them have ruled the others.

During the 1960s the country was heading for political as well as economic chaos and the military, representing the middle class, took over. Their aims, supported by a majority of "whites by definition," professionals, and students, are to create a multiracial society which will include both the traditional and cholo Indians and permit the development of pluralistic but compatible social structures in rural and urban areas, and to work out complementary roles for state and private interests suitable to Peruvian conditions.

The Industrial Community Legislation

The problem with which the author was concerned arises from legislation introduced in 1970, setting up Industrial Communities (ICs) as collective legal personalities in all enterprises in the private sector. There were some

2000 ICs in 1972, employing some 200,000 people at all levels. Although the private sector represents only a small part of the Peruvian economy and population, the legislation is intended to create conditions which will foster its accelerated development in consonance with the ideas of decentralization, social justice, and social as well as private property, to which the government is committed.

An IC is composed of all employees of a given enterprise—management, supervision, white-collar and blue-collar workers—who, meeting in assembly, elect a council with a president and secretary. By the provisions described below, the IC gradually acquires up to 50 percent of the shares in the enterprise as well as up to half of the seats on the Board of Directors. The chairmanship then rotates between representatives of private and IC shareholders. Private owners may be members of the IC if they are also employees when they share in its rights and obligations.

The basic legal instruments are two forms of profit sharing, which together give IC members 25 percent of profits before taxes annually:

Form A provides 10 percent (according to salary) to each individual as a bonus. The effect of A is to widen income distribution and so to increase purchasing power and therefore to enlarge the overall size of the market.

Form B provides 15 percent to the IC as a whole (as a collective legal personality) to purchase shares in the enterprise. After 50 percent has been acquired, funds may be invested in other enterprises. Former shareholders are bound to sell to the IC and also invest elsewhere. The effect of B is to increase the rate of capital formation and widen the basis of shareholding on a communal principle. Both more purchasing power and more investment are essential if economic development is to proceed. The priority given to B should, moreover, generate internal funds which will make the country less dependent on foreign capital.

Initial Discussions with the Ministry Planning Staff

The author felt these two measures effectively embody recent thinking in development economics by various Latin American economists but, from a sociopsychological point of view, they were incomplete. Instrument A gave an employee a personal monetary incentive; B, a control incentive.[1] In themselves they would not create the conditions allowing an employee personally to participate in the concrete decisions which affect his daily work. Only so far as he could do this would his creative resources be released. On such release would depend in substantial measure the level of his work satisfaction and of his productivity—indeed, his capacity to learn and grow as a human being and to contribute fully to his society.[2]

The need was emphasized to make a clear distinction between participation in ownership and participation in conducting the operations of the enterprise. One can have the former without the latter, vice versa; or one can have participation in both. Moreover, the degree of participation can vary enormously in both respects. Failure to distinguish between these two basic forms of participation has created immense confusion in the discussion of industrial democracy.[3]

Government planners were responsive to these points. They had become concerned lest the passage of laws which instituted ICs and established the rules for their economic regulation should be taken to mean that nothing more need be done; that all else would follow from the act of legislation. Under present arrangements, IC councils had little to do other than financial monitoring, with assembly meetings in all likelihood turning into poorly attended rituals and the board becoming remote, even with elected IC directors. It was agreed that the creation of the conditions required to realize the full potential of the human resources of the enterprise constituted a task distinct from that of increasing the level of personal income (A) or of widening the basis of ownership (B). In subsequent discussions this distinct task was referred to as C, which became the code word for quality of working life. It was postulated that

> if A and B provide the necessary conditions, then only when C is added will the necessary and sufficient conditions be created for optimum industrial development.

The Decision to Experiment

Among the key issues regarding the development of ICs whose discussion led to acceptance by planners of the idea of operational experiments was the potential inability of the Peruvian work force to participate actively in the direction of their work. The Peruvian worker has been brought up to be passive and dependent, the Peruvian manager to be patriarchal and authoritarian. These traits are built into their "social character" which cannot easily be changed.[4] There was also the question of low educational level. Literacy (in Spanish, moreover) has still to be fully established in the Indian urban population.

These and similar problems have led many to maintain that less developed countries have a poor chance of developing C capability. However, a study undertaken by the Tavistock Institute[5] in the Calico Mills, Ahmedabad, India, where the workers, many of whom were illiterate and had only recently come into the city from the countryside, showed an amazing ability to develop self-organizing autonomous work groups in the textile industry. Productivity, quality control, wage levels, career opportunities, and job satisfaction all increased substantially. They were able to obtain these results, it was postulated, because they brought with them deep experience of a more organic pattern of life, lost by those urbanized and industrially regimented for a generation or more. The preservation of this experience enabled them rapidly to learn holistic and flexibly interchangeable work roles. Moreover, cooperation seemed natural to them through customs largely intact in the Hindu joint families to which they still belonged.

Against this background, it seemed worthwhile to propose and test a hypothesis: Third World populations undergoing industrialization are likely to bring with them unsuspected talents which will hasten rather than hinder C developments. If one assumes that such talents do not exist, one will never try to develop them. Or, if one confronts Third World workers with organizations characterized by extreme job breakdown and close supervision on bureaucratic and authoritarian lines, any talents that may be there will begin to wither. In view of these alternatives, those concerned with industrial development in the less developed countries must address themselves to the issue of building the conditions for a high quality of working life into the job designs and organizational practices being evolved.

The Indian communities of Peru possess outstanding and well-preserved traditions of cooperative work and artisanship. It is unlikely that these have been entirely forgotten, even by those who have moved into the marginal *barriadas* of the urban centers. With their fellows remaining in the highlands they comprise the majority of the population. One either learns to work constructively with human resources of this kind or gives up hope for reasonably rapid and successful industrial development in a country such as Peru. Preferring the former option, the author made the following recommendations for experimentation with type C development:

Recommendations

1. At least one pilot experiment concerned with establishing the condition for realizing a high quality of working life would be set up in a selected enterprise containing an IC, under the auspices of the Ministry of Industry whose sanction and commitment were regarded as absolutely essential to protect and nourish the endeavor.

2. At the site selected, key individuals, committed to the values of industrial democracy, should be well known personally to the ministry so that an understanding of what would be involved could be worked out informally under protected conditions. They should come from all levels of the enterprise and include members of the board, IC council, management, and trade unions. Members of the ministry would act as the ex-

ternal resource group in developing and monitoring the project to gain direct experience for future developments and for diffusion of results.

3. The selected enterprise should be in an industry having priority for development, underlining the importance attached to the project by the ministry and supporting the use of scarce resources for such innovation.

4. The selected enterprise should also be one in which a new technology was being diffused, linking the endeavor to the country's technology transfer program so that one could enrich the other. It is most important that technology transfer programs acquire an understanding of quality of working life factors. What has to be "transferred" is not simply a technology but a sociotechnical capability adapted to the conditions of the host country. Indeed, the idea of transfer is in itself a misleading concept. Sociotechnical remodeling would better express what needs to be undertaken.[6]

5. The enterprise selected should be of medium size—not less than 100 or more than 300 employees—assuring a certain differentiation and complexity of internal organization as well as manageability while allowing the enterprise to be affected as a whole.

6. The nature of the work done and of the new technology being introduced should be such that clear opportunities for work restructuring would arise, entailing detailed sociotechnical analysis and design and permitting comparison of results with traditional forms of organization.

7. After these choices are made, the project should be discussed formally with the board, the trade unions involved, the management, and the IC council. Thereafter, the project should be discussed at the IC assembly, and agreement to proceed obtained from the entire body based on progress reports, feedback, and ultimate choice as to further continuation.

8. The trade unions should be assured that negotiated agreements involving wages or working conditions would not be abrogated during the period of experiment.

9. The board, the IC council, and the trade union representatives should jointly appoint an action group, as the Norwegians have done in their experiments, to do the work needed to carry out the actual changes. (This group would work in conjunction with a small team from the ministry and would report to the board, the ministry, and the IC assembly.)

10. The action group would proceed from urgent and manageable problems to achieve early success to more difficult and more general ones. Its work should be closely linked to the planning processes of the organization, eventually affecting general policies and the design of new installations.

11. Great care must be exercised to provide suitable means of conflict resolution as the project proceeds and of justly and humanely dealing with groups or individuals likely to be harmed. Misperceptions, prejudices, and fears must be "worked through" in open discussions—as indeed also unrealistically high expectations and overexcitement.

12. The object of the experiment would be not only to raise productivity and work satisfaction, but to transform the whole organization into an adap-

tive learning system capable of self-sustaining improvement and relevant innovation, and by so doing to increase these capabilities in each individual not merely as an employee, but as a man and as a Peruvian.

13. Finally, the selected enterprise should be located in the Greater Lima area so as to be readily accessible to the ministry and other government agencies and national organizations headquartered there, as well as to universities and students.

The Extension of Ministry of Industry's Leadership Role

In insisting on the ministry's involvement in the pilot experiment, the author envisioned a continuing role for that body in fostering the C component of industrial democracy, as well as the A and B aspects of profit sharing throughout the country. C capability will not develop spontaneously; it must be planned and led, and in Peru only the ministry could do this. Therefore, as the first priority, it must develop C capability within its own staff with the help of learning missions abroad to universities, institutes, and innovative enterprises in a number of countries.

Another role for the ministry would be to foster the development of relevant courses in Peruvian universities, especially in schools of management and engineering. Those now in the labor force—both management and union members—must be reached through "post-experience courses" or other forms of adult education. Important groups such as industrial engineers, organization planners, and operations researchers have all been trained (on approved Western models) in absolete, atomistic, technocratic, and bureaucratic concepts reflecting the machine theory of organization. Only a thorough change of attitude through a massive reeducative effort is likely to make them into a valuable source of support.

In the next two or three decades, there will be a very great increase in manufacturing industry in the less developed countries. Some of this growth will be initiated by these countries themselves, but some will be introduced by multinational enterprises, with the goal of extending their business in countries which provide the most economical location for production for the world market. A great deal of the work will consist of component assembly and other fabricating or process activities which account for so many of the jobs in which the quality of working life is the poorest—jobs designed in the ways which have become standard in the industrial engineering traditions of the advanced countries.

It is urgent, therefore, to bring to the attention of the governments of the less developed countries, multinational corporations, and international agencies the need to consider job design—a kind which will foster a high quality of working life—as an integral part of industrial development and of the planning and educational processes associated with it. The Peruvian initiative represents a first step in opening up the field.

NOTES

1. I. Sachs, *La Découverte du Tiers Monde* (Paris: Flammarion, 1970).

2. In advanced countries alienation of blue-collar and white-collar workers, line and staff middle managers has become the more evident as so-called affluence has increased. The young, particularly, with a higher standard of education and higher life expectations, are becoming increasingly intolerant of narrow monotonous jobs and authoritarian forms of management. In the science-based industries the work on the shop floor is problem solving rather than physical labor. These industries are creating what is often called the second industrial revolution—whose core activity is information handling. Its coming has revealed the extent to which the older industries can have more flexible organizations allowing for more autonomy, power of decision, and participation at the lower levels than has been traditionally accepted. Could not the less developed countries take advantage of this realization? In fact, do they not need to do so to further their own development?

3. In the workers' councils of the decentralized enterprises of Yugoslavia, there is full participation in ownership but almost none in the conduct of operations and management has remained authoritarian. By contrast, there are a growing number of plants in the United States and Britain where ownership remains in private hands but where extensive use is made of autonomous work groups and participatory modes of decision making at various levels of management. The results as regards job satisfaction and productivity have been encouraging, whereas the results in these respects in Yugoslavia have been disappointing, indicating there is a decided limit to what can be achieved unless operational participation takes place. There is also a limit to what can be achieved by operational participation alone, for in the United States and Britain there has recently been a recrudescence of interest in profit-sharing schemes.

4. E. Fromm, and M. Maccoby, *The Social Character of the Mexican Peasant* (Englewood Cliffs, N.J.: Prentice-Hall, 1970).

5. A. K. Rice, *Productivity and Organization: The Ahmedabad Experiment* (London: Tavistock, 1958); A. K. Rice, *The Enterprise and Its Environment* (London: Tavistock, 1963).

6. See discussion by Cherns and Davis of sociotechnical assessment in selection 1.

PART
II

Defining and
Measuring
the Quality of
Working Life

THE authors in this section tackle different but inevitably overlapping aspects of the problems of definition and measurement of quality of working life. All accept that different people will have different perspectives on what makes for a high quality of working life and that some components are pre-potent; that is to say, you can give little attention to such questions as the potential for learning in your job if the physical conditions are appalling or the prospect of layoffs is always imminent. In this respect, spokesmen who point to the elimination of continued pockets of poor working conditions, poor pay, and low job security as prior objectives to pursuing quality of working life are surely right; they may be wrong, however, if they argue that any talk about quality of working life is a dangerous distraction from the "real" needs of the worker. That kind of argument would devalue any attempt to im-prove the flavor of beef on the ground that some people have too little to eat. As several contributors show, the impact of his work life on the individual is the outcome of many interacting factors, the salience of each of which can differ from group to group and from time to time. Walton proposes that we look for possible tradeoffs between factors so as to optimize the situation for as many as possible. His selection is an attempt to disaggregate the concept of quality of working life to expose those elements which could be separately measured and subsequently reaggregated when their inter-relationships have been established.

Another way of approaching this problem of dealing with the multi-dimensional nature of the criteria exposed by Walton is explored by Dyer and Hoffenberg. We can take it for granted that any process, whether manu-facturing or organizational, will have some negative as well as some positive consequences. Faced with multidimensionality, many decision makers retreat into using a single criterion, then trying to patch up by remedial action the damage done on the remaining criteria. Our aim, then, is clear: to enable decision makers to use more criteria. While Walton proposes tradeoffs, Dyer and Hoffenberg suggest a more thoroughgoing and theoretical approach to boiling down and putting in order some forty variables culled from the quality of working life literature. Their "cluster" method offers possibilities not only of making measurements of key variables, but also of using these to define quality of working life itself.

All the authors agree that quality of working life is not just job satisfac-tion, which is only one among its many aspects. Job satisfaction has far too long stood surrogate for a true measure of quality of working life. Nor is it a unitary factor, requiring a considerable amount of disaggregation before its components can be used in a wider framework. Furthermore, job satisfaction, not alone among attitudinal measures, has a flavor of the self-fulfilling prophecy. Most of us can react only to what we know. If our expectations of work are realistically adapted to what work provides, we will be "satisfied" because our expectations are met. And, the more we identify ourselves with our jobs, the less willing we are likely to be to express a dissatisfaction that can only injure our own self-perception.

The three selections by Seashore, Sheppard, and Lawler are all concerned with the present status of measurement. Inevitably, they are obliged to make use of the data collected over the years concerning job satisfaction as this is the only measure available. All three are critical of the rather narrow conceptualization of job satisfaction used in that measure and suggest other parameters which must be taken into account if we are successfully to measure and monitor changes in the quality of working life.

The only longitudinal data available, however, are of the disaggregated job satisfaction concepts. These data, limited in scope though the authors point out, nonetheless provide valuable signposts to the shifts in sentiment and concern of large samples of workers over time toward the qualitative aspects of work life. That some of the most important changes are recent is shown by the fact that, although Seashore points to several decades in which the proportion of dissatisfied workers in the United States has remained low and fairly constant, Sheppard, examining the record over the last decade, describes a decline in satisfaction among employed white Americans.

Seashore and Sheppard both review existing data on job satisfaction measures. Sheppard suggests a new measure of frequency of job satisfaction. He regards this principally as an outcome variable for which the inputs are, of course, those making for a high quality of working life. Seashore emphasizes that satisfaction and dissatisfaction are not just output measures, epiphenomena, but act as motivators, thus entering into the processes of change and accommodation, as agents entering into interaction with jobs and the environment. We do not know all that much about the strategies workers use to accommodate to events which from their point of view are normal recurring features of their lives. We suspect that some strategies are too costly in terms of the health both of workers themselves and of their organizations.

A full conceptualization of the definition and measurement of quality of working life necessarily takes us far beyond studies of job satisfaction as a single parameter. Analytical studies such as those of Enid Mumford[1] enable us to disaggregate the concept of job satisfaction. She identifies five "contracts" between the employee and the firm: the Knowledge Contract, the Psychological Contract, the Efficiency (Rewards) Contract, the Ethical

(Social Value) Contract, and the Task Structure Contract. Job satisfaction is the degree of fit between the individual's needs, expectations, and aspirations and his work experience in these five areas.

More knowledge and better measures are good, but they are not enough by themselves. Sheppard and Lawler both maintain that the problem is less the difficulty of measuring or obtaining useful indicators of quality of working life than of its neglect. Managements, unions, and governments have all accorded a low level of importance to quality of working life; if it had been seen as important, the difficulties of measurement would have been overcome. The development of concern with social indicators offers one means of increasing the visibility of the problem by seeking longitudinal measures which can serve as major indicators of the quality of life.

If, however, managements are to obtain *and to use* such measures to improve the quality of working life in their organizations, they may need urging and even regulation by government. Lawler makes some interesting suggestions for such regulation; the least controversial and probably the easiest to ensure would be the requirement that in designing new plants managements should file a "psychological impact statement" in the same way as environmental impact statements are now mandatory. Goodale et al. are also concerned to relate quality of working life better to quality of life. In their view, measures of job satisfaction have been conducted within what is essentially a closed-system framework. The concept of "job" itself is one which relates to the work situation and measures commonly refer to the individual's relationship to his job rather than to the place of the job within his whole life space. As these authors point out, quality of working life must be seen as a component of the quality of life in which its salience may indeed be high, but not overwhelmingly so. Social indicator movements seek to subsume measures of quality of working life within a hierarchy of measurements, but so far no satisfactory way of doing this has been found. Goodale et al. attempt to relate quality of life and quality of working life by suggesting a model, but empirical testing must follow with a view to modification of this model.

NOTES

1. Enid Mumford, *Job Satisfaction: A Study of Computer Specialists* (London: Longman, 1972).

5

Criteria for Quality of
Working Life

Richard E. Walton

EIGHT major conceptual categories relating to the quality of working life are proposed, each including specific considerations—for example, autonomy, multiple skills, information and perspective, whole tasks and planning. Examples are presented of how the eight categories lend themselves to various types of analysis: some criteria are especially salient for one employee group, while others are salient for the identification and deficiencies affecting different groups. There are complex relationships among the categories, some pairs of which contain apparent inconsistencies while others permit tradeoffs. There may be curvilinear relationships between certain categories and between productivity and quality of work experience; there is no consistent relationship between job satisfaction and productivity. The current trend in redesigning work assumes that opportunity to use and develop capacity is presently underdeveloped rather than overemphasized. In considering bases for deriving quality of working life criteria related to the eight categories, combinations

A partial version of this selection has been published as "Quality of Working Life: What Is It?", *Sloan Management Review*, Fall 1973, pp. 11–21.

are suggested of various empirial methods—for example, surveys, observations, and depth interviews. Criteria could also be derived from ideological systems or from theories of human development. Differences in subcultures and life styles are accompanied by different definitions of what is a high quality of working life. Three ways are suggested of allowing employees a free and informed choice that takes into account some of the more subtle aspects of the quality of working life.

In the United States and in other industrially developed countries, there is a growing interest in the possibilities of redesigning the nature of work. Evidences of this interest are the many organizational experiments currently under way, intended to improve both productivity for the organization and the quality of working life for its members.

Although the broad productivity criterion contains some dilemmas—for example, short-run versus long-run effectiveness—it appears to be relatively straightforward when compared with the quality of working life, which is the focus of this selection. How should the quality of working life be conceptualized, and how can it be measured? What are the appropriate criteria, and how are they interrelated? How is each related to productivity? Are these criteria uniformly salient for all employee groups? How can quality of working life criteria be derived or rationalized? These questions are central to both research on the quality of the human experience in work organizations and action programs which seek to improve that experience.

The phrase "quality of working life" suggests comprehensiveness. The concept embraces—but is broader than—the aims of a long series of legislative acts that began in the early twentieth century: for example, child labor laws; the Fair Labor Standards Act establishing the 8-hour day and the 40-hour work week; and workmen's compensation laws which protect the job-injured employee and have led to the elimination of many hazardous working conditions.

The concept is also broader than the aims of the unionization movement which made rapid headway in the 1930s and the 1940s, when emphasis was placed on job security, due process at the workplace, and economic gains for the worker. And it is broader than the notion of the 1950s, when psychologists proposed that a positive relationship existed between morale and productivity and that improved human relations would lead to the enhancement of both. Finally, the concept is broader than any of the attempts to reform in the 1960s, such as the drive for equal employment opportunity and the numerous job enrichment schemes.

The concept of the quality of working life in the 1970s must, however, include the values that were at the heart of these earlier reform movements, and it must include other human needs and aspirations, which have only now come to the fore, such as the preference that one's employer be socially responsive.

Eight major conceptual categories are now proposed, ranging from adequate and fair compensation for work to the social relevance of work; they provide a framework for analysis of the salient features that together make up the quality of working life.

Adequate and Fair Compensation

The typical impetus to work is to earn a living. It is fundamental, therefore, that the quality of working life is affected by how well this aim is achieved. What level of earnings is adequate for a particular job or for any individual is the most relative of all aspects of the quality of working life discussed here. Also, there is at present no consensus on objective or subjective standards of adequacy of compensation.

"Fairness" in compensation, on the other hand, has various operational meanings: job evaluation specifies certain relationships between pay and such factors as training required, job responsibility, and noxiousness of working conditions. By other approaches, supply and demand for particular skills or community averages determine the fair level of compensation. Another standard of fairness relates to ability to pay—more profitable firms should pay more. A variant of this standard is that when work rule changes increase productivity of employees, it is only fair that the economic fruits of productivity be shared with the employees involved. But it may be that the application of one standard of fairness produces a pattern of compensation judged unfair by another standard.

The adequacy and fairness of pay are partly ideological questions. For example, a twenty-to-one ratio between the pay of the top executive and the hourly worker of a firm may have been generally accepted in the recent past, but it may become widely regarded as too large in the near future.

Even though accepted operational measures are not available to judge the adequacy of income from work and the fairness of compensation, the two factors are important determinants of the quality of working life:

Adequate income: Does the income from full-time work meet socially determined standards of sufficiency or the subjective standard of the recipient?
Fair compensation: Does the pay received for certain work bear an appropriate relationship to the pay received for other work?

Safe and Healthy Working Conditions

It is widely accepted in our society that workers should not be exposed to physical conditions or hourly arrangements that are unduly hazardous or detrimental to their health. Legislation, union action, and employer concern have worked continuously to raise the standards of satisfactory working conditions, some aspects of which include the following:

Reasonable hours enforced by a standardized normal work period beyond which premium pay is required.

Physical working conditions that minimize risk of illness and injury.

Age limits imposed when work is potentially destructive to the welfare of persons below (or above) a certain age.

It is possible that in the future, more stringent standards will be imposed where health is less the issue than comfort, that is, minimizing odors, noises, or visual annoyances. On the other hand, the general improvement in the quality of working conditions and the earlier maturation of youth may lead to a relaxation of age limits in some areas of working life.

Immediate Opportunity to Use and Develop Human Capacities

As to the content of work itself, the industrial revolution and a simplistic extension of its underlying logic has taken much of the meaning out of work. To varying degrees work has become fractionated, deskilled, and tightly controlled; planning the work has often become separated fom its implementation. Thus jobs differ in how much they enable the worker to use and develop his skills and knowledge, affecting his involvement, self-esteem, and the challenge obtained from the work itself.

Autonomy: Does the job allow for substantial autonomy and self-control relative to external controls?

Multiple skills: Does the job permit the learning and exercise of a wider range of skills and abilities, rather than a repetitive application of narrow skills?

Information and perspective: Can the worker obtain meaningful information about the total work process and the results of his own actions, in order to appreciate the relevance and consequences of his actions as a basis of self-regulation?

Whole tasks: Does the job embrace a whole task in order to provide meaningfulness, or is it merely some fragment of a task?

Planning: Does the job embrace planning as well as implementation activities?

Opportunity for Continued Growth and Security

Here the focus shifts from the job to career opportunities. Although the opportunity of self-improvement through education and hard work has been considered an American birthright, the typical industrial job can now be completely learned within a few weeks or a few years, after which the blue-collar worker has reached nearly the peak of his earnings and can look forward only to minor improvements. The same is true of white-collar workers. Most professional workers tend to peak somewhat later, but they frequently confront an additional source of discouragement—the obsolescence of their knowledge and skills. Thus attention needs to be given to the following aspects of working life:

Development: The extent to which one's current activities (work assignments and educational pursuits) contribute to maintaining and expanding one's capabilities rather than leading to obsolescence.

Prospective application: The expectation to use expanded or newly acquired knowledge and skills in future work assignments.

Advancement opportunities: The availability of opportunities to advance in organizational or career terms recognized by peers, family members, or associates.

Security: Employment or income security associated with one's work.

Social Integration in the Work Organization

The preceding categories relate to the worker's immediate and long-range opportunities of expressing and developing individual abilities. However, since work and career are typically pursued within the framework of social organizations, the nature of personal relationships becomes an important dimension of the quality of working life. Whether the worker has a satisfying identity and experiences self-esteem will be influenced by the following attributes in the climate of his workplace:

Freedom from prejudice: Acceptance of the worker for work-related traits, skills, abilities, and potential without regard to race, sex, creed, and national origin, or to life styles and physical appearance.

Egalitarianism: The absence of stratification in work organizations in terms of status symbols and/or steep hierarchical structures.

Mobility: The existence of upward mobility as reflected, for example, by the percentage of employees at any level who could qualify for higher levels.

Supportive primary groups: Membership in face-to-face work groups marked by patterns of reciprocal help, socioemotional support, and affirmation of the uniqueness of each individual.

Community: The sense of community in work organizations that extends beyond face-to-face work groups.

Interpersonal openness: The way members of the work organization relate to one another about their ideas and feelings.

Constitutionalism in the Work Organization

A member of a work organization is affected by many decisions that are made on his behalf or about his status in the organization. What rights does he have, and how can he protect his rights? The labor unions have brought constitutionalism to the workplace to protect employees from arbitrary or capricious actions by employers. But in unorganized employment, there may be wide variations in the extent to which the organizational culture respects personal privacy, tolerates dissent, adheres to high standards of equity in distributing organizational rewards, and provides for due process in all work-related matters. These aspects of constitutionalism are key elements in providing quality of working life:

Privacy: The right to personal privacy, for example, withholding from the employer information about the worker's off-the-job behavior or about actions of members of his family.

Free speech: The right openly to dissent from the views of superiors in the organization without fear of reprisal.

Equity: The right to equitable treatment in all matters including, for example, the employee compensation scheme, symbolic rewards, and job security.

Due process: Governance by the "rule of law" rather than the rule of men with respect to such matters as equal opportunity in all aspects of the job, privacy, dissent, and so on, including procedures for due process and access to appeals.

Work and the Total Life Space

An individual's work experience can have positive or negative effects on other spheres of his life, for example, his relations with his family. Prolonged periods of working overtime can have a serious effect on family life. Also, if frequent transfers are required, there are psychological and social costs when families are uprooted from their networks of friends, acquaintances, and local affiliations. But, even beyond that, the more direct relevance of work to the total life space is best expressed by the concept of balance:

Balanced role of work: Work schedules, career demands, and travel requirements that do not take up leisure and family time on a regular basis. Likewise, advancement and promotion that do not require repeated geographical moves.

The application of this criterion is often debatable. When a person invests enormous time and energy in work at the expense of family, it is unclear whether this pattern is a cause or symptom of deficiencies in the family situation. Sometimes the employing organization is imposing demands that seriously affect the employee's ability to perform other life roles such as spouse or parent. In other cases, however, these demands are in fact largely self-imposed to escape the responsibilities and strains of family roles; if work did not absorb this time and energy, the person would shift his attention to other pursuits outside the family, such as hobbies or civic activities.

The Social Relevance of Work Life

The socially beneficial roles of the employing organization and the socially injurious effects of its activities have increasingly become salient issues for employees. Organizations seen not to be acting in a socially responsible manner will cause increasing numbers of workers to depreciate the value of their work and careers which, in turn, affects their self-esteem. The concept of social relevance raises some of these social responsibility questions:

Social Responsibility: Does the worker perceive the organization to be socially responsible, for example, in its products, waste disposal, marketing techniques, employment practices, relations to underdeveloped countries, participation in political campaigns, and so on?

Some Perspectives on the Criteria of the Quality of Working Life

The scheme of eight conceptual categories outlined above invites several types of analyses, including (1) how some criteria tend to be associated with the purposes of a given type of change agent or are especially salient for one employee group, but not for others; (2) how each quality of life attribute tends to be related to the others in practice; and (3) how each relates to productivity. Below, each of these analyses are briefly described in order to gain additional perspective on the whole scheme.

Deficiencies Affecting Different Employee Groups

Currently, various employee groups seem to experience different deficiencies in the quality of their respective work lives. Some nonunionized employees have suddenly become aware that the lack of constitutionalism in their particular work organizations is a key defect in the quality of their work lives. Engineers have been laid off according to criteria different from those which they had understood determined their job security. Faculty members despair at the lack of due process in decisions affecting tenure. Primary teachers in nonunion school systems often have no recourse when they are fired for certain activities off the job. Recent growth in unionization among teachers and university professors probably results more from concerns about this aspect of work life than from concerns about the level of compensation.

Also, in recent years the restlessness and alienation of blue-collar and office workers has extended to employees who already enjoy what is called here constitutionalism; this indicates a priority need to alter the content of the work itself to provide challenge and more satisfying contact among workers.

A number of young doctors and lawyers have recently demanded that their employing organizations adopt policies and practices more responsive to certain acute social problems. Some engineers and scientists have expressed similar opinions, while others have become increasingly concerned about technical obsolescence. Even stockbrokers, advertising agency executives, and business managers whose work lives would have scored high on most of the criteria set forth above have made the news by dropping out of the career "rat race" in order to redress the imbalance between work and other aspects of their lives.

Interrelations among Quality of Working Life Criteria

There are complex relationships among the eight conceptual categories. Several pairs tend to be positively correlated; for example, the quality of the immediate work challenge not only affects current job satisfaction, but can offset the tendency toward skill obsolescence. Other pairs contain apparent inconsistencies; for example, heavy emphasis on the rule of law in work organizations has tended to promote impersonality and impede some forms of social integration; the elaborate rules governing job rights, arising to provide job security and prevent arbitrary treatment by superiors, have limited the flexibility to make work more challenging; the high involvement of employees which results from such job attributes as autonomy, whole task responsibility, and membership in a cohesive face-to-face group occasionally works against a balance between work and other life roles advanced as an important quality of working life.

The question arises, are there inherent tradeoff relationships among some of these qualities of working life, occasionally necessitating a decline in quality in one respect in order to improve it in another? Perhaps not. It may be that mechanisms yet to be invented or cultures yet to be developed can provide constitutionalism without encouraging impersonal relations and rigidity in roles and responsibilities.

Relationship to Productivity

Another question is how changes in each of these aspects of working life may affect the productivity and longer run effectiveness of the employing organization. Probably, general positive or negative correlations between productivity and changes in the quality of a particular dimension of work life cannot now be proposed; the relationship depends to some extent upon the particular employees' awareness of certain deficiencies. Also, productivity seems to have some form of curvilinear relationship to most of these dimensions of work life. Two general criteria are examined below:

Considering the productivity for any given class of work and group of employees, there is probably some optimal level of opportunity to use and develop capacities (created by autonomy, multiplicity of skills required, work information, and planning responsibility). It should also be recognized that increasing autonomy, multiplicity of skills, and so on, does not have a linear effect even on the quality of the work experience. Considering employee satisfaction and self-esteem derived from this aspect of work, there will be some optimal amount of opportunity to use and develop one's capacities. Figure 1 illustrates these points, showing the experience on quality of work

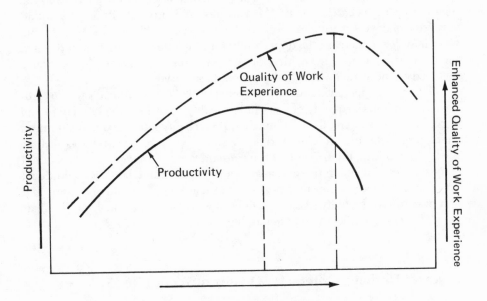

Figure 1. Effect of the Opportunity to Use and Develop Human Capabilities on the Quality of Work Experience and on Productivity

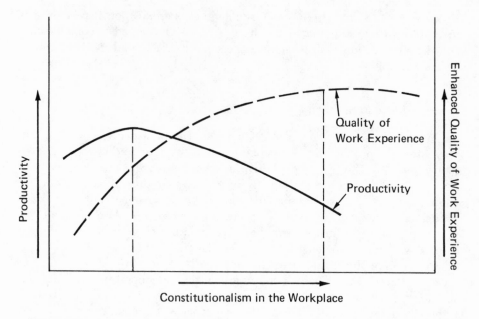

Figure 2. Effect of Constitutionalism in the Workplace on the Quality of Work Experience and on Productivity

life continuing to rise with increases in "opportunity" after the maximum effects on productivity have been realized. The particular slopes of the curves and the relationship between the quality of work life and productivity curves would vary from one work setting to another. However, current interest in redesigning work in order to increase the opportunity for employees to utilize and develop their capacities indicates a widely held assumption that the employee groups involved are now somewhere to the left on these curves.

The curves portraying the direct effects of "constitutionalism" on productivity and on the quality of work life probably have a relatively small region of coincidence between them (Figure 2). It can be hypothesized that situations characterized by only minimum rights would depress productivity as well as quality of working life because of the consequences of insecurity, anxiety, and employee resentment on performance. Beyond some point, however, additional forms and degrees of constitutionalism will continue to improve quality, but at a price to productivity. At a still higher level of constitutionalism, the marginal effect on quality is zero or negligible.

Bases for Deriving Criteria for Quality of Work Life

The categories and criteria proposed in this selection are the result of this author's personal observations, experiences, values, and assumptions about human nature; each has an ad hoc justification. However, there are more systematic ways to derive criteria for quality of working life, for example, some combination of empirical methods—surveys, observations, and depth interviews—to identify what aspects of the work situation significantly affect the overall quality of human experience in work roles. Undoubtedly, this method would yield different sets of criteria for different groups of workers. A composite set of criteria could then be constructed. Or criteria can be derived from ideological systems or theories of human development, physical and mental health, social integration, community development, and the like. This approach is illustrated below by exploring how criteria for the quality of work life could be derived from two theories of individual psychology.

One theory, Abraham Maslow's "hierarchy of needs," has frequently been employed in a way similar to that proposed here: therefore, it is treated briefly. A person must first meet security and economic needs before he can attend to and will be motivated by social needs; finally, if these other needs are met satisfactorily, he may seek self-actualization. Presumably those aspects of work, work context, and work careers can be identified which would enable—indeed, encourage—an employee to ascend this hierarchy; those aspects would provide one set of criteria for the quality of working life, having a theoretical rationale and a logical internal structure.

Thus, in assessing the quality of working life provided by a particular organization, two questions could be asked: First, what *potential* situation exists for employees to reach each successively higher level of the need hierarchy? Second, what percentage of employees *are currently operating* at each of these levels of need fulfillment in their working roles?

A quite different framework which could be employed in a similar manner is Erik Erikson's "eight ages of man." [1] He proposes that paralleling the stages of psychosexual development emphasized by Freud are psychosocial stages of ego development, in which the individual seeks to establish new basic orientations to himself and to others. He believes that personality development continues throughout the entire life cycle, and identifies several stages which occur during adulthood. The five preadult stages are stated in terms which make their relevance to the work situation almost self-evident. The three adult stages make his scheme especially pertinent, for it could reasonably be hypothesized that the work organization has a kind of influence over how a working adult comes to terms with self and others during these later stages corresponding to the influence that parents and siblings had over early developmental stages.

In each of Erikson's stages a new dimension of social interaction becomes possible; there may be a negative outcome or a positive resolution. Briefly, the five preadult stages involve the following issues:

1. *Trust versus mistrust.* In this first stage, the degree to which the infant comes to trust others and himself depends largely on the care he receives.

2. *Autonomy versus doubt.* During the second stage—ages 2 to 3—autonomy becomes a most salient issue. The child develops new motor and mental skills and wants to do things for himself. If parents allow him to do what he is capable of doing, he develops a sense of self-control and autonomy.

However, if others are impatient and continue to do everything for him, they induce a sense of shame and doubt.

3. *Initiative versus guilt.* In this stage—years 4 and 5—the child not only has mastered skills, but can initiate activities. If parents react by providing the freedom and opportunity for these initiations to be expressed, and by themselves respond when they are directed to them (e.g., answering the child's questions), then the child's sense of initiative will be enhanced. However, if the child is made to feel that his play (including fantasies) is silly and his questions a nuisance, then he will tend to develop a sense of guilt over self-initiated activities.

4. *Industry versus inferiority.* The fourth stage covers ages 6 to 11. The child develops deductive reasoning ability, learns to play by rules, and can acquire an interest in making things. If children are encouraged to take on and complete projects and are rewarded for results, then the sense of industry will be reinforced. But if the child's efforts along these lines are criticized as "mischief" or because they make a mess, the result will be a sense of inferiority.
    It is at this stage that socializing agents other than parents typically come strongly into the picture. A child whose sense of industry is blunted at home can have it stimulated by a sensitive teacher.

5. *Identity versus role confusion.* Stage five covers the age period from 12 to 18. The child's task is

> to bring together all of the things he has learned about himself as a son, student, athlete, friend, Scout, newspaper boy, and so on, and integrate these different images of himself into a whole that makes sense and that shows continuity with the past while preparing for the future. To the extent that the young person succeeds in this endeavor, he arrives at a sense of psychosocial identity, a sense of who he is, where he has been and where he is going.[2]

Erikson's treatment of these five preadult stages has two aspects of special significance for the present analysis: First, he goes beyond the immediate family in assigning responsibility for personality growth. While parents have a large role in determining the result of each developmental crisis—they can help the young person develop a vital sense of trust, autonomy, initiative, and industry and in turn a meaningful sense of ego identity—they also bear a large share of the responsibility for a youngster who enters adolescence with considerable mistrust, shame, doubt, guilt, and inferiority, and who subsequently shows role confusion. However, throughout the period of these five stages, the classroom and the total social milieu of the school play an increasingly influential role in facilitating or inhibiting effective ego development.

Second, Erikson has emphasized that confronting psychosocial issues at one stage in life is no guarantee that they will not reappear again at later stages. They can be reawakened by threats, challenges, and impoverished situations encountered in later life; for example, in the work setting.

Criteria for the quality of working life can be derived by analyzing how various elements of work, work context, and career potentialities strengthen or · weaken the worker's capacity for trust, autonomy, initiative, and industry, and his claim to a unique identity. Such analysis on a broad scale would probably show that the working lives of much of our adult population tend to reinforce or reawaken mistrust, shame, doubt, guilt, and inferiority. Comparative assessment would indicate how different job designs, for example, would relate to the primary types of ego development.

Even more provocative are the three adult stages of ego development proposed by Erikson. They help us understand why certain aspects of working life become important for an adult as he must deal with new development issues.

6. *Intimacy versus isolation.* The sixth stage is young adulthood. Erikson uses the term intimacy to refer to the ability to care about another person without fear of losing one's own identity in the process. If the young adult fails to establish sharing and caring relationships with friends or a marriage partner, the result is a sense of isolation.

He may agonize over the discovery that he is unable to share with and care for others with whom he is in close contact. Or he may attempt to develop his capacity for intimacy, an effort that could be greatly facilitated or inhibited by organizational factors such as types of task interdependence, incentives for collaboration and competition, and norms about interpersonal openness.

7. *Generativity versus self-absorption.* Middle age can bring a sense of "generativity" wherein the person's concerns extend beyond his family to the nature of society and to future generations. The alternative is a state of "self-absorption" in which the person is preoccupied with his own needs and comforts.

The generativity stage at the workplace reflects, for example, a middle-aged manager's newly acquired concern for subordinates and for the maintenance of a healthy organization to benefit future generations of employees. If a middle-aged worker or manager has no opportunity to help train or develop others and no role to play in shaping a better future for others, the working life denies him an important arena in which to work constructively through the developmental issues of generativity versus self-absorption.

8. *Integrity versus despair.* This stage occurs when a person is nearing the completion of his life's major activities.

The sense of integrity arises from the individual's ability to look back on his life with satisfaction. At the other extreme is the individual who looks back upon his life as a series of missed opportunities and missed directions; now in the twilight years he realizes that it is too late to start again. For such a person the inevitable result is a sense of despair at what might have been.[3]

The integrity versus despair crisis is vitally affected by the organization's manner of handling employees who have made fine contributions in the past, but who in their years before retirement are moved aside in various ways. This either tends to confirm their sense of worth and give integrity to their work career or leads to a sense of injustice, bitterness, and despair.

Accommodating the Diversity of Human Preferences

Regardless of how one approaches the issue of the quality of working life, one must acknowledge the diversity of human preferences—diversity relating to culture, social class, family rearing, education, and personality. It seems we are becoming more conscious of the quality of work life at a point in time when there is a growing heterogeneity in life styles in America. Differences in sub-cultures and life styles are accompanied by different definitions of what is a high quality of working life. And the young person with a college degree who elects to work as an auto mechanic, a taxi driver, or a mail carrier is saying something significant about his or her preferred pattern of working life. Of two employees equally skilled in performing basic elements of their work, one may prefer autonomy and the other to be instructed in detail. Similarly, one may prefer to be closely integrated into a work team and the other relatively unencumbered by work relations. How are differing preferences such as these to be accommodated?

We can attempt to accommodate diversity within a work unit by tailoring individual work assignments to fit individual preferences. We can try to accommodate diversity within an organization by organizing work differently from one work unit to another, allowing employees to select the pattern of work life they prefer. Or we can provide diversity among organizations by encouraging each to develop a unique and internally consistent pattern of work life and providing persons on the job market with enough information to choose an organization that is a good fit for them. The principle is one of allowing employees to exercise a free and informed choice that takes into account some of the more subtle aspects of the quality of working life.

NOTES

1. The discussion in this paper of these ages of man draws heavily on a summary of Erikson's scheme by David Elkind, "Erik Erikson's Eight Ages of Man," *New York Times Magazine*, 6 (April 5, 1970), 25. (The original source is Erik H. Erikson, *Childhood and Society*, 2nd rev. ed. [New York: Norton, 1963].)

2. Elkind, *op. cit.*, p. 90.

3. *Ibid.*, p. 112.

6

Defining and Measuring the Quality of Working Life

Stanley E. Seashore

THE testing of a simple set of propositions about job satisfaction has distinct limitations. Available evidence suggests that about half of the variance in present measures of job satisfaction is explained by a relatively small number of environmental conditions and that there are systematic and predictable individual differences in satisfaction. This is a narrow perspective which assumes a very limited time horizon. It is a static paradigm with little allowance for changes in organization, jobs, and persons. The quality of working life is better considered in relation to effectiveness in work roles; three distinct perspectives for evaluating such effectiveness are those of employers, workers, and the community. Measures of the quality of working life must consider the past, changes and current trends, and expectations about the future. Because of the *dynamic* nature of the problem, satisfaction must be included in both theory development and research and treated as a cause, not merely a consequence of quality of working life. Attitudes can be potent factors in modifying

The preparation of this selection was facilitated by discussions with valued colleagues (Robert P. Quinn, Robert L. Kahn, Ephraim Yuchtman, Burkhard F. Strumpel) and by support from the Employment Standards Administration, U.S. Department of Labor, and the Netherlands Institute for Advanced Study in the Social Sciences and Humanities.

behavior, and individual differences in relation to differing job qualities account for much of that dynamic aspect. Job satisfaction is an individual phenomenon, and both satisfaction and dissatisfaction are potentially of positive value in the maintenance of an effective society. In the normal worker there is a persistent force toward experiencing satisfaction and avoiding the experience of dissatisfaction—the latter being generally an unstable and transitional state. The dissatisfied worker will seek ways to change his job or rationalize a change in his evaluation of it. Accommodative processes to assure job satisfaction include changing the job environment, goal reduction, cognitive distortion, resignation, aggression, and withdrawal. Some of these strategies reduce dissatisfaction at heavy personal, organizational, and societal cost.

The dominant paradigm of the quality of working life in recent research and theory is based upon the assumption that the individual's own experience of satisfaction or dissatisfaction defines the quality of his working life. This proposition is usually elaborated with two associated ideas: (1) that the objective characteristics of the work situation induce corresponding attitudes of satisfaction or dissatisfaction; and (2) that the association between working conditions and satisfaction is not constant, but is moderated by attributes of the individual that bear upon his abilities, values, and expectations. A further elaboration proposes that some conditions of work can be defined or discovered which are so linked to universal human needs that subminimal gratification insures dissatisfaction.

While few would want to defend this simple set of propositions as an adequate basis for understanding and improving the quality of working life, most of what is known derives from a persistent testing of ideas that flow from or are expressions of these propositions. For the immediate future, they and the quantitative data resulting from them will be the major source of guidance in efforts to improve the quality of working life.[1, 2]

The evidence bearing upon the validity and potency of these propositions is impressive and incontrovertible. It is estimated that approximately half of the variance in the present measures of job satisfaction of individuals is "explained" by a relatively short roster of objective environmental conditions, with respect to which jobs vary.[3] It is known that the degree of satisfaction with a given working condition varies among individuals in ways that are systematic, measurable, and predictable from differences in individual attributes.[4] And it is also known that differences in significant public forms of behavior (e.g., quitting a job, changing a job, becoming ill, etc.) are linked with job satisfaction.

This selection, however, will be addressed to the limitations of such a conception of the quality of working life, and to the directions of elaboration and supplementation that are needed.

Limitations of the Paradigm

The chief limitation of this dominant paradigm in past inquiry is its almost exclusive reliance upon the expression of satisfaction by the individual worker as evidence of high quality of working life. This is a very narrow perspective because (1) it assumes a very limited time perspective and does not invite consideration of past conditions or future consequences; (2) it assumes a very narrow scope of relevant factors, with relevance defined by reference to the "job" (as compared with "working life") and to the present attributes of the person as compared with the changing and potential attributes of persons as they progress through a life cycle; and (3) it assumes that a job is an adequate entity for description and analysis of the environment associated with a person's working life, despite the obvious fact that jobs occur in sets, sequences, and interdependencies with other jobs in organizations, and in interdependency with other nonjob roles for the individual. It is thus a static paradigm, with few allowances for inquiry or purposeful action with respect to *changes* in organizations, jobs, and persons.

The common feature of these limitations is their invitation to enlarge the consideration of quality of working life beyond the confines set by the individual worker's reaction to immediate experiences of an environment narrowly bounded in time, and in physical as well as social space. While high importance, if not primacy, must be given to the individual's personal values in assessing the quality of his own experiences of working life, it can be taken for granted that they are not sufficient. First, the individual is in many ways incapable of an optimum assessment of his experiences; second, there are other value perspectives to be invoked.

The individual worker, whatever his background and status, is in important respects incapable of optimum judgment of his own life situation. His report of job satisfaction or dissatisfaction contains elements of expediency, self-deception, ignorance, social pressure, and perceptual distortion. Hence, in most such studies of the quality of working life, individuals can—and do—report satisfaction with work situations that (from information not accessible to the respondents) are found to abbreviate their lives, threaten their family relationships, and unnecessarily narrow their future options. Others can—and do—report dissatisfaction with work situations that display in high degree virtually all of the attributes generally valued by others, and no attributes that are plausibly accessible for "improvement."

These are not trivial individual aberrations in judgment, but extreme opinions reflecting the frailty of all evaluations based exclusively upon the person's own values and information resources. The quality of working life, however, cannot be considered a wholly private affair of the job occupant, for there are at least two other perspectives that must be employed, each with distinctive and legitimate values—that of the employer and that of the community or society as a whole. These additional perspectives must be taken into account when developing guidelines for ameliorative actions and programs.

It is suggested that exclusive dependence upon individual satisfaction as a definer of the quality of working life should be replaced by a broader conception, which might be given the label "effectiveness in work roles."

Meaning of Effectiveness

If priorities are to be assigned to various policies and programs intended to improve working conditions, their development and execution will obviously be very costly. To justify the cost of any such policy or program, some resulting benefit must be anticipated. But who should be the beneficiary? Clearly, priorities should be assigned to improving quality of working life with respect to those job facets that heighten the effectiveness of each worker. But from whose perspective should such effectiveness be judged? There are at least three distinct perspectives for evaluating effectiveness.

The first, *that of employers*, assigns priorities to needs more relevant to those doing the employing than to those who are employed. As a result, many previous investigations of the determinants of employee effectiveness emphasize productivity, quality of output, cost per unit of work, and similar indicators of effectiveness.

The second perspective is *that of the worker himself*. Workers form conclusions or expectations about their effectiveness in their work roles not only as to actual work performance, but also in more general terms of costs and benefits associated with their work roles. Thus, a worker normally includes such familiar terms as earnings, access to promotions, avoidance of accident or discomfort, security, intrinsic satisfactions from the work, and the like. Also he engages in something like a cost-benefit calculation, with consequences that involve behavior changes such as quitting, working harder, seeking improvement in rewards, or seeking qualifications for a "better" job.

A third perspective can also be invoked: *that of the community or the society*. Some of the costs and benefits associated with work role effectiveness do not enter into the limited formal or informal accounting of employer or worker. For example: underutilized skills are lost to the economy; the laid-off worker drains the public budget; a local "cost" of advanced skill training accrues to the manpower capital of the nation; the economic impact of a work stoppage falls in the end upon the public; the income-deficient worker is likely to burden society with a family prone to illness, future welfare costs, and substandard economic contributions.

Which of these three perspectives is the most appropriate for dealing with issues of costs and benefits in the allocation of priorities to policies and programs is not a question that can be resolved by research. It is fundamentally one of values; research can at best help social planners to recognize which perspectives may at present be incompatible.

For purpose of priority setting, the importance of any aspect of a work role, therefore, depends ultimately upon the magnitude of its impact on a variety of effectiveness criteria, the differential significance of which is largely a matter of a somewhat arbitrary, but hopefully informed and humane, selection from among a possibly incompatible set of values. If future research is to establish causal relationships between working conditions and their quality of working life outcomes, upon which outcomes should this research focus? Employers would probably suggest that attention be paid first to those directly affecting the productivity of their workers. This view is, however, a very narrow one unless it can be demonstrated that once productivity is raised or maintained all other desired outcomes will follow. More defensible is a broader-based investigation to determine the antecedents of working conditions valued according to not one, but all three, of the perspectives described above. A brief listing of examples of such outcomes or consequences is presented in Table 1, and is organized according to the perspectives most likely to be represented by each outcome.

Structure of Effectiveness

The assignment of an indicator to a particular perspective in Table 1 is at times somewhat arbitrary, even uncharitable. It does not mean to imply, for example, that from the employer's point of view the physical or mental disorders of his workers are of no importance, only that from the perspectives of most employers there are other more important outcomes. Conversely, the assignment does not imply that employees are necessarily indifferent to productivity. Indeed, the harder it is rationally to assign an outcome to a particular perspective, the more important that outcome is likely to be. According to this rule of thumb, priorities might profitably be assigned to improve those working conditions that affect outcomes patently relevant to all three perspectives. Work-related illnesses and injuries are a case in point. They are obviously important to the ill or injured worker, represent a cost to his employer (e.g., sick pay and filling the worker's position while he is laid up), and are costly to society as well (e.g., a drain on a nation's scarce medical resources).

Few would debate the assignment of a high priority to a particular improvement in working conditions that simultaneously effects a desired change with regard to *all* the outcomes listed in Table 1. However, there is probably no such

TABLE 1.

Examples of Indicators of Work Role Effectiveness as Viewed from Three Perspectives

---

From the perspective of a worker
- Job satisfaction assessed both generally and with regard to specific aspects of job and job environment
- Job-related feelings of excessive strain or tension
- Self-esteem
- Affective states, such as anxiety, depression, resentment, hopelessness, etc.
- Physiological states, such as fatigue, work-related illnesses or injuries, coronary heart disease risk symptoms, drug dependency if work-related, etc.
- Satisfaction with work-role potential for personal development, adaptability, career-long value realization, etc.

From the perspective of an employer
- Productivity, including quantity and quality of output, innovative behavior, initiation of new techniques or procedures that increase productivity, etc.
- Adaptability to changing work procedures, skill acquisition
- Turnover, absenteeism, lateness
- Counterproductive behaviors, such as theft, sabotage, work stoppage, etc.
- Alienation from work
- Identification with work organization

From the perspective of society
- Gross national product
- Increasing value of manpower pool
- Cost of welfare protection for workers and their dependents
- Political behaviors and attitudes
- Consumer behaviors and attitudes
- Societal adaptability
- Life satisfaction rates in society
- Alienation
- Quality of life with regard to nonwork roles and situations

---

"miracle cure," and attention therefore will have to be directed toward action programs with more circumscribed effects, each of which would achieve desired results with regard to some outcomes, none with regard to some others, and even undesired consequences with regard to still others.

For this reason knowledge is essential about the relationships among possible outcomes. Only when the possible side effects are known of improving some of working conditions to effect a positive change with regard to an outcome call all perspectives realistically be invoked; the unforeseeable side effects of any change need to be foreseeable. Therefore, a major requirement of future research is to provide better data than are presently available concerning the interrelations among outcomes such as shown in Table 1.

Time Span of Measurement

A further consideration in the definition and measurement of the quality of working life is the time span. With very few exceptions, past efforts, regardless of the value framework for assessment, have referred to a relatively brief time period. It is self-evident, however, that individuals, employing organizations, and societies in fact operate within a long time span; the quality of working life must accordingly be defined and measured with consideration for past events and conditions, changes and trends, delayed consequences, and predictions and expectations about the more distant future.

There is evidence that the physiological consequences of job stress in a certain occupation are cumulative over a period of at least fifteen years, with chronic heart disease deaths and the rates of chronic heart disease risk factors increasing throughout that period; it is plain that any short-term association between working conditions and health in this and similar occupations would grossly underestimate the health outcomes.[5] The reported high satisfaction of individuals in certain work roles (medical intern, for example) that embody normally unacceptable working conditions (low pay, low status, long hours) can be readily understood by viewing the work role in the span of a lifetime, with short-term, negatively valued conditions outweighed by confidently expected, positively valued future conditions. There is evidence that certain descriptors of organizational work environment are more closely associated with later than with concurrent outcomes.

The definition and measurement of the quality of working life thus requires consideration not only of diverse value perspectives, but also of value realizations with differential time lags that must be determined. Another research priority is thus identified.

Role of Satisfaction in Measuring the Quality of Working Life

Earlier in this selection the limitations of individual satisfaction were pointed out as a basis for assessing the quality of working life. For some time, however it will probably prove necessary and desirable to give a prominent place to satisfaction both in theory development and in research plans. The following section introduces some considerations to stimulate a more realistic and analytically powerful conception of the relationship of satisfaction to the quality of working life. The essential ideas are that (1) job satisfaction must be treated as a *dynamic* rather than a static concept, and (2) job satisfaction must be treated as a potential *cause* of enhanced or diminished quality of working life, not merely as a consequence.

Dynamic Aspects of Job Satisfaction

The measurement of job satisfaction assumes that, first, the experience of satisfaction or dissatisfaction is an attitude that arises in part from the objective qualities of jobs and job-associated conditions and, second, that such attitudes may be potent factors in the cause or modification of certain kinds of behavior.[6] In short, it is assumed that objective conditions provide a partial "explanation" of such behavioral outcomes as illness, turnover, absenteeism, and counterproductive behavior. It is further assumed that members of the work force are not wholly uniform in their perceptions of and responses to objective working conditions. Additional satisfaction and behavior variance is explainable by taking into account individual differences, as well as the interactions between these differences and the working conditions.[7] For example, it may be possible that individuals of different educational attainments or degrees of economic need might respond differently when exposed to the same objective conditions.

This elementary assumption is one basis for searching for individual differences in satisfaction and in satisfaction-related behavioral outcomes, as well as between categories of the work force defined by common demographic or measured personality characteristics. Thus one may ask of survey data whether men respond differently than women, blacks differently than whites, or older workers differently than younger ones. Similarly, in the personality domain, one may ask whether persons relatively high in need for affiliation respond differently to the same working conditions than do those relatively high in need for achievement.

More important, there is a third type of assumption underlying the measurement of job satisfaction and its consequences—the assumption that a given individual is not constant in his responses to working conditions, but is subject to highly individualistic differences and short-cycle changes. That is, in addition to explaining his reactions arising from his existence as a normal human being in the work force, and in addition to further explaining his possession of certain specific attributes which he shares with many, but not all, other members of the work force, there is still further degree of explanation to be sought in terms of transitional and changing attributes which he shares for a time with relatively few other members of the work force.

These three assumptions can be summarized as follows, along with illustrative and *highly* speculative percentages that represent the accumulative explanatory power of inquiries encompassing all three levels of explanation:*

---

* Ignored here are two further sources of variance: one arises because the "objective situation" itself is somewhat inconstant due to short-term changes in working conditions that normally occur in "the same" job; for example, a machine operator may acquire a new supervisor, or be assigned to a newer model machine, or be confronted with unusual deadline pressure. The other arises from interactions among the factors treated above as being strictly additive.

Percent of Variance in Experienced Satisfaction (or Dissatisfaction) to Be Explained 100

Components of Job Satisfaction
Stable portion attributable to characteristics of the objective situation 40*
Portion attributable to relatively stable demographic and personality characteristics 30
Portion attributable to unstable demographic and personality characteristics 20
Portion representing measurement errors not explainable 10

Job Satisfaction as an Adaptive Psychological Process

A worker's experience of job satisfaction, and the generation of behaviors consequent on job satisfaction, is undeniably a *psychological* phenomenon, therefore, in all cases an *individual* phenomenon. This view is valid even though there may be, and indeed are, constancies arising from the realities of the external world and from human uniformities in psychological processes. It follows that a conception of the research issues must rest fundamentally upon biopsychological propositions.

The formulation set out by Locke[8] and others is useful here. In essence, it holds that the human capacity to form attitudes of satisfaction or dissatisfaction regarding a job serves the essential biological function of behavior regulation in the interest of maximizing life-sustaining and life-enhancing values. Two features of this view are emphasized: (1) job satisfaction and dissatisfaction are of interest in the long run not so much as intrinsic ends to be maximized or minimized by society, but because they affect behavior and thus have important social implications; (2) job satisfaction and dissatisfaction are *both* to be regarded as potentially and normally of positive value in the maintenance of an effective society. These features are emphasized because they are at odds with the casual presumption that job satisfaction is "good" and job dissatisfaction "bad." Job satisfaction is better regarded as an attitude—"merely" an attitude—resulting from two concurrent, continuing evaluations in which the individual assesses his job and work environment *as he perceives them*; that is, whether they are likely to aid or undermine the realization of his basic values (relatively constant for an adult) and their associated experienced needs (changing in priority with life experiences), as well as their associated concrete life goals (mainly short-run and changeable as subgoals are achieved, abandoned, or substituted). Job satisfaction is thus *dynamic*, although at any given time of measurement it can be treated as a static attitudinal state; the

---

* According to data from the 1969 Working Conditions Survey, this figure should be 53 percent. Because the survey's presumably "objective" measures were based on workers' reports of their working conditions, the biases of which are at present unknown, the 53 percent figure is possibly an overestimation. In the spirit of the purely speculative percentages presented here, the 53 percent estimate has therefore been arbitrarily reduced to a more conservative 40 percent. The "true" percentage could be 30 percent or even less—or, for that matter, 70 percent or more.

fluctuation of satisfactions and dissatisfactions is emphasized as an expected condition, to be considered in explaining the behavior of individuals in relation to their jobs.

This argument may at first seem unnecessarily global and abstract; it is advanced to make clear that it is essential in future inquiries dealing with job satisfaction at three complementary levels of generalization:

1. Assessment of the prevailing levels of satisfaction and dissatisfaction for the work force as a whole, and description of conditions of the workplace that, as a general rule, are associated with satisfaction and dissatisfaction.

2. Assessment of the prevailing levels of satisfaction and dissatisfaction for large defined subsets of the work force—categories defined by common demographic and personality characteristics—and descriptions of the manner in which conditions of the workplace differentially affect these categories.

3. Assessment of the *changes* in job satisfaction and dissatisfaction that accompany typical changes in the person or the work environment of persons, with a view toward discovering regularities (predictability) in such changes.

Accommodative Patterns

Attention must be paid to those individual differences and changes of a dynamic, accommodative, and transitional kind, setting aside those that, because of their relative stability over a lifetime, are called "personality." In considering these differences and changes, the following paragraphs ignore differences of fluctuating kinds associated with stable personality differences —for example, individual differences in perceiving and cognizing the environment, and differences in patterns of abilities that moderate responses to the environment. These rather arbitrary exclusions are made because the focus is upon types of individual differences and similarities that are *induced by the normal and recurring events of life in any society*, and thus can provide generalizations useful for predicting or influencing the satisfaction of other individuals going through similar normal life-experience changes. The differences in question are thought to be most pertinent to the understanding of association between qualities of the job and job environment, on the one hand, and responses of satisfaction, on the other.

The "normal and recurring" events of life and life-experience changes need not be detailed here; the most obvious are those that most or many people expect as members of the work force. A worker takes his or her first job and experiences satisfaction or dissatisfaction. Few people remain in their initial job, and choice of and response to a new job may be influenced by the experience in the preceding one. If the job is within an established promotional sequence or a career ladder with known advancement stages, response is no doubt altered by knowledge of future potentialities and normally scheduled career events, and by gradual awareness that these will or will not be realized. An initially challenging job may become less so as the occupant gains competence by experience; change in satisfaction may occur with the gradual realization of relative success or failure in its performance. A person satisfied with pay and security benefits may have altered his experiences of job satisfaction with the acquisition or loss of dependents through marriage, birth and maturation of children, employment of spouse, or approach of retirement. Normal life experience increases, with aging, the range of available comparative information about alternative jobs and their characteristics. Abrupt changes of economic inflation or changing levels of employment may alter the meaning of the characteristics of a worker's own job.

What such normal changes have in common is the potential for inducing substantial changes in the experienced satisfaction with a given job, and a potential for changing the relative salience of the values, needs, and goals invoked by a person in the process of forming and changing attitudes of satisfaction or dissatisfaction. A study of the impact of such normal life changes upon job satisfaction must take into account not only the more-or-less directly observable facts (e.g., tenure in job, change in number of dependents), but also the psychological process of accommodation. To this end, a proposition is advanced and some alternative forms for its expression are indicated.

The proposition assumes there is in the "normal" worker a persistent force toward experiencing satisfaction and the avoidance of experiencing dissatisfaction; it assumes as well that, experiencing dissatisfaction with the job or some aspect of it, the worker will seek and find accommodation in some fashion. Thus, *dissatisfaction is generally an unstable and transitional state*, one that is *changed*. In support of this assertion, over a span of several decades, estimates of the proportion of "dissatisfied" workers in the United States work force generally or in specific occupations have remained surprisingly low and only moderately variant; data from the 1969 Working Conditions Survey are typical in this respect,[9] with perhaps 15 to 20 percent of the respondents reporting overall dissatisfaction (more or less depending upon the form and content of the job satisfaction measure or the questions). Further evidence lies in the fact that many workers feel and report satisfaction with jobs that on their face do not merit that kind of attitude, being grossly deficient in pay, safety, security, intrinsic interest, and other qualities commonly valued. This dissatisfied job occupant will normally find ways to change his job or rationalize a change in his evaluation of it. An individual's accommodative processes and actions undertaken to assure job satisfaction may include any or several of the following:

1. *Changing the job environment.* A worker may change his job and job environment through promotion or transfer, seeking new employment, or exploiting the ever present latitude for altering the "same" job within limits allowed by his employer and his own resources and ingenuity. The

many devices to make a job situation more interesting, fulfilling, secure, more (or less) responsible, and so on, are richly documented.[10] Few jobs are fixed in their properties, as implied by labor contracts, job specification, managerial directives, and the like. An essentially unsatisfactory job may, within limits, be made more satisfactory by the occupant within the terms of employment.

2. *Goal reduction.* A worker may modify his expectations and aspirations, reducing his goals, to bring them into consonance with his perception of the realities of his situation and of feasible alternatives.

3. *Cognitive distortion.* A worker may alter his perceptions of the situation and of himself to attain consonance between his values and his experience of the job. The processes of perceptual and cognitive distortion are well established and potent. For example, a worker may come to regard his essentially routine and inconsequential job decisions as "really critical" to the enterprise; he may revise his assessment of his pay by shifting reference groups.[11]

4. *Resignation.* A worker may adapt to what he sees as necessity by simply accepting the situation, usually preserving self-esteem by allocating blame to others, to "the system," or to past chance events not now in his control. Such an accommodation may be accompanied by adverse consequences in, say, health or effectiveness.

5. *Aggression.* A worker may respond by aggressive attitudes and acts, directed toward himself, with consequent mental and physical health pathologies, or toward the situation, with consequences ranging from minimal job performance to disruption and sabotage. The acting out of aggression is itself satisfying and may become a permanent feature of the job.

6. *Withdrawal.* A worker may gain partial psychological escape from a dissatisfying situation, usually by altering his values (e.g., regarding income, skill usage) or seeking primary value realization in off-work activities or leaving the work force.

These and other actions for minimizing job dissatisfaction can be differentiated with respect to their implications for work performance, manpower utilization, public health, community/family welfare, and other outcomes listed in Table 1. While all of the strategies serve the immediate and compelling function of dissatisfaction reduction, some accomplish this end with a by-product of personal, organizational, and societal enhancement, others, at a heavy cost.

Concluding Comments

The aim of this selection has been to promote three themes that seem essential to future efforts toward the definition and measurement of the quality of working life. These themes arise from: (1) the existence of different and possibly conflicting values with respect to working life; (2) the existence of significant delayed consequences arising from working conditions; and (3) the existence of some diversity among individuals in their affective and behavioral responses to any given set of working conditions.

It is argued that the improvement or optimizing of the quality of working life should take into account the interests of employers and of society at large, as well as the interests of the employed person. While such an idea may at first seem platitudinous, it draws attention to the fact that "improvements" initiated from each of the three perspectives lead to quite different priorities of action and may in many situations lead to conflicts of interest. The approach to definition and measurement should reveal and explicate such differences, rather than conceal them or assume that one or another perspective should be dominant.

The issue of delayed consequences arises because most of the existing approaches to measuring the quality of working life rely on short-term consequences—for example, concurrent employee satisfaction or concurrent productivity. A warning is provided by recent inquiries which demonstrate that the consequences of the conditions of working life may be long delayed for the individual, as in the case of accumulative health consequences, or may be discernible only under later conditions which take time to unfold, as in the case of transient short-term costs and losses that may accompany improvement programs. One could be grossly misled by short-term consequences alone.

Finally, it is argued that the prevailing conception of job satisfaction, while useful for many purposes, is quite unrealistic for others. Specifically, the experience of job satisfaction may be taken as sound evidence of the goodness of the quality of working life for particular populations at particular times (as in comparative studies or change experiments), but the experience of job satisfaction may be deceptive in individual cases and useless for measuring longer term trends and societal changes. It is proposed that job satisfaction should be regarded in a more dynamic way as an aspect of the process of accommodation of individuals to their work environment, with particular attention to the motivational properties of transient dissatisfaction and to the societal implications of "pathological" satisfaction—that is, satisfaction achieved at the cost of longer-term personal, organizational, and societal enhancement.

NOTES

1. Robert L. Kahn, "The Work Module: A Proposal for the Humanization of Work," unpublished background manuscript for *Work in America*, U.S. Department of Health, Education, and Welfare, 1973.

2. Robert P. Quinn, Stanley E. Seashore, Ephraim Yuchtman, and Burkhard F. Strumpel, "The Personal, Corporate, and Societal Implications of Quality of Employment: Some Issues of Strategy, Theory, and Methods," multilith, 104 pp. A technical

report submitted to the Workplace Standards Administration of the U.S. Department of Labor, 1972.

3. J. Thad Barnowe, Thomas W. Mangione, and Robert P. Quinn, "An Empirically Derived Model of Job Satisfaction," unpublished manuscript for a chapter in *Final Analytic Report of the 1969 Working Conditions Survey*, Employment Standards Administration, U.S. Department of Labor, 1972.

4. Survey Research Center, *Survey of Working Conditions: Final Report on Univariate and Bivariate Tables*, Document No. 2916–0001 (Washington, D.C.: Government Printing Office, August 1971), page 484.

5. Sidney Cobb and John R. P. French, Jr., personal communication regarding a study in progress.

6. As indicated earlier in this selection, the *1969 Working Conditions Survey* showed, for example, that 53 percent of the variance in job satisfaction was "explained" by the job occupant's report of working conditions and job-associated conditions.

7. Such inquiries within the *1969 Working Conditions Survey* data (largely excluding "personality" measures) demonstrated that there were significant differences in response to working conditions for such categories of persons, and that these differences were sufficiently regular and stable to aid in explaining satisfactions and behavioral outcomes *in addition to* the explanations applicable to the whole of the work force. Survey Research Center, *op. cit.*

8. Edwin L. Locke, "What is Job Satisfaction?," *Journal of Organizational Behavior and Human Performance*, 4, no. 6 (1969), 309–336.

9. Barnowe, Mangione, and Quinn, *op. cit.*

10. William F. Whyte (ed.), *Money and Motivation* (New York: Harper, 1955).

11. Martin Patchen, *The Choice of Wage Comparisons* (Englewood Cliffs, N.J.: Prentice-Hall, 1961).

7

Some Indicators of Quality of Working Life: A Simplified Approach to Measurement

Harold L. Sheppard

THE author suggests a simple readily usable indicator of work satisfaction in the form of a job satisfaction frequency measure. This measure when used with a four-way paradigm related to employment provides a typology that can be used at national level.

This selection has been condensed by the editors. The original paper, "Measuring the Quality of Working Life," presented at the International Conference on Quality of Working Life, is available from the author.

There is growing acceptance in our society of the *qualitative aspects* of employment becoming a major "social indicator." As a result, there is growing recognition of the need to consider quality of working life itself as a desirable societal goal, as an index *sui generis* of "individual well-being." (Any interest in "individual well-being" includes, of course, an acceptance of the individual's own judgment of that well-being.) Today, for a large proportion of the country's work force, steady employment at high wages, while a necessary condition for satisfaction with one's work, may no longer be the *sufficient condition* that perhaps it was in the past.

Work satisfaction has been shown to relate to a number of personal, organizational, and societal outcomes including mental health, productivity, turnover, retirement propensity, family relations, alienation, morbidity, and longevity, Although objective outcomes affecting the goals or organizations are important, personal well-being within work has a legitimacy all its own.

There is much to be said for the position that concern with the economic effects—for the firm or the society—of "job well-being" should not be included in any justification for measures of work conditions and satisfaction as a part of social indicators. While productivity, absenteeism, and turnover, profit and loss, and other factors involving the goals of organizations may be important for various reasons, concern with measures of personal well-being with the work sphere—to repeat—has a legitimacy all its own.

Overcomplication and the preference for multi-item test "batteries" for measuring such a subjective phenomenon as work satisfaction are a major obstacle in our progress toward conclusive efforts in this area. There is also confusion between the measurement of work satisfaction and the identification and measurement of "correlates" or "bases" of satisfaction—for example, degree of autonomy, and so on. And the frequent use of substitute or "proxy" measures, because they provide "hard" data (for example, income and the possession of certain goods) for indicating or predicting well-being, presents serious limitations. These are not substitutes for direct measures of working life satisfaction.* Indeed, changes in income (and in *satisfaction* with income) are not always accompanied by corresponding changes in *work* satisfaction.

The least complicated measure of work satisfaction is a job satisfaction *frequency* measure, derived from answers to the question, "How much of the time are you satisfied with your job?" This measure should be treated as an *outcome*, for the purpose of developing an *indicator* of the quality of working life.† (The reader may recall Seashore's argument, in selection 6, that job

---

* Emphasis on working life satisfaction as a "primary goal area," deserving *direct* measurement, does not, of course, exclude the recognition that societies as well as individuals may pursue multiple goals and multiple values. Thus needs, expectations, values, and assessments are changing with time. The most dramatic recent evidence relevant to this topic of working life satisfaction can be found in the behavior and attitudes of young workers of all social classes.

† This one measure correlates very highly with a *multi*-item "battery" of other job satisfaction questions, which suggests the "parsimony" of the simple job satisfaction frequency question.

satisfaction and job dissatisfaction should be regarded as causes as well as outcomes of the quality of working life.)

A four-way paradigm is presented below, providing a *typology* which takes into account the physical and economic attributes of work life and can differentiate sixteen "types" of quality of work satisfaction and allow for a modified rank ordering of these types.

Measures of Work Satisfaction	*Measures of Economic Concern*			
	STEADY EMPLOYMENT		UNSTEADY EMPLOYMENT	
	Wages or Salaries		Wages or Salaries	
	High	*Low*	*High*	*Low*
	(u)	(x)	(y)	(z)
Frequency of Job Satisfaction				
HIGH (JSF) a) in standard or above-standard physical work environment (PWE)	I			
b) *below* standard PWE				
LOW (JSF) a) in standard or above standard PWE				
b) below standard PWE				XVI

NOTE: Each of the attributes or variables in this typology is, of course, not operationally or quantitatively defined here, e.g., "high" vs. "low" wage, "standard," PWE, etc., but they would and could be.)

This typology could be used to obtain valuable information: First, to determine the proportion of a nation's (or an enterprise's) work force in each of the categories, from (I) the presumably "ideal" type with good physical work environment, high job security, high wages, and high job satisfaction, to (XVI), the presumably "least ideal" type with low job security and wages, low job satisfaction, and so on. The remaining categories could be compressed into an intermediate classification (or type), but other combinations or aggregations are possible too.

Second, changes over time in each of these categories could be monitored within an industry's, a region's, or a country's labor force, examining shifts in the proportion which is in the most or least ideal category.

Third, at any time the distribution of each of the types can be determined according to other socioeconomic criteria of a country's work force, such as occupation, industry, age, sex, region, and so on, as a basis of the need for, and choice of, "intervention strategies."

There are obviously *sub*concerns involved in this focus on the quality of working life, such as the difficulty of individual job tasks; fringe benefits; degree of autonomy, feedback, variety, and responsibility; nature and quality of social interaction at the workplace; kind and degree of supervision, and so on. And, indeed, perhaps these subconcerns should now become an equally major focus in attempts to develop social indicators in the area of work life satisfaction.

In sum, so far as the question of measuring the quality of working life is concerned, the viewpoint governing this approach is obviously one of pragmatic inductionism. It is an attempt to persuade governments, as well as employers and union leaders, to take some first steps toward becoming concerned about the quality of work life of their labor force. It is an attempt to persuade these institutions to devise and use relevant measures—just as they have already been persuaded to do in other primary goal areas, such as health, education, the physical environment, employment, income, and productivity. At issue is the recognition of the qualitative experience of work life as a hard fact of economic and social reality.

8

Measuring the Psychological Quality of Working Life: The Why and How of It

Edward E. Lawler III

THE present concern with the quality of working life will produce little significant social change until valid measures are developed and carefully used. Such measures would aim to be valid, have face validity, be objective, and take account of individual differences in response to a given work environment. But, since no measure meets all these requirements, subjective measures may provide better data on individual differences than do many objective ones. Groups with varying interests have legitimate albeit somewhat different reasons to be concerned with quality of working life. Management can benefit from measures of satisfaction and motivation as well as from objective measures (e.g., turnover, absenteeism); human resources accounting can complement data on quality of working life. Stockholders and investors are affected in terms of long-range financial success of the enterprise. At present the public and the government have only economic indices with which

The preparation of this selection was facilitated by a research contract with the U.S. Department of Labor, Manpower Administration.

to assess a high quality of working life, but economic growth is no longer a sufficient indicator. Self-report measures of workers' feelings, while appropriate to build national indicators, should not be used to regulate or influence the behavior of organizations. Government efforts to improve the quality of working life could take several forms: charging organizations for negative social outcomes or taxing organizations whose employees are dissatisfied; requiring organizations to prepare psychological impact statements when plants are modified or being built; awarding contracts to organizations which provide good quality of working life; supporting experimentation with and demonstration of new methods and taking an active role in disseminating new findings.

An interesting and important phenomenon has occurred in the last five years—the emergence of a major concern about the quality of working life. There are some obvious reasons why this has happened (e.g., the U.S. balance-of-payments problem, the rising education level of the population), but it is still difficult to understand why it happened at this particular time in history. It is clear that if the present concern with the quality of working life is going to produce any significant social change, valid measures of it must be developed and used adroitly.

Unfortunately, there is no well-accepted or well-developed definition of the term quality of working life, a fact that is not surprising since the various groups interested in life in organizations have quite different vested interests in what such life is like. Some of these groups are primarily concerned with the degree to which an organization's work environment motivates effective job performance, others with the degree to which it safeguards the physical as well as psychological well-being of employees, and still others with the degree to which it decreases the alienation of people from work and society. Discussions in the popular literature have focused on all of these aspects of the individual/organization relationship. For example, a high quality of working life has been equated with high employee motivation and also with a high level of employee satisfaction.

Satisfaction, alienation, and motivation, however, are quite different and often unrelated phenomena that should be and are of differential importance to those who desire information on the quality of working life in organizations. Management, stockholders and investors, the public in general, and the government all have legitimate and somewhat different reasons to be concerned about the quality of working life. This selection deals with only one aspect of the quality of working life, the psychological quality of work life that organizations provide for their employees; however, it is an aspect that deserves the close attention of everyone. While much progress has been made in providing work environments protecting the worker's physical well-being, there is very little agreement on what kind of working conditions and organizational practices are important to provide a psychologically good work life, despite the fact that the whole society is injured when employees work in environments harming their mental health and sense of well-being.

The psychological quality of working life will be discussed, first in relation to job satisfaction. Then some approaches to measuring it are analyzed in terms of impact and potential usefulness to management, investors, and the public in general. Finally, some ways are proposed in which the government can intervene to assure the broad improvement of the quality of working life in society.

Job Satisfaction and the Psychological Quality of Working Life

As traditionally defined, job satisfaction has focused upon the degree to which people feel adequately rewarded and fairly treated in their work environment. Many writers seem to end up equating high satisfaction with a psychologically good working life.[1] Admittedly, feelings of job satisfaction are an important part of a psychologically good working life, but can the two be equated? Probably not, for despite the fact that satisfaction is an important part of a high quality of working life, other elements must be considered too.

First, as Maslow and others have pointed out, mentally healthy individuals are often motivated to seek personal growth and development by dissatisfaction with their present level of self-development.[2] Second, equating satisfaction with good mental health is like accepting a kind of "contented cow" view of how man should exist, and there is no evidence to indicate that man is best off when he has reached the cud-chewing stage. In an organizational setting, this view would require that everyone be happy, which could cause serious performance problems since satisfaction is more likely to reduce performance than to increase it.[3] Finally, any definition of a psychologically good working life should include some measurement of the stress and tension level present in the workplace. Thus far research on job satisfaction has usually ignored this issue, but other research has suggested that a slightly dissatisfying tension may be desirable if it encourages personal growth, but that too high a level can cause serious mental and physical problems.

Still, it probably does make sense to equate a psychologically good work environment with one in which the individuals' *basic* needs are satisfied. There is evidence[4] that these basic needs must be satisfied before people can be motivated by *higher-order* needs, and for some people psychological well-being and growth are facilitated when they are so motivated. It may seem inconsistent to argue that it is psychologically acceptable when people are dissatisfied with their degree of self-actualization, but unacceptable when they are dissatisfied with the amount of security they have. However, these are two quite different types of dissatisfaction; they often motivate different kinds of behavior, and they can produce different kinds of psychological effects. Feelings of insecurity, for example, are more likely to cause such physiological disorders as ulcers and high blood pressure and lead to mental illness.

Despite the fact that satisfaction of higher-order needs cannot be equated with a high quality of psychological life in an organization, it is important to consider them in any definition of the quality of working life. The most defensible way to do this is to argue that, with respect to higher-order needs, a high quality of working life is one where the pursuit of higher-order need satisfaction is within the grasp of those individuals who desire it.

Characteristics of Measures

Any method of measuring the psychological quality of the working life an individual experiences should ideally include four characteristics. First, the measure should be valid in the sense that it measures accurately all the important aspects of the psychological quality of working life. Second, it should have enough face validity so that it will be seen as a legitimate measure by all involved. Third, it should be objective, and therefore verifiable, and not subject to manipulation. Finally, it should recognize and take into account differences in how individuals respond to the same work environment.

Unfortunately, no measure possesses all four of these characteristics. Thus, if we are to measure the psychological quality of work life, we must settle for suboptimal measures. Which characteristics can we afford to give up? In some cases, we may be able to give up objectivity. While always desirable, objective measures may be less useful than subjective self-report measures of the psychological quality of working life in some cases. Despite their subjectivity, they represent the most direct data available about the psychological state of a person. Further, they provide better data on individual differences than do many objective measures of working conditions. For example, repetitive assembly-line jobs or authoritarian supervision are not negatively regarded by all workers. Quite the contrary; some individuals see them as part of a high quality of working life, while others see them as very negative and as part of a low quality of working life.

One way to take individual difference factors into account is to use self-reports of satisfaction and need strength and to compare what people want from the job situation with what they actually receive. This is a satisfactory method in those situations in which the individual is not motivated to report false data; but, when there is such motivation, this approach has problems because of the subjective nature of the data. Some uses to which measures of the quality of the psychological life in organizations might be put would create conditions inviting motivation for distortion. In such situations, self-report data would seem inappropriate unless measures are developed that cannot be manipulated. At the moment, no such measures exist, although some commonly used ones are more difficult to manipulate than others. For example, some difference measures (e.g., subtracting people's feelings of what they should receive from what they feel they do receive) are more difficult to falsify than are measures which simply ask people how satisfied they are or how much opportunity they have to grow and develop on the job.

An alternative approach would focus on the behavioral outcomes produced by psychologically harmful jobs. Phenomena such as rates of turnover, absenteeism, drug abuse, mental illness, tension-related physical illnesses, and alcoholism would be measured. This has the advantage of focusing on more "objective" outcomes; however, it has the disadvantage of identifying bad conditions only after they have done their damage. Poor individual/organization environment fits produce dissatisfaction and a psychologically poor work environment. This, in turn, contributes to outcomes like mental illness and alcoholism. Thus, where possible, it is important to identify poor work environments before there are serious negative outcomes, and self-report data can serve this function because the feelings they measure often precede outcomes like mental illness, turnover, and absenteeism. Potentially, measures of the actual physical work environment can also be used to identify bad conditions before problems arise. They also have the advantage of being objective. However, they do not take into acount individual differences in how people react to the same work environment. With the strengths and weaknesses of the different measures in mind, the uses to which they might be put will now be considered.

Managerial Decision Making

A number of writers have stressed the potential usefulness to management of self-report measures which assess satisfaction and motivation.[5] Merrihue and Katzell have taken a slightly different approach, arguing that organizations should develop an objectively based "Employee Relations Index" to reflect the overall quality of the relationship between the employees and the organization and to include among other things measures of absenteeism, tardiness, and turnover.[6] By regularly collecting systematic data on the kind of psychological quality of life employees are experiencing, organizations could determine how various policies and practices influence it; and, when called for, they could correct those policies and practices that produce a psychologically negative work life before they lead to excessive and expensive absenteeism and turnover (among other outcomes).

How important is it that only objective measures be used for managerial decision making? Probably not too important. Self-report measures of satisfaction and opportunities for self-development, for example, are potentially useful to managers for decision-making purposes; and experience has shown that generally people give valid self-report data if they are assured of anonymity.

In short, measures of this type should in many instances enable organizations to make decisions that may improve both the psychological life of their employees and reduce costs by reducing absenteeism and turnover. However, there are also likely to be some situations where improving the quality of work will not contribute to greater organizational effectiveness or profits. In some situations the cost of turnover and absenteeism, associated with a poor organizational environment, may be more than offset by the additional production that can be gained from the use of an assembly line or some other dissatisfying practice.

The new technique of Human Resource Accounting is prospectively an objective approach to measuring the human assets of an organization, but it does not directly measure the quality of life in that organization.[7] It is a potentially useful tool for management. A combination of this technique and indicators of the quality of working life should provide management with the information upon which to base decisions about improving the organizational environment since they provide complementary data. Human Resource Accounting allows organizations to place a financial value on many of their personnel practices and procedures and financially to value the consequences of a high-stress, dissatisfying work environment. The indicators of the psychological quality of working life, on the other hand, would help identify the causes of the stress and dissatisfaction and provide a measure of their long-term trend as well as means for improvement.

Potential Use of Measures by Stockholders and Investors

At the present time, publicly owned companies must provide their stockholders and potential investors with data about their financial situation, but they are not required to give or collect information about the kind of working life they provide for their employees. Since the psychological quality of life in an organization can influence its long-term financial success because of its impact on absenteeism, turnover, and the ability of organizations to attract talented employees, investors should have this information. Further, since it is also related to such socially important issues as mental illness, alcoholism, drug abuse, and various physical illnesses, some stockholders motivated by social concern might want to know something about the impact of their organization on the people who work for it. Other similar information on discrimination and pollution are being demanded by stockholders, as are changes in corporate policy on the environment and discrimination. Some changes are even being made that will decrease corporate profits. Similar demands intended to enhance the quality of working life may soon appear.

If there were Human Resource Accounting data would they be sufficient? Such data are insufficient since only the worth of employees to the company is indicated. Nothing is said about ability of members to work together (organizations are not always equal to the sum of their parts) and about whether the organization treats them in destructive ways that make them less valuable, either through turnover or reduced psychological and physical fitness. Such data are clearly needed.

Organizations could provide their stockholders with data on turnover, absenteeism, and grievances rates, as well as with information on the rates of job-related physical and mental illness. These data could be subject to audit, just as are financial data, and they might be combined in a single "Quality of Work Life Index" that would provide an indication of the kind of work environment existing in a company. It is questionable whether an index should include self-report data. Because these data might affect the value of the company's stock, there could be a tendency for employees (particularly those holding stock) to distort their answers in order to make conditions in the company look good.

Stockholders should also have measures of the quality of the interpersonal relationships in the organization since these reflect whether the members are able to work together effectively. To some extent this could be measured by self-report, but people often do not realize what their impact is on others. Thus measurement by skilled observers may be needed. These measures could then be combined into a simple measure of the quality of the interpersonal relations in the organization.

Reporting to stockholders on the condition of the human aspects of organizations raises the question of who would prepare these reports. Probably behaviorally trained human system auditors would be needed to audit the human system, just as the accountant audits the financial system. And, as in financial accounting, over time a standardized procedure could be developed so that comparable data would become available from different firms. If a standardized index were agreed upon, it would be possible to report a percentile score for each company. Thus, in addition to reporting its earnings, each company would report where it stands on the "Quality of Work Life Index."

Potential Use of Measures by the Public and Government

At the present time a number of indexes provide measures about what life is like in the United States; almost without exception, however, they focus on the economic aspects of life. While these indexes provide valuable information and serve as guidelines for setting national economic policy, information is also needed on how various government policies affect the psychological quality of life in the United States. Although for a long time we assumed that economic growth was synonymous with a high quality of life, we now realize this is not necessarily true. But before we can act in ways that we are confident will improve the quality of life, we need measures of it. There can be no question that, in order to measure the quality of life, we require measures of the quality of working life.

How difficult is it to develop psychological quality of life measures for this purpose? Not too difficult if they are to be used only for the purpose of building national indicators of the quality of life and as guides to governmental decision making. Self-report measures of workers' feelings with respect to satisfaction and opportunities for growth could form a major part of any such measure because there would be a relatively low level of motivation to give invalid data. However, if the measures were to be used for regulating and influencing the behavior of the organizations for which the people work, the situation would be quite different. There might well be some motivation to distort self-report measures, just as there would be if the information were designed for stockholders.

Probably the most interesting potential use for psychological quality of working life indicators would be to influence and control those organizational practices that affect the psychological life workers enjoy. It may seem remote to envision the government's prohibiting certain practices because they reduce the psychological quality of work life, or penalizing organizations because they provide a poor quality of life for their employees; but it can and may happen. The long history of governmental regulation of conditions and practices affecting physical health and safety coupled with the regulation of environmental pollution establish important precedents for government regulation of the psychological quality of working life.

In the area of physical safety, there has been a long history of legislation regulating those organizational practices and working conditions that are likely to affect a person's physical health. Such things as hours of work and equipment design are specified in considerable detail in order to protect the physical health of employees. Without this legislation, an organization could reduce its cost and gain a competitive advantage by having a substandard work environment.

In the area of environmental pollution, organizations that pollute the air, water, and soil are now subject to fines and in some cases shutdown. The economic logic underlying this legislation is as follows. It costs organizations more to produce many products in ways that will not pollute. Thus any organization that tries to produce a product without polluting is at a competitive disadvantage in the market. The reason for this is that pollution control equipment is expensive and therefore adds to the company's costs. In a real sense, however, when goods are produced in a way that pollutes, their actual price tends to be too low because the full costs of producing them are not charged to the customer. They are borne by the society as a whole because the society as a whole bears the costs of pollution (e.g., rivers to clean up, air that increases illness, etc.).

There is a parallel between the economics of pollution and safety and those of providing a poor psychological environment for workers. Dissatisfying and meaningless jobs, without question, are a form of pollution (psychological and mental pollution) that causes health problems, the cost of which is borne by the society as a whole, rather than by the organizations engaging in such pollution. Evidence indicates that mental illness, alcoholism, shorter life expectancy, and less involvement in the community are sometimes caused by poor work environments, and their cost is partly borne by society. Just as was the case with environmental pollution, because these costs are absorbed by the society, some goods are underpriced relative to their real costs. And, just as with environmental pollution and safety, an organization which acts unilaterally to reduce the human pollution it causes may find itself at a competitive disadvantage. Thus a case can be made for government intervention designed to correct this situation. Of course, there are some situations where improving the quality of working life would not increase an organization's costs so as to put it at a competitive disadvantage. Research on job design[8] suggests that job enrichment can even reduce costs by leading to higher quality products and lower turnover rates, at the same time improving the psychological quality of working life. However, when increased costs are involved, the government may have to intervene in meaningful ways to change the economics of the situation in order to motivate organizations to improve the quality of employees' working lives.

Governmental Intervention to Improve the Quality of Working Life

Government could intervene in two very significant ways. First, it could charge organizations for the negative social outcomes that result from the psychological work life they create. For example, if a company was found to have an unusually high rate of alcoholism, drug addiction, and mental illness among its employees, the government could proportionately increase its taxes. This is not dissimilar to what it does now in the area of unemployment insurance. Alternatively, organizations with dissatisfied employees could be taxed more highly; but reliance on workers' self-reports could pose problems.

The second approach resembles those usually taken in the areas of physical safety and environmental pollution. Here organizations are fined and controlled not on the basis of the outcomes they produce (e.g., accidents, dead fish, sick people), but on the basis of the practices in which they engage (e.g., air pollution, unsafe work practices). This could be adapted to the area of the psychological quality of work life by fining or taxing organizations if they engage in psychologically harmful practices (e.g., repetitive jobs, punitive supervision). The major problem with this approach is that few practices have a negative impact on everyone's psychological life. Some people enjoy working on assembly lines; should organizations be penalized for having them work on assembly lines?

At the present, our knowledge of how many specific practices and environmental conditions affect the psychological quality of working life and our knowledge of how to measure them is sufficiently incomplete that we are probably not ready for any of the types of intervention just discussed. There are, however, some interim approaches (in addition to sponsoring research) that government can begin to take. It can, as has been done in the area of pollution, require organizations to prepare psychological impact statements when they modify existing or build new plants and facilities; this would at least force organizations to think about how the physical design of a plant and its administration affects their employees' lives. While these psychological impact statements would have no direct sanctions attached, they would be made public, which might cause public pressure to be brought on those organizations that engage in deleterious practices.

The government could also direct its business toward those organizations that do provide a high quality of life for their employees, just as now it directs its business toward organizations that do not discriminate. This would require federal standards so that the quality of life in organizations could be audited and, if found deficient, government contracts withheld. This represents a potentially powerful intervention strategy for the government and one that could be made operational in the not-too-distant future if work on it were to begin now.

Another immediate thing the government can do is to provide partial financial support for experimentation with and demonstration of new methods and practices that promise to improve the quality of working life. It can also take an active role in disseminating new findings about the effects of different management approaches. In short, it can offer a service to businessmen similar to the one currently offered to farmers by the Department of Agriculture. This approach should have a significant effect in those situations where improving the quality of work life will increase corporate profits.

In sum, clearly there is no shortage of potential ways in which the government can intervene to improve the psychological quality of working life. However, the operationalization of the most powerful of the intervention strategies discussed above (i.e., those involving legislated penalties) requires the development of better measures of work life quality, and further requires research on how this is linked to the practices and policies of organizations. Still, these are things the government can do now.

NOTES

1. H. L. Sheppard and N. Q. Herrick, *Where Have All the Robots Gone?* (New York: Free Press, 1972).

2. E. E. Lawler, *Pay and Organizational Effectiveness: A Psychological View* (New York: McGraw-Hill, 1971).

3. E. E. Lawler and J. L. Suttle, "A Causal Correlational Test of the Need Hierarchy Concept," *Organizational Behavior and Human Behavior*, 7 (1972), 265–287.

4. L. W. Porter and E. E. Lawler, *Managerial Attitudes and Performance* (Homewood, Ill.: Irwin-Dorsey, 1968).

5. W. V. Merrihue and R. A. Katzell, "ERI—Yardstick of Employee Relations," *Harvard Business Review*, 33 (1955), 6, 91–99.

6. J. G. Rhode and E. E. Lawler, "Auditing Change: Human Resource Accounting." A chapter in M. Dunnette (ed.), *Work and Nonwork in the Year 2001* (Monterey, Calif.: Brooks/Cole, 1973).

7. C. Argyris, *Intervention Theory and Method* (Reading, Mass.: Addison-Wesley, 1971).

8. E. E. Lawler and J. R. Hackman, "Corporate Profits and Employee Satisfaction: Must They Be in Conflict?" *California Management Review*, 14, (1971), 46–55.

9

Evaluating the Quality of
Working Life—Some Reflections
on Production and Cost and a
Method for Problem Definition

James S. Dyer and Marvin Hoffenberg

CONVENTIONAL criteria of productivity and cost are insufficient to
determine *problem structure* in organizations for the examination of issues
relating to the quality of working life and the evaluation of alternatives.
Because an organization's output is a sector of *joint products* multiple criteria
are required, but organizations may be reluctant to abandon a single criterion
as a basis for decision making, maintaining that consistency in decisions is
more difficult with multiple criteria. While members of organizations impose
penalties on decision makers in order to express their displeasure with decisions
affecting their quality of working life, the underlying causes of dissatisfaction
may not be identified—a situation that could be improved by the use of multiple
criteria. In complex problem situations there may be so many potential criteria

We are indebted to M. Milne for providing access to his CLUSTR computer program and
for his advice in using it.

that the decision maker's system definition is crucial because it determines the elements to be considered as decision variables and those to be taken as fixed, exogenously determined parameters. Forty "requirements" are suggested, illustrating the importance of problem definition in job-organization design. A computerized method was designed in which these requirements are clustered in terms of the analyst's consideration of every pair of requirements and whether they *interact*. The clustering program produces simplexes—sets of items in such manner that each item interacts with every other item in the set. simplexes are then clustered according to ratios of interactions, producing a branching or tree-like structure which allows a quick search to isolate those aspects relevant to a particular problem. This procedure is a potential tool for problem definition in evaluating quality of working life.

The phrase "quality of working life" invokes a sympathetic response among many, but consensus has not yet developed on a definition of the problem that is implied. Thus those who attempt to improve the quality of working life are grappling with an ill-defined problem that occurs in the context of complex systems, and no generally accepted basis exists for the evaluation of their efforts. Also, while efforts to develop indexes and other measures for the more general concept of the "quality of life" have been valuable in provoking thought and discussion, none of the results holds much promise for widespread adoption in the near future.[1] The "appreciative process" required for a convergence of views and values on such concepts can be expedited, but it cannot be hurried.

This selection is concerned with facilitating the process of problem definition. Specifically, a computerized design method has been adapted to determine a problem structure for viewing issues related to the quality of working life. The structure aids in identifying those aspects of a problem that should be considered in the evaluation of alternatives.

It must be stressed that this problem structure for the quality of working life is not presented in hopes that it will be adopted by others. The purpose in illustrating the design method is to present a process that may assist others in enhancing and sharpening their own appreciation of this problem. As study and research in this area continue, disparate views of different individuals will probably converge toward a more generally accepted problem definition; a rush to closure, therefore, seems premature at this time, and perhaps even dysfunctional in the long run.

A review of the literature for criteria suggested for evaluation of alternative solutions to problems related to the quality of working life indicated that those most commonly occurring are productivity and cost, both linked to the concept of production. However, organizations not only turn out conventional commodities and services; the same productive processes have effects on their societal and physical environment, and on those individuals associated with the processes who may view and evaluate these different "products" in various ways. Thus a single criterion, such as labor productivity, cannot be considered sufficient as the only evaluative measure. An organization's output is a vector of "joint products," to be evaluated by multiple criteria.

Criteria Considerations

Production, Productivity, and Cost

"Production" is defined in traditional economic theory as "the creation of valuable utilities." A productive act increases utility by altering the form, place, or time availability of something; the outputs of such an act may have many attributes and may be valued in different ways. Customarily, a monetary value (actual or imputed) is associated with output, but it may also be valued relative to the satisfaction derived from it by ultimate users, or from the standpoint of its social value. As another alternative, it may be valued in terms of how the necessary productive activities affect those individuals involved in them. Thus the value of production may be viewed as a physical, monetary, utility, or normative concept.

The physical concept for defining and valuing production is used to determine labor productivity—the ratio of output to labor input; psychological and behavioral factors that may affect the quality of working life are ignored in such a measure. Productivity measures are important, but users should understand their limitations. For example, if the output of a particular production process could be valued simultaneously in terms of a physical, a monetary, a utility, and a normative concept, and the valuation repeated for a subsequent time period, four productivity indexes could be computed that correspond to the four production concepts. If all the changes are either positive or negative, it can be said that productivity has increased or decreased, respectively. However, if some changes have different signs, the answer to the question of whether there was a positive or a negative change in productivity is totally dependent on the concept chosen as the basis for valuing the output.

This concept also determines "cost," since the cost of an event is the most highly valued alternative forsaken in order to achieve the chosen event. Any event is an amalgam of desirable and undesirable consequences, whether or not it is expressed in a common unit, for example, dollars. Since an event is valued by comparing "goods" and "bads," there is a tendency to consider the undesirable aspects as costs. The distinction between *valuation* and *costing* is overlooked by this practice; value is obtained by comparing good and bad consequences, but the cost is still unknown and must be identified as the highest-valued forsaken alternative.

Valuing (and, consequently, costing) is subjective, not completely described by pricing objects such as labor, capital, raw materials, and so on. When the operations underlying any measure of production or cost are examined critically, it becomes evident that one of many possible concepts has been used. Consequently, all measures are appraisals of production and cost, rather than value-free factual statements.

The Need for Multiple Criteria

In order to allow for different views of the same productive process, the output of an organization is defined here as a vector of "joint products." It consists of the commodities and services produced by the organization for consumption, of measures of the effects of the organization on the psychological and social attitudes of individuals (members, consumers, and others), and of measures of other, secondary effects (e.g., pollution) that results from the organization's activities.[2]

The operational use of the concept of multiple outputs does present certain obstacles since it requires that decisions be based on multiple criteria. Organizations may be reluctant to abandon a single criterion as the basis for decision making; maintaining consistency in decisions is more difficult with multiple criteria; and a mechanism must be found for sharing within the organization the values necessary for establishing the perhaps nonlinear tradeoff rates (or marginal rates of substitution) among the criteria.[3]

A more fundamental problem concerns the identification of the individual(s) whose values should be adopted as the basis for decision making. Alternative decisions may produce consequences (costs and benefits) borne by others; if these are not considered by the decision maker, his choices may be at odds with their needs and values. For example, members of organizations indirectly impose penalties (increased absenteeism, prolonged strikes, or even sabotage) on decision makers to express their displeasure with decisions that affect the quality of working life. However, while these tactics can effectively communicate a divergence between the value placed on the work experience by the decision makers and the value placed on it by other members of the organization, they do not aid in identifying the underlying causes of dissatisfaction. An analysis of the multiple criteria related to the quality of working life is required to determine the responses which more effectively deal with the needs of members of the organization.

Criteria for Evaluating the Quality of Working Life

It was stated that the output of organizations should be regarded as a vector of joint products, consisting of the commodity of service produced, of changes in psychological and social attitudes and behavior, and of measures of other secondary effects. In addition, it is now assumed that the quality of working life can be defined in terms of the organization's contributions to the economic and sociopsychological needs of those individuals actively engaged in furthering its goals.

Examples of potential criteria for evaluating the quality of working life on this basis are rich in the literature regarding organization theory and job design.[4] In fact, the list of potential criteria is so long that it may be considered infinite. The decision maker or analyst must exercise his judgment in carefully selecting from this list those criteria which seem most relevant for a particular problem. The criteria thus selected are affected by the analyst's perception of the "system" with which he is concerned. This "system definition" is crucial since it determines, among other things, which elements of the problem are to be considered as decision variables and which are to be taken as fixed, exogenously determined parameters.

The complex interrelationships among the many aspects of a particular problem require the analyst to delimit the system in some way: it is important to enhance his understanding of the system *a priori,* so that crucial relationships are not excluded from the research design. This understanding would also be helpful in synthesizing the results of previous studies that have concentrated on different aspects of questions related to the quality of working life.

Structuring the Problem

Requirements of Job-Organization Design

After a careful study of the relevant literature, forty "requirements" (listed in the Appendix) were selected as representative of the concerns in job-organization design.[5] (Since the distinction between constraints and criteria is often not clear and may be artificial, the term requirement is used here to include both concepts.) For example, the literature survey produced an initial list of fifty-six candidates for inclusion as personal need requirements. An analysis indicated that all could be subsumed under four broad categories of needs: material, social, self-esteem, and self-actualization, a group related to that of Maslow, but not implying a need hierarchy.[6] In addition, a requirement has been included that the organization must provide for differences in personality traits and values among its members.[7]

This list of forty requirements is not complete. Some requirements arise only from design errors recognized in other organizations and are to be avoided. This perception and the concerns represented by these requirements are very much functions of one's unique personal experiences and values. Also, while generality has been maintained in this list, a more specific and detailed list may be more appropriate for a particular problem. However, the forty requirements are sufficiently rich to illustrate the importance of problem definition, and to provide results with some significance for the study of the quality of working life.

Identification of Interactions

Many models of systems have been proposed in which links are drawn among boxes that identify important subsystems, such as the individual, the organizational structure, the environment, and so on. These links correctly indicate that interactions exist among certain elements of the subsystems, but the diagrams have serious limitations as a basis for the analysis of such problems as concern for the quality of working life. Their primary defect is that they do not aid in identifying the elements, perhaps from different subsystems, that are interrelated and that should be simultaneously considered in an effort to resolve a specific problem. Worse, these models may inhibit the analyst's understanding of the system if they incorrectly focus his attention on each subsystem as an appropriate unit of analysis.

As may be seen from the list of requirements in the Appendix, each of the subsystems we have identified generates a series of demands on the design problem, and many of these demands interact strongly with those from other subsystems. What is required is a means of regrouping these demands, or requirements, into clusters that define the important problems to be solved.

A computer-aided process for achieving this recombination of design requirements has been proposed by Alexander, and implemented by Alexander and Manheim and by Milne.[8] This process requires the analyst to consider each possible pair of design requirements, and to indicate whether or not they interact (for n requirements, a total of $n(n-1)/2$ comparisons). No distinction is made between "one-way" and "two-way" interactions. The self-posed question we found helpful in specifying an interaction between two requirements was the following: If actions are taken to satisfy the first requirement, will the degree to which the second requirement is satisfied be significantly affected, or *vice versa*. A response of "yes" that could be rationalized was the basis for indicating the existence of an interaction.

This "yes" or "no" specification does not include any measure of the intensity of the relationship. Given the current state of knowledge concerning the quality of working life, this restriction has certain advantages. While analysts may disagree over the intensity of a relationship, they may be able to agree that a "significant" relationship either does or does not exist.

Again, it is important to emphasize that these responses reflect only the opinions of the analyst. The significant relationships among the requirements that have been suggested are also indicated in the Appendix. While empirical data may be available in some cases as a guide to the decisions, many of the responses are based on a combination of personal experience and intuition. This approach is similar to the use of subjective probabilities as a basis for decision making when empirical data are unavailable.

The Structure of the System

The interactions among the requirements were input into a computer program named CLUSTR, an extension of Alexander's approach to design problems. The procedure differs in significant ways from Alexander and Manheim's HIDEC programs, and will yield different results.[9] Briefly, the program generates all of the possible "simplexes" existing in the system. A simplex is defined here as a set of requirements with the property that each requirement interacts with every other requirement in the set. In addition, no simplex is completely contained within another simplex. Further, a requirement may appear in more than one simplex, a feature which represents an important difference between the CLUSTR and HIDEC programs. These simplexes identify those aspects of the system which exhibit complete interdependencies, and which should be considered simultaneously in any effort to affect any one of them.

After the simplexes have been identified by the computer program, a clustering process begins. Every simplex is compared with every other simplex and a coherency ratio is computed, based on the number of interactions in the union of the two sets of requirements divided by the theoretical maximum number of interactions. The two simplexes with the highest coherency ratio are then combined to form a cluster (a slightly larger set of requirements which are no longer completely connected). New coherency ratios are computed for this new cluster compared to all the remaining simplexes. Again, the two simplexes or clusters with the highest coherency ratio are combined into a new cluster. The process continues until the last two clusters have been combined, and a "tree-like" structure results.

The forty requirements and the interactions listed in the Appendix generated a hierarchy with eleven levels, which included 72 simplexes and 29 second-level clusters. It may be argued that the creation of 72 simplexes from a list of forty requirements does not represent a simplification of the problem; however, the complexity of this system does not stem from the number of requirements, but rather from the maze of interactions among them. The structure provided allows a quick search through this maze to isolate those aspects relevant to a particular problem. In other words, the analyst can easily discover the simplexes containing requirements identified as related to a particular problem; considered either individually or as part of a closely related cluster, they provide the problem definition that he seeks.[10]

Possible secondary effects, some perhaps considered "good" and others "bad," are also illuminated by the interactions among the requirements, suggesting other criteria for evaluation to augment the set implied by the primary objectives of the effort. Thus the proper means of evaluation will evolve naturally as a part of the problem definition process.

Since the simplexes include only requirements identified by the analyst as interacting with each other, there can be no surprises in the computer output about them. Some of the simplexes are easily explained since they merely illustrate well-understood relations, but others include requirements that are seldom simultaneously considered and their implications may be far from obvious. The former are reassuring since they reinforce conventional wisdom; the latter require much thinking and perhaps some change in appreciation before becoming acceptable.

Use of the Structure

Identification of Relevant Requirements

The selected set of requirements and the specified interactions shown in the Appendix are based on our understanding of the general job-organization design problem. The derived complex system structure can be used in the analysis of problems other than those associated with the quality of working life. Ultimately, its usefulness depends upon the analyst's skill in identifying the parts of this general structure that are important for a particular area of concern.

We have assumed that the quality of working life can be defined in terms of the organization's contributions to the economic and sociopsychological needs of those individuals actively engaged in furthering its goals. These contributions may accrue to individuals either directly, while they are on the job, or indirectly through the influences of the organization on society. For the purpose of analysis, we may elect to concentrate on both the direct and indirect consequences, or on either subset. As an illustration, we shall restrict the discussion to the direct contributions of the organization to the needs of its members. The requirements that relate to this restricted problem are numbers 25 through 28 in the Appendix.

These four requirements also suggest classes of criteria that should be used in the evaluation of alternatives. Although this simplifies the task considerably, the identification of those specific criteria that are both appropriate for evaluation and operationally practical to use still requires careful thought.

At least one of these four requirements appears in 29 of the 72 simplexes that are the basic building blocks in the structure of the system described here. Several of these 29 simplexes contain a number of common requirements. The clustering process that produces the tree-like structure of the system provides a convenient means of identifying two or more simplexes that share a high proportion of common requirements. Instead of focusing on each simplex in isolation, additional insights into a problem may be obtained by simultaneously analyzing two or more similar simplexes that form a cluster.

An Example of the Analysis of Simplexes

Space limitations do not allow us to present each of the 29 simplexes of interest. Therefore, one cluster was chosen from the structure of the system to provide an example of the information generated by the computerized design procedure. This cluster contains 4 of those 29 simplexes that include at least one of the requirements 25 through 28. The brief discussions of the implications of each simplex are provided only as illustrations, since other interpretations are possible. In fact, the reader is encouraged to develop his own rationalizations for the relationships among the requirements shown. The attempts to provide these rationalizations lead to the insights that in our judgment justify the effort required by this approach.

Figure 1 indicates that simplexes 1020 and 1039 were grouped into a second-level cluster, as were 1012 and 1013. These two second-level clusters were then combined to form a third-level cluster. Abbreviated descriptions of the requirements that appear in these simplexes are included in Figure 1, while the associated numbers refer to the more complete descriptions given in the Appendix. Those requirements which appear within a particular simplex are contained within an appropriately labeled figure.

Figure 1 draws attention to those requirements common to all four simplexes. These common requirements (numbers 6, 19, 27, 29, and 37) suggest that if we consider differences in the personalities and the competences of the available work force in defining the appropriate variety of tasks to be included within each job and in determining the means of controlling the work, then we can provide an environment in which the self-esteem of the individuals will be enhanced. An inspection of the individual simplexes provided further indications of how this might be best achieved, and suggests other requirements that should be considered.

For example, simplex 1020 emphasizes that the degree of uncertainty inherent in the technology involved may affect the choice of mechanisms for controlling the work, as well as the required skill and knowledge among the organization's members. Specifically, the degree to which automatic control of operations may be feasible will be affected by the uncertainty in the system.

Simplex 1039 recognizes that in some cases it may be impossible to achieve the desired match between the individual and the job, or that an appropriate variety of tasks within a "job" may not be feasible. As an alternative, job rotation or some means of additional compensation should be considered to provide the individual with the opportunity for self-actualization.

According to simplex 1013, if consideration is given to the desired degree of specialization of labor (in addition to merely matching skill requirements

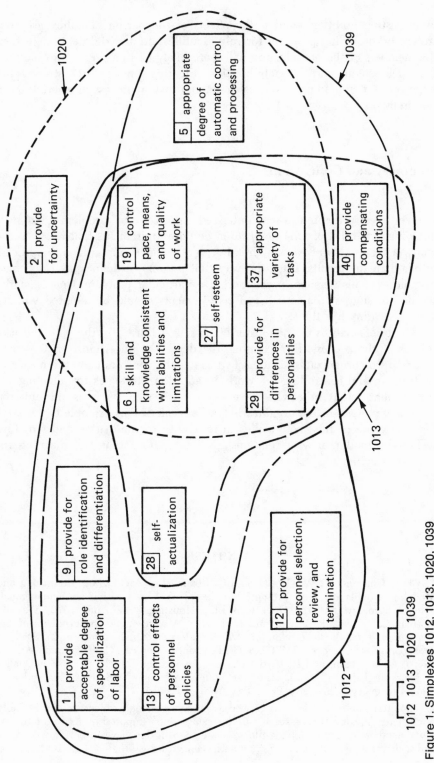

Figure 1. Simplexes 1012, 1013, 1020, 1039

with existing abilities), and if the effects of the personnel policy are controlled by providing properly for role identification and differentiation, then the members of the organization will more likely be in a position to increase their self-esteem and self-actualization. Finally, simplex 1012 stresses the importance of a good personnel selection and review process in meeting these requirements.

Summary and Conclusions

We have presented a computerized approach to problem definition, applying it to a list of job-organization design requirements that relate to the study of the quality of working life. Further, we have emphasized the process rather than the results, since the way that an analyst defines a system may be unique to his personal perception of a particular problem. Consequently, we do not suggest that our list of requirements should be adopted without serious scrutiny by others.

The brief analysis of the cluster of simplexes illustrates the potential usefulness of the process. For example, the degree of uncertainty in the technology of the organization is identified as placing constraints on the means of performing and controlling the work. In addition, strategies for affecting the system that might otherwise have been overlooked, such as through the personnel policies of the organization, are revealed. This example emphasizes that the value of this method lies in its ability to summarize and structure well-understood pair-wise relationships into a form that has meaning for problem solving.

NOTES

1. Cf. A. Charnes, W. W. Cooper, and G. Kozmetsky, "Measuring, Monitoring and Modeling Quality of Life," presented at the TIMS XIX Meeting on Management, Science, Ecology, and the Quality of Life, Houston, Tex., April 1972. See also Norman C. Dalkey, R. Lewis, and D. Snyder, *Measurement and Analysis of the Quality of Life: With Exploratory Illustrations of Applications to Career and Transportation Choices*, RM–6228–DOT (Santa Monica, Calif.: Rand, August 1970); S. M. Mann, and Richard Hobson, "Toward the Development of a Quality of Working Life Index," Division of Man-Environment Relations, Pennsylvania State University, University Park, Pa., April 1972.

2. Too often the organization is viewed as pursuing a single objective—profitability or efficiency in some form—subject to the "constraints" imposed by its commitments to its members and to society. Although concern with this view on both a normative and a descriptive basis is not new, it has been growing rapidly. (Cf. R. M. Cyert

and C. L. Hedrick, "Theory of the Firm: Past, Present, and Future; An Interpretation," *Journal of Economic Literature*, June 1972, pp. 398–442; M. Shubik, "A Curmudgeon's Guide to Microeconomics," *Journal of Economic Literature*, June 1970, pp. 405–434.) Suggestions of other criteria for evaluation also occur in the literature on organizational behavior, job design, and worker satisfaction. (See, e.g., R. Likert, *New Patterns of Management* [New York: McGraw-Hill, 1961]; C. Argyris, *Integrating the Individual and the Organization* [New York: Wiley, 1964]; F. Herzberg, *Work and the Nature of Man* [New York: World, 1969].) Organizations in societies of the postindustrial era can no longer afford this simplistic view of a single criterion as being adequate for evaluating organizational change. (See L. Davis, "Job-Satisfaction Research: The Post Industrial View," *Industrial Relations*, May 1971, pp. 176–179, and E. Trist, "The Relation of Welfare and Development in the Transition to Post-Industrialism," *Proceedings International Seminar on Welfare and Development*, Canadian Centre for Community Studies, Ottawa, 1967.)

3. H. Raiffa, *Preference for Multi-Attributed Alternatives*, RM–5868–DOT/RC, Rand Corporation, Santa Monica, Calif. April 1969.

4. For example, Herzberg ("One More Time: How Do You Motivate Employees?", *Harvard Business Review*, January-February 1968, pp. 53–62; and *Work and the Nature of Man*) assumes that the technology and the basic organizational structure are only incidentally related to job enrichment and, consequently, are treated as being largely predetermined. Therefore, the decision variables are the elements of the task activities which may be combined in various ways to define a "job." Morse ("The Myth of Job Enlargement," Graduate School of Management, UCLA, June 1972) argues that it is important to achieve a "fit" between the job design and the personality characteristics of the individual assigned to the task. (See also, e.g., J. Morse and J. Lorsh, "Beyond Theory Y," *Harvard Business Review*, May-June 1970, pp. 61–68 and M. Myers, "Who Are Your Motivated Workers?", *Harvard Business Review*, January-February 1964, pp. 73–78.) Other researchers have shifted their attention from the worker and his job to an analysis of the organization in terms of a "sociotechnical" system. (See, e.g., Davis, *op. cit.*, and "The Design of Jobs," *Industrial Relations*, October 1966, pp. 21–45, by the same author; see also F. Emery and E. Trist, "Socio-Technical Systems," in Emery [ed.], *Systems Thinking*, Penguin Modern Management [Penguin Education X 71] [Baltimore: Penguin Books, 1969], pp. 241–260.) They refer to the organization as an "open system" to emphasize the fact that it interacts with its external environment and can effect social change. McWhinney and Eldon ("Not Industrial Democracy, But a Reticular Society," Graduate School of Management, UCLA, March 1972) have extended this open systems concept by suggesting that jobs and organizations can be viewed as instruments to achieve social change objectives. (Cf. F. Emery and E. Thorsrud, *Industrial Democracy: Some Experience from Norway and Other European Countries* [London: Tavistock, 1969].) Finally, Pateman (*Participation and Democratic Theory* [Cambridge, Eng.: Cambridge University Press, 1970]) has linked the democratization of the workplace to democratic political theory.

5. See C. Alexander, *Notes on the Synthesis of Form* (Cambridge: Harvard University Press, 1964); and Murry M. Milne and Charles W. Rusch, "Systematic Design as an Educational Experiment," draft, School of Architecture and Urban Planning, UCLA, n.d.

6. A. Maslow, *Motivation and Personality* (New York: Harper & Row, 1954).

7. Cf. Morse, *op. cit.*

8. Alexander, *op. cit.*, and C. Alexander and M. Manheim, "HIDECS 2: A Computer Program for the Hierarchical Decomposition of a Set with an Associated Graph," M.I.T. Civil Engineering Laboratory Publication No. 160, Cambridge, Mass., 1962. Murry A. Milne, "CLUSTR: A Program for Structuring Design Prob-

lems," *Proceedings* of the SHARE-ACM-IEEE Design Automation Workshop, Atlantic City, N.J., June 28–30, 1971.

9. Cf. Milne, *op. cit.*, and Alexander and Manheim, *op. cit.* Several other computer programs written for the same purpose also exist, and are reviewed by Milne and Rusch, *op. cit.*

10. For example, they should include those requirements that restrict his ability to offer alternative solutions. In some cases, other requirements may suggest means of affecting the system that could have been overlooked. Thus the procedure provides a "check list" of constraints and feasible strategies for solutions.

APPENDIX: REQUIREMENTS AND INTERACTIONS

Technology

1. The required degree of specialization of labor (differentiation of tasks) must be within limits acceptable to the organization. Interacts with 2, 3, 6, 7, 9, 10, 12, 13, 15, 18, 19, 26, 27, 28, 29, 34, 37, 38, 39, and 40, and appears in 15 simplexes.

2. Provide for the degree of uncertainty which exists in inputs, the process, and outputs. Interacts with 1, 3, 4, 5, 6, 7, 8, 9, 10, 12, 13, 15, 16, 17, 18, 19, 21, 23, 27, 29, and 37, and appears in 27 simplexes.

3. Provide for the desired degree of flexibility in the sequencing of tasks. Interacts with 1, 2, 5, 6, 7, 8, 9, 13, 15, 19, 26, 29, 37, and 40, and appears in 8 simplexes.

4. Provide appropriate degree of nonhuman power (reduce physical fatigue). Interacts with 2, 5, 6, 7, 8, 19, 34, and 35, and appears in 5 simplexes.

5. Provide appropriate degree of automatic control and processing. Interacts with 2, 3, 4, 6, 7, 8, 19, 34, and 35, and appears in 5 simplexes.

6. The degree of skill and knowledge required for tasks should be consistent with the abilities and limitations of the available and potential work force. Interacts with 1, 2, 3, 4, 5, 7, 9, 10, 12, 13, 15, 19, 25, 27, 28, 29, 34, 37, and 40, and appears in 19 simplexes.

7. Provide for adequate long- and short-run flexibility and adaptability of physical facilities and the technological process. Interacts with 1, 2, 3, 4, 5, 6, 8, 9, 10, 15, 16, 19, 23, 29, 37, and 40, and appears in all simplexes.

8. Provide for control of all aspects of the physical process including secondary effects perhaps not directly related to primary mission (e.g., disposal of waste, etc.). Interacts with 2, 3, 4, 5, 7, 18, 19, 21, 23, 35, and 37, and appears in 8 simplexes.

Organization

Formal Structure

9. Must provide for role identification and differentiation. Interacts with 1, 2, 3, 6, 7, 10, 11, 12, 13, 15, 16, 18, 19, 20, 21, 26, 27, 28, 29, 37, 38, 39, and 40, and appears in 23 simplexes.

10. Must provide clear decision assignments. Interacts with 1, 2, 6, 7, 9, 11, 12, 15, 16, 18, 19, 20, 21, and 29, and appears in 8 simplexes.

11. Must provide compatibility between authority and accountability. Interacts with 9, 10, 16, 18, 20, and 23, and appears in 2 simplexes.

12. Must provide for personal selection, review, and termination. Interacts with 1, 2, 6, 9, 10, 13, 14, 15, 16, 18, 19, 21, 22, 25, 27, 28, 29, 34, and 37, and appears in 21 simplexes.

13. Provide for control of the effects of the personnel policies of the organization, including secondary effects not directly related to the primary organizational goals. Interacts with 1, 2, 3, 6, 9, 14, 15, 18, 19, 21, 22, 23, 25, 26, 27, 28, 29, 34, 37, and 40, and appears in 5 simplexes.

14. Must provide incentives for individual participation (room for advancement, etc.). Interacts with 12, 13, 17, 22, 25, 26, 27, 28, 29, 37, and 38, and appears in 5 simplexes.

15. The organizational structure must be adaptable to changes within the limits of perceived potential needs as determined by the goals and environment of the organization (e.g., project or functional organization). Interacts with 1, 2, 3, 5, 6, 7, 9, 10, 12, 13, 16, 17, 18, 19, 20, 21, 23, 29, and 37, and appears in 18 simplexes.

Decision-making and Control System

16. Provide a goal-setting mechanism leading to mutually reinforcing internal goals (including a means of conflict resolution). Interacts with 2, 7, 9, 10, 11, 12, 15, 18, 20, 22, 23, 28, and 29, and appears in 11 simplexes.

17. Provide a means of generating new goals, policies, and strategies regarding the primary organizational mission (while recognizing that some organizations may be temporal by choice). Interacts with 2, 14, 15, 18, 21, 23, 25, and 32, and appears in 3 simplexes.

18. Must provide a clear basis for establishing decisions at levels where the relevant tradeoffs are visible. Interacts with 1, 2, 8, 9, 10, 11, 12, 13, 15, 16, 17, 19, 20, 21, 22, 23, and 29 and appears in 17 simplexes.

19. Provide for the control of the pace, means, and quality of work. Interacts with 1, 2, 3, 4, 5, 6, 7, 8, 9, 10, 12, 13, 15, 18, 21, 27, 28, 29, 37, and 40, and appears in 25 simplexes.

20. Provide a means of implementing decisions and obtaining their acceptance. Interacts with 9, 10, 11, 15, 16, 18, 22, and 29, and appears in 3 simplexes.

Information System

21. Must provide a match between decision level and available information. Interacts with 2, 8, 9, 10, 12, 13, 15, 17, 18, 19, 22, 23, 27, 32, and 37, and appears in 13 simplexes.

22. Must provide a mechanism for obtaining feedback from members of the organization regarding their feelings and perceived needs. Interacts with 12, 13, 14, 16, 18, 20, 21, 25, 26, 27, 28, 29, 31, 33, 37, and 38, and appears in 12 simplexes.

23. Must provide a mechanism for obtaining feedback from consumers and society. Interacts with 2, 7, 8, 11, 13, 15, 16, 17, 18, 21, 24, 32, 34, 35, and 38, and appears in 13 simplexes.

24. Must provide external communication channels to consumers and society. Interacts with 23, 32, and 38. This element appears only in simplex 1063 where it is completely defined because it contains all of the other elements with which it interacts.

Personal Needs

25. Provide for satisfaction of material needs (for food, clothing, and shelter). Interacts with 6, 12, 13, 14, 17, 22, 27, 28, 29, 31, 33, 34, 35, and 40, and appears in 7 simplexes.

26. Provide for social interaction. Interacts with 1, 3, 9, 13, 14, 22, 30, 33, and 40, and appears in 4 simplexes.

27. Provide for increasing self-esteem (self-confidence, potency, control, personal influence, independence, autonomy, adaptability, freedom, security). Interacts with 1, 2, 5, 6, 9, 12, 13, 14, 16, 19, 22, 25, 27, 29, 30, 31, 32, 33, 34, 36, 37, 38, 39, and 40, and appears in 21 simplexes.

28. Provide for self-actualization (growth, personal identity, self-realization). Interacts with 1, 5, 6, 9, 12, 13, 14, 16, 19, 22, 25, 27, 29, 30, 31, 32, 33, 34, 36, 37, and 40, and appears in 15 simplexes.

29. Provide for the differences in personality traits and in moral and social values. Interacts with 1, 2, 3, 5, 6, 7, 9, 10, 12, 13, 14, 15, 16, 18, 19, 20, 22, 25, 27, 28, 34, 37, and 40, and appears in 29 simplexes.

Needs of Society and the Physical Environment

30. Increase potential for meaningful social interaction off the job and for community-citizen involvement. Interacts with 26, 27, 28, and 33, and appears in 2 simplexes.

31. Increase effectiveness in the home life. Interacts with 22, 25, 27, 28, 33, and 34, and appears in 2 simplexes.

32. Produce a product perceived to have significant social value. Interacts with 17, 21, 23, 24, 27, 28, 35, and 38, and appears in 6 simplexes.

33. Reduce habits that result in physical and mental ill health and in antisocial behavior. Interacts with 22, 25, 26, 27, 28, 30, 31, and 34, and appears in 5 simplexes.

34. Provide employment opportunities for all individuals seeking work (including groups such as the young, disadvantaged, and minorities). Interacts with 1, 4, 6, 12, 13, 23, 25, 27, 28, 29, 31, 33, and 35, and appears in 8 simplexes.

35. Reduce air, water, noise, and visual pollution (preserve wilderness and scenery, increase beauty of environment). Interacts with 4, 8, 23, 25, 32, and 34, and appears in 6 simplexes.

36. Provide for increased learning and personal growth not related to the workplace. Interacts with 27 and 28. This element appears only in the simplex 1071 where it is completely defined because it contains all of the other elements with which it interacts.

Job Design

37. Provide an appropriate variety and pattern of tasks within the job. Interacts with 1, 2, 3, 5, 6, 7, 8, 9, 12, 13, 14, 15, 19, 21, 22, 27, 28, 29, and 40, and appears in 18 simplexes.

38. The tasks in the job should provide a basis for respect in the community. Interacts with 1, 9, 14, 22, 23, 24, 27, 32, and 39, and appears in 4 simplexes.

39. The job should make some perceivable contribution to the utility of the product. Interacts with 1, 9, 27, and 38. This element appears only in simplex 1015 where it is completely defined because it contains all of the other elements with which it interacts.

40. Provide for job rotation or other compensating conditions (including interlocking tasks or physical proximity) on jobs high in stress or with little obvious end-product contribution. Interacts with 1, 3, 5, 6, 7, 9, 13, 19, 25, 26, 27, 28, 29, and 37, and appears in 7 simplexes.

10

Some Significant Contexts and Components of Individual Quality of Life

J. G. Goodale, D. T. Hall, R. J. Burke, and R. C. Joyner

AN ONGOING study measuring the relationship between the quality of working life and the quality of life is reported in this selection. Work ranked third in importance in respondents' lives and was mentioned most often as a source of disliked activities but ranked second for most liked activities.

This selection has been condensed by the editors with permission of the authors from the paper by the same title, describing a preliminary study giving considerable procedural and analytic detail presented at the International Conference on Quality of Working Life, September 1972. Copies of the paper are available from James G. Goodale.

This selection deals with the important issue of the possible relationship between quality of working life and other components of quality of life. Sharing the increasing general concern for the development of methods to monitor social change and to diagnose society's well-being, the two factors are emphasized: the individual's perception of his quality of life and the person in his various contexts, for example, work, family, community, and recreation. It is observed that while work may be an important facet in a person's identity, it is not the only, or even the most important, one.

Concerning the components of quality of life, seventeen variables have been chosen, shown on Table 1. The variables describe either quality of life outcomes or environmental factors influencing these outcomes. The variables can also be divided into four categories, each viewed as having three basic elements: a task, a social, and a self-oriented component. The categories are: *personal characteristics* (e.g., self-control, self-esteem, and self-identity); *activities* (e.g., task, social, and self-development activities); *objective outcomes* (e.g., task and social success and physical and economic well-being); and *perceived outcomes*, that is, the individual's subjective assessment of his objective outcomes (e.g., task involvement and felt security).

TABLE 1.

Components of Quality of Life

Self-control
Self-esteem
Self-identity
Task activity
Social activity and participation
Self-development activities
Task success
Physical health
Physical and economic security
Task involvement
Task satisfaction
Social involvement and feelings of relatedness
Self-reported health
Perceived security, fears, anxieties
Perceived growth and mastery
Global evaluative feelings
Fulfillment-in-context $\times$ value of context

One aim of the ongoing project is to estimate the impact of these components in the four specific contexts of work, home, community, and recreation. The model presented in Figure 1 shows a causal chain leading from the environment to objective outcomes thought to produce the relatively transient, perceived outcomes which, in turn, affect more stable personal

Environmental Factors* ——→ Objective Outcomes ——→ Perceived Outcomes

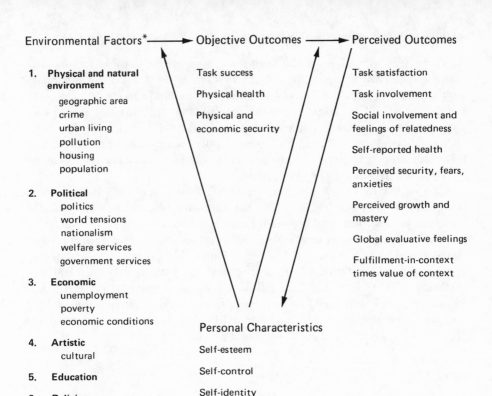

1. **Physical and natural environment**
   geographic area
   crime
   urban living
   pollution
   housing
   population

2. **Political**
   politics
   world tensions
   nationalism
   welfare services
   government services

3. **Economic**
   unemployment
   poverty
   economic conditions

4. **Artistic**
   cultural

5. **Education**

6. **Religion**

7. **Social**
   friendships, relationships
   youth
   neighborhood
   community

8. **Family**

9. **Work**
   organizational climate
   labor relations climate
   technology
   bureaucratization
   working conditions

10. **Leisure**
    recreation
    hobbies

11. **Personal**
    health
    civil liberties
    establishment "the system"
    financial

Task success

Physical health

Physical and
economic security

Task satisfaction

Task involvement

Social involvement and
feelings of relatedness

Self-reported health

Perceived security, fears,
anxieties

Perceived growth and
mastery

Global evaluative feelings

Fulfillment-in-context
times value of context

Personal Characteristics

Self-esteem

Self-control

Self-identity

*Not included in Quality of Life questionnaire.

Figure 1. Model of Quality of Life Variables

characteristics. The latter are seen to act as moderators on the relationships among the other three components. The research to be reported deals only with perceived outcomes and personal characteristics.

The study has two main objectives: first, to obtain information about the generality and applicability of the model (e.g., if interviews yielded constructs not covered, the model could be made more comprehensive and valid); second, to explore how groups differing on certain dimensions (e.g., employed or unemployed, high or low degree of personal control over job and life activities) might describe their quality of life. The groups studied and the conditions to which they were assigned are shown in Table 2.

TABLE 2.

Samples of Interview Study

	Variable	
	EMPLOYED	UNEMPLOYED
High degree of control	College professors Telephone construction workers*	Counterculture youths* College students
Low degree of control	Junior chartered accountants* Assembly-line workers Computer engineers* Telephone operators*	Immigrants Executives Housewives

* Groups marked with an asterisk are discussed in the present selection; the remaining groups are presently being interviewed. The complete results will be reported at a later date.

In this preliminary study, fifty-three people from five organizations were interviewed; each completed a questionnaire comprising demographic information, global estimates of satisfaction with life, and rated importance of contexts. The data reported here should be considered tentative and is provided as a condensed, qualitative description. The plan is to interview another hundred people.

Asked "How would you define the phrase 'quality of life' ?," all 53 persons were able to respond; 48 provided an abstract response (e.g., the value placed on life and living); 21 used concrete referents such as relating with other people, and 15 of this latter subgroup provided definitions with both concrete and abstract referents.

The most frequently mentioned components of quality of life were psychological well-being, the work environment, realizing or working on one's aim in life, and the social environment provided by other people. Almost all respondents answered affirmatively to "Do you ever think about the quality of your own life?" It was the interviewer's impression, however, that defining quality of work took considerable time and hard thinking.

Responses to the question "What do you really enjoy doing?" were categorized as to the contexts mentioned—most commonly mentioned were leisure or nonwork-setting work and social relationships with friends. Asked why these activities were enjoyed, between 11 and 17 percent of the respondents mentioned at least one of the following: satisfaction, challenge or mastery, communication with other people, and relaxation or decrease in stimulation.

Asked whether their quality of life had gone up or down in the last year, a sizeable majority reported an increase and only four indicated a decline. The reasons given may have been a function of the age (mean age 27.4) or position in the life cycle of the respondents. Such matters as getting married or buying a new home were mentioned.

Each person was asked about the most satisfying and the most dissatisfying part of his job. Greatest satisfaction was felt on contact with clients and co-workers, challenge, and autonomy (freedom). The most dissatisfying aspects were problems with supervisors and co-workers, shift work or working hours, and repetitive or dirty jobs.

Of eight contents ranked for their importance in a respondent's life, family came first, followed by personal relationships, work or school, and spare time activities.

Group differences in response to the same questions are examined. Because of the very small sample size in each group, the differences are useful only as indicators for further research.

The results of the interview study led to some changes in the quality of life model (Figure 1). A number of categories were added both to content and component outcomes, and a recombination of categories was necessary for contexts: for example, "community" was hardly ever mentioned and was dropped, whereas "family" was broadened to "family and home" to include nonfamily members with whom respondents were living; "recreation" was broadened to "nonwork," solitary activities often mentioned were put into a "self" context, and "outdoors" was mentioned often enough to be listed as a separate context. "Work" was the only context not modified.

The work context was mentioned most often as a source of disliked activities, but ranked second for most-liked activities.

Initially, fourteen components of quality of life had been generated by the authors. Only one additional component, "relaxation or decrease in stimulation," was mentioned often enough to warrant inclusion in the model.

It had been predicted that the three personal characteristics—self-esteem, self-control, and self-identity—are factors of which people would be less consciously aware and thus would mention less as influencing quality of life. The expectation was correct except for self-esteem, mentioned quite often.

PART
III

Changing
the Quality of
Working Life

In this part the processes of change in organizations are considered. Most organizations have some experience with "intervention" from the outside in the form of consultants of one kind or another and evolve a role model for such interventions. But consultants are usually engaged to tackle a reasonably well defined "problem," the methods they will use are familiar or at least understood, the nature of the outcome is appreciated, and some measures, however crude, are seen to be appropriate to evaluate its success.

The engagement of an organization with researchers from the outside with the aim of evolving new organizational forms and methods which will enhance the quality of working life of its members contradicts almost all the expectations described in our last paragraph. The problem cannot be precisely defined; indeed, its nature changes with every step. The methods, predominantly those of action research, are unfamiliar and little understood. The nature of the outcome is unpredictable and, particularly if some advance is made toward new forms, the organization will evolve new ways of operating which cannot be foreseen. Not least, its view of itself and its missions will undergo change. Thus any measures of evaluation cannot be static in the usual before-after model.

The four selections which follow tackle all these questions. Alfred Clark is concerned mainly with the problems that arise during the engagement of two organizations—the "client" and that of the "practitioner." The client's role model of the consultant is inadequate to a joint enterprise of two organizations—the client's and the consultant's. Instead of the researcher-consultant operating within the value system of the client organization, agreed values to govern the relationship have to be sought and found. Churchman and Emery[1] have described the need for a temporary "cover" organization with values superordinate to those of each separate organization. Clark also describes the difficulties which arise as a result of the different organizational structures —the tall pyramidal shape of the capital-intensive client and the flat shape of the labor-intensive research organizations. Cherns[2] has described how this exerts strain on the researchers to operate in a more hierarchical mode than they wished. The appropriate model of the relationship between client and consultant-researcher will, of course, vary with the nature of the problem, the extent to which it is defined, the freedom of the researcher to select methods of approach, and the nature of the expected outcome. As Peter Clark describes, the appropriate model for the engagement aimed at enhancing quality of working life is likely to be the "collaborative/dialogic" one which governs the conduct of action research.

As Thorsrud emphasizes, action research still possesses a "pioneering" quality. In view of Peter Clark's analysis, we would expect not only a good deal of potential confusion about the role of the action researcher, but also that this confusion would become critical at the points where the implicit model held by the client is contradicted. Thorsrud describes three "critical incidents" of this kind where points of stress occurred and how these stresses were relaxed or resolved. As we would now expect, difficulties arose at the time of setting the original objectives and in testing out the commitment of the researchers.

In a subsequent period of difficulty for the client, the researcher was looked to for consulting help to establish role relationships that would only have hindered subsequent developments. Finally, difficulties arose within problems of diffusion, linking learning with that from other projects where again the more familiar role models make little provision. As Thorsrud concludes, the role requirements of this kind of engagement call for the development of an appropriate role culture within the institutions of social science itself. The universities encounter great problems in incorporating action research within their value framework. As discussed in *The Quality of Working Life: Cases and Commentary* (section 3), action research offers a mode of generating and validating knowledge which is not assimilable into the familiar canons of scholarship. The problems that this poses in terms of the organization of research are described in that chapter where the need for boundary institutions to cope with them are outlined. A more detailed analytical view of the challenge action research poses for science is in Cherns, Clark, and Jenkins.[3]

The problems for methods of evaluation are described by Faxen and Hansson who show the inappropriateness of the before-after model. As they explain, the taking of measures before and after implies that one knows precisely what the goals are and that these will not change as the research or experiment progresses. Furthermore, they do not answer the really important questions Why does the change occur? Will it last? This is really crucial. Changes that have become part of the culture of an organization lead to further change, unpredictable but sharing and supporting the values of the original change. If they have not become part of the culture they will not last. If our goal, then, is, as it must be, the creation of self-developing forms of organization, we cannot afford to neglect the creation of self-developing forms of evaluation.

NOTES

1. C. W. Churchman and F. E. Emery, "On Various Approaches to the Study of Organizations," in J. R. Lawrence (ed.), *Operational Research and the Social Sciences* (London: Tavistock, 1966).

2. A. B. Cherns, "Models for the Use of Research," *Human Relations*, 25, no. 1 (1972), 25–33.

3. A. B. Cherns, P. A. Clark, and W. I. Jenkins, "Action Research and the Development of the Social Sciences," in A. W. Clark and P. M. Foster (eds.), *Experiences in Action Research* (London: Malaby Press, 1975).

11

The Client-Practitioner Relationship as an Intersystem Engagement

Alfred W. Clark

CLIENT-PRACTITIONER (C-P) relationships are considered at the system rather than at the individual level. Conditions influencing the interdependence between the client and practitioner systems include the "openness" of each, a condition which enhances adaptability to environmental variance. However, there is not total congruence of the two systems and each needs to realize that contradictory inputs can lead either to creative engagement or, if poorly handled, to destructive conflict. Other conditions influencing C-P interdependency are located in the task, external, value, reward, and power systems. The primary task is to maintain the C-P relationship and to help the client system change in an agreed direction. The task should thus be defined, collaboratively and not unilaterally. The practitioner must analyze his and the client's environment and locate any mismatches. Both confront environments ranging from placid to turbulent; the more disturbed the environment, the more conflict there is likely to be in the C-P relationship, but the more creative will also be the solutions. Existing patterns of hostilities and affections within the client system, vested interests in skill and territory, and whether the practitioners are seen as "management's men" are all relevant. The nature of the technical system of the action researcher is likely to be very different from that of the client. It is labor-intensive and highly technical. Researchers have interchangeable roles and high independence, but they must also be committed to shared objectives and there must be criteria for the achievement of objectives. Client system technologies vary greatly, but they are predictable, explicit, and rather inflexible. Few industries have a well-developed set of ethical constraints. The social systems have developed to match the technical systems—for example, tall hierarchical structures. There is seldom an appreciation of the principle of joint optimization of the social and technical systems, and seldom an accounting system which includes social indicators.

The C-P relationship is conceptualized as a sociotechnical system with various inputs and transformation processes, which act not only as resources but also as potential sources of variance. The operational steps in converting inputs to outputs and questions to be asked concerning intolerable variances are listed. It is imperative that the key variances and their sources be located and deliberate mechanisms established to control them. In all of these tasks the practitioner must combine social and technical skills.

EDITORS' INTRODUCTION

The issues raised by this selection acquire special significance when we are dealing with the quality of working life. To begin with, the client system with which we are concerned is very complex, including not only the management of the organization but also the workers and their unions. The practitioner system has to engage with all of these, all of which have their own "projects," each of which is also likely to gain or lose power and influence as the engagement proceeds.

The practitioner system is operating in a special environment. It is oriented not solely toward solving the problems of its client, but also toward values and goals for the community. It is impossible to work in this field without strong commitment to enhancing the quality of working life, to humanistic values in the workplace, and to the community benefits which derive from them. This endeavor, if successful, will have impact on other components of the client system and on other work organizations, themselves potential clients. It is more likely than not under these conditions that the practitioner system will experience such an environment as turbulent or at least as disturbed reactive.

The client's environment must also be analyzed. The client is involved either in a deliberate attempt to promote quality of working life because of a value commitment on the part of leading members of the system or in response to difficulties experienced or foreseen in managing the work force. In the latter case these difficulties are likely to be severe. One variant is the expectation of difficulty due to perceived societal developments. These scenarios identify client systems as themselves being in environments of turbulent or disturbed character.

The choice by the client of practitioner is of course influenced by his perception of what aim the latter is pursuing. If the client is purposely seeking an enhancement of quality of working life, this creates no special difficulty. On the other hand, if the client has first to be convinced that his interests will best be served by humanization of the work of his employees, a further degree of uncertainty is imported into his already difficult situation. While the author does not specifically follow these points through, his client-practitioner paradigm allows us to analyze these situations with greater insight.

Introduction

The client-practitioner relationship is a key element in the change process directed toward enhancing the quality of working life. It may be viewed as an engagement between individuals, between an individual and a system, or between systems. This selection explores some implications of viewing it as an intersystem engagement, providing a framework that may encourage the systematic development and testing of hypotheses in this area, as well as pointing to gaps in knowledge and to directions of research needed to close them.

The paper describes the internal and external environments of the client and practitioner systems and the transformation of inputs, including information, that must take place in the relationship between them. Next, task interdependency is isolated as the critical condition that both brings about and sustains the collaborative relationship. Then the external, value, reward, and power systems are considered as other key areas influencing the interdependency between the systems. In the section following, the key characteristics of the social and technical systems are described, emphasizing the need to monitor and control the variance that develops in the operations making up the change program. Exchange theory and role theory are shown to provide useful guidance in managing variations in participants' expectations and pay-offs. The final section indicates the main hypotheses stemming from the theoretical approach that has been outlined.

An Intersystem Engagement

Figure 1 shows the possible models within which client-practitioner relations may be viewed. On the left, a closed relationship exists within the separate organizational systems, each of which is bounded by a solid line. Each system operates as if it has no interdependence with its environment and there is no perception of a shared environment between the two systems. The center part of the diagram shows the systems as open to their own environment, but there is as yet no overlap between them. There is no clear perception that they share parts of a common environment. On the right of the diagram each of the systems is open to its environment and they have also created an overlap between themselves. In addition, they have come to perceive that they share common parts of the environment, as well as being in environments unique to their own structures.

The question, then, is how to understand the conditions that influence the interdependency between the client and practitioner systems; without some interdependency there is no basis for their relationship. The openness of both

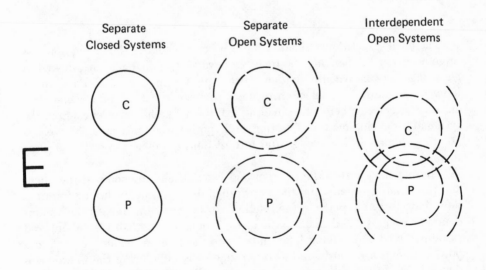

Figure 1. Relationships between Client and Practitioner Systems and Their Environments

systems heightens the chances of a perceived interdependency. This is because each of the systems will be attempting to create a negentropic situation that keeps it alive, in a state of poised stability, as it were, that enhances its adaptability to environmental variance. Insofar as each system is open and alert, it will be interested in new inputs that can be transformed into outputs to increase the possibility of survival. The systems will be looking for bits of information, in information theory terms, to reduce their uncertainty in a turbulent environment. They will not be concerned with congruence between themselves because that would give them no new information. They need inputs that will reduce uncertainty, thus enabling them to adapt constructively to dimly perceived environmental requirements as well as to those looming on the horizon or completely unknown at that point. Congruent information is likely to be redundant and may not further this goal, although it may add to the critical mass in an adaptive direction. It is more likely that contradictory inputs will lead to creative emergents. They do, however, carry the danger, if not handled carefully, of provoking destructive conflict.

As both the client and the practitioner system come to appreciate their interdependency, they will be able to take advantage of the properties of open systems. For instance, they will be able to think in terms of a variety of paths toward desired outcomes, the principle of equifinality; they will also be able to capitalize on the growth of the system through internal elaboration, as well as use the capacity for self-regulation to variations both in the internal and external environment. At a broader level, they will be able to maintain a constancy of direction even when there are technical changes in position.

According to the analysis by Emery and Twist, the interdependency within one organization follows a variety of patterns.[1] As the present analysis involves multiple organizations, the number of lawful connections are increased. For simplicity the overlap could be treated as if it were one organization, but this is misleading and the additional lawful connections must be considered. For example, one set of connections is between the internal environment of each of the systems. Another set is between the external environment of one system and that of the other. Then there are the connections between the internal environment of one system and the exernal environment of the other, in terms of the environmental sections that are shared and those that are unique to either system.

To reach creative solutions, the practitioner and the client have to locate the particular interdependency they are concerned with at any point of the change program.

Bases of System Interdependency

The conditions influencing the interdependency between the systems will now be considered. They are located in the task, external, value, reward, and power systems.

Task System

The primary task of the overlapping systems is to create and maintain the relationship between them and to help the client system change in a generally agreed direction.[2] This provides the basis for the interdependency between the systems, holding them into a relationship against forces that pull them apart. Without some primary task, there is no basis for intervention by the practitioners. In addition, it may well be that "behavior takes the shape of the task."[3]

To perform this task, the two parties have to share information and action. Each party must come to respect the distinctive competence of the other and the complementary nature of the skills they possess. Churchman and Schainblatt describe unilateral and collaborative ways of defining tasks.[4]

Polansky and Kounin showed that clients in psychotherapy and counseling made two kinds of judgment:[5] first, an appraisal of the change agent's ability to help with the specific problem; second, an estimate of how much satisfaction could be expected from a relationship with him. The results determined the degree of willingness to commit oneself to the relationship.[6] Previous experience with professionals, personal recommendations, fashion, stereotypes, and preconceived definitions of respective roles—for instance, layman-expert, passivity-activity—as well as the degree of distress and image of potentiality, are involved in these types of judgment. In addition, it has been shown that the task cooperation extended to a researcher in an industrial organization was inversely correlated with the degree to which the manager felt threatened by the relationship.[7]

To some extent both client and practitioner are each other's victim. On the one hand, the client has little basis for judging the competence of the practitioner. A practitioner who presents a single package is as likely to be judged competent as one with a wider repertoire. On the other hand, the practitioner is dependent on the client. Whereas the client has a task that is independent of the practitioner, the practitioner has no task unless it is given to him by the client.

External System

Interdependency is also influenced by the properties of the external system which may prompt the relationship in the first place. An industrial or commercial client under market pressure may seek help to think problems through, or may cling to outworn practices. It is not unusual for them to be so cost-conscious that they cannot manage the client-practitioner interface appropriately, thus reducing the quality of the job. These forces also tend to constrict clients' time horizons. They are often so concerned with daily problems and short-term firefighting operations that they cannot think in longer terms.

The practitioner's environment includes his professional ethic. Usually he does not advertise or approach clients directly. Although word-of-mouth recommendations bring work to particular practitioners, very little is known of the precise mechanisms involved. It has been found that search processes are relatively loose, with few clear expectations of costs and returns, and with chance playing a large part in the final selection.[8] The effect, however, is to leave the practitioner ignorant about the state of his market; he does not know where his next job might come from and what it might be like. Practitioner systems go through waves of high elation when they are receiving plenty of approaches from prospective clients, to troughs of deep depression as the sources seem to dry up. This holds most forcibly when the practitioner is completely dependent on this source of income. It puts him into a state of desperation, akin to that of his client's system, so that he will take on jobs in which he has no special competence or agree to unworkable relationships.

The onus is on the practitioner to analyze the character of his own environment and that of his client, noting the matches and mismatches. He must also assess the possible effects on the relationship and on the solutions that may be reached. Then he must use his professional competence to cope with these variations, converting potential disasters and routine outcomes into creative and successful solutions.

Both the client and the practitioner encounter the range of environments described by Emery and Trist.[9] Table 1 summarizes the type of environment of each of the systems and its possible effect on their relationship with each other. It will also influence the type of solution that they reach. In Table 1 all environments are matched, that is, the client system and the practitioner systems are operating in a similar environment. When they are both embedded in a placid randomized environment, the relationship is likely to be serene but the solution routine. There is no thrust toward creativity. The same holds, although to a somewhat lesser extent, when they are both sharing a placid clustered environment. On the other hand, when they are involved in a disturbed reactive or a turbulent environment the relationships are likely to be far more confused and the solutions more creative. The uncertainty of these environments forces both systems into a state of confusion and possibly conflict, but also enhances the possibility of a creative and novel solution.

Mismatches also occur between environments. The client environment may

TABLE 1.

Environments of Client Systems and Practitioner Systems and Their Effect on the Relationship

Environment	Effect on Relationship	Solutions
placid, randomized	serene	routine
placid, clustered	serene	routine
disturbed-reactive	conflicted	creative
turbulent	conflicted	creative

be placid and randomized whereas that of the practitioner may be turbulent. Here the client may be expecting a serene relationship with a fairly straight-forward solution. The turbulence of the practitioner's system may, however, be projected onto the client situation, so that the typical confusions and drives toward creativity will be imposed on the relationship. If the environment were truly placid and randomized, this would be inappropriate. At the other end, the client may be caught up in turbulent fields, whereas the practitioner is operating in a placid, randomized environment. The client would then be pushing toward creativity, whereas the practitioner would be hanging back for the security of a serene and routine existence.

Value System

Values also affect interdependency.[10] The client system may be concerned with profit, efficiency, production, achievement, self-control, independence, and endurance of distress. In contrast, the practitioner system may be concerned with service or a science component, self-actualization, self-expression, interdependence, and possibly capacity for joy.[11] If there are such splits in organizational philosophy, then superordinate values will have to be developed and shared by the two parties to hold them in the task relationship.[12]

As part of the value system, the preferred shape of the client-practitioner relationship is influenced by the theories held about organizational functioning, both by the client and by the practitioner. At the extremes, these are organic and mechanistic. An organic theory views the organization as an entity composed of interrelated parts which act together to adapt to variations in environmental conditions. This model implies an active stance toward variations both in the organization and in the environment, in terms of scanning the present situation, drawing on past experience, and attempting to anticipate future developments. A mechanistic theory views the organization as a hierarchically arranged structure with precise allocation of responsibility and authority. The organization is seen as a closed and stable system, somewhat independent of its environment. Subscribers to this theory operate with a short time perspective, a passive delayed reaction to change, and a faith in routine ways of solving problems. A client or practitioner subscribing to either of these views or organizational structure and process prefers a relationship with a person of similar views. Mismatches may lead to conflict and rejection of either one or the other of the parties, or working through to a new and agreed-on formulation of respective roles.

A similar analysis can be made of the matches between the value systems of clients and practitioners. The possibility of a creative solution comes from the overlap of values to the extent that a working relationship is possible, augmented by a difference in values or experience that introduces a new input into the relationship between the two systems.

Clients and practitioners tend to differ in their evaluation of the relative importance of theory and practice. Despite Kurt Lewin's oft-quoted dictum that there is nothing so practical as a good theory, most clients still distrust

theory. Crawford et al. bridged the gap between theory and practice successfully by getting nurses to put classroom theory to work in solving their own
management problems.[13] When necessary, their efforts were supported by concrete actions on the part of the hospital executive. Clients rarely appreciate
the reasons why practitioners ask general and fundamental questions that
seem remote from the problem as they have defined it. Organizations engaging in redundancy exercises are more concerned to arrange alternative employment, retraining, and separation conditions than to ask the question why
they have redundancies at all.

Two contrasting practitioner styles reflect different values. One adopts an
aloof objective stance; the practitioner controls his own emotional reactions
and regards the emotions of members of the client system as noise rather than
as information. He takes the role of observer and attempts to minimize the
influence of his presence on the behavior of the client system or on the data
that he is attempting to collect. The other type of practitioner accepts the
feelings of both the client and the practitioner as valid data to be fed into
the ongoing relationships and problem-solving activity; the practitioner must
have ready access to his own emotional reactions as well as be sensitive to
those of his client.[14] His "feelings of pleasure and pain, anxiety and relief,
excitement and sobriety are frequently the only measures we have available
to assess what is real and what unreal in a difficult situation." [15] This approach
implies a reciprocal relationship between equals rather than any subject-
expert type of relationship.

Both styles are required in complex situations. If they cannot be encom-
passed in a single individual, a team approach may be appropriate. Both
approaches will introduce variance into the operations depending on how well
they are perceived and accepted by the client system. For instance, a highly
intuitive style will not mesh with the expectations of a traditional management, nor will a technical style mesh with a management attempting to focus
on process rather than structure. The constant bind of working inside the
acceptable limits as the organization perceives them, while at the same time
pushing the organization toward innovation, increases the difficulty of monitoring the effects of different expectations.

Timing is no problem if consulting is viewed as a mechanical process. One
step follows another without any search for appropriate conditions for their
introduction. Timing is critical if consulting is viewed as an art which depends
as much on experience as on theory. The practitioner will constantly evaluate
the readiness of the client system for particular interventions, acting quickly
when he feels the time is right, or holding up new initiatives until previous
ones have been worked through. To supplement his intuitions, he must probe
to test reactions and obtain feedback.

Reward System

The reward system also influences interdependency. In the client system,
the superior's judgments are the typical basis for reward. In the practitioner

system, while the superior's judgments may still play a part, the influence of scientific peers and one's own judgment plays a larger part. In addition, a reciprocal reward system comes into play in which both the client and the practitioner system reward each other.[16] They also come to share an interest in the progress of the task they have created for themselves. This traction is an important source of continued effort.

However the relationship began, it acquires a character of its own called forth by the task. A successful relationship is marked by the identification of each party with the goals of the other.[17] It is unlikely that a continued forced compliance situation would be profitable. The greater the internal commitment to both the relationship and the task, associated usually with free choice, the more likely the relationship is to be creative and the solutions novel and constructive.

The temporary nature of the relationship influences the extent to which members of either system will look to the rewards that emerge from the engagement itself. The ground for each set of members is their own system, with its role senders who control resources and rewards. The more clearly the rewards are linked with behavior produced in the client-practitioner relationship, the more the negative efforts of its transitory character are overcome.

Power System

As Wolin says, every move of a person in an organization has implication for changes in the aggregations of power.[18] This holds equally for the practitioner, even when he thinks he may be operating as a pure scientist. From this point of view, it is deceptive to operate too much under the mantle of the expert or the technician with special skills. Practitioners' personal orientations as actionist, activist, reformer, advocate, servant, scientist, therapist, or professional are hidden agenda that may act as a possible source of misunderstanding. Members of the client system also introduce their agenda into the relationship, allying themselves with or distancing themselves from the practitioner.

Practitioners' assumptions about the needs of their client systems stem from their own political views. Linked with the underlying assumptions of the practitioner as politician will be a matching set of assumptions about his client systems. The elitist practitioner assumes that his clients need firm guidance. The egalitarian allows his clients to be responsible for their own judgments. For instance, they might be allowed to make their own errors if there are no consequences for other people either within the organization or outside it; as this is rarely the case, the practitioner must take professional responsibility for members of the client system unprotected by a well-sinewed form of democracy. He must guard both against false certainty that pushes him toward imposition of solutions and undue modesty that prevents him from playing his proper role in the process.

However carefully the terms of the relationship are specified and their respective roles made explicit, there will still be a need for the development of trust.[19] A period of testing is necessary to establish, beyond a verbal level, that the other person is trustworthy as well as competent. For the practitioner this includes eluding capture, a process well documented in anthropological literature. He must be careful of the special relationships that members of the client organization attempt to create. These carry with them the danger of alienating other people within the system, particularly as there are differentials in power within and between systems. Because practitioners are usually called in by people at the top of the hierarchy of the client system, they are viewed with suspicion. At worst, seen as management's men, they are hard put to convince people located elsewhere in the system that they are independent professionals carrying responsibility for the welfare of the total client system. The existing patterns of hostilities and affections within the client system will also be brought into play. Besides processes of power and interpersonal liking, the practitioner will also be caught up in the processes surrounding tasks of the organization and the vested interests of skill and territory. Any perceived threat of interference in these preserves will spark off negative reactions. Often power struggles are fought under the guise of task-related activities.

The underlying process in many of these relationships may be analyzed by using exchange theory.[20] A check may be kept on the course of a project by mapping the range of relationships caught up in the overall client-practitioner relationship, estimating both the outcomes for the various parties and their potential for disrupting the project. To help in the mapping process of power relations, role expectations, and payoffs matrices, it is necessary to list the actors, in terms of both their position in their own system and in the client-practitioner system. One needs to construct an organizational chart for each of the systems. The various actors are then located in their official role within their own organization; this immediately draws attention to the series of values and behaviors expected of them. As enriching material comes to hand about their own characteristic way of enacting their role, this can be summarized and added. The second role designation is somewhat more difficult because it is less institutionally bound. One or more of the following actors appear in the client system: the sponsor of the project, the mediator, the day-by-day contact person, members of the steering committee, members of the working committee, catalysts and pacemakers and project managers. In the practitioner system there are project officers, the front men concerned with the political management of the engagement, the field workers carrying the responsibility for interviews and questionnaire administration, for instance, and the team members providing conceptual and technical skills. Even further in the background is "grandfather" practitioner who acts as a sounding board and support agent, provider of the enabling insight. Not only must this range of relationships be attended to in terms of expectations and payoffs, but they also provide the source of crosscurrents which can have a destructive outcome or can be brought to good use.

The essential trick in the development of a fruitful client-practitioner relationship is to create enough overlap between these two systems for communication and action to take place, without sacrificing the differences that enhance the possibility of a creative tension. To the extent that either system dominates or swallows the other, the value of the complementary relationship is reduced.

Key Characteristics of the Technical Systems

Among the variables influencing interdependency are certain key characteristics of the technical systems involved in the relationship. These affect both the social systems and the variance. The technical system of the action researcher is labor-intensive and expensive, spread geographically out of the client's sight and highly technical, both in terms of model building and of tools used for data gathering and analysis. In addition, there is a set of abstracts which imply emergent solutions, unpredictability, and implicit and rather mysterious flexible approaches to problems. This amounts to a meta-level of the technical system, an aura of mysticism bounded by ethical constraints, that is difficult to communicate to clients and introduces variance in the relationship.

This technical system implies a matrix-type social system with a flattened hierarchy and an interchange of roles. This will facilitate the flexible use of resources. It also requires a high degree of independence in activity, balanced by a concern for the welfare of other members of the research team. As researchers usually operate in settings with completely different approaches to the world, they have particular need for support mechanisms. They must be internally motivated and committed to shared objectives, both technically and ethically. Within this professional practitioner organization they have an obligation to translate and communicate their values, theories, and techniques to other parties in external systems.

It is, then, necessary to develop criteria for the achievement of objectives. Publications, citations, and inclusion of material in courses, for example, may indicate achievement of the goal of furthering social science knowledge. Client satisfaction and recommendation and evaluation of client's present and future problem-solving behavior may indicate the achievement of the goal of helping society cope with its affairs.

The technical system of clients ranges through craft, batch, mass production and assembly, and process production. Less obviously, service, financial, administrative, and professional organizations also have technologies in the form of systematic transformation processes. Technologies will probably be highly routinized in their operations and their rules will be consolidated into manuals. They will be predictable and explicit, somewhat inflexible and non-mysterious in their approach. At a metalevel, therefore, even in the science-based industries, there will be an aura of rationality and explicitness. Few industries have a well-developed set of ethical constraints; their managers operate by testing the limits of what can be done, with an underlying adherence to a laissez-faire political doctrine.

Where clients regard their technical systems as predictable and explicit, their social systems will be designed or have evolved to match the definition. Tall hierarchical structures with clear lines of command and accountability characterize many organizations. Members may be seen as isolated individuals slotted into jobs, and the existence of a social system as a set of interdependencies between people is not perceived or is attacked as irrelevant.

Many organizations employing advanced technologies and many complex service organizations have not yet fully appreciated the type of social system that matches their technology; more specifically, they have not yet appreciated that the principle of joint optimization may imply changes in their technology to make it more appropriate to the characteristics of individuals and social groups. For instance, in the long run it is uneconomical to have a technology that violates human characteristics. Either the human beings have to be designed out of the system or their characteristics must be appreciated and used fully. This may involve using the technology suboptimally, but in terms of overall systems functioning it is more efficient. Lacking here is a set of indices and instruments to measure social as well as monetary costs. At present many of the social costs of an organization are transferred into the external environment. They become hidden costs to be paid by society through its agencies.

The criteria for evaluating the performance of the client system involve the development of an accounting system that includes social indicators as well as material and technical ones, in addition to measures of the transfer of costs into the external systems. It should also include the costs of the use of scarce physical resources, as well as considerations of recycling. It may be that some client and practitioner systems lack understanding of their objectives and their evaluation, and of the match of their technical system with their social system, including the steps that should be taken for joint optimization. In these circumstances the engagement is likely to be hazardous with increased variance to be controlled.

Controlling the Variance in a Sociotechnical System

The bases of interdependency and the characteristics of the technical systems may be summarized as being part of the input/transformation/output processes. To start with, separate inputs come from the practitioner system and from the client system. In the transforming process, some of these inputs will be treated collaboratively and others will be hived off, either to be transformed in the practitioner system or in the client system. The outputs will then be a function of these three potential transformation processes.

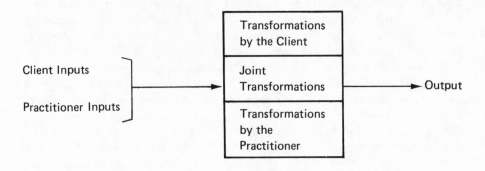

From this point of view, the client-practitioner relationship is a sociotechnical system enmeshed in an intersystem engagement, influenced by different internal and external environments and characterized by splits and overlaps. The resources brought into the transformation process are economic, technical, social, and political; these not only act as resources but are also sources of variance. If this variance is not controlled, the smooth transformation process will be disturbed. Any errors introduced early in the system, such as a hidden objective that is not worked through, will be carried into later transformation processes. When this happens it is much more difficult to detect its source and to bring its effects back within limits.

The following operations are involved in the process of converting inputs to outputs: (1) the presentation of a problem and the initial testing out of the degree of fit between the two systems; (2) the negotiation of some contractual relationship; (3) a first scanning of the client's setting and its environment by the practitioner, matched by reciprocal scanning of the practitioner's system by the client; (4) the working toward and agreement upon a definition of the problem (this may amount to a redefinition of the presenting problem); (5) a diagnostic phase, again approached as a collaborative exercise, which treats the diagnosis as a working hypothesis that may be altered later on; (6) the planning and implementation of change; (7) the evaluation of its consequences; (8) the assessment of the effectiveness of the client-practitioner relationship and its activities to this point; and (9) the consideration of the need to repeat operations in new cycles.

The general question relates to what is to be controlled and how this is to be done. This involves defining the output at any point in the process and the criteria that will be used to evaluate it. It must then be decided what is the zone of indifference, that is, the acceptable range within which the output will be considered satisfactory. Once this is defined, any observation that exceeds this limit, either above or below it, enters the zone of intolerance.[21] The questions are: (1) Where does the variance occur? (2) Where is it observed (which may be different from its origin)? (3) Where is it controlled? (4) By whom? (5) What tasks does one have to do to control it? (6) What information does one get and from where to enable control activities to be carried out?

These questions require a distinction between those processes that are related to others and those that are relatively independent. The location of areas of high interdependence gives increased leverage on the control of variance. If, for instance, the client's initial expectations are not being met by the process of the engagement, this becomes interdependent with every other process, insofar as it affects the outcome of client satisfaction. On the other hand, the technical aspect—for example, of a questionnaire—may not affect any other process and can be treated as a relatively independent source of variance.

The key variances must be located. These affect the type and quality of solutions or scientific contributions, the operating costs—for example, over-running a project—and the social costs, such as stress on the research team or on members of the client system. The throughputs can come from the client system, either internally or externally, or from the practitioner system, again either from within the system or from its environment; or they can come from the shared overlap between the client and practitioner systems and the environment in which they operate. The character of the information or energy inputs can be seen as benign and useful, as threatening, or as irrelevant; they may be seen as creating or as solving a problem.

The competence of the practitioner includes the twin strands of technical and social skills. These must be looked at throughout each of the operations, always with an eye toward joint optimization. For instance, in the diagnostic or evaluation phase, it is no use developing a beautiful instrument if the path is not prepared for its introduction; nor, on the other hand, is it any use gaining acceptance for a poor instrument. Elsewhere the author has traced out the consequence of inadequately monitoring the effect of sanctioning from various quarters through the stages of a change program.[22] Davis and Valfer have shown the payoff which results from the control of variance.[23] One way is to create exchanges and accommodations between the client and practitioner systems so that they come to view their fates as interdependent.[24] This rests on their acceptance of the proposition that the final output of the process has implications for their well-being; they will then have an interest in controlling the variance, both from their own inputs and from the inputs of the other party. They will come to avoid breaks in the relationship by, for instance, violating the values or expectations of the other party. They will also wish to preserve the capability of working together in this particular task and in later tasks.

Deliberate mechanisms must be established to control variance; for example, mapping outcomes for participants and their relative influence, and developing steering committees to span interest groups. Information can then be fed into loops that keep the system under control. It is advisable to draw a graph, however roughly, setting the limits of variance that will be tolerated. The actual course of the study is then plotted against this margin. When variance is going out of tolerance, special steps must be introduced to bring it under control.

Conclusion

The foregoing analysis points up the importance of a primary task which creates sufficient interdependence to hold the parties in a relationship when the supporting forces are too weak to do so or when the forces pulling them apart are too strong. It also highlights the need for an exchange process in which there is sufficient give-and-take so that the payoffs for the various parties are satisfactory.

The following main hypotheses emerge from the present effort:

1. The greater the difference in values and skills between the client and practitioner systems, the more difficulty there will be in maintaining the relationship. If the relationship survives, however, the change will be more effective and more novel than if there were smaller initial differences.

2. Collaborative specification of tasks and methods will lead to greater change than a unilateral approach.

3. The higher the task interdependency between the parties, the more resilient the relationship will be to disruptive forces.

4. The systematic location and monitoring of key variances throughout the operations of the change program will lead to a better outcome than focusing on the outcome of individual operations.

5. The more effective the monitoring of payoff matrices of participants in both the client and practitioner systems, the more successful will be the change program.

It is suggested that refining these general hypotheses into a testable form and following them through in systematic programs of research, including the collection of sets of case studies, should contribute further to our understanding of the client-practitioner relationship.[25]

NOTES

1. F. E. Emery and E. L. Trist, "The Causal Texture of Organizational Environments," *Human Relations*, 18; (1965), 21–32. Also in F. E. Emery (ed.), *Systems Thinking* (Harmondsworth, Middlesex, England: Penguin, 1969).

2. J. C. Glidewell, "The Entry Problem in Consultation," *Journal of Social Issues*, 15 (1959), 51–59.

3. H. A. Simon, *Sciences of the Artificial* (Cambridge: M.I.T. Press, 1969).

4. W. Churchman and A. H. Schainblatt, "The Researcher and the Manager: The Dialectic of Implementation," *Management Science*, 2 (1965), 69–87.

5. N. Polansky and J. Kounin, "Clients' Reactions to Initial Interviews, a Field Study," *Human Relations*, 9 (1956), 237–264.

6. R. Lippitt, J. Watson, and B. Westley, *The Dynamics of Planned Change* (New York: Harcourt, Brace, 1958).

7. C. P. Alderfer, "Organizational Diagnosis from Initial Client Reactions to a Researcher," *Human Organization*, 27 (1968), 260–265.

8. S. C. Hollander, *Business Consultants and Clients: A Literature Search on the Marketing Practices and Problems of the Management Research and Advisory Professions*, Bureau of Business and Economic Research, Graduate School of Business Administration, Michigan State University, East Lansing, 1963. See also R. M. Cyert, W. R. Dill, and J. G. March, "The Role of Expectations in Business Decision Making," *Administrative Science Quarterly*, (December 1958), 307–340.

9. See n. 2 *supra*.

10. T. R. Vallance, "Social Science and Social Policy: A Moral Methodology in a Matrix of Values," *American Psychologist*, 27 (1972), 107–113. See also P. J. Shipp, *Client Relations*, Tavistock Institute of Human Relations, Doc. IOR 552, 1970; P. J. Shipp, *A Study of Client Relations*, Tavistock Institute of Human Relations, Doc. IOR 676, 1972.

11. E. L. Trist, *Urban North America: The Challenge of the Next Thirty Years*, address to Annual Conference of Canadian Institute of Town Planners (Minaki, 1968), published as Working Paper No. 2, Socio-technical Systems Division, Western Management Science Institute, University of California, Los Angeles, 1968. Also, revised version: E. L. Trist and F. E. Emery, *Towards a Social Ecology* (London: Plenum, 1972).

12. C. W. Churchman and F. E. Emery, "On Various Approaches to the Study of Organizations," in J. R. Lawrence (ed.), *Operational Research and the Social Sciences* (London: Tavistock, 1966).

13. L. E. Crawford, F. L. Ritchie, and B. A. Herriott, "Replanning Sydney Hospital," *Medical Journal of Australia*, December 1971.

14. A. W. Gouldner, "Engineering and Clinical Approaches to Consulting," in W. G. Bennis, K. D. Benne, and R. Chin (eds.), *The Planning of Change: Readings in the Applied Behavioral Sciences* (New York: Holt, Rinehart, & Winston, 1961), pp. 643–653. See also R. Lippitt, J. Watson, and B. Westley, *The Dynamics of Planned Change* (New York: Harcourt, Brace, 1958); and E. H. Schein, *Process Consultation: Its Role in Organizational Development* (Reading, Mass.: Addison-Wesley, 1969).

15. A. K. Rice, *The Enterprise and Its Environment: A System Theory of Management Organization* (London: Tavistock, 1963). See also C. Sofer, *The Organization from Within* (London: Tavistock, 1961).

16. H. H. Kelley, "Interpersonal Accommodation," *American Psychologist*, 23, no. 6 (1968), 399–410.

17. H. C. Kelman, "Processes of Opinion Change," *Public Opinion Quarterly*, 25 (1961), 57–78.

18. S. S. Wolin, *Politics and Vision: Continuity and Innovation in Western Political Thought* (London: Allen, 1961).

19. M. Deutsch, "Psychological Alternatives to War," *Journal of Social Issues*, 18 (1962), 97–119.

20. G. C. Homans, *The Human Group* (New York: Harcourt, Brace, & World, 1950). See also J. W. Thibaut and H. H. Kelley, *The Social Psychology of Groups* (New York: Wiley, 1969); and H. Turk and R. L. Simpson (eds.), *Institutions and Social Exchange: The Sociologies of Talcott Parsons and George C. Homans* (New York: Bobbs-Merrill, 1971).

21. P. H. Engelstad, *Socio-Technical Approach to Problems of Process Control*, chap. 23 in L. E. Davis and J. C. Taylor (eds.), *Design of Jobs* (London: Penguin Books, 1972).

22. A. W. Clark, "Sanction: A Critical Element in Action Research," *Journal of Applied Behavioral Science*, 8, no. 6 (1972), 713–731.

23. L. E. Davis and E. Valfer, "Controlling the Variance in Action Research," in A. W. Clark (ed.), *Experiences in Action Research* (London: Malaby Press, 1975).

24. See n. 16 *supra*.

25. R. E. Walton, "Advantages and Attributes of the Case Study," *Journal of Applied Behavioral Science*, 8 (1972), 73–78.

12

Intervention Theory: Matching Role, Focus, and Context

Peter A. Clark

FOUR models of intervention strategies are described in terms of the expectations of practitioner and client, and the different conditions are suggested in which each may be most appropriate. (1) The collaborative/dialogic model has a number of variations: mutual determination of goals and joint effort in a voluntary relationship; maximum participation by those affected by any change; or joint discussion of policy, joint evaluation of alternatives, and utilization of action research by the client for diagnosis and other activities. (2) The unilateral expert model seems inappropriate for indepth interventions designed to bring about changes in attitudes. (3) The delegated or do-it-yourself method, well known in the area of work simplification, is required for some aspects of the use of Blake and Mouton's managerial grid. (4) In the subordinate technician model the client specifies the service required, the practitioner then obtains and reports the information to the client who then decides on the next step(s).

This research was financed by a grant from the Social Science Research Council (UK) to A. B. Cherns and P. A. Clark, 1967–1972 (HR 86.1).

Despite controversy and some contrary evidence relating to participation, the collaborative/dialogic model has considerable empirical support, is itself consistent with the emphasis on creating more authentic relationships within work organizations, and, because of the participants' readiness to work with uncertainty, can be innovative (cf. Alfred W. Clark's contingency approach to client-practitioner relationships). The unilateral expert approach may be relevant when there is high specificity of the practitioner's goal, great urgency on the client's part, low availability of resources of time and money, and the client's felt lack of competence to deal with the problem. The delegated approach has possibilities for the diffusion of quality of working life solutions. The focus taken by a practitioner to achieve quality of working life intervention may involve all or some of the following issues:

one or more of four interacting organizational variables of technology, structure, actors, and objectives;

the depth of intervention into the attitudes of organizational members;

the relative emphasis on experiential and cognitive factors; the formalization of the practitioner-client relationship;

the scope of the problem, which is relevant to the formalization and cognitive/experiential issues.

Although there is a wide variety of known forms of intervention strategy, social scientists seem to prefer strategies of equal influence between practitioner and client, characterized by open and free exchange and by deliberateness from each party. This *role* model is most appropriately used when the *focus* of the intervention involves solely the social system variable of improving interpersonal relations and authenticity, and when the *context* is characterized by a confident client with ample resources of time and money, with a commitment to deep penetration of attitudes, one who occupies an integer power center. Conversely, other role models are appropriate when the focus is different, for example, in the case of indirect social system change through intervention in the technical system, and when the context varies from that described above. It is implied here that no single strategy is universally appropriate, a point that applies to differences between stages of the same project as well.

Four Role Models for the Practitioner

An important aspect of intervention strategy is the belief which practitioners and clients have about the appropriate role relationship that should exist between them. In this section four main role models will be examined advocated by practitioners or, alternatively, criticized as inadequate. Each model has a complementary set of client expectations:

1. *Collaborative/dialogic* approach of diagnosis and intervention. This model has been advocated by a number of leading social science practitioners and is widely regarded as universally appropriate.

2. The *unilateral expert* approach is frequently pilloried as ineffective and inappropriate.

3. The *delegated*, or do-it-yourself, approach has been popular in the social sciences and in management science, as well as in work simplification efforts.

4. The *subordinate technician*, or engineering, approach is frequently criticized because the social scientist is not involved in the definition of the problem.

Each of these models will be described to present the key characteristics but two points should be kept in mind: First, a great deal of social science research seems to show that the collaborative/dialogic approach is the most appropriate. For example, Greiner, in a retrospective analysis of eighteen published cases, argues that these provide an adequate basis for presuming that intervention is less successful when it is unilateral, that is, by indirect manipulation of the structure.[1] This is an important contention because structuralists like Chapple and Sayles have argued for indirect manipulation through alterations in the work flow and structure.[2] And O'Connell, in an extensive study of intervention, has shown that this approach has a measure of success.[3] Second, the choice of intervention strategy is best made with a view to achieving congruence between the role model, the focal variables to be manipulated, and the organizational context.[4] In order to illustrate this contention more clearly, a description of the focus and context in each of the four models follows below:

The collaborative/dialogic model is best known through the writings of leading American practitioners and commentators. Five subtypes are quoted to give the full flavor of the range of this category. First, Bennis advocates a relationship which is best described as including *mutual determination of goals and joint effort; equal opportunity to influence (eventually); deliberateness on both sides; a voluntary relationship conducted in the spirit of inquiry.*[5] He argues that collaboration is especially appropriate when making interventions to improve the authenticity of relationships within organizations, and that authenticity cannot be imposed coercively or through exposition as in human relations training lectures.

Second, Schein suggests a process model into which *the consultant is willing to enter without a clear mission; there is joint effort.*[6] He contends that this model is appropriate in situations in which managers know exactly how to define and articulate the problems they are confronted with and, further, that it saves diagnostic time.

The third example is from Argyris, who is highly critical of mechanistic approaches to intervention, preferring organistically oriented intervention in which *the subjects participate; the interventionist acknowledges that he is a stranger; participation is encouraged in the design of the instrument; costs and rewards of the program are defined jointly; the aim is to minimize dependent relationships.* Argyris, like Bennis, is taking authenticity in interpersonal relationships as the focus for the intervention, and is implicitly arguing that authenticity cannot be established by means of "rigorous research." [7]

Fourth, Gouldner advises the use of the clinical role, in which the practitioner *takes a highly active role in the definition of the problem.* He argues that the social scientist's conception of the problem must be introduced into the relationship.[8] In his critical analysis of the coming crises in Western sociology, he is especially conscious of making the social scientist's substantive concepts about human behavior an integral part of the practitioner's activities; he suspects much applied work.[9] In some respects, Gouldner's polemic for the clinical role, and the examples he gives, may seem to argue from his later writing that this is not the case.

The fifth subtype is taken from the Loughborough program, led by A. B. Cherns and P. A. Clark, especially the project undertaken by John Player and Sons on the design of organizational aspects of a new cigarette factory.[10] The intervention commenced very shortly after a top-level design group had been formed to guide and plan the new installation. When asked by the client how the intervention would proceed, Cherns emphasized that the relationship would be a dialogue, by which he meant *joint discussion about policy; joint evaluation of the alternative plans advanced for examination; the building into the research strategy of a strategy for utilizing the research and gaining its dissemination and the commitment of resources by the client to diagnosis and other activities.* These five examples provide a useful picture of the collaborative/dialogic approach.

The unilateral expert model is frequently criticized as being ineffective and inappropriate to the focus of social science interventions. It is therefore important to note that the critics most typically are concerned with in-depth interventions designed to achieve alterations in attitudes.[11] The knowledge base is sociopsychological and does not include the perspectives of socio-organizational analysts. In fact, Argyris has specifically attacked organizational sociologists for advocating mechanistic forms of organization in some situations.[12]

One reason why social scientists may be uneasy with the expert role model is that being employed as facilitators for the smooth introduction of innovations rather than as active agents in the design of such systems does not easily fit into their experience. There is an abundant literature of poor outcomes of the expert role in classical management changes which does not commend the role highly to social scientists.

O'Connell describes the behavior of a management consultant as follows:

> He
> performed as an experienced expert, acting like a man who was expected to advise the client on what to do and how to do it;
> He
> carried out the diagnosis himself with two professional assistants from the consulting agency.[13]

It is important to stress that the consultant did not impose his solutions on an unwilling executive and that there were elements of a dialogue, but the author also points out that the role relationship was sharply in contrast to both the collaborative/dialogic and the subordinate technician models.

The notion of the social scientist as expert, albeit *in a less unilateral fashion* than in the case described by O'Connell, is suggested in important studies by Paterson, reporting his experiences with the Royal Air Force in battle conditions; by Flanders, describing the work of an Emerson consultant; and by Hutte in a retrospective analysis of his experiences as consultant in various settings.

Paterson was requested by his commanding officer to investigate and resolve a high accident-rate problem among pilots. His initial approaches concentrated upon training, but were not taken seriously. However, his diagnosis of relations among groups on the station indicated the major problem lay in the pilots' frustration because of lack of contact with the enemy. Paterson was not able to utilize the support of senior staff, who did not comprehend his analysis; so he made subtle use of his role to refocus aggression upon a symbolic enemy.[14]

Flanders describes how a consultant, trained in the social sciences and in anthropology, questioned the beliefs which underlay the existing arrangements governing the planning and allocation of work in the Esso refinery in Fawley, England.[15] He was sharply critical of management's reactive approach to problems and worked hard to bring conflicts out into the open. His method of questioning was by *patient reasoning* (a point also made by O'Connell, but rarely emphasized); and by *gaining personal authority by weakening the authoritarian arguments of his critics.*

Hutte's examination is especially interesting[16] because, although he is primarily concerned with finding an effective solution to the problems of growth in organizations, his analysis of the practitioner-client relationship is considerably detailed and offers a balanced discussion of the problems of maintaining an impact as well as achieving entry.[17] He argues, "It is being realised more and more that the relationship between an expert and (organisation) should be of a co-operative nature, be it that the expert can, at certain points, possess so much knowledge and experience, *that he will be directive out of a sheer sense of responsibility.*" [18]

Delegated interventions are typified by training full-time members of an enterprise to implement an innovation or a new approach by themselves. This method is well known in work simplification, as mentioned earlier, but there is little information about whether it works satisfactorily, and if so, why. An interesting version of the delegated approach is found in some aspects of the use of Blake and Mouton's Managerial Grid, in which the approach is highly formalized. By way of contrast, the action learning approach was introduced, through the initiative of R. W. Revans and others, to a small sample of hospitals in London.[19] The senior members of the three main groups in the hospital were introduced to social science technology and research findings relevant to hospital administration. Their subordinates then received one month's training before returning to initiate research studies on live problems in their own hospitals. The main features of this approach include: *Social scientists train clients to recognize and diagnose particular problems through the application of research technology; the client is typically in control of the entire process and its evaluation; in this respect, the London hospitals project was exceptional, because there was an external evaluation.*

The *subordinate technician* model typically takes the following form: *The client specifies the service required from the practitioner; the practitioner undertakes studies to discover the information required and sends this to the client in the form of a report. The client then decides on the next step(s).*

The best-known examples arise when the client hires a survey agency to collect information from employees on their attitudes to predetermined problems. The survey agency's role is sometimes restricted to sampling, and the content of questions is strongly influenced by the sponsor's perceptions of the situation; few surveys are systematically designed as a confirmatory step, following initial diagnosis of problems.

These four role models have been presented in a somewhat exaggerated form to highlight the options and provide the broad lines for further and more focused discussion below.

The most preferred role model—the collaborative/dialogic—has three major points in its favor. First, there is a fair amount of research and practice which provides direct and anecdotal confirmation for the efficacy of the approach. The notion of participation is more controversial, however, than supportive research suggests; there is much contrary evidence and argument.[20] Second, it may be argued that there is consistency between the role and the selected focus upon creating more authentic relationships within work organizations; that is, consistent at least within the Anglo-American value system. Third, given that using elements of social science is a new experience for many clients, it may be expected that the activity is nonroutine, the problems obscure, and the pathways to solutions strewn with false leads and turns. Therefore, the decision-making process between practitioner and client may have many of the characteristics of innovative situations. However, if the theoretical perspective of the contingency theorists were to be applied,[21] or the findings of decision-making studies,[22] it might be argued that collaboration and dialogue provide a theoretically justifiable mode of operation for tackling the uncertainties in the situation.[23] This is an important point, because there seems to be some confusion about the position which contingency theorists would advocate as appropriate.[24]

Confusions and uncertainties about using social science consultants have probably led to the constriction of the cognitive inputs. For example, Bennis, after a thoughtful comparison of three variants on collaboration—organic, equilibrium, and developmental models—observes that cognitive inputs are, with the exception of the constructs about managerial styles implicit in the Managerial Grid (organic model), largely neglected.[25] In fact, he goes somewhat further and suggests that the discussion of consulting styles has led to a neglect of the problem-solving process.

The collaborative/dialogic role model makes certain important assumptions about the clients and the problems which require explication: First, the clients must have some confidence in their ability to relate as equals in the relationship; otherwise the spirit of inquiry is merely a charade, barring transformation in the key paradigms held by the client. The presumption here is that the client's cognitive map of the organization is not sufficiently differentiated or accurate for adequate comprehension of the problem. Sayles has argued that it is constructs which policy makers and executives adopt in examining the human aspect that will crucially affect the industrial relations climate.[26] Frequently, the practitioner has to directly confront these conceptions. For example, Flanders reports the various ways in which one consultant questioned the beliefs held by executives about customs and practices through patient reasoning, and also by weakening rival arguments held in an uncritical fashion.[27] Unless the client has confidence in the handling of concepts and arguments, this approach could easily deteriorate into a fight/flight situation.[28]

Elsewhere, it was argued that the continuance of the Loughborough dialogue with the key design group in John Player and Sons over a period of more than three years was dependent upon that group's ability to adopt a design and a long-term perspective, and be at ease with lengthy examinations and investigations.[29] Second, and closely related, the client must be in a position effectively to deploy the resources of time and money so that the dialogue may be based upon sound judgment. Third, the client must have a role model which approximately fits his expectations of collaboration. In this case, the key figures in the design team worked with a variety of external resources in a collaborative manner. Fourth, dialogue must be dependent upon the existence of subject matter which is considered problematic.

In situations where these conditions are not present, collaboration may be ineffectual and inappropriate. This point is emphasied by O'Connell in his advocacy of the relevance of the unilateral approach expert. He suggests that the expert role is appropriate when the following conditions exist: high specificity of the practitioner's goal; great urgency of the problem for the client; low availability of the resources of time and money; the client's feeling of incompetence to tackle the problem.[30] Implicity, these four aspects direct our attention to the matching of intervention strategy to the context. However, O'Connell may, in some respects, be underestimating the importance of learning for the organization. In the specific assignment described by him, the consultant enters, provides an apparently viable solution, implements it, and then departs. Perhaps this approach cuts across one of the objectives of collaborative intervention, namely, that members of the organization should learn enough from the encounter to meet similar situations later on without outside assistance. On the other hand, those practitioners who claim they cannot be effective in resolving the client's problems unless "it hurts" would advance a contrary solution.

The delegated approach has, in principle, a number of valuable possibilities for the diffusion of quality of working life solutions. Optimism must, however, be tempered considerably in view of the findings of recent research, an excellent example of which is the failure of an educational innovation attempt, the catalytic role model.[31] The context was a school in which the staff was sympathetic to the innovation, yet it failed. This is an important finding because delegated approaches are intimately involved in theories of diffusion and the implementation of organizational innovations, but in these areas practice tends to be restricted—in part because policy makers and social scientists tend to regard implementation as an event rather than a process, and to interpret failures as exemplifying resistance to change. As was noted, however, the catalytic role model failed even when its potential users were sympathetic. Why?

The answer to this question holds considerable implications for the popularizing of analysis and solutions in the quality of working life area. Few social scientists are knowledgeable in sociotechnical analysis, yet few regard it as complex. Banks, for example, regards it as simplistic, while R. K. Brown is more sympathetic and yet hesitant; C. P. Hill recommends further simplification for general use.[32] However, in some respects sociotechnical analysis probably is one of the best known, highly relevant, least understood, and rarely applied perspectives. This author feels that its application is far beyond the area of comprehension of many executives and policy makers, and that its implications can be realized only by those with access to top-level decision making where they can sanction changes in structure and authority. In contrast to sociotechnical analysis, the approach of job enrichment is more easily comprehended by the layman because it deals with individual jobs. Further, it is more easily implemented, although its consequences for relativities of rewards are not foreseeable.

These features of job enrichment and of sociotechnical analysis have been noted in order to define more closely the conditions under which delegated approaches may be initially defined as having been successful. Job enrichment has many of the features of easily diffusible practices, as outlined by Rogers:[33] it is comprehensible to the user, divisible for partial experimentation, and low in cost for implementation. A delegated approach is then possible but these conditions do not really exist for sociotechnical analysis. Consequently, a delegated approach seems less promising.

Revans' approach of action learning in hospitals, in a number of respects, has seen a popular phase and now come under criticism.[34] There is an aspect which the critics seem to have underplayed, namely, the problems of gaining intervention in arenas where professional competences are overtly displayed. It is quite possible that the delegated approach may facilitate later interventions of a more directed kind.

Focus

Focus refers largely to the variables chosen by the practitioner to manipulate to achieve the quality of working life intervention. Five major points about focus are noted in this section, each of which contributes toward the development of an intervention theory. However, at the present level of understanding, some of the relationships between the factors are problematic.

First, the practitioner's focus may be a single or a multiple one. That is, the practitioner operates on, or *takes into account*, one or more of the four interacting organizational variables suggested by Leavitt:[35] technology, structure, actors, and objectives. "Takes into account" is emphasized because there seems to be some neglect of the contextual factors which may facilitate any intervention.

The importance of Leavitt's formulation is that it alerts thinking toward the possibility of indirect change, a possibility that would seem to receive support from the careful examination of the role of technology in planned change by J. C. Taylor;[36] he argues that technological change facilitates structural change and low-depth impact on attitudes.

Second, and following from the comments above, is the depth of intervention into the life span and attitudes of the organizational member. Not all quality of working life interventions will aim to make in-depth changes. Therefore, it seems appropriate to recognize this and follow Harrison's suggestion that this conceptual distinction should be utilized to consider more appropriate matchings of *role* and *focus*.[37]

The third point concerns the relative place of experiential and cognitive emphasis in the focus. Much of the intervention literature and, possibly, practice is given to experientially shaped foci. This may be appropriate when the knowledge base is sociopsychological and the experiences of intragroup process can be connected to the appropriate concepts; but even here are problems of timing the cognitive clarification, as Bowers clearly notes.[38] It is, however, less easy to provide a comparable experience for the knowledge base of organizational sociology.

The importance of doing so is emphasized by Katz and Kahn in their conception of the role of the social scientist in policy formation, an area of direct interest for quality of working life activities.[39] Bennis acknowledges the lack of emphasis upon cognitive inputs but, in his critique of all other approaches except his own vision of planned change, tends to neglect the crucial role of the formal media in disseminating ideas and practices.[40] Rogers, on the other hand, would give considerable weight to formal media in the early stages of diffusion.[41] But diffusion is neither application nor internalization of the repertoire of approaches which an organization comes to possess; a number of factors involve the relative success of cognitive inputs.[42]

The fourth aspect is formalization. Bowers suggests that it can be viewed as existing or being absent in diagnosis and therapy stages of the relationship. Thus this simple 2-by-2 matrix provides a range of possible combinations: formalization is important because its appeal lies in the ease of its application (e.g., delegated and economical interventions), but its existence alters the relationship with the client and may be inappropriate. The degree of formalization, for example, envisaged in the contract negotiation affects the relationship between client and practitioner. The decision to use a survey, as contrasted with the decision to undertake organizational design, for example, implies quite different ways of interaction.

Fifth, the problem scope is of considerable relevance, directly connected with formalization and the cognitive/experiential dilemma. If the scope is narrow, the exceptions presented (à la Perrow)[43] to the parties may be resolved by a simple search process reaching a solution through the rearrangement of existing knowledge.[44] In such situations it is possible to use established tools, such as questionnaires and confrontation groups. The writer feels that the role implied is unlikely to be joint; it is more likely to be delegated or technocratic. On the other hand, in broadly conceived and diffusely specified projects the problem scope is broad; there are two possibilities depending upon the context. If the client is confident, is in a noncrisis situation, and can deploy resources, the role may be collaborative; but, under opposite circumstances, the appropriate role is that of expert.

Having looked at five facets of focus and alluded to some of the ways in which the emergent intervention theory suggests they should be combined with role and context, the latter is now examined in more detail.

Context

Eight aspects of the context must be considered, namely: client's expectations, timing, existence of a problem, impact studies, integer power centers, knowledge-using style, societal patterns of conflict resolution, and organizational problems of the research agency.

First, the client's expectations of focus and role are rarely mentioned, and there is little evidence of a conceptual framework to identify the main possibilities. In some respects, the analysis of bargaining suggested by Walton and McKersie provides broad clues to assumptions of client expectations which particular role models imply.[45] As mentioned above, the dialogue suggested by Cherns to one particular client anxious to implement quality of working life goals closely reflected the client's expectations.[46] However, in another study on a somewhat similar problem of organizational design for a new factory, the client expected the social scientists to behave like experts.[47] In that case, the prior commitment to a collaborative/dialogic approach of joint problem solving was troublesome and unsatisfactory in the client's view.

Second, and leading on from above, is the issue of timing. It has been suggested that in crisis and emergency situations the expert approach is most appropriate, the dialogic approach being more suited to situations in which the client is dealing with anticipated future problems. The point has strong theoretical justification but cannot, in the absence of good longitudinal studies, be easily illustrated.[48]

Third, it is argued that context must include a problem, but not necessarily a crisis. This argument arises from experience where it was not possible to attach action research to a generally perceived problem. There is a potential danger for quality of working life insofar as there may be a tendency to transfer research strategies to nonresearch situations, and also to gaining entry without involvement.

The fourth issue concerns impact of the intervention. The collective researchers of Greiner, Barnes, and Dalton point to the importance of preexisting structural cleavages which facilitated impact; intervention was perceived as having contributed to the resolution of these internal conflicts.[49] Impact implies that the practitioner carefully selects the point of intervention. Again, there is little knowledge about how practitioners make such selections—except in the documentation of a failure: management scientists in a packaging firm had selected a department most subject to fluctuations in work as the starting point for making their activity effective and meaningful; it was in just that department that the rationality of the consultants was most sharply exposed to local and traditional knowledge.[50]

Fifth, impact and continuance of an intervention depend upon internal support and sanctioning. There is some danger of preoccupation with sanctioning, following Jacques' account of the work at Glacier; however, that was an unusual circumstance.[51] The importance of internal support is expressed in most reports, and very persuasively so by Hutte, who suggests that the practitioner should map the power centers in the organization and devise a strategic pathway through these, returning always to what he terms the integer power center. He argues that in the absence of such a center the intervention is unlikely to succeed.[52] There is good circumstantial evidence to support this contention in, for example, Greiner's secondary analysis of eighteen cases of organizational change.[53]

Sixth, it may be observed that clients have particular styles of utilizing knowledge. Feld has documented the military's increasing attempts to absorb outside inventions and ideas, suggesting considerable changes since 1900.[54] Other researchers have initiated some carefully thought through examinations of the knowledge-using style of the Office of Naval Research and of the military in general, which point the way to future theories.[55] It was noticed in the Loughborough project that public bureaucracies frequently have highly formalized procedures for handling external intervention, irrespective of its format. A useful contribution would be a classification of styles to show their appropriateness to other characteristics of context and focus.

The seventh issue involves societal patterns of conflict resolution. It is frequently observed that there are distinctive cultural patterns of manners within and among nations, yet thus far intervention theory has not sufficiently accounted for the influence or other impact of this dimension. There is an apparently strong interest of Dutch administrators in the social sciences. If this is so, why? Goudsblom states that the patterns of manners and conflict resolution in the Netherlands are distinctive and place considerable emphasis upon the absence of overt conflict. He also points to the nature of rationality in Dutch thinking.[56] Could there be a connection between potential intervention and these features; if so, what implications arise?

Eighth, and not least important, is the intersystem contextual aspect of the research agency, or Laboratory in Dispersion. Much has been written about research agencies and their crises. In a recent account of gaining entry for interventions and managing relationships within the intervening agency, there was strong emphasis on the problems faced by the negotiator working from a university base, which is teaching-oriented, when engaging with clients, who are practice-oriented, and where work has to be undertaken by staff who are research-oriented in the belief that this will lead to future teaching posts.[57] This exaggerates the difficulties, but it points to some of the confusions in the context faced by both practitioner and client.[58] There are other problems, such as the range and balance of skills in a project team requiring that different situations be handled by different roles; or the relationship between the agency and the client is likely to change in the progression of the project thereby requiring different skills at various stages.[59] This creates considerable problems, particularly for the internal organization of the agency and the careers of members, and the problems are heightened by a proliferation of independent and competing agencies when some form of federation could be profitably employed.[60] This list of eight facets of the context is not exhaustive, but it does point toward a realistic assessment of the difficulties of matching interventions to the context.

Role, Focus, and Context

In this final section some of the main themes and propositions implicit in the preceding sections are drawn together in four approaches, to spell out the conditions under which particular strategies are appropriate.

1. *The collaborative/dialogic approach is appropriate when:*
    either a multiplicity of interacting variables is involved or the focus is upon interpersonal relations with respect to openness, and so on;

the intervention is intended to achieve some in-depth transformation of attitudes;

the problem scope is broad;

formalization of diagnosis and solution is low;

there is both cognitive and experiential emphasis at different times;

the problem is not clearly articulated;

there is no immediate crisis or it is a situation of anticipated problems;

an integer power center exists;

knowledge-using style is characterized by a spirit of inquiry;

the client expects a joint relationship and can allocate resources;

the research agency is multiskilled and flexible.

2. *Unilateral and expert approaches apply mostly when:*

the focus is on a single variable (e.g., production process, attitudes, etc.);

the intervention is not intended to create a deep transformation in attitudes;

the problem scope is narrow;

formalization is high;

the emphasis is cognitive (i.e., instruction about new ways);

the client is willing to let the expert define the problem and the solution;

the situation is critical;

an integer power center exists;

the client expects direction;

the agency is specialized in particular skills.

3. *The delegated approach applies when:*

the focus is on a single variable;

depth of intervention is moderate (loosening-up process);

the problem scope is broad, possibly ill defined;

or narrow scope and well defined;

formalization is high;

a problem exists or a general desire for learning;

there is no immediate crisis;

there are multiple power centers;

the client expects to purchase a solution, but is nervous about experts;

the agency exists to make initial presentations and intermittent support.

4. *The subordinate technician approach applies when:*

there is a single set of variables;

a minimum impact on attitudes;

a narrow problem scope;

high formalization of procedures (e.g., brief writing);

there is cognitive emphasis (e.g., information);

a felt problem exists;

the timing is not relevant;

an integer or multiple power center exists;

a purchase model of knowledge utilization is operated by the client;

the client expects information.

These profiles are tentative; they have been constructed from a digest of the literature, comparative research, and personal experience in an effort to tackle the problems set out in the program of the Task Group on Intervention Strategies. A number of problems are not covered, such as those of the diffusion of new practices and demonstration studies which involve particular role models; it may well be that different role models are required at different stages. This point has considerable implications for the social organization of quality of working life participants of all categories, and for the context of this work.

In sum, the profiles do suggest the relevance of several models, and do suggest *some* consistent patterns. Further discussion might critically examine the four main approaches and the aspects of focus and context selected, and then proceed to the formulation of propositions and the testing against published research and experience.

NOTES

1. L. E. Greiner, "Antecedents of Planned Organizational Change," *Journal of Applied Behavioral Science*, 3, no. 1 (1967), 51–85.

2. E. O. Chapple and L. R. Sayles, *The Measure of Management* (New York: Macmillan, 1958).

3. J. J. O'Connell, *Managing Organizational Innovation* (Homewood, Ill.: Irwin-Dorsey, 1968).

4. P. A. Clark, *Action Research and Organizational Change* (London: Harper & Row, 1972). Cf. chaps. 7–10.

5. W. G. Bennis, "Theory and Method in Applying Behavioral Science to Planned Organizational Change," in J. R. Lawrence (ed.), *Operational Research and the Social Sciences* (London: Tavistosk, 1966).

6. E. H. Schein, *Process Consultation: Its Role in Organization Development* (Reading, Mass.: Addison-Wesley, 1969).

7. C. Argyris, *Intervention Theory: A Behavioral Approach* (Reading, Mass.: Addison-Wesley, 1970).

8. A. W. Gouldner, "Applied Social Science: Clinical and Engineering Models," in W. G. Bennis, K. D. Benne, and R. Chin (eds.), *The Planning of Change* (New York: Holt, Rinehart, & Winston, 1961).

9. A. W. Gouldner, *The Coming Crisis in Western Sociology* (London: Routledge & Kegan Paul, 1971).

10. P. A. Clark, *Organizational Design: Theory and Practice* (London: Tavistock, 1972). Permission to refer directly to John Player and Sons is gratefully acknowledged.

11. R. Harrison, "Choosing the Depth of Organizational Intervention," *Journal of Applied Behavioral Science*, 33 (1970).

12. C. Argyris, *The Applicability of Organizational Sociology* (Cambridge, Eng.: Cambridge University Press, 1972).

13. O'Connell, *op. cit.*

14. T. T. Paterson, *Morale in War and Work* (London: Parrish, 1955).

15. A. Flanders, *The Fawley Productivity Agreements, A Case Study of Management and Collective Bargaining* (London: Faber, 1964).

16. Based on *Sociatie van de Arbeid* (Assen: Royal Van Gorcum, 1966).

17. H. Hutte *The Sociatry of Work*, MS, Institute voor Sociale Psychologie, University of Groningen, The Netherlands, mimeo, 1967. Cf. R. Lippitt, J. Watson, and B. Westley, *The Dynamics of Planned Change* (New York: Harcourt, Brace, 1958).

18. The emphasis is mine, as is the decision to include Hutte in the expert category. My objective is to counter the preference for delegated and collaborative approaches without reference to the context.

19. R. W. Revans (ed.), *Hospitals: Communications, Choice, and Change; The Hospital Internal Communication Project Seen from Within* (London: Tavistock, 1972). See also G. F. Wieland and H. A. Leigh, *Changing Hospitals: The Hospital Internal Communications Project* (London: Tavistock, 1971).

20. N. Morse and E. Reimer, "Report of Organizational Change," Survey Research Center, University of Michigan, mimeo, 1955. See also F. Herzberg, B. Mausner, and B. Synderman, *The Motivation to Work* (New York: Wiley, 1958), p. 127.

21. The contingency theorists may be said to include March, Simon, Woodward, Burns (early work with Stalker), Perrow, Bell, Lawrence, and Lorsch as representative examples.

22. G. B. Cohen, *The Task-Tuned Organization of Groups* (Amsterdam: Swets & Zeitlinger, 1969).

23. E. Litwak, "Models of Bureaucracy Which Permit Conflict," *American Journal of Sociology*, 67 (1961), 177–184.

24. We refer to recent critique of organizational sociology by Argyris, and to his suggestion in an earlier account of intervention theory that contingency theorists would support his organic approach. Cf. Argyris, *Intervention Theory* and *Organizational Sociology, op. cit.*, pp. 85–86.

25. W. G. Bennis, "A New Role for the Behavioral Sciences: Effecting Organizational Change," *Administrative Science Quarterly*, 8 (1964), 125–165.

26. L. R. Sayles, "The Change Process in Organizations: An Applied Anthropology Analysis," *Human Organization*, 21 (1962), 1–17.

27. Flanders, *op. cit.*, pp. 72–98.

28. W. R. Bion, *Experiences in Groups and Other Papers* (London: Tavistock, 1951).

29. See n. 10 *supra*, p. 265.

30. O'Connell, *op. cit.*

31. N. Gross, J. B. Giacquinta, and M. Bernstein, *Implementing Organizational Innovations: A Sociological Analysis of Planned Change* (New York: Harper & Row, 1971).

32. J. A. Banks, Review of "The Enterprise and Its Environment," *Sociological Review* (New Series), 11 (1963), 374–375. See also R. K. Brown, "Research and Consultancy in Industrial Enterprises: A Review of the Contribution of the Tavistock Institute of Human Relations to the Development of Industrial Sociology," *Sociology*, 1, no. 1 (1967), 33–60 and C. P. Hill, *Toward a New Management Philosophy* (London: Gower Press, 1972). Cf. n. 10, *supra*, chap. 7.

33. E. Rogers, *Diffusion of Innovation* (New York: Free Press, 1961).

34. Revans, *op. cit.*

192   CHANGING THE QUALITY OF WORKING LIFE

35. H. J. Leavitt, *New Perspectives in Organizational Research* (New York: John Wiley and Sons, 1964).

36. J. C. Taylor, "Technology and Planned Organizational Change," University of Michigan Institute of Social Research, 1971.

37. Harrison, *op. cit.*

38. D. G. Bowers, "Perspectives in Organizational Development," Institute for Social Research, University of Michigan, mimeo, 1970.

39. D. Katz and R. L. Kahn, *The Social Psychology of Organizations* (New York: Wiley, 1966).

40. Cf. Bennis, "Organizational Change," *op. cit.*

41. Rogers, *op. cit.*

42. My personal view is somewhat jaundiced as frequently there seems to be a conspiracy of avoiding the differences in perspective which quality of working life goals imply; as a number of authors have observed, an important aspect is the replacement of inappropriate paradigms by new ones—and that may imply confrontation. Cf. D. Schon, *Invention and the Evolution of Ideas* (London: Tavistock, 1963).

43. C. Perrow, *Organizational Analysis: A Sociological View,* (Belmont, Calif.: Wadsworth, 1970).

44. Argyris, *Intervention Theory, op. cit.*

45. R. E. Walton and R. B. McKersie, *A Behavioral Theory of Labor Negotiations* (New York: McGraw-Hill, 1964).

46. See n. 10 *supra.*

47. See n. 4 *supra,* chap. 9, p. 3.

48. A. Etzioni, *A Comparative Analysis of Complex Organizations* (New York: Free Press, 1961), p. 383; see also T. Parsons, F. R. Bales, and E. Shils, *Working Papers in the Theory of Action* (New York: Free Press, 1953), chaps. 3, 5.

49. Greiner, *op. cit.*

50. S. Dalziel and L. Klein, *The Human Implications of Work Study* (London: DSIR, 1960).

51. E. Jaques, *The Changing Culture of a Factory* (London: Tavistock, 1950).

52. Hutte, *op. cit.*

53. Greiner, *op. cit.*

54. M. D. Feld, "Military Self-Image in a Technological Environment," in M. Janowitz (ed.), *The New Military* (New York: Russell Sage Foundation, 1964).

55. P. F. Lazarsfeld and J. G. Reitz, "Towards a Theory of Applied Sociology," *Report,* Bureau of Applied Social Research, Columbia University, 1970.

56. J. Goudsblom, *Dutch Society* (New York: Random House, 1967). See also N. Elias, *Uber den Prozess der Zivilisation* (Bern, 1969), as cited by Goudsblom.

57. A. B. Cherns, "Negotiating the Contract," in A. B. Cherns et al., *Utilisation of Social Science Research,* Monograph no. 1, Department of Social Sciences, Loughborough University of Technology, 1972.

58. Cf. L. B. Barnes, "Organization Change and Field Experiment Methods," in V. H. Vroom (ed.), *Methods of Organizational Research* (Pittsburgh: University of Pittsburgh Press, 1967).

59. G. N. Jones, *Planned Organizational Change: An Exploratory Study Using an Empirical Approach* (London: Routledge & Kegan Paul, 1969).

60. Cf. A. B. Cherns, "Relations Between Research Institutes and Users of Research," *International Social Sciences Journal,* 1, no. 2 (1970), 226–242.

13

Collaborative Action Research to Enhance the Quality of Working Life

Einar Thorsrud

THIS selection looks at requirements for the organization of collaborative action research and at the roles and capabilities of researchers
engaged in enhancing quality of working life. Because there can be problems
in establishing and maintaining relationship with clients, the "critical incident"
technique is applied to an example of programmatic action research in Norway.

The first critical incident focuses on the development of an action research
project following the formulation of a national industrial democracy research
program. Objectives of the project were discussed in terms of creating conditions for personal participation.

The second critical situation emerged from the decision to carry out a
sociotechnical analysis in a specific department.

The third critical incident developed around the visit from a study group
concerned with a similar project in another country. At both the intellectual
(scientific) level and at the interpersonal and professional level, a series of
problems were confronted and some remain unresolved. Seven sequential
steps constitute the applied research program: consideration of alternative

problem formulations—a phase critical for building trust and testing the common value basis of the collaborators; preliminary collection of both "soft" and "hard" data to test alternative approaches; further clarification of theory and method, which is unlikely to be a "pure" scientific task and may call for more knowledge and time than available; data collection and analysis which demand much time and energy; preliminary feedback of results, often linked to the formulation of change programs; reporting of results to collaborators, the scientific community, and other groups; and follow-up, evaluation, and diffusion.

There is a need to experiment with a differentiated social science role culture to improve recruitment, training, and professional careers in applied social research. The tasks are discussed within three roles: the applied social science trainee, the professional applied research team member, and the program director.

Introduction

This selection raises requirements of collaborative action research organization and of the roles and needs of researchers if suitable capability is to be available in the future to engage in enhancing quality of working life. Ten years of experience in applying social science research to the problems of the work organization in industry underlie the observations. Such research is distinct from research where access is mainly on a private basis as in the family and from research where access is highly controlled as in prisons or in the military. The purpose here is to pool experience regarding alternative research strategies and principal roles to be filled to insure the success of collaborative research activities.

If we are concerned with selecting people suitable to occupy the positions or with training people to perform satisfactorily in them, we need to locate those aspects of roles which impose a special demand on their occupants. The "critical incident" technique has been used for this purpose and for evaluating people's performance in their roles. In this paper it is used to identify some crucial features of the action research role. Although action research is not new it still has a pioneering quality. Action researchers are mainly self-taught, each has developed a "style." Yet despite apparent differences there are aspects common to all successful action research engagements. In all of them there are dangerous corners in the road of establishing and maintaining collaborative relationships with cilents. The three critical incidents described here exemplify points in the client-researcher relationship which pose crucial problems for both.

First Incident

The first incident focuses on developing a new action research project. In 1964, following a year and a half of formulating a national industrial democracy research program with a joint national research committee representing labor and employers, a pulp and paper firm was selected as a prospective site for a field experiment and was being visited to ascertain participation.

After brief contacts with management and with union representatives jointly and separately, the researchers met with people from production management and from the service departments; two researchers discussed with production management problems of technology, markets, organizational structure, and so on, while the third met with the personnel department and with the local union.

A second meeting during the visit took place with the president of the company, the personnel manager, the technical director, the local chairman of the main union, and a representative of the foremen's union. Several crucial questions were discussed without seeking to reach a decision.

1. What would be the response and potential involvement among different groups in the firm in this project? The trade union chairman openly questioned the company's policy on supervision, indicating that there would likely be very slow worker involvement.
2. How would the researchers handle the collection of information in the face of possible opposition to participation? Would one person in the firm be permitted to stop everything?
3. If an experiment led to specific recommendations, would the firm and the union be committed to follow them?
4. How would decisions be made during each developmental stage of the project and who would sanction these decisions?

In retrospect, the role problems of the professional social scientist seem implicit in all four questions; they could not have been solved once and for all by explicit formulations of goals and norms of conduct. What could be done, however, took place at the third meeting on the following day.

First, the objectives of the project were discussed in terms of creating conditions for personal participation. It was useful to distinguish between these conditions and those governed by collective bargaining between organized power groups.[1] Members of these groups were in the plant and represented in the national research committee. The human values which would be important in judging the possible outcome of the project were spelled out in terms of psychological criteria for jobs.[2]

Second, the research objective was explained in concrete terms, what was what in analyzing the company situation, and why. It was made clear that people could only be expected to commit themselves to the first steps, and then judge continued collaboration in view of their *concrete experience, that is, what they did to achieve some goals and the way they handled their tasks.* The question of sharing the results of productivity was a good way of testing the researchers as professionals, that is, did they know what they were talking about, and were they used to handling controversial matters? If not, it would clearly have come out when they explained how the sanctioning body had agreed that productivity would be a basic constraint to be controlled in experiments, but not an objective in itself.

Second Incident

About a year and a half after the first incident, a critical situation emerged in the project. Agreement had been reached with the national committee and at the company level to carry out a sociotechnical analysis; a specific department had been selected for potential experimentation and an outline of an experiment submitted. The researchers had completed most of the analysis; one researcher and an assistant had spent more than half a year in the plant; the program director spent a few days at the site after a month or during the year; the Tavistock Institute adviser had made three visits. The emerging crisis was compounded of the following:

1. Concern by the researchers that continuing to play an active role would constitute assuming responsibility for actual change.
2. Some operators in the experimental department, the shop-steward committee, and top management had begun to commit themselves to a change program, while other operators directly involved and most supervisors were either indifferent or negative toward the program.
3. Strong empirical evidence showed the incongruity between the traditional work role and status system, on the one hand, and the departmental task structure, on the other. By contrast, there was little empirical evidence for the outline of alternative roles at the supervisory and middle-management level.
4. The market position of the firm had worsened and management was under strong pressure to achieve some immediate change. The researcher experienced delays in getting data and things done for the project. He was doing more than he was supposed to do according to the agreed roles. Simultaneously, the importance of the research program had increased at the national level and the demands for new ideas on work organizations based on empirical evidence were becoming very strong. Also, workers wanted proof that the project would mean something more than promises.

Some things took care of themselves; workers demanded a vote about continuation and got it—against the advice of the researchers. After the voting, which showed a slight majority in favor of the project, a stronger demand came from the shop floor to put the experimental changes into operation; that is, pressure mounted on management to act on suggestions for change. In a confrontation with everyone involved in the project, a top management official made some very explicit statements regarding principles of job security, training, and payment policies, while union representatives committed themselves to specific aspects of the change program. A local action committee was established (consisting of one worker, one [assistant] foreman and a training officer) which assumed most of the action tasks of the researcher. (From then on, the latter withdrew and acted as an expert adviser and project manager. His main task was to collect data on the consequences of change. The program director, in close contact with the Tavistock adviser, counseled a top management policy group and trade union representatives, and reported periodically to the national research committee.)

The two basic changes which took place after the confrontation can be seen as a restructuring of roles triggered off by tensions over the tasks to be carried out within the agreed framework of the project as well as by the company. The most striking developments in the experimental department took place during those six months when the research group was not directly involved in the activities at the field site.

Third Incident

Approximately three years after the initiation of the project, another critical incident took place. A similar project had been developed in England, and a study group composed of management and union members wished to visit the paper and pulp company. There was some hesitation about the invitation since there were signs of stagnation at the experimental site. In spite of this, however, management and the union set up a new experiment in the paper plant, and gradually introduced new organizational principles based in part on autonomous work groups in the company as a whole.

The project manager had worked a few months with the Tavistock research team on the English project. The program director had visited that team when a major step was made toward an integration of theory at the level of the work organization and at that of the corporation and its wider societal networks.[3] This had some impact on the research strategy at the company and the national level in Norway. On the other hand, the English study group that had come to Norway experienced a quite different work culture and a strong sense of leadership among Norwegian trade unionists as well as employers regarding democratization of the workplace.

A confrontation between the English union-management study group and various key persons in the Norwegian project raised a number of issues.

1. What lessons could be learned from various approaches to achieve the same type of basic changes in work organizations in two different cultures?
2. Who was most capable of translating experience from one field experiment to another: the researchers or the managers, shop stewards, and others from the work organizations?
3. How would the various interpretations of results obtained by the researchers and others in the Norwegian experiment be represented in the project report under preparation?
4. How could an international network be created between researchers and between collaborative partners in industrial social research?

Some time after the visit, an English member of the corporation research staff returned to Norway with one of his colleagues and worked in collaboration with the Norwegian research team. This was an important phase in the development of a nine-point program in organizational change, later published in England.[4] The Norwegian program director circulated this program and reports on policy making in the English firm among Scandinavian researchers, and company and union representatives engaged in similar activities.

The managers and union representatives in the Norwegian paper and pulp firm learned a great deal from the presentation and discussion of their own project with outsiders. They agreed to repeat such presentations to visiting groups from Norwegian firms and union representatives from abroad, as well as in conferences and so on at the national level.

Within the firm, some policy decision had to be made regarding alternative roles for supervisors, for middle management, and specialists. For example, the foremen of the plant participated in an experiment with their employment guaranteed by the company aimed at a work organization without traditional foremen roles. (In fact, this was established about a year later; the production managers and several staff specialists changed their work roles, three taking jobs outside the firm.)

The Research Reports

Tensions between the research staff and one of the managers increased, and a confrontation occurred over the approval of drafts of the research reports. Several aspects of social science research policy were involved in the analysis and evaluation of research data, in the writing of the reports, and in the diffusion of information. At the intellectual level—in terms of theory and method—and at the interpersonal and professional level, the research group had to work its way through a series of difficult problems, some of which remained unresolved.*

---

* The research report was published with the consent of those involved. Some problems on interpersonal level within the firm were left unsolved since further engagement might have endangered the impartial position of the researchers.

These were the specific and general problems involving research roles and research policy. Now, a look at the functions and objectives of social science institutes, and at the task sequence of applied research may help to provide a more complete frame of reference in this area of study.[5]

The Task Sequence of Action Research

Outlined below is the sequence of steps or phases involved in a social science program, though a given project may have fewer steps or phases. Also, the realities of an actual program are usually much less orderly and logical.

1. *Consideration of alternative problem formulations* and frames of reference with corresponding research designs and strategies: in action research this phase may be critical in terms of building trust among those involved, that is, testing the common value basis and the sanctioning system necessary for a collaborative relationship.

2. *Preliminary data collection* to test alternatives. Typically in applied research, complementary types of "soft" and "hard" data are more likely to be used than one type of data and method. The type of data is often decisive for choice and, thus, attendant values.

3. *Further clarification of theory and method.* This may be primarily a "pure" scientific task, but quite often in action research it is not. Problems of theory are often related to the values and objectives of research, and methods, to the degree of trust that can be built and maintained. Purely technical matters— for example, measurement problems—are less complicated to deal with from the point of view of roles. To resolve such problems, knowledge and time may be serious constraints.

4. *Data collection and analysis*, usually based on field work or experimentation, are always a major strenuous and time-consuming phase in action research. Since the primary task of those in the field is not research, the value of data is limited by that fact and by one's patience; the analysis of data is tedious and requires persistence. The novice usually relies entirely on the type of data he knows from textbooks, while the experienced researcher tends more to use data already accumulated in the field (untouched by social scientists).

5. *Preliminary feedback of results* means involvement in social change, even when this is consciously reduced to a minimum. In most collaborative action research the feedback process is linked to formulation of change programs.

6. *Reporting of results.* Depending on the type of research, this phase can be very complex and time-consuming, involving a number of roles; for example, when problems of theory and method or measurement and application in social change are to be reported to collaborators, to the scientific community, and to

other groups. At the very least, there must be some account of what was done and what was learned within what frame of reference. Also, the reporting of results usually raises a number of questions regarding rights and responsibilities.

7. *Follow-up, evaluation, and diffusion.* In most action research, if conducted professionally, there is an urgent need for follow-up; one reason is that verification cannot be accomplished overnight. One also has a responsibility for those with whom one has worked. Moreover, it is often in the form of by-products from the first phases of applied research that the most valuable ideas and innovations appear. If follow-up does not take place, very little may have been learned.

Collaborators in applied social research usually take it for granted that the scientists will be responsible or at least somewhat involved in the diffusion of new knowledge. If social scientists are really becoming involved in emerging major problems of man and society, then follow-up, evaluation, and diffusion means involvement in policy making. This cannot occur without considerable risks for all involved unless a great deal of care and consideration is spent on planning and development of an appropriate role culture within the institutions of social science. At least this aspect of policy making, the social scientists cannot leave to others.

Complementary Roles in Collaborative Research

The main tasks of applied social research form a set of key roles. There is need, however, to experiment with a differentiated role culture to improve recruitment, training, and professional careers within the social sciences.

The action research trainee may have the following tasks:

1. data collection and analysis under the guidance of a senior research team member;
2. contribution to theory, methods, and techniques in the context of a project or program;
3. participation in social process building and analysis;
4. participation in evaluation and feedback of results.

The first task should be shared with an experienced field worker; too often, the trainee plans a very extensive data collection without considering the limitations and the unknown possibilities in the field. Long questionnaires, standardized interview guides, or predefined experimental variables may look very good in advance, but not so good after testing. Much valuable data are already available but trainees have to learn where to look. Although a trainee may learn by making mistakes, the client may learn to stop collaborating. The more experienced field worker should help the trainee to organize his data in such a way that it can be analyzed in a step-by-step accumulation of knowledge.

Quite often these tasks will be handled by a project leader. The need within client systems or "user" organizations to have one person to relate to when rights, responsibilities, and sanctioning must be clarified should not be underestimated. If planned social change is part of a research project or program, a project leader or someone with his support must be able to build the trust and in some cases face the necessary confrontations without unduly risking the integrity of those involved or the continuation of the collaborative relationships.

One of the many reasons for having more than one researcher on a project is the impossibility of planning a research project fully in advance. If this were done, it would result in tasks more like production tasks or routine learning than scientific research and innovative problem solving.[6] If more than one person is involved with a project, he can pick up new leads and pursue them without leaving behind too many unfinished jobs.

The second task (theory and method) is not such a difficult one to share among researchers; here the contribution of the trainee may be underestimated. Even when textbooks or journals have not been of much help to match theory and methods, on the one hand, with the blooming, buzzing confusion in the field, on the other, the research trainee may be the one who can really take a new look at both aspects and the relations between them.

The two last-mentioned tasks (process building and feedback) can seldom be left to the trainee, and only in exceptional cases can be carried out by one individual researcher. Two or three people working together have a much better chance to build into these interaction processes the optimal mix of shared learning and control. The senior researcher can certainly benefit from having a junior colleague question and challenge him back at base on such points as power, professional ethics, and personal skill.

The professional action research team member may have the following tasks:

1. Collaboration with users of research to formulate problems in alternative ways so that they are researchable, and in such ways that alternative goals and values can be pursued.
2. Search for relevant theory as a frame of reference for the formulation of research problems and projects. Contribution to cumulative improvements in theory and methods should follow from any project. (Often these tasks can be approached in collaboration with scientists in academic institutes.)
3. Project planning in terms of content, models, strategies, methods, and manning.
4. The organization and performance of field work or experimental work or any other research activity to collect data.
5. Analysis of data, report writing, and collection of complementary data, possibly after preliminary feedback of results.
6. Feedback of results and diffusion of information, possibly in connection with planned social change.

The tasks of the professional applied research worker cannot be effectively carried out unless two basic conditions are fulfilled: one is the development of a set of complementary roles within the research institute, the other is the design and development of professional careers across the boundaries of different kinds of research institutes. However, there are many obstacles. A serious problem; for example, is competition for resources between social scientific institutions, which could be *complementary*. Trist has offered a description of three types which would have different, distinctive competence and would not really compete, although there would be several kinds of overlapping activities.

The program director's role has no meaning unless a distinction is made between a project and a program; the former usually covers a shorter time period, perhaps two to three years, whereas a program may cover at least five and sometimes fifteen years. The project is more limited in its objectives; one knows in what directions to look, and the content of the problem is often defined in terms of manifest rather than emerging problems. (However, more and more, the manifest problems are not what advanced applied social science will concentrate on.) The research program covers a fairly broad problem area and usually represents a continuation of a project which branches out after a phase of two to three years. Within the *later* phases of such projects and programs, there are generally openings for trainee and student roles, but the key roles have to be filled by social scientists at the professional level.

The primary task of the program director is policy making and resource building within the institute, on the one hand, and creating institutional networks, on the other. His main contributions as a scientist will probably have to be made within the framework of projects, or perhaps in adjunct roles, or as adviser outside his home base.

Some Thoughts on Future Research

From the experience involving the project in the paper and pulp mill discussed earlier, a number of questions emerge:

1. What minimum requirements should be set up by the action research institute (with respect to alternative personnel with complementary skills for different roles in different phases of a project or program) before committing the institute within a wider institutional network?

2. What is the mutual support needed for academic and applied institutes to improve social science research in terms of adjunct roles, exchange of trainees, educational activities, and career lines based on known citeria for evaluation of competence at different levels and in different areas of knowledge?

3. What is the mutual support needed from user organizations and applied institutes in terms of selective interdependence between professionals in

two types of institutions (adjunct roles, exchange of trainees, overlapping career lines, and training activities)?

4. The *need for clarification of professional ethics* is behind the three questions above; it is not easy to discuss the more fundamental problems of the power or lack of it and the integrity of the social scientists, unless it is done in the framework of complementary (or conflicting) forms of institutional roles.

The critical incidents discussed in the selection pose many problems which can be solved only in a differentiated role culture, in which different people play different roles in different projects. In no other type of work should a matrix organization be more functional. Without alternative matrix relations it is very difficult to see how individuals can move constructively into different primary tasks and new roles as their work develops and as they develop as researchers. With these points in mind it is quite clear that the individual researcher, his institute, and the collaborating institutions are running great risks if a researcher has no guarantee that he can call on other team members during certain phases of research.

The career pattern within the social sciences is constrained by the present structure of the scientific establishment. One aspect of this problem is the inadequacy of the present role system for building and maintaining a responsible relationship between the researchers and the researched. It is not easy to discuss what the scientist can be involved in as a scientist, unless there is an exchange of viewpoints with people in fundamentally different roles and institutions. Another lies within the social science role culture itself, which may create tensions and insecurity at the personal and group level, as well as within this new profession.

In this context, it can no longer be claimed that the majority of social science researchers are primarily concerned with the pursuit of knowledge for its own sake. Rather, the effective accumulation and utilization of scientific research is hampered by the lack of appropriate strategies and roles among the scientist and the users. One aspect of this problem may be the gap between what is known and what is done. Another, however, may be the gap between the frame of reference of the social scientist and the problems emerging in society at large.[7]

NOTES

1. F. E. Emery and E. Thorsrud, *The Form and Content in Industrial Democracy* (London: Tavistock, 1969). Cf. pp. 85–86.

2. *Ibid.*, p. 105.

3. Paul Hill, *Towards a New Philosophy of Management* (London: Gower Press, 1972).

4. *Ibid.*

5. Publication of reports in research and professional journals was inadequate; development of new professional social science competence within the user organizations proceeded far too slowly, as did recruitment of social scientists from universities.

6. P. G. Herbst, "Characteristics of Research Tasks and Research Organizations," AI doc. 30/69, Oslo.

7. E. Thorsrud, "A Strategy for Research and Social Change in Industry," *Social Science Information*, 5, no. 9, (1970) 65–90.

14

Research on Self-Developing Forms of Organization

Karl-O. Faxen and Reine Hansson

THIS research is undertaken by the Working Group for Research of the Union-Management Development Council for Collaborative Questions (URAF) whose principal aim is to bring about balanced increases in productivity and job satisfaction. The group is also experimenting with new forms of cooperation for the establishment of wage levels within an enterprise relative to collective agreements concluded at the national level. Of central importance in the URAF research is the role of joint consultation in the total learning of the enterprise "learning how to learn." It is more important in this regard to examine conditions for consultation and joint decision making in the management of large development steps than to study the same processes in relation to gradual development in localized sections. Job satisfaction expresses the relationship between individual experience and emotion, and between work and the work environment. More recently, it is seen as the degree to which a worker's needs and expectations are fulfilled by his actual experiences: the individual's ideas about himself, his values, abilities, and identity and how he sees his job and work environment corresponding to the ideas about himself.

Another version of this selection was published in A. Silberston and F. Seton (eds.), *Industrial Management: East and West.* (New York: Praeger Special Studies, 1973).

Lack of agreement between expectations and their fulfillment leads to tension, which then becomes a "cause" of the next phase in the adjustment process between the individual and his work. In this sense, job satisfaction and dissatisfaction do not denote a permanent state but form the emotional driving force of a continuing adaptation.

The URAF's emphasis on "self-developing forms of organization" is meant to draw attention to internal dynamics as well as to adaptation to external conditions. By analyzing changes within a certain time phase into those which are discrete and those which are continuous, some idea can be formed as to when a given development will stabilize or whether it will continue toward higher levels of productivity and job satisfaction.

It is noted that once a given experiment has concluded, there are prospects for development in that area if management draws conclusions from what has happened and brings new groups into the process.

The fundamental goal of the research effort in Sweden of the Working Group for Research of the Union-Management Development Council for Collaborative Questions (URAF) is to bring about greater productivity and greater job satisfaction. These two objectives are contained in the collective agreement of 1966 between the SAF, the LO, and the TCO (*Svenska Arbetsgivareföreningen*, the Swedish Employers Association; *Landsorganisation*, the Confederation of Manual Workers Unions; and *Tjänstemännens Centralorganisation*, the Swedish Central Association of Salaried Employees). The full meaning of realizing these objectives is difficult to put into words, but it can be said that URAF will not follow a line of reasoning in which greater job satisfaction is accomplished at the expense of productivity or, conversely, in which improvements in productivity can only be attained at the expense of job satisfaction.

Another important consideration in URAF's experimental activities on new forms of cooperation within the enterprise is the Swedish approach to establishing wage levels, which are formulated through collective agreements concluded mainly at the national level. This procedure limits the freedom of movement of the individual enterprise on wage questions. It is true that special collective agreements are often concluded between management and local union representative structure in the enterprise, but the scope of these negotiations is restricted by the provisions of the national collective agreements in force. This applies also to a number of other questions which are subject to negotiations and to collective agreements. Management's contacts with the local representatives about negotiation questions are normally far more intense than about questions for joint consultation in the works councils.

Thus, in those enterprises which are experimentally making decisions about organizational changes in special development groups containing elected representatives of workers and salaried employees together with "management representatives," the related questions about forms of payment, wage levels, and so on have to be settled through negotiations between management and local representatives.

Productivity and Job Satisfaction—The Base for Research

A considerable part of the work within the URAF has been devoted to a closer analysis of the interpretation of the fundamental concepts of productivity and job satisfaction, as given in the 1966 agreement between the SAF, the LO, and the TCO.

The Concept of Productivity

The development of productivity in an enterprise, an industry, or in the total economy can be divided into three components: labor productivity, capital productivity, and a "residual factor." Labor productivity means the conditions which affect the individual employee's way of performing his job, such as his utilization of time, and his skill on the job—how often he commits errors ruining materials or having to repeat certain tasks.

Capital productivity means conditions which affect the qualities of the particular capital good. For example, a new lathe which runs at greater speed is more productive than an older one; a big pulp digester is more productive than a small one since the volume increases by the cube of the size when capital costs increase by the square. The production capacity of the individual capital good is not proportional to the cost, and this relationship develops in time as a consequence of technological progress. A certain part of the productivity increase in industry derives from these two factors: the educational level of the labor force rises and professional skill grows; capital goods become more efficient through technological progress.*

---

* In measuring the size of the share of the total productivity increase which can be attributed to labor and capital, the variables volume of labor and volume of capital must also be considered in the course of "technological progress." We cannot here enter into these well-known, fundamental difficulties but make the assumption that they have been solved in one way or another, e.g., through an index measuring the volume of capital on the basis of historical costs, corrected by a price index.

As to the residual factor—the part of the total productivity development that is of primary interest to the URAF research—the analysis begins with the following hypotheses:

1. The so-called residual factor represents an independent cause (or number of causes) of productivity development. Consequently, it does not rest (except possibly in part) on errors of measurement in the variables volume of labor and volume of capital, or on interaction effects which arise when these two variables change. It accounts for a considerable part of the total productivity increase.

2. The residual factor can only be associated with developments in a "system" as a whole, not with any particular part of it. By "system" is meant a division of a certain complexity in an enterprise, or an enterprise as a whole, or an industry, or the total economy.

3. The residual factor is purely dynamic, and a dynamic method is necessary to study it; a method comparatively static will not detect it. Consequently, the residual factor in the productivity of an individual enterprise may be associated with the ability of the enterprise as an organization, to utilize market changes and changes in production techniques, to develop new methods for internal organization, and so on. It may take the form of assimilating a new production technique which is already applied elsewhere; it may be coordinating production and sales internally; it may be recruiting staff. The aim of research here is to identify the organizational forms or patterns of behavior which characterize a certain enterprise as an organization, regardless of who occupies the various positions in the enterprise or which capital goods the company owns at the moment. Attention is directed to the ability of the firm, seen as an organizational unit, to increase its productivity continuously.

  The same dynamic process that characterizes continuous adaptation between enterprise and environment is assumed to be important when the internal development in an enterprise is studied. It is assumed there are internal factors in its organization (some of which will be discussed more closely under the heading "Job Satisfaction") which, under certain conditions, release productivity growth that can be ascribed to the residual factor. It is not only a question of interaction between the enterprise and the environment, but also one of internal interaction.

4. The theory of learning may contribute to the comprehension of the interactive processes sketched above, that is, complex learning processes which solve problems. Attention is directed not only toward learning itself, but also toward how the organization as a whole increases its ability to learn.

  Of central importance in the URAF research problems is the role of joint consultation in the total learning of the enterprise. It is not enough to study how joint decision making between workers and supervisors in a certain production process may lead to increased productivity under stable conditions, that is, where technology and market demand are concerned. Since each production process is exposed sooner or later to important changes in technology or market conditions, it is far more important to examine the conditions for consultation and joint decision-making processes to manage large development steps than to study the decision-making process in the course of a continuous development. Is it possible for an organization to "learn how to learn" during a period of stable conditions, in such a way as to improve its ability to solve the problems arising from large changes in technology or market conditions?

5. In a varying environment subject to great changes, that are of primary interest here, the criterion of increased productivity in an enterprise can hardly be expressed by the productivity measures based on static theory. The changes in the product mix, in the composition of the labor force, and so on, is so great that such measures are inadequate. Profitability must then replace productivity as an indicator, which is easier to measure in an enterprise since they are divided into smaller units for which separate profitability measurements are undertaken.

Finally—beyond the profitability criterion—it becomes a question of the organization's ability to survive in competition with other organizations in the economy. The criterion is to increase its productivity continuously in order to survive and develop further.

Thus, no attempts are made to measure the productivity growth in experimental enterprises or special departments within them by ratios of index numbers for input and output during certain periods, but profitability is used as a criterion at an early stage. The accounting system and internal organization of the enterprise should then provide relevant profitability estimates for the decision-making units which have been created during the period of experimentation. These estimates should comprise the aggregate effect of all change which the experimental activities bring about in job organization, marketing, the interplay between production and sales, the methods for investment decisions, and so on. An important part of the effects of an altered organization of work may be a change in the sales method, such as shorter times of delivery and better service for customers, which cannot be covered by productivity measures in the form of index numbers, but shows up in profitability measures. Nevertheless, the decisive question is the organization's ability to survive; profitability is not an ultimate aim in itself, but only a criterion.

The Concept of Job Satisfaction

Job satisfaction expresses the relationship between human experiences and emotions, and work and work environment; satisfaction or dissatisfaction is experienced by the individual employee. In research as well as general discussion, the concept of job satisfaction has developed gradually, and has increasingly taken on a dynamic meaning. During the 1940s and 1950s, there was a "debate on well-being," which aimed largely at the physical work environment; research efforts were directed at physiological and medical factors and at questions of industrial safety. As a result, various norms were established of what could be characterized as a good or acceptable work environment. This research continued and has intensified in the last few years, in response to widespread concern with the environment and was directed at flowers, color schemes, music-while-you-work, and so on. In the 1950s and 1960s, sociological research broadened and the result was to supplement the concept of job satisfaction as seen from a physiological and medical point of view.

Job Satisfaction: Attitude toward Environment

This area of sociological research on work deals with the employees' attitudes to various aspects of work and work environment (external physical environment, work tasks, fellow workers, work supervision, time studies, staff policy, wages, etc.). The workers are asked, usually in questionnaires, whether they find conditions of work and work environment satisfactory or unsatisfactory. The answers are then subjected to statistical analysis, comparing different groups of employees, and attempts have been made at expressing the degree of job statisfaction for whole enterprises or parts of enterprises. The co-variation between the replies to attitude questions and independent judgments of various aspects of work and work environment has also been studied. In this kind of research the concept of job satisfaction is mainly defined with the help of attitude questions. Job satisfaction is usually measured in percentage numbers of the group which expressed satisfaction-dissatisfaction with aspects of their work and work environment or as averages (or corresponding measures) on an attitude scale.

Surveys of this kind attempt to clasify jobs and work environments as, generally speaking, more or less satisfactory. With a few exceptions, they begin with work and work environment, and it is then assumed that some jobs and environments give rise to satisfaction while others lead to dissatisfaction and negative answers to the attitude questions.

In many of these surveys there is a built-in idea about cause and effect, which implies that satisfaction-dissatisfaction is an effect of work and work environment. It is possible to go even further and classify jobs and work environments on a general job satisfaction scale. This point of view agrees with the position of industrial physiology and medicine, which formulates standard values, for noise, light, and so on. The concept of job satisfaction is then linked to the "average individual" or a similar standard and is given the character of a rational empirical concept, primarily based on environmental conditions. Results of these research activities have yielded a great deal of important information about various jobs and work environments. However, experiences have appeared here and there which cannot be explained within the framework of the concept of job satisfaction used. There are, for example, jobs and work environments which, seen from the outside, have been judged as decidedly negative, but which have nevertheless yielded positive replies. In many cases, employees in simple, repetitive, strictly supervised jobs state in response to the attitude questionnaires that they are on the whole satisfied with their work and work environment. Similarly, these attitude surveys have shown that one work environment yielded both positive and negative judgments, both satisfaction and dissatisfaction, as defined by the questions. Some results also indicate that middle-aged and elderly workers are generally more satisfied than younger fellow workers doing the same kind of work and in the same work environment.

Job Satisfaction: Expectations—Experiences

These observations have given rise to the development of both theory and methods of job satisfaction. New ideas have come from different aspects of psychological and sociopsychological research, and one result is that job satisfaction is regarded as the expression of a relationship. This relationship contains the individual's needs and personal expectations of his work, on the one hand, and his experience of how his work and work environment fulfill these expectations, on the other. If the expectations are too high or too low in relation to what work and work environment can offer, the result is a feeling of dissatisfaction. If the expectations agree reasonably with what work and environment can fulfill, the result is a feeling of satisfaction. Consequently, job satisfaction is an expression of the individual's subjective expression of himself and his job situation. This expression includes:

the individual's idea about himself, his value, his ability, his chances of development, his integrity, his identity;

how job and work environment correspond to his idea about himself;

his emotional experience of satisfaction-dissatisfaction with himself and his work situation.

The "degree of job satisfaction" is expressed from these bases as the difference between expectations and experiences. A comparison of job satisfaction between individuals or between groups of individuals can be made through measuring subjective expectations and experiences, and estimating the difference between them. Such measures and measurement of job satisfaction then become more complicated than traditional attitude measurement.

Satisfaction–Dissatisfaction: Cause and Effect

The individual or subjective interpretation of the concept of job satisfaction has also led to a growing interest in how the experience and feeling of satisfaction-dissatisfaction changes in individuals over time; the dynamic aspects of job satisfaction have attracted greater attention. In earlier research and discussions, job satisfaction was regarded:

as an effect of job and work environment in research oriented toward environment;

as an effect of differences in expectations related to fulfilled expectations in research oriented toward relationships.

When job satisfaction is seen as an emotional result of the adaptation process between the individual and his job, the feeling of satisfaction-dissatisfaction also becomes an important part of that process; this feeling forms a large part of the driving force, the motivation in this process. Lack of agreement between expectations and their fulfillment in work and work environment leads to dissatisfaction—a conflict, or a tension which the individual tries to resolve; consciously or unconsciously he tries to flee from this situation.

The "effect," dissatisfaction, then becomes the "cause" of the next phase in the adjustment process between the individual and his work and work environment. This phase, in its turn, leads to an "effect," a feeling of dissatisfaction or satisfaction, which then forms the driving force in a subsequent phase, and so on.

In the course of the adaptation process, the individual forms opinions about himself, his ability, his chances of development, his identity. In accordance with, among other things, the demands which work and work environment make, his needs and expectations are adjusted. If the demands are too one-sided and simple, if his job is seen as uninteresting and unqualified, the individual tends to adjust his expectations downward, withdrawing and becoming passive. If these demands are more varied and complex, if he finds his job meaningful and interesting, he will adjust his expectations upward, becoming active and engaged in order to live up to expectations and demands.*

From this point of view, the concept of job satisfaction does not denote a permanent state, but forms the emotional driving force in a continuous adaptation process between the individual and his work and work environment. Consequently, job satisfaction turns into not only a goal, a state to be reached, from the individual's point of view, but an instrument, a driving force which may lead to different courses of action in the adaptation process.

A Sequence Analysis of the Interplay Between Increased Productivity and Increased Job Satisfaction

A before and after comparative study of an organization undergoing change toward a more democratic decision-making form of operation during an experiment contains no analysis of why the changes have taken place and of the course of events while they took place. Consequently, it does not

---

* This dynamic element in the adjustment process between the individual and his environment is well documented empirically. There are a great number of clinical studies among children and adults and also many experiments with the so-called level of aspiration (K. Levin, *Field Theory in Social Science* [London: Tavistock, 1952]) and expectations and subjective probability (J. W. Atkinson [ed.], *Motives in Fantasy, Action, and Society* [New York: Van Nostrand, 1958]).

supply a basis for forecasting the future development after the experimental period is over. Nothing is known of how the new organization would react if there were a change in its market conditions or production technique. Can the new organization cope with such a changed environmental state, or will it regress to its earlier form of operation? What would be the effect on productivity and job satisfaction after such a change, which might be imagined to occur after the specialist change agents left the enterprise to its own devices?

The main objective of the URAF's "self-developing forms of organization" draws attention to the ability of the organization to adapt itself, both when there are changes in external conditions and as a result of internal dynamics; the latter is not the least important element. When these questions are discussed, it is too easy to concentrate on adaptation to external conditions, for instance, the rising educational level of the labor force, the increasingly rapid development of technologies which shortens the average life of products, the increasing difficulty of forecasting the direction of consumers' preferences, and similar factors.

The problems of analyzing self-developing forms of organization and their dynamics become visible when using the concepts of the dynamics theory, developed in the Stockholm School of Economics in the 1930s. It rests on a division of time into periods. There is, further, a distinction between discrete changes which take place at the boundary point between periods, and another type of continuous change which takes place within the periods. Among the latter would be found, for instance, a successive learning of a new production organization and a gradual shift of the level of ambitions, so that the tension between the level of ambitions and the actual experience of the job situation changes. The discrete changes, at the beginning or end of periods, could be the precipitating factors in organizaticnal changes.

Naturally, this is only a pedagogic model which is not intended as a record of what actually happens. But it serves to systematize the subject matter and explains the concepts. The course of events can now be described as certain shifts in a number of continuous variables, which develop gradually during each time period so that certain tensions at the end of the period release an organizational change (a noncontinuous change) at the beginning of the following period. When the following period begins with a new organization, a number of new learning and adaptation processes start, which run up to the next period, and so on. In this way, there is an interplay between the continuous and the noncontinuous changes. URAF's work rests on the assumption that the research workers will be able to determine the character of the process by studying developments during a limited number of periods—two or three of them. Indicators can be developed of when the development will stabilize or continue toward higher levels of productivity and job satisfaction.

A concrete example would be a change in shop floor, work organization, such as a new way of arranging for sickness substitutes. Earlier this was done by supervisors; now the members of the working group arrange it between them. Is it likely that a change of this kind is the first step in a cumulative process of change, which later will mean changes, for instance, in the functioning of the time study department? Or is it likely that this change will become permanent without releasing any impulses to a continued self-development within the organization?

Another example of an initiating change would be a broadened consultation process for long-term planning of an enterprise. Is the choice of initial change decisive to the course of events that follow? And, further, what are the similarities and differences in processes of learning for different categories within the enterprise or the shifts in attitudes and levels of ambition, which accompany initial changes of various kinds? The fundamental hypothesis of this way of reasoning is that some types of initiating activities for self-development lead to a similar kind of dynamic process, regardless of other conditions in different kinds of enterprises. Alternatively, these other conditions may possibly be analyzed and taken into account, so that experiences can be systematized.

Presumably an initial change in a manufacturing company which only brings about changes in attitudes and altered levels of ambition among the workers, but has no corresponding effects among the groups of salaried employees who do time studies, planning, preparation, and similar tasks, will not lead to a cumulative process. It remains an initial change, the effects of which will disappear relatively rapidly; it will not lead to continuous self-development in the organization. Such development would probably require that impulses to change pass on in an efficient way to other groups of technical and managerial staff and that these impulses alter the way of thinking and working among the affected groups in the following time period. Thus a change in the job organization for workers leads in turn to new impulses reaching planners, and others at various organization levels.

A cumulative process of this kind probably runs its course after a number of periods if it does not reach other parts of the enterprise, for example, the accounting or sales departments. It runs the risk of being halted by the accounting system, when the changes effected during the process are of such a kind that the old accounting methods can no longer adequately measure their effects on profitability. Each accounting system is adapted to a certain kind of work organization and through a process of development must become compatible with the newly evolved form of work organization if it is not to be inhibited. The same applies to sales. When a new method of production has been initiated, it must also affect the method of selling. So, for example, when the enterprise learns to switch more quickly and smoothly than before between different models within a given period, it must then utilize this advantage in market competition so that it can offer new varieties more rapidly than its competitors. In turn, a new, more flexible way of selling then affects the production organization.

The general aim of planning research must be to create opportunities to follow a process of change through the various departments of an enterprise. Efforts should be directed at identifying and analyzing the systematic causal relationship through which one function influences another in a cumulative process, so that the organization as a whole develops toward achieving greater productivity and greater opportunities of providing job satisfaction for the individual employee.

In this context, there is a central question for URAF: Is there a recurring pattern in the process of change so that certain features are repeated? For instance, in the dispersion from the shop floor to the planning department and back to the shop floor, in the further dispersion to the construction department and from there back to planning, back to the shop floor, then from there perhaps to sales, and so on.

In actual practice, the specialists engaged in this research cannot stay in an enterprise for more than a few of these time periods or phases of dispersion. Consequently, no particularly long sequence periods can be observed in a single project. But knowledge of what a long chain in an actual process of change looks like may be obtained by combining systematized, abstract information about different components, for instance, from a project on the shop floor, from one on supervision, from one on time study departments, and so on.

To support the research URAF has developed a scheme in which projects are begun at different starting points. The next step is to find out from the various projects if there are similar courses of events—if any regularly recurring patterns can be discerned in those parts of the processes in different departments of the enterprise where changes have been introduced. Consequently, the interesting and generally valid question is not whether a certain step of progress leads to a large or a small increase in productivity and job satisfaction, measured in a certain way, but whether it may be a link in a longer chain of changes. For example: When assembling a certain kind of engine, workers, supervisors, and production technicians carry out an experiment together, which leads to a relatively limited increase in productivity and job satisfaction. This is what happens in the first period.

In the second period, the production technicians analyze their experiences and draw certain general conclusions. Then the interesting element enters, that is, the production technicians transform these conclusions into a new expansion of production, thus gaining an entirely different degree of freedom than they had in the old manufacturing process. They can order new machinery and design a new layout according to their new ideas.

In the third period the new plant is being put into operation. There may not be a very great increase in productivity and job satisfaction in this period either, but a new pattern of joint consultation has been established on a much larger scale. Now perhaps several hundred workers are affected, involving a considerable volume of production. The pattern of joint consultation leads to a new form of organization, which in the fourth period utilizes the new machinery and the new layout of the factory in a better way than the production technicians had devised for the third period. Only then—in the fourth period—does the truly significant change take place in productivity and job satisfaction.

But the experiment ends at this stage and the question arises, Are there prospects for further development? Yes, there are, if the management draws conclusions from what has happened and brings new organizational groups into the process, initiates new joint consultation processes, and so on. If the experience is to be meaningful, the pattern for self-development formed during the first four periods of the process should be transposed to other relationships within the enterprise—for instance, those between production and sales —to gain positive effects in productivity and job satisfaction.

What is important in this research is to identify the mutual causal relationships between, on the one hand, the gradual shifts in knowledge, levels of ambition, and whatever variables are used in the periods and, on the other, the changes in organization which take place between the periods. In this way the conditions are created for continuing self-development. A basis is also laid for review of the stability of the processes.

This approach is important from another point of view. The form of industrial organization and the fundamental ideas which characterize it have a very long history. They did not develop randomly. Rather they fundamentally reflect in a fundamental manner the structure of society as a whole. Thus, largely the same pattern of organization recurs, whether it is the way of governing of the school system by the Ministry of Education, the way military organizations face problems of command, or the way corresponding problems are resolved in enterprises. If real democracy at the place of work is to be created, rather far-reaching shifts in attitudes, ambitions, and expectations must be effected among employees in different positions. There are no formulae or panaceae which will yield important useful new relationships.

The only possibility of obtaining a lasting improvement over what already exists lies in finding feasible initial changes, relatively marginal changes of previous forms, which can actually be carried out—with agreement of the parties involved—but which can trigger the change sequence described above. For instance, there may be many ways of changing the organization of work to bring about a better adaptation to the higher educational levels of the labor force, but which do not contain the ability for self-development. However, external changes are not as meaningful as those which are largely propelled by their own dynamics. Only the latter kind can start a continuing process of self-development, a stable cumulative process of interaction between increased productivity and greater job satisfaction.

Technology and Quality of Working Life

THERE is a fashionable form of technological determinism which maintains that just as the technology of the first industrial revolution was responsible for all the evils of alienation so the technology of the second industrial revolution will return the skill and self-management that its predecessor removed. This three-act opera proceeds to its inevitable end depending, like Greek tragedy, not at all on the will and choice of man but on the will of the gods of technology.

Davis and Taylor attack this technological determinism on two grounds. In the first place, the shape of technology was not predetermined by its own developmental "laws" but in substantial part by the psychosocial assumptions which its designers planned into it. Once its requirements were planned in and then regarded as a given, behavior followed the only path available, amply fulfilling the prophecy implied in the design.

In the second place, what advanced technology provides is not an automatically enhanced quality of working life but a new opportunity. For example, the shorter span of control characteristic of advanced technology *can* result in supervision whose role is mainly that of technical resource, or in supervision concerned with boundary maintenance. The poverty of extant measures of technological complexity and the persistence of psychosocial assumptions which remain in systems after whatever underlying technological rationale supplied them has ceased to exist inhibit forceful response to the new opportunity.

Davis and Taylor show how technological design incorporates assumptions about human behavior, the relative value of man and machine, and the nature of organizational design. Thus, organizations betray in their design the values dominant in society at the time their technology evolved.

Susman's selection provides an explication of the degree of system choice within a particular level of technology. He stresses that the technology of a system is *one* constraint in a network of constraints, only *some* of which need be regarded as given. He argues that certain types of work system, which he characterizes by "intrinsic" system preparation, demand technically required cooperation. If the locus of uncertainty is in the time of arrival of "signals" across the work group's boundary, elected leadership is required; if the locus of uncertainty is in the system of conversion, some form of sharing of leadership roles is required. Similar reasoning is applied to the relationship between organizational levels which facilitate autonomous group functioning.

Remembering Davis and Taylor's warnings against the use of gross techno-logical variables and about the dangers of treating organizations as techno-logically homogeneous, Susman attempts to follow through technological constraints to detailed levels of group functioning. His approach is systematic and logically self-contained, but for practical use requires to be linked with some algorithm for translating this conceptualization into measurable para-meters.

15

Technology Effects on Job, Work, and Organizational Structure: A Contingency View

Louis E. Davis and James C. Taylor

THE view of technological determinism current for the last 150 years is dangerously simplistic as the postindustrial era approaches, for it holds that technology evolves according to its own inherent logic and needs regardless of social environment. Although there are correlations between technology and organizational structure and process, there are choices available based on social system values and assumptions. It is important to make implicit the economic and social as well as technical factors included in the decision process. While it is not known to what extent psychosocial assumptions affect the design or choice of a work system, it is clear that a designer carries with him and expresses the values and assumptions of his culture. Four cases are described, each representing a different cell in a two-by-two table in which the independent variables are (1) psychosocial effects at the system and at the job level, and (2) whether or not manifestations of psychosocial effects are considered. Lack of consideration at the system level produced unexpected negative social outcomes; a similar lack at the job level is apparent in many assembly lines but folklore belief that such repetitive work is desired by and suited to some workers accommodates comfortably the exclusion of other psychosocial considerations.

Scarcity and disparities are noted in reviewing the literature on technological effects on job content and structure which may result from difficulties in measuring technology and from discontinuities among studies concerning the transitional needs of new technologies. Automated, computer-aided production calls for fewer craft skills in favor of mental, perceptual and decision-making skills. However, computer-assisted, white-collar work is becoming similar to blue-collar work of the industrial era.

Automation calls for better technically trained foremen and, frequently, an upgrading of nonsupervisory jobs in which supervision of machine systems by operators is more critical than supervision of workers by supervisors. Technological change can call for greater group cooperation and coordination and can link the emerging needs of workers with greater responsibility and discretion on the job. When designing jobs to meet the requirements of automated technology, their quality is frequently enhanced. This fact becomes visible to other workers in that industry who demand more meaningful jobs. Thus, it becomes difficult to maintain a distinction in job design solely on the basis of a distinction in technology.

There is some evidence that as work becomes more technically complex, more involvement of lowest level workers, more coordination among work groups, and more horizontal communication are required. Other studies find organizational size is more relevant to these latter features than is technological complexity. Difficulties of interpretation arise from the grossness of measures of technological sophistication and the resistance to changing psychosocial assumptions operative at the system level.

Introduction

We are living in a period of rapidly increasing, wrenching social and technological change. Organizations and job structures are undergoing change in response to these developments and because of our increased knowledge of the behavior of organizations and individuals Western industrial society is in transition from one historical era to another, and the environmental characteristics of the emerging era will lead to crisis and massive dislocation unless there is some form of adaptation. The structures of most purposive organizations, based as they are on concepts of the industrial era, are becoming increasingly dysfunctional because they stand at the confluence of changes involving technology, social values, the economic environment, and the practices of management.

As we approach the evolving postindustrial era, ways must be found to aid in developing a new appreciation of the relationships between technology, organization, and job structure, based on assessments garnered from research and state-of-the-art innovations, with special attention to changes in the technological environment.

A New Appreciation of Interactions Between Technical and Social Systems

The present view of the relationship of technology to organization and job structure, carefully nurtured for the past 150 years, is that of technological determinism—and it is dangerously simplistic.[1] It holds that technology evolves according to its own inherent logic and needs, regardless of social environment and culture. Further, it holds that to use technology effectively and thus gain its benefits for society requires that its development and application be uninhibited by any considerations other than those that its developers—engineers or technologists—deem relevant.

Technological determinism has generally been invoked to support the organizational and institutional status quo of the industrial era. For example, the claim is made that organizational structure and behavior are predetermined by technology and unalterably locked into its needs. Doomsayers predict the impending doom of society as we know it given the negative consequences of a substantial number of technical developments. While it has been shown that there are some correlations between technology and organizational structure and organizational process[2], there are choices available based on social system values and assumptions. Additionally, it is part of our new learning that the determination of technological form and its unalterable application is both misleading and defeatist. It is well known that many technological alternatives are considered by technical system planners, of which only one form is put forth in an instance. The new learning alerts us to look at the design process of production technology itself to see which social system planning and psychosocial assumptions were considered in the design of various technical system alternatives. Further, we have learned that we need to have made explicit what economic and social as well as technical factors were included in the decision process of choosing a technological form.

In the design and development of technology, we are dealing with the application of science to invent technique and its supportive artifacts (machines) to accomplish transformations of objects (materials, information, people) in support of certain objectives. The invention of technique may be engineering to an overwhelming extent, but in part is also social system design. If, then, we look at work, we can see two sets of antecedent determinants that constrain the choices available for design of tasks and job structure. First, there are the social choices already contained within the technological design; second there are the social choices contained within the organizational design undertaken to use the technology. Our present appreciation is that one rarely finds technological determinism in the pure sense of technological or scientific variables exclusively determining the design or configuration of a technical system. On the contrary, most frequently technical system designs incorporate social system choices, made intentionally or included accidentally either casually or as the result of some omission in planning. In this sense, engineers or technologists can be called social system engineers, and they are crucial to evolving new organization forms and job structure.

For the very same reason, we are led to the position that it is impossible at present to draw many cause-and-effect or even correlative conclusions about the causal effects of technology on the structure and process of organizations and jobs. Yet, today, in study after study, we are confidently offered such conclusions despite the fact that the researchers did not undertake appropriate analyses of the technological systems to ascertain incorporated psychosocial purposes and assumptions.[3] There are innumerable instances in which psychosocial assumptions indirectly or subconsciously become part of a technical system design. It is unknown to what extent psychosocial requirements or assumptions are wholly ignored in the design or choice of a technical system (particularly a work system), except insofar as the designer inevitably carries with him and expresses the values and assumptions of his culture.

Technological Alternatives in Social System Choices

Cultural or subcultural values and assumptions held by the designers of the technical systems referred to above can be manifest in at least several ways. Table 1 shows the effects of technical systems on jobs as specific elements, or on organizations or systems at a broader level; the social system effects of technology are separated into those which were consciously considered from those not considered by the designers.

Thus, the table presents four different cases or effects: cell 1 contains psychosocial system effects of technology at the system level which were not considered by the designers; cell 2 shows psychosocial system effects at the system level which were considered; cell 3 effects are at the job rather than the system level and are considered; and in cell 4 these specific job and work

TABLE 1.

| | | **Manifestations of Psychosocial Effects** | |
		CONSIDERED	NOT CONSIDERED
Levels of Psychosocial Effects	System	2	1
	Job (Task)	3	4

effects are not considered. Some brief examples of each of these four conditions are given to describe the ways in which systems designers can affect
psychosocial systems.

The case of cell 1 is illustrated in enlargement and relocation of a series
of distribution terminals in the British trucking industry. In effect, such
changes in size and location of terminals or depots are a direct function of
the changes in size and speed of the motor vehicles involved. The effects on
psychosocial systems were both unintended or not considered by the
designers of the new terminal system, but were also very widespread because
not only the jobs of the truckers, but their extra-work activities, their home,
family, and leisure time activities were greatly affected. In fact, the connection between the changes in the terminal size and location and the subsequent changes in worker behavior was not realized for some time following
the changeover.

An example of cell 2 is the case of the Norsk Hydro fertilizer plant in
Norway, already documented, in which the systems of jobs and work and
outside activities were considered in advance of implementing the technical
design of the new factory.[4]

When technical systems designers do consider psychosocial system
effects of technology, the outcome is not necessarily the enhancement of the
quality of working life. Cell 3 is an example in which the systems designers'
consideration of technical effects on humans, given their assumptions about
people, leads to greater dehumanization of work rather than to its ameliora-
tion. A number of parallel operating, automated machines for filling and
capping aerosol spray cans, with one operator attending each machine, are
arranged far enough apart so that there is no communication among the
operators. The most frequent human intervention in terms of sheer time and
effort required is the insertion of a small plastic tube into a large hole at the
top of the upright cans which pass on a circular conveyor belt in front of
the operator. The second human intervention and the basic reason for the
presence of the operator in the first place is to press a stop switch placed on
a post directly in front of him. In the event of perceptible trouble anywhere
in the machine, the operator is expected to shut off the machine and seek
help to resolve the problem. In this case, the machine design did not include

the needed sophisticated sensing devices requiring human intervention as a substitute for them. At the present time, however, it was clear that workers were designed into the system as human machine elements to perform the isolated, technologically unnecessary, and tedious task of inserting tubes which could be easily done by the machine. The decision is one in which the human task of inserting tubes into cans was developed simply because the primary task of sensing and diagnosing required human eyes and ears and, by hiring those, one also acquired a set of hands which were not to be left idle.

Cell 4 represents a situation where the psychosocial effects at the task level are not considered specifically in advance, one which in our estimation is most frequently found in industrial era organizations. On assembly lines the technological needs for material transfer are considered to the exclusion of the psychosocial task demands, which are monotonous and often unpleasant.[5] The psychosocial assumptions about people working at repetitive, machine-paced jobs are present, of course, even if technical systems planners have not explicitly considered them. Indeed, there is a veritable folklore to the effect that repetitive assembly-line work is desired by some workers and suited to the limited human capacities and aspirations of most American workers. This belief accommodates comfortably the exclusion of other psychosocial alternatives in the design of such technical systems.

The Emerging Postindustrial Era

In Western societies, the urgency implicit in the new appreciation of the relationship between psychosocial assumptions and technological choices arises because the dominant and long-held beliefs about people at work are growingly being called into question not least by workers themselves. It is the emergence of some new values and the change in the relative importance of others that lead to the recognition of an approaching epoch—the postindustrial era.

The emergence of the postindustrial era is stimulated by an ever increasing rate of change in organizations and institutions and by changes in technology. The latter contribute to changes in values, not only by evoking new social systems and roles for organizational members (for this is, if anything, a minor effect), but also by stimulating the rising level of expectations concerning material, social, and personal needs. The changes in technology also provide the wealth to support the continuously rising levels of education in Western countries which, in turn, are changing the attitudes, aspirations, and expectations of major segments of society.[6] The seeming ease with which new (automated) technology satisfies material needs, coupled with the society's provision of subsistence-level support for its citizens, has stimulated a growing concern on the part of groups and individuals about their relationship to work, its meaningfulness, and its value—a concern for the quality of working life.[7]

In the United States, questioning the relationship between work and satisfaction of material needs is widespread among university students, younger workers, women, and even among unemployed members of minorities. For industrial workers, there is a revival of concern with the questions of alienation from work, job satisfaction, personal freedom and initiative, and the dignity of the individual at the workplace. Although on the surface the frequently expressed concern involves the effects of automation on job availability and greater sharing in the wealth produced, there are indicators—restlessness among the rank and file in unions, and the latter's image as being "establishment"—that, in the United States at least, there is a changing view stemming from the increasingly tenuous relationship between work and satisfaction of material needs.

Additionally, the effectiveness of technology has shifted employment from goods production to services. The vast majority of our work force is now engaged in providing services and the same issues are important here. Our former and naïve expectation that the shift to white-collar work will bring with it a high quality of working life is now revealed as an unfounded assumption as white-collar work is increasingly organized on the principles of production technology.

Changes in Technology

Man once played three roles in any goods production technology, two of which can now be preempted by machines. His first role, as energy supplier, is now virtually nonexistent in Western industrial societies. His second role, as a guider of tools, is increasingly being transferred to machines as part of a continuing process of mechanization. Man's third traditional role is the only one that remains in existence in advanced technology or in automated work processes: that is, man as controller or regulator of the working situation or system and as diagnoser and adjuster of difficulties. Similar changes are taking place in service industries based on information technology.

Characteristics of the New Technology

Technology as developed during the industrial era has had a powerful impact on the organization of work. This trend began about 150 years ago with a number of developments in England which led to the gradual replacement of human and animal power sources and which brought about the factory system and the coordination of man and machines, stimulating the movement to rationalize or streamline the utilization of labor—and the notion of division of labor (for economic purposes). The latter was made possible by the deterministic character of industrial technology; that is, what is to be done, how it is to be done, and when it is to be done are all specifiable factors.

Organizations evolving out of the design processes implied in the industrial era reflect both this deterministic technology and the values and beliefs of Western society. A new kind of specialization of labor emerged in which jobs were deliberately fractionated so that unskilled people could perform them.[8] Under such organizational arrangements, management is reinforced in its belief that workers are unreliable, interested only in external rewards, and regard their work as a burden. This is largely a self-fulfilling prophecy because the more planning, control, and supervision management undertakes, the less is there for workers to be interested in and the less they are willing to accept responsibilities. Thus, they come to see their jobs only as an instrumental means to other ends.

The most striking characteristic of the new sophisticated (automated) technology is that it absorbs routine activities into machines rather than leaving them for people, which creates a new relationship between a technology and its embedded social system. Workers in automated systems are interdependent components required to respond to *stochastic*—not deterministic—conditions; they operate in an environment where the important events are randomly occurring and unpredictable raising needs for commitment and wide competence.

Once again, the table presented earlier can be considered in the context of this technology. That modern technology can have more varied effects on jobs and work and that the impacts on the psychosocial system may be different do not necessarily mean that those additional assumptions or alternatives will be considered by the designers.

In fact, the illustration provided for cell 3 indicates this situation rather clearly, a case of more advanced technology being coupled with industrial era assumptions about workers being considered rather directly by the designers of the equipment. Any potential for changes in human skills or demands for those skills in the illustration provided is totally ignored. As will be noted below, the new sophisticated stochastic technology requires skills related to regulation, skills in monitoring and diagnosing, skills in the adjustment of processes. These skills can be related more to group efforts and tasks rather than to individual jobs and tasks. In turn, these group activities can have an impact on organizational structure. However, referring back to the above appreciation, the designers of the technology and their implicit assumptions about people, mediate between the new stochastic technologies and their behavioral, job, or organizational effects.[9] Unfortunately, there are instances of organizations and job structures evolved to suit deterministic technology being used with stochastic technology.

Technological Effects on Job Content and Structure—A Review of the Literature

The following sections are devoted to an examination of the literature purporting to measure the effects of technology, jobs, works, and organization in order to see the extent to which contingency or mediating concepts may reconcile the differences found in those writings. This undertaking may be presumptuous since these ideas have received little attention in literature discussed, with the exception of several very recently published papers. It may also be presumptuous because there are two other explanations for the disparity of results. The first disparity is created by a lack of confidence in measures of technology such as those that cannot be replicated either because they are specific descriptions of a particular technology in a particular organization or because so little reference is provided as to exclude any potential replication of the measurement involved.

The second disparity stems from the discontinuities among the empirical studies of technology involving the traditional needs in application of a new technology. Some workers may experience job demands characteristic of the ultimate stable system, whereas job demands on other workers are transitional or temporary in relation to the ultimate stable system. For example, machines or processes may have become fully automated but transitional tasks may be maintained even though they are redundant. If these transitional jobs are in themselves not disruptive or dehumanizing, they are likely to become destructive of the system at large by virtue of invidious comparisons between what was required before and what is required after the transitional period is over.

Automation and Skills

Automated computer-aided production systems are bringing about crucial changes in the skill requirements of the job occupants. From the earliest studies of the effects of automation, shifts in skill demands have emphasized a reduction in requirements for the traditional high-coordination motor skills or craft precision skills, in favor of mental skills, perceptual skills in monitoring dials and gauges, as well as decision-making skills regarding machine adjustment or repair.[10] Other studies have found it useful to consider increased responsibility, increased need for attention and decision-making discretion as, in fact, new skill demands. It can be concluded from this early literature that demands for traditional skills are reduced in part while demands for new skills are increased.

More recent studies of the effects of technology on skills strongly support earlier findings. The aptitudes required in advanced production technology as examined in 1969, 1970, or 1971 still include aptitudes such as close attention to work processes or instruments, rapid response to emergency situations, ability to stay calm in attention-producing environments, and early detection of malfunctioning or of conditions leading to it. In addition to these characteristics such as freedom for social contact, decision-making power and variation in tasks are associated with modern technology. However, these recent studies have also noted that control over the work methods or planning of work sequences is found to be no greater in process-monitoring tasks than it was in the repetitive work tasks of the industrial era.[11]

Throughout the literature, although a number of studies deal with the white-collar area, few are concerned with jobs and skills. To summarize what is available, however, the following can be advanced.

Studies of white-collar work in computer-assisted work organizations tend to suggest that it is becoming more similar to blue-collar work of the industrial era. For example, much of this involves the replacement of manual clerks with keypunch operators.[12] Some longitudinal studies tend to suggest that job enlargement can take place in conjunction with white-collar automation.[13] The authors of these results caution, however, that these changes may not necessarily follow in other cases, and that some of the positive effects of the present case were offset by negative demands such as shift work in white-collar organizations. Also, aggregate skill demands have increased slightly while the demand for man-hours is reduced rather remarkably with white-collar automation.[14]

Worker Autonomy and Discretion; and the Redefinition of Supervision

The issue of the effect of technology on supervision has been of interest for a good many years. More particularly, at issue is the continuance—or perhaps the resurgence—of coercive, close supervision in automated industries versus the opportunity to develop supervisory styles which are more participative. Evidence collected over the past decade can be presented in support of either side. It should be noted as well that there is also a body of literature on supervisory styles which tends to negate the technological influence entirely. In turn, in other sets of studies conflicting hypotheses are supported that differences in supervision and their effectiveness are a function of subcultural values: for example, differences between rural and urban upbringing and residence. Finally, there are data that go beyond the simple test of whether or not the effect of technology on supervision is manifest.

As early as the late 1950s, but more so during the early mid-1960s, a number of studies presented evidence in favor of the position that automation leads to close and coercive supervision.[15] At the same time, other studies suggested that the reverse was true, namely, supervision was becoming more participative, open, and democratic with the introduction of automation.[16] The studies pointing to increased closeness of supervision and increased punitiveness with advanced technology had an advantage in that they could explain at least some additional portion of the variance remaining after associating supervisory style with the subcultural position being advanced by Hulin and Blood, Turner and Lawrence, and others.[17] This position, held rather strongly for a period of time, tends to support the position of managerial and engineering emphasis on industrial era values.

A number of isolated studies conducted during that period tended to suggest an absence of subcultural effects, while more recently other researchers have begun to hypothesize and test these effects more rigorously.[18] They have concluded that if there were a difference between rural and urban workers as recently as ten years ago, that difference is disappearing. As there is now a period of massive realignment of values and urban centers are increasingly transmitting values to the rural areas, there may be a leveling of regional and rural-urban differences that were noted and assumed to be valid not more than a decade ago.[19]

A number of the above studies tend to show "negative" effects of supervision as a function of automation—that is, tend to emphasize the emergence of close supervision, and tend also to couple that phenomenon of close supervision with coercion. Though it is true that span of supervisory control can become smaller with automation, this shortened span of control in itself is not necessarily close supervision nor is close supervision by itself punitive.[20]

If, in fact, a small span of control is to represent the production management of the future, it could follow that supervision becomes increasingly closer and more highly skilled until industry returns once more to the crafts notion, namely, that the supervisor is merely the most skilled of the workers—and, if work groups continue to decrease in size, they may eventually be considered as either leaderless work groups or autonomous groups of workers. This raises the question of difficulty in distinguishing supervisors from workers. The early literature, as noted above, cited evidence of changes in worker skills showing increased discretion and responsibility replacing motor skills and crafts. These new skills would seem to be more typical of supervisory than nonsupervisory employees in previous periods.

Given this, the findings relating technology to supervisory style can be roughly summarized as follows: With the coming of automation, better technically trained foremen are more frequently needed and the remaining nonsupervisory jobs are upgraded, which combines the element of worker skill with the phenomenon of close supervision and smaller supervisory control spans. It could well be postulated that higher skills in the sense defined earlier in this selection may be automation's new skill requirements of machine process supervision—supervision of machine systems by operators rather than supervision of workers by supervisors.[21]

Increasingly, however, the more recent literature describes a different role for supervisors, one that is basically a shift from controlling internal variances in the work group to controlling variances impinging on the work group from the outside; that is, coming from outside the unit or the organization as a whole.[22] Other results tend to suggest that although the supervisor may seem more concerned with technical aspects of the work process, such concern is characteristic of his role at the beginning or early in the introduction of a technological innovation and is in great measure eliminated later on.[23]

There is little direct evidence that the social system assumptions held by managers and engineers can modify the effects of technological sophistication and effects on supervision. An organizational design study conducted in Norway highlights the problem of assessing the technological effects on worker autonomy and supervision.[24] It points to management's insistence on maintaining a newly developed foreman role with strong internal group controls, together with a design for creating greater worker discretion on the job. The change achieved some measure of success in creating worker autonomy and discretion, but the company itself decided to eliminate the foreman role for this type of work after four years' experience with the internal conflict it created.[25]

Automation and Work Group Behavior

Several studies of the impact of technological change on supervisory style also looked at work group behavior.[26] These studies tended to show that changes in the direction of more meaningful group cooperation and coordination developed in conjunction with changes in the technology.

There is some causal logic which can be used in describing technological effects on work group behavior, although it is not well supported by empirical studies. This logic suggests that stochastic technologies provide a functional synthesis of formerly separated occupations. This diffusion of roles makes for less separation or overlap, forcing more contact and cooperation among members than was previously the case.[27]

Another and larger body of data uses a more associative, empirical logic, which looks at the degree of success of implementing more participative democratic and autonomous group structure with changes in technology.[28] These are not only important for the correlative evidence they provide, suggesting strongly that new types of work group behavior can be used to advantage in situations where technology is changed or changing, but they also furnish a link between the emerging needs of workers, as noted above, and greater responsibility and discretion on the job.

How far a work group is capable of responsible autonomy and can adapt itself to ongoing conditions indicates the extent to which its social structure is appropriate to the demands of the work situation. At least one researcher suggests that the difference between autocratic management and autonomous work organization lies not in the amount of control exercised by the supervisor, but in applying control to external factors affecting internal stability.[29] When technology makes it easier to evaluate results, it is then easier to supervise on the basis of results, and autocratic management of work activities is less likely.[30]

A comparison between an industry that is highly automated and one that is not demonstrates these differences very clearly. In the oil-refining industry, the tasks that remain to be performed by operators consist almost entirely of control and regulation, and the line between supervisor and worker is tenuous. The construction industry, on the other hand, still retains prominent roles for man as a source of energy and tool guidance, and supervision (often at several levels) mediates all system actions. Industrial relations officers in the oil industry are proud of their "advanced and enlightened" personnel practices. These practices may indeed be described as such, but they were not adopted for the sake of their enlightenment. They were adopted because they were, and are, a necessary functional response to the demands of process technology.[31]

Here is the point at which both the social and the technological forces can be seen working toward the same end, for "job characteristics that develop commitment." Thus requirements that promote the economic goals of the highly automated organization are exactly those beginning to emerge as demands for "meaningfulness" from the social environment: participation and control, personal freedom, and initiative.

Nor is this linking of the two threads confined to industries as highly automated as oil refining and chemicals. Most industries are neither all automated nor all conventional; they utilize a mix of the two modes of production. If an industry has some employees whose enhanced jobs were designed to meet the requirements of automated technology, then the enhanced quality of their work life is visible to all the employees of the organization and creates demands by all employees for better, more meaningful jobs. It becomes very diffcult to maintain a distinction in job design solely on the basis of a distinction in technological base.

Some recent reports argue against the position stated earlier, that work in automated technology is shifting from single jobs to a set of jobs (or group of performed activities).[32] One, a comparative survey of British companies representing several different levels of technological sophistication, concludes that in automated lathe operation, as well as continuous process operations, social interaction and group relations are less frequent than in more traditional industrial technology—as well as involving lower skill levels, as traditionally defined.

In view of the earlier discussion of the influence of social system assumptions on the design of a technical system, a possible explanation for the absence of any meaningful group structure in automated operations is the following: If the managers and technical system planners imposed job and organizational structures which flow from the assumption that people (or parts of people) are merely parts of the machine or work process, then whatever potential the technology could provide for formation of group activities would be negated.

It seems reasonable to speculate that whereas management may change some psychosocial assumptions toward higher individual worker responsibility in more automated systems, it is likely to offer more resistance to changing its assumptions about delegating authority and reducing supervision of worker behavior. In other words, it is an issue of imposing "managerial authority structure" regardless of the "work authority requirements." [33]

In reviewing the impact of technological effect on organizational structure, the literature is divided into those studies that tend to show some effect of technology on organizational structure and those that tend to show little or no relationship between technology and organizational structure. In the former case, the studies can be separated again into two categories: In the first, it is concluded in general that positive involvement of the lowest level persons in the organization, coordination among work groups, and horizontal communication are required when the technical system becomes complex.[34] Although the definitions of technological complexity vary from one study to another and, further, rely on a small amount of impressionistic data, it is interesting that the conclusions show a great deal of similarity.

In the second category are data that not only support the findings regarding communication and responsibility but tend to show more flexible organizational design as well.[35] Very tentative conclusions based on these studies and several others would affirm that more modern technologies are associated with feasible, adaptive, more formless organizations or with a bureaucracy based on a consensus and a sense of industrial community.[36]

The other studies, showing that technology is slightly or not at all related to organizational structure, consider the structural effects of a number of variables, such as organizational size and technology.[37] Both are related to organizational structure in general, but size is a better predictor. Thus the empirical evidence for technological effects on organizational structure is not only conflicting, but in even greater disarray than the results presented earlier for effects of technology on job and group structures. This is not surprising, for at least two reasons: First, the available studies utilize fairly gross, unquantified comparative judgments of degree of technological sophistication at the organizational level.[38] Such gross categorization of technological sophistication makes comparison difficult and replication impossible. Second, there seems to be considerable resistance to changing psychosocial assumptions operative at the system level. It was noted earlier that whereas management may be less willing to allow modification of group structural arrangements and more tolerant of individual job and task changes, it is likely to resist even more strongly any attempts at changing organizational form or control structure, since such modification comes even closer to touching the organizational life space of managers themselves.

Summary and Conclusions

Our review of technology in the organizational setting is based on a new appreciation that technology design implicitly or explicitly includes certain psychosocial assumptions. A wide range of studies provides some direct evidence of considerable flexibility in the design of technology in response to psychosocial assumptions, which challenges the widely accepted notion of technological determinism.

The position has been taken here that the psychosocial assumptions related to postindustrial technology are at present the most crucial (and the most useful) elements in meaningful change in organizations. This position translates into action in designing jobs and larger social systems in organizations by considering emerging values toward people and work together with extant potentials of the technology. This implies a recognition that nearly all technology is designed by exercising certain assumptions about people and work. In almost every case in the past, these have been the psychosocial assumptions of the industrial era.

This review has dealt with studies of technological effects on job and skill requirements, worker autonomy and supervision, effects on group relations, and, finally, impact on organizational structure. And, in going from the specific topics of jobs and skills to the more diffuse topics of organizational structure, agreement among results of studies has diminished. In the area of organizational structure, little direct evidence is available so far—there has been no specific effort to look for it—for establishing managerial discretion as an important variable conditioning the relation between technology and organization.[39]

The remaining studies reviewed have not directly supported the model of technological determinism or that of the decision-maker intervention model. In the former case, methodological limitations of measuring technology, at least, create enough inconsistency across studies to obviate any monolithic support for technological determinism. At the same time, these inconsistencies might themselves provide indirect evidence for the latter model as managerial discretion may account for some of the inconsistencies noted.

Evidence has been presented that, although vastly different social systems have been associated with similar technologies, these differences have typically been less than the differences among technologies. This, we reason, is probably as much a function of the dominant social values extant at the time of a technology's introduction as it is of the constraints of the technology itself. If, for example, designers considered workers to be "parts of machines" by virtue of the values of the culture at that time, then this would have an effect upon all the similar technological installations of the period. Dramatic changes in technology over the past twenty years have been associated with a general shift toward jobs, work, and organizations, which are different from those that preceded them and reflect the changing value patterns of society, as well as of technological designers specifically. Such value shifts occur slowly, however, and are by no means universal.

That many engineers and managers continue to operate with industrial era assumptions about people at work is obvious. One element evidencing the shift is the greater degree of agreement among results of studies reporting new individual worker skill-level demands of automation compared with lower agreement among results of associations between automation and psychosocial effects at the work group and organizational system levels. This, we believe, can be explained by greater tolerance on the part of managers, designers of technology, and operating systems for psychosocial changes affecting the lower levels of the organization and the individual worker, and by less tolerance for psychosocial changes with general effect on the organization as a whole or upon higher organizational levels.

Accepting that technology design also involves social system design, when psychosocial assumptions contained in the technology design are revealed, the conclusions drawn from a review of the existing literature make even more ambiguous the effects brought about by changes in technology. We have, therefore, weakened the cause-and-effect linkages previously stated by many authors.

Starting with the position that psychosocial assumptions are a part of technical system design, the effects of technology are seen in the light of a self-fulfilling prophecy. That is, the observed effects on workers and on organizations of technology reflect the assumptions held by the designers of the technological systems about men and social systems. Hypotheses held about the nature of man embedded within a technical system are operationalized in the design of the technical system. For example, when assumptions are held that a system is composed of reliable technical elements and unreliable social elements, then, to provide total system reliability, the technical design will call for parts of people as replaceable machine elements to be regulated by the technical system or by a superstructure of personal control. On the other hand, if the system designers' assumptions are that the social elements are reliable, learning, self-organizing, and committed elements, then the technical system will require whole, unique people performing the regulatory activities. Experience has shown that in the latter case such a technical system design produces effects markedly different than in the former.

We, therefore, have no alternative but to consider technical systems and social systems to be *joint* systems with elements of one system residing in the other. The consequence, then, is that in designing organizations or jobs, these two subsystems have to be jointly optimized if there is to be a mutually effective organization or job result.

The conceptualization of correlated sociotechnical systems has been supported by the experiences in action research where researchers are forced to accept the complexity of the field as an outgrowth of a triple responsibility, namely responsibility to the created system, to science, and to the greater social environment rather than merely the responsibility to science alone. Such researchers have been forced to accept the reality of how technology is designed, and of how designs of technological alternatives get to be made. From these experiences has developed the learning or appreciation that is central to this review. Future research must go beyond the limited focus of positivistic science, yet at the same time lend itself to the descriptions of the real world complexities long experienced in applied science. What is called for is an end to the acceptance of technology as given and of unidimensional concepts or effects. One important variable stressed in this report is the interaction of the decision maker's discretion both in the design of technologies and in the organization of jobs based on the assumptions about people. That the inclusion of this variable increases analytic complexity and reduces elegance in research design is accepted as necessary if we are going to develop useful causal models of organizational functioning and behavior.

Opportunities Presented by New Technology

Technology is changing, and doing so at a very high rate. This is reflected in the rate of introduction of both new porducts and new processes or techniques which are growing in sophistication, that is, more highly science based. The high rate of change has consequences for organization and job structure. On the product side, frequent new developments are leading to the growth of shorter production runs with the resulting need for adaptability of organization and workers to more changes. On the production side, there is the phenomenon of more sophisticated machines and simpler manual activities embedded within automated complex production processes, which blurs the boundaries of jobs and organization units as conventionally conceived.

Advanced technology presents us with a number of opportunities to develop new, more humane organizational forms and jobs leading to a high quality of working life.[40] First, although it poses new problems, highly sophisticated technology possesses an unrecognized flexibility in relation to social systems. There exists an extensive array of configurations of the technology that, within limits, can be designed to suit the social system's needs.

Second, the new technology both increases the dependence of the organization on individuals and groups and requires more individual commitment and autonomous responsibility in the workplace. These requirements for mutual dependence and independence provide opportunities to redress past deep-seated errors in social organization and member's roles. Such opportunities may now be at hand to overcome alienation and provide humanly meaningful work in sociotechnical institutions providing for both organizational needs and for the personal and social needs of those who work.[41] The development, over a period of nearly twenty years, of a body of theory concerned with the analysis and design of interacting technological and social systems permits a research-based examination of the organization and job design in complex environments. Advanced technology, and its mismatch with conventional industrial organization, have further stimulated this examination. The diffusion of knowledge about applications of these theories is itself changing the environment of other organizations.[42]

NOTES

1. This position has been reified in a spate of recent pronouncements, some by those seeking to show that although there be change, all is still the same, for example, see Herbert Simon, *The Shape of Automation* (New York: Harper & Row, 1964); and by those predicting impending doom, for example, J. Ellul, *The Technological Society* (New York: Knopf, 1964).

2. On technology and organization structure, see Joan Woodward, *Management and Technology* (London: Her Majesty's Stationery Office, 1958); on organizational process, see T. Burns and G. M. Stalker, *The Management of Innovation* (London: Tavistock, 1961).

3. The rare examination (L. E. Davis, R. R. Canter, and J. Hoffman, "Current Job Design Criteria," *Journal of Industrial Engineering*, 6 [1955], no. 2, 5–11) of decision rules and precepts underlying technical production system design should alert us to the trap of the self-fulfilling prophecy. As indicated subjectively, it appears that all production technologies, whether designed or selected, include social system choices. Social system requirements derived from scientific and empirical bases, from values, or from commonly held assumptions can be and are designed into technical systems or their applications (R. Boguslaw, "Operating Units," chap. 4 in L. E. Davis and J. C. Taylor (eds.), *Design of Jobs* [London and Baltimore: Penguin, 1972]).

4. E. Thorsrud and F. Emery, "Mot en Bedriftsorganisasjon," chap. 6 in *Norsk Hydro Plant* (Oslo: Tanum Press, 1969); and P. H. Engelstad, "Socio-Technical Approach to Problems of Process Control," chap. 23 in Davis and Taylor, *op. cit.*

5. The general case in cell 4 is illustrated by the assembly-line studies of Charles R. Walker and Robert H. Guest, *The Man on the Assembly Line* (Cambridge: Harvard University Press, 1952).

6. D. Bell, "Notes on the Post-Industrial Society (I and II)," *Public Interest*, nos. 6, 7 (1967); and Robert J. Heilbroner, "The Future of Capitalism," *World*, September 12, 1972.

7. L. E. Davis, "Job Satisfaction Research: The Post-Industrial View," *Industrial Relations*, 10 (1971), 176–193.

8. Charles Babbage, *On the Economy of Machinery and Manufacturers*, 1835; Frederick W. Taylor, *The Principles of Scientific Management*, 1911; and Davis and Taylor, *op. cit.*

9. The important point to remember is that these stochastic technologies are becoming more prominent in the industrial organizations of today as well as that people themselves, the workers in the labor pool, are beginning to expect more responsibility, discretion, and use of mental capabilities in jobs rather than steadfastly accepting routine, monotonous, or tedious work so characteristic of the industrial era deterministic technology.

10. W. A. Faunce, "Automation in the Automobile Industry," American Sociology Review, 23 (1958), 401–407, and "Automation Applied to the Automobile Industry," in H. B. Jacobson and J. S. Roucek (eds.), Automation and Society (New York: Philosophical Library, 1959); J. R. Bright, Automation and Management (Boston: Division of Research, Harvard Business School, 1958), and "Does Automation Raise Skill Requirements?", Harvard Business Review, 36, no. 4 (July-August 1958), 85–98; C. R. Walker, Toward the Automatic Factory (New Haven: Yale University Press, 1957).

11. Two other recent studies (Hazelhurst, Bradbury, and Corlett, 1971; and Wedderburn and Crompton, 1972) both provide evidence that skill demands of sophisticated technology can be mediated by managerial actions or attitudes. The Wedderburn and Crompton article describes the case of continuous process technology in three plants owned by the same organization. The examination of skill demands of the jobs in these three plants suggested, to these authors at least, the strong effects of individual management within the plants on the resulting nature of the jobs.

Hazelhurst, Bradbury, and Corlett studied relationships between numerically controlled machines and job characteristics, concluding that policy decisions on the part of management affect the job skill demanded of the operators as much if not more than the technology itself. R. J. Hazelhurst, R. J. Bradbury, and E. N. Corlett, "A Comparison of the Skills of Machinists on Numerically-Controlled and Conventional Machines," Occupational Psychology, 43 (1969), 169–182; and Dorothy Wedderburn and Rosemary Crompton, Worker's Attitudes and Technology (Cambridge, Eng.: Cambridge University Press, 1972). E. H. Burack, "Industrial Management and Technology Theory and Practice," unpublished paper (Chicago: Illinois Institute of Technology, Spring 1969); Bertil Gardell, Produktionsteknik och arbetsgladje [Production technology, alienation, and mental health; with English summary] (Stockholm: Personaladministrativa radet, 1971).

12. Among the studies that tend to confirm this reduction in number of skills and replacement of tedious and monotonous demands of keypunch operation are the following: Ida R. Hoos, "When the Computer Takes Over the Office," Harvard Business Review, 3, no. 4 (1960), 102–112, "Impact of Automation on Office Workers," International Labor Review, 82 (1960), 363–388, and Automation in the Office (Washington, D.C.: Public Affairs Press, 1961); W. A. Faunce, Problems of an Industrial Society (New York: McGraw-Hill, 1968); E. Hardin, "Computer Automation, Work Environment, and Employee Satisfaction: A Case Study," Industrial and Labor Relations Review, 13, no. 4 (1960), 559–567, and "The Reactions of Employees to Office Automation," Monthly Labor Review, 83 (1960), 925–932; E. Jacobson, D. Trumbo, G. Cheek, and J. Nangle, "Employee Attitudes Toward Technological Change in a Medium Size Insurance Company," Journal of Applied Psychology, 43 (1959), 349–354.

13. F. C. Mann and L. K. Williams, "Organizational Impact of White Collar Automation," Industrial Relations Research Association Proceedings, 1959; "Observations on the Dynamics of a Change to Electronic Data Processing Equipment," Administrative Science Quarterly, 5 (1960), 217–256, and "Some Effects of Changing Work Environment in the Office," Journal of Sociological Issues, 18, no. 3 (1962), 90–101.

14. E. R. F. W. Crossman and S. Laner, "The Impact of Technological Change on Manpower and Skill Demands: Case-Study Data and Policy Implications," Research Document, Department of Industrial Engineering, University of California, Berkeley, February 1969.

15. R. Dubin, "Supervision and Productivity: Empirical Findings and Theoretical Considerations," in R. Dubin, G. C. Homans, F. C. Mann, and D. C. Miller (eds.),

Leadership and Productivity (San Francisco: Chandler, 1965); Faunce, "Automation in the Automobile Industry," *op. cit.*, and L. W. Gruenfeld and F. F. Foltman, "Relationships Among Supervisor's Integration, Satisfaction, and Acceptance of a Technological Change," *Journal of Applied Psychology*, 51 (1967), 74–77.

16. R. Blauner, *Alienation and Freedom* (Chicago: University of Chicago Press, 1964); Joan Woodward, *Management and Technology*, *op. cit.*, and *Industrial Organization: Theory and Practice* (Oxford: Oxford University Press, 1965).

17. C. L. Hulin and M. R. Blood, "Job Enlargement, Individual Differences, and Worker Responses," *Psychological Bulletin*, 69, (1968), 41–55; and A. N. Turner and P. R. Lawrence, *Industrial Jobs and the Worker* (Cambridge: Harvard University Press, 1965).

18. F. H. Harbison, E. Kochling, F. H. Cassell, and H. C. Ruebmann, "Steel Management in Two Continents," *Management Science*, 2 (1955), 31–39; G. I. Susman, "Worker's Responses to Job Enlargement by Location of Childhood and Current Residence," unpublished paper, Pennsylvania State University, University Park, 1972.

19. The case of the Lordstown, Ohio, auto assembly plant (*Newsweek*, February 7, 1972) is relevant, showing that auto assembly technologies are at least as alienating to young, primarily rural workers as to the older unionized urban workers of Detroit.

20. K. E. Thurley and A. C. Hamblin, *The Supervisor and His Job* (London: Her Majesty's Stationery Office, 1963) L. K. Williams and B. C. Williams, "The Impact of Numerically Controlled Equipment on Factory Organization," *California Management Review*, 7, no. 2 (1964), 25–34; and L. E. Davis and E. S. Valfer, "Studies in Supervisory Job Design," *Human Relations*, 19, no. 4 (1966), 339–352.

21. Bright, *Automation and Management*, *op. cit.*, and "Does Automation Raise Skill Requirements?" *op. cit.*; Dubin, *op. cit.*; and Harbison et al., *op. cit.*

22. Jon Gulowsen, *Selvstyrte Arbeidsgrupper* (Oslo: Tanum, 1971) T. U. Qvale, *Etterstudier ved N O B Ø fabrikker* (Trondheim, Norway: 1967); Institute of Industrial and Social Research, Judith T. Archer, "Achieving Joint Organizational, Technical, and Personal Needs: The Case of the Sheltered Experiment of Aluminum Casting Team," selection 16, in L. E. Davis, A. B. Cherns, and associates, *The Quality of Working Life: Cases and Commentary*, (New York: Free Press, 1975).

23. Thurley and Hamblin, *op. cit.*; Mann and Williams, *op. cit.*; and Walker, *op. cit.*

24. Engelstad, *op. cit.*

25. This contingency model of technological effects on supervision has indirectly been examined by persons more involved and interested in purely supervisory activities. Cf. House, Rossel. Essentially, the present position of stochastic technological effects is congruent with Fiedler's contingency theory of leadership, at least insofar as task aspects are at best partial determinants of the leader's human relations or task emphasis. Moreover, as Fiedler himself has stated, perhaps the most important implication of his theory is that the degree to which the organization defines the group tasks directly defines what particular leadership orientation will be successful. R. J. House, "Leader Behavior and Subordinate Satisfaction and Performance: A Motivational Theory of Leadership," in E. A. Fleishman and J. G. Hunt (eds.), *Current Developments in the Study of Leadership* (Carbondale, Ill.: Southern Illinois University Press, forthcoming) R. D. Rossel, "Required Labor Commitment, Organizational Adaptation, and Leadership Orientation," *Administrative Science Quarterly*, 16 (1971), 316–320; and F. E. Fiedler, "Style or Circumstance: The Leadership Enigma," in F. E. Kast and J. E. Rosenzweig (eds.), *Contingency Views on Organization and Management* (Chicago: Science Research Associates, 1973).

26. F. C. Mann and L. R. Hoffman, *Automation and the Worker* (New York: Henry Holt, 1960); Walker, *op. cit.*; and A. J. Marrow, D. G. Bowers, and S. E. Seashore, *Management by Participation* (New York: Harper & Row, 1967).

27. Bright, *Automation and Management, op. cit.*; H. Hanke, *"Wissenschaftlich-technische revolution und berufsausbildung"* [Implications of scientific and technical change for vocational training], *Berufsbildung* (Berlin), 19, no. 1 (1965), 3–5; *I. L.O. Automation Abstracts*, 93, no. 2 (February 1966); P. G. Herbst, *Autonomous Group Functioning* (London: Tavistock, 1962); F. E. Emery, "Characteristics of Socio-Technical Systems," unpublished paper (London: T.I.H.R., January 1959); E. J. Miller and A. K. Rice, *Systems of Organization* (London: Tavistock, 1967).

28. A. K. Rice, *Productivity and Social Organization, the Ahmedabad Experiment* (London: Tavistock, 1963); and E. Thorsrud, "Industrial Democracy Project in Norway, 1962–1968," unpublished paper (Oslo: Work Research Institutes, 1968).

29. Herbst, *op. cit.*

30. Woodward, in a case study of technical change, reported that there was more delegation and decentralization at the workplace in process industries than in mass production industries. More of the machine-made decisions characteristic of the process industry were accepted over decisions made by management production planning staff because output measures became the "law of the situation" (Woodward, *Industrial Organization, op. cit.*).

31. In two studies of different oil refineries, Susman and Taylor found that relatively self-supervising work groups developed in this continuous process technology to an extent not evidenced in other industries having less sophisticated technologies. In the case of Taylor's research, it was also found that groups with more sophisticated technology were also more amenable to change in the direction of even greater autonomy and self-direction, which suggests that the original assumptions of managers and production system planners were such that they greatly undervalued the self-direction capabilities of their workers. G. I. Susman, "The Concept of Status Congruence as a Basis to Predict Task Allocations in Autonomous Work Groups," *Administrative Science Quarterly*, 15 (1970a), 164–175, and "The Impact of Automation on Work Group Autonomy and Task Specialization," *Human Relations*, 23 (1970b), 567–577; J. C. Taylor, "Some Effects of Technology in Organizational Change," *Human Relations*, 24 (1971), 105–123, and *Technology and Planned Organizational Change* (Ann Arbor: Institute for Social Research, 1971).

32. J. H. Goldthorpe, D. Lockwood, F. Beckhofer, and Jennifer Platt, *The Affluent Worker: Industrial Attitudes and Behavior* (Cambridge, Eng.: Cambridge University Press, 1968).

33. Thorsrud, *op. cit.*

34. M. Janowitz, "Changing Patterns of Organizational Authority: The Military Establishment," *Administrative Science Quarterly*, 3 (1959), 473–493; E. Litwak, "Models of Bureaucracy Which Permit Conflict," *American Journal of Sociology*, 67 (1961), 178–179; A. Touraine, C. Durand, D. Pecant, and A. Willener, *Workers' Attitudes to Technical Change* (Paris: OECD, 1965); J. D. Thompson, *Organizations in Action* (New York: McGraw-Hill, 1967); and J. D. Thompson and F. L. Bates, "Technology, Organization, and Administration," *Administrative Science Quarterly*, 2 (1957), 325–343.

35. Burns and Stalker, *op. cit.*; Blauner, *op. cit.*; and Woodward, *Management and Technology, op. cit.*, and *Industrial Organization, op. cit.*

36. In this regard Woodward's data have been used in a variety of ways: to show that (counter to her own conclusions) continuous process production can best be served by bureaucratic organizational structure (Perrow). Additional studies meant

to replicate or parallel Woodward's data suggest (like Perrow) that technologically more sophisticated or complex organizations tend also to have more rigid organizational structures (Harvey). It should be noted that Harvey's data examined the nature of product change and subunit specialization. The differences between Harvey's findings and those of Woodward may reflect an inadequate sampling of firms or may reflect the fact that Woodward did not study subunit specification or product change directly in her studies. See Charles Perrow, *Organizational Analysis: A Sociological View* (Belmont, Calif.: Wadsworth, 1970), p. 90; and E. Harvey, "Technology and the Structure of Organizations," *American Sociological Review*, 33 (1969), 247–259.

37. D. S. Pugh, D. J. Hickson, C. R. Hinings, K. M. Macdonald, C. Turner, and T. Lupton, "A Conceptual Scheme for Organizational Analysis," *Administrative Science Quarterly*, 8, (1963), 189–315.

38. Burns and Stalker, *op. cit.*; Woodward, *Industrial Organization, op. cit.*; Thompson, *op. cit.*; and Blauner, *op. cit.*

39. John Child, however, in reviewing the work of the Aston group and Joan Woodward's research program, like Cooper, suggested that ideology and the perceived interest of organizational decision makers may well influence interactions between technology and structural aspects. John Child, "Organizational Structure, Environment, and Performance: The Role of Strategic Choice," *Sociology*, 6 (1972), 1–22; John Child and Roger Mansfield, "Technology, Size, and Organizational Structure," *Sociology*, 6 (1972.), 369–393; and R. Cooper, "Man, Task, and Technology," *Human Relations*, 25 (1972), 131–157.

40. For a report of cases and description of methods and requirements for design of jobs see Davis and Taylor, *op. cit.*

41. To this end, directions that may be taken are suggested by Fromm; similarly, strategies for grasping the present opportunity are suggested in Emery. See E. Fromm, *The Revolution of Hope: Toward a Humanized Technology* (New York: Harper & Row, 1968), chap. 5; and F. E. Emery, "The Next Thirty Years: Concepts, Methods, and Anticipations," *Human Relations*, 20 (1967), 199–235.

42. The concepts were first developed in Britain (cf. Emery and Trist) and followed by developments in the United States (cf. Davis and Taylor) and recently in Norway, Holland, Canada, and Sweden. They are far from having come into common practice. Their most comprehensive application is taking place in Norway, and their most extensive application is taking place in Sweden, on a national scale, as a basis for developing organizational and job design strategies suitable to a democratic society. F. E. Emery and E. L. Trist, "Socio-Technical Systems," in C. Churchman and M. Verhulst (eds.), *Management Sciences, Models and Techniques*, vol. II (London: Pergamon, 1960), pp. 83–97; and Davis and Taylor, *op. cit.*

16

Technological Prerequisites for Delegation of Decision Making to Work Groups

Gerald I. Susman

A MODEL is presented for analyzing the technological conditions under which performance can be enhanced by delegation of decision making to work groups. Evidence is presented to support such delegation when group members must perform their tasks under conditions of reciprocal interdependence. Also, recommendations for more limited delegation are presented when group members must perform their tasks under pooled or sequential interdependence. Delegation of decision making is considered a necessary condition for reducing alienation by increasing the worker's sense of control over his immediate environment. It is not a sufficient condition, because autonomy is not equated with complexity of the decisions made. Many situations which permit the former do not provide opportunities for maximum testing of one's capabilities. The position taken here is that autonomy alone does not provide sufficient opportunities to perform challenging tasks and to participate with higher organizational levels in making the decisions which immediately affect work group behavior.

This selection offers a framework by which an organizational designer can evaluate the consequences of technological decisions for their compatibility with delegation of decision making to work groups. Autonomy refers to decisions that work group members make and carry out themselves; the greater the number of decisions made and carried out by work group members, the greater the autonomy of the work group. Compatibility of technological conditions refers to conditions which enhance or at least do not hinder effective work group performance. While, on the one hand, every concrete work place has technological conditions which require, prevent, or permit varying degrees of work group autonomy, on the other hand, this does not imply that technological conditions are "givens" which inevitably compromise the degree of autonomy that work groups can be delegated. That they may appear to be givens at a particular workplace results when decisions over major components or processes of production have been made by those who are unaware of the implications of their decisions or do not wish to acknowledge that work group autonomy is possible in their organization. The former decisions result from ignorance of the effects of technological conditions on permitting work group autonomy or because of lack of imagination concerning alternative ways of arranging technology to effectively and efficiently turn out products in a manner that makes maximum use of work group decision making (see Davis and Taylor, selection 15).

The term technology, as used in this selection, refers to "technique," which Ellul describes as "nothing more than *means* and the *ensemble of means*" and "includes every operation carried out in accordance with a method in order to attain a particular end." [1] Technique evolves as man's knowledge of his environment increases and as he develops skills to alter his environment to attain desired outcomes.[2] In addition to skills, technique includes *artifacts* which refer to inanimate objects such as tools, machines, mechanical conveyances which may assist the worker or in some cases substitute for him in performing the operations which produce desired outcomes.[3]

Technology is viewed as one constraint in a network of constraints in a particular concrete environment. Other constraints include the level of training of group members, the nature of raw materials, and uncertainty over the arrival of orders and raw materials for processing by the work group. Decisions may be made to alter any of these constraints based on a change in market strategy or the nature of products or services produced or an explicit organizational decision to alter priorities in favor of improving the job experiences of workers. Whatever the reasons for such alterations, it is important that there is an awareness of the impact these decisions have on the autonomy permitted at the workplace.

It is important to point out also that this analysis focuses on determining what kinds of decisions are compatible with given technological settings, not with whether the delegation of decisions will reduce alienation from the job or organization or increase job satisfaction. As important as this problem is, it is beyond the province of this selection. However, evidence suggests that to increase job satisfaction and motivation to improve productivity, autonomy must be accompanied by other factors such as good working conditions[4] and tasks which challenge the worker's capabilities.[5,6] Also, reduction of alienation is enhanced by permitting workers an opportunity to participate with higher organizational levels on decisions affecting their work which they are unable to make alone. Work group autonomy is considered here as a necessary but not sufficient condition for reducing alienation—in this case, by increasing the worker's sense of control over his immediate environment.

A. The Work Group as an Open System

This approach to the design of autonomous groups considers the work group as an open system, which is in dynamic interaction with its environment. The environment contains flows of materials and/or information, which may originate from parallel work groups, groups or persons in the organization's external environment, or higher organizational levels. These other systems are collectively referred to as the work group's environment.

The materials and/or information which flow across the group's boundary are of two kinds. Those flows which are processed by the work group to produce outputs acceptable to its higher organizational levels are called *signal inputs*;[7] those flows which prepare or maintain the system to process signal inputs are called *maintenance inputs*. The group processes which alter the shape, size, location, or pattern of signal inputs are called *conversion activities*.[8] Those activities which procure and replenish maintenance inputs are called *maintenance activities*.

A model is presented in Figure 1 that abstracts the processes by which the group produces products or services acceptable to higher organizational levels. This model represents the general case for all groups that perform work activities; thus, the recommendations derived from it are applicable to manufacturing or service organizations. Higher organizational levels, through their decisions, pattern the flow of signal inputs (orders, raw materials) to the work group whereupon conversion activities are undertaken to produce an output which is then returned to the work group's environment. The flow of maintenance inputs (machines, tools, members) is also patterned by the decisions of higher organizational levels. The figure shows that part of the flow of outputs is returned to the work group in the form of *feedback*, permitting the group to engage in *regulatory activities*, which relate conversion activities to each other, maintenance activities to conversion activities, and all internal activities to the external environment.

B. Regulatory Activities

Work group members can make three types of decisions which relate conversion activities to each other: (a) what activities to assign to a particular

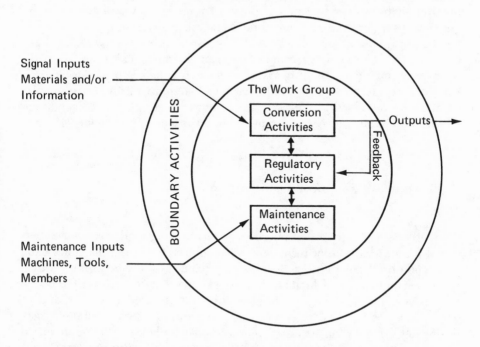

Figure 1. The Work Group and Relationships Between Its Internal Activities and Environment

member, that is, *position content*; (b) the relationship of activities within a position to each other, that is, *intraposition decisions*; (c) the relationship of activities between positions to each other, that is, *interposition decisions*. Decisions which relate maintenance activities to conversion activities are (d) what maintenance activities to assign to a *particular member*. Decisions which relate internal activities to the external environment involve (e) *boundary maintenance*.

This selection is primarily concerned with the conditions under which decisions regarding conversion activities are most effectively made by work group members. The other decisions will be discussed where appropriate.

C. Intrinsic and Extrinsic System Preparation

System preparation is the process by which a system readies itself to accept and transform the signal inputs entering it. Signal inputs may take the form of raw materials and/or information and are what the system converts into outputs. Preparation may consist of no more than activation of programmed conversion activities which were prearranged in a particular spatiotemporal configuration. In that case, system preparation is merely the recognition that an appropriate signal input has crossed the system's boundary; decisions (a), (b), and (c) can and did take place before the entry of signal inputs. This preparation process is called *extrinsic system preparation*. When decisions (a), (b), and (c) cannot take place before signal inputs cross the work group boundary, the preparation process is called *intrinsic system preparation*. The technological conditions which require intrinsic system preparation are discussed in the next two sections, the technological conditions which permit extrinsic system preparation are discussed in section H.

D. Technically Required Cooperation

A necessary condition for interdependence among work group members is that for a given state of technology (techniques, tools, and machines) and production time; any or all of the group's products[9] *cannot* be produced by a single person because of limits in individual capacities to perform the necessary conversion activities. Therefore, responsibility to produce the product or service must be assigned to two or more individuals. These limitations may be due to the size of the area for simultaneous surveillance or action, required physical strength, or multiplicity of skills. These are limiting factors in the short run although sufficient learning time may lead to innovations in technology or improved skills that alter these limiting factors. Under this condition cooperation among individuals is necessary which, to quote Barnard, "justifies itself . . . as a means of overcoming the limitations restricting what individuals can do."[10]

Meissner describes cooperation as "a relationship between two or more parties where the parties share certain properties of their environment and their behavior displays certain arrangements which regulate the distribution of whatever is shared."[11] More specifically, he uses the term *technically required cooperation* "when . . . operators perform acts necessary for the attainment of technical ends," and when operators must share, in addition to time, either the same equipment or "work piece." Equipment is a maintenance input and does not generally have, by itself, properties which are conditions requiring intrinsic system preparation; this matter will be taken up in a later section concerned with regulating maintenance activities. As to the term "work piece," Meissner notes that it refers to any material worked on and may not have the discreteness implied by the term (for example, petroleum flowing through a cracking plant or coal moving on a belt). For the purposes of this analysis, his term is considered a special case of signal input which may consist of matter and/or information to be converted by the group.

E. Conditions under Which Intrinsic System Preparation Is Required

In addition to technically required cooperation, either of the two following conditions is necessary for intrinsic system preparation:

1. The group deals with more than one class of signal inputs requiring an (a), (b), or (c) decision, for example, as usually occurs when the group is responsible for producing more than one product or service, but the time or sequence in which signal inputs cross the group's boundary is highly uncertain or the nature of the signal input cannot be specified until it crosses the group's boundary because it is poorly coded or requires expertise to interpret it. Uncertainty occurs when higher organizational levels cannot buffer demand uncertainty through rationing, forecasting, or smoothing out activities[12] and plan for a regularized flow of signal inputs. This may occur in batch-type factories which produce a number of products in small lots[13] or in groups whose primary function is boundary-spanning activities—sales, dispatching centers, and so on.[14] Signal inputs are well coded when they unambiguously inform group members of what is to be done; for example, if only one product which the group produces is made of plastic, then introduction of plastic raw materials tells the group what conversion activities are to be engaged in.

2. After signal inputs have crossed the group's boundary, the production of the group's products or services requires conversion activities whose sequence or timing is highly uncertain. This occurs when raw materials are unstable or contain properties unknown to group members requiring search to discover appropriate conversion activities. Unstable raw materials exist for teams responsible for semiautomated equipment[15] in which human interventions are required at uncertain times and in uncertain sequences. Raw materials with unknown properties exist for psychiatric teams[16] with therapeutic rather than custodial goals for their patients or for research teams developing new products.

Condition E1 refers to signal input *arrival uncertainty* and is the result of a low ability to control or interpret signal inputs *before* they cross the work group's boundary. This condition corresponds with Barnard's classification of observations which "are outside the area bounded by lines joining the positions of the observers centrally located." Condition E2 refers to signal input *properties' uncertainty* or *conversion uncertainty* and is the result of a low ability to control signal inputs or predict the consequences of actions on them after they cross the work group's boundary. This condition corresponds with Barnard's classification of observations which are "inside the area bounded by lines drawn between the positions of observers. The thing [signal input] observed is more or less centrally located." [17]

Under technically required cooperation and either or both of the above conditions, group regulation requires continual and rapid exchange of information between group members about signal inputs and conversion activities. Under these conditions, group members are in *reciprocal interdependence*; that is, the output of any group member may serve to modify the conditions of work for any or all group members. Coordination occurs under reciprocal interdependence by *mutual adjustment*; constant updating about the state of the task must be communicated to all group members to maintain effective performance.[18]

F. Group Decision Making under Reciprocal Interdependence

The recommendations in this and the following section are generalizations based on studies of group decision making where all or parts of the group's conversion activities take place under reciprocal interdependence.

1. Under reciprocal interdependence, decisions regarding conversion activities require a frequent exchange of information of varied content between group members and a decision maker. The boundaries between positions become blurred and it is difficult to distinguish (a), (b), and (c) decisions from one another. Under these conditions, decision making is enhanced when decisions concerning conversion activities are made by members of the work group rather than by a decision center external to the group. If the decision center is external to the group, that is, assigned to a position at a higher organizational level, the cost of transmitting information to the decision center is highly relative to the cost of time lags which may be critical for effective work group functioning. Moreover, the channel capacity of an external decision center is unlikely to be adequate to the varied and complex information which must be transmitted to it under reciprocal interdependence. A decision center with an inadequate channel capacity will distort, confuse, omit, filter, or abstract information that it cannot process[19] and thus be less effective under uncertain task conditions than if decisions were processed by work group members. Group members who are close to the information do not have to develop elaborate codes for transmission and they also have redundant channels for processing nonverbal and kinesthetic cues as well as verbal ones.

2. Under condition E2 information about task conditions necessary for coordination decisions may not flow from the same source, that is, same spatiotemporal location. Thus, different group members may be better placed at a given point in time to process and evaluate the information for coordination decisions. Under such circumstances, the most effective decision making may take place with a decision center whose location shifts from time to time depending on the information in the

system. McEwen calls this type of structure *redundancy of potential command*.[20]

3. Under condition E1, information about signal inputs which cross the group boundary may best be processed and evaluated by an internal nonshifting decision center occupied by an elected member of the group. The function performed by the elected "leader" is boundary maintenance (e).

G. Group Structure to Complement Autonomous Decision Making

1. A necessary condition for the effective use of redundancy of potential command is a communication network in which each member can communicate, at least serially, with other members—for example, the circle (O) network;[21] it is most effectively used, however, when each member can be in direct communication with every other member—for example, the wheel network.[22]

2. Coordination by mutual adjustment is facilitated in work groups whose members have flexible role boundaries. Studies by a number of researchers suggest that rapid adjustment to unexpected contingencies is hindered by rigid job descriptions which specify that only certain tasks are to be performed by the occupant of a particular position.[23] March and Simon present propositions which state that, under conditions of variability and contingency, specialization is sacrificed to secure greater self-containment of activities.[24] Using these propositions, this writer concludes that work groups whose members are in reciprocal interdependence are most effective when they are conditionally autonomous and their members multiskilled.[25]

3. Coordination by mutual adjustment is facilitated in work groups in which status differentiation is low. The implementation of flexible role boundaries, as suggested above, is facilitated by leveling the skill differences among group members through equal opportunities for training in all tasks. Minimal wage differences among group members also diminish status distinctions and facilitate internal mobility among the positions.

H. Task Conditions Permitting Extrinsic System Preparation

Extrinsic system preparation is possible under any of the three conditions below. The word "possible" is used rather than "required" because higher organizational levels may make (a), (b), or (c) decisions as effectively as, or more effectively than, work group members. However, if the former make such decisions, overall work group performance may be lower because of an adverse effect on the motivation of group members. The decision to delegate such decisions to work groups depends on the organization's commitment to implement work group autonomy, and its success will depend, in part, on implementing the recommendations in this and the following section.

Extrinsic system preparation is possible when:

1. Conditions exist for technically required cooperation and uncertainty over arrival of signal inputs and conversion activities is both low or absent.
2. Conditions do not exist for technically required cooperation and uncertainty over arrival of signal inputs and/or conversion activities is high.
3. Conditions do not exist for technically required cooperation and uncertainty over arrival of signal inputs and conversion activities is both low or absent.

Under condition H1, conversion activities may be either simultaneous-independent or sequential-dependent. Simultaneous-independent activities can be assigned to two or more positions with no relationships between positions other than that conversion activities occur during the same time period. This type of interdependence occurs when the limiting factor is *time:* that is, one worker cannot perform all the required activities in the allotted time; for example, two workers may be needed to simultaneously perform two or more separate actions on semimolten billets in a hot-strip rolling mill in a time period too short for one worker to perform these actions.

Sequential-dependent activities can be assigned to two or more positions, but the activities of the second position cannot begin until completion of the activities in the first position. A different worker will be assigned to each of the different positions when the limiting factor is *skill.* This may be due to lack of training or to union restrictions over which workers can be assigned to which positions; for example, a craftsman such as a glass etcher may lack the skills of a glass blower and must wait until the latter has completed his activities before beginning his own. Organizations may, of course, create sequential-dependent activities—for example, mass production assembly lines —even though it may not be necessary to do so. When this occurs, it frequently results from scientific management assumptions held by technical staff rather than from technological limitations. Assembly-line production may also be set up under condition H3 when alternative arrangements exist; this will be discussed below. In both kinds of activities, members share the same "work piece" and regulation of conversion activities consists of *scheduling*[26] their occurrence.

Whether conversion activities are simultaneous-independent or sequential-dependent, the decisions regarding their coordination can be made before signal inputs cross the work group boundary. Coordination decisions under condition H1 concern both position content and scheduling the performance of conversion activities. Work group members have a greater opportunity to make these decisions when (1) conversion activities are manual; (2) transfer operations are manual; (3) decisions do not influence parallel work groups or higher organizational levels; (4) decisions require little information about long-range organizational plans; and (5) group members have access to specialized knowledge required for decisions. If, contrary to the recommendations given above for E1 and E2 conditions, an external decision center insists on making coordination decisions that cannot be determined before signal inputs cross a work group's boundary, group members can still engage in *technically permitted cooperation*. This is, according to Meissner, worker behavior not necessary to complete an operation as technically designed but behavior still varying in relation to the behavior variations of others and regulated by mutual obligation.[27] Workers may do this if the technology, work flow, and so on do not reduce the time/distance ratio between positions (fixed by A, B, and C decisions) below a minimum value or raise the noise level above a minimum value, thus permitting workers to exchange materials and/or information in ways other than those prescribed by the external decision center.

Under conditions H2 and H3, each individual within a work group can be assigned all the conversion activities necessary to produce a complete product. Under condition H2, the natural interdependence between activities required to produce a complete product favors assigning activities to workers by product rather than by other types of specialization. The criteria for allocating complete products to positions parallel those under section I1 for allocating complete products to work groups.

The greatest choice concerning alternative ways to group activities exists under condition H3. No clear-cut discontinuities in interdependence exist between activities which favor assigning activities by product or other criteria. It is hypothesized that the jobs offering the greatest choice of design alternatives to give workers an opportunity to fashion a complete product will be found under condition H3.

When complete products are assigned to positions, the occupants of those positions are in pooled interdependence,[28] that is, each group member makes an independent contribution to the group output. Under such conditions, coordination is by *standardization* which, according to Thompson, "involves the establishment of routines or rules which constrain [the] action of each unit or position into paths consistent with those taken by others in the interdependent relationship." [29] Coordination by standardization can take place before the entry of signal inputs. Once position content decisions are made, adherence of group members to standards can be accomplished by encouraging commitment to a common objective—for example, by group payment for production.

When group members are in pooled interdependence, there is a minimal relationship between positions as regards conversion activities. However, positions may be indirectly related through maintenance activities. Decisions concerning the assignment of maintenance activities to positions may be handled by an elected group member or assigned as a responsibility of higher organizational levels. Section I4 discusses these decisions.

I. Relationships Between Higher Organizational Levels and Work Groups Which Facilitate Effective Autonomous Group Functioning

1. Self-containment of Conversion Activities

Research evidence suggests that motivation is positively affected when the work group produces a complete product,[30] that is, the group contains a repertoire of conversion activities necessary to produce the product or products for which it is held responsible. If the number of workers and resources necessary to accomplish this is greater than can be contained within a group (a decision center without echelons),[31] then products or services should be divided into subproducts and placed within separate boundaries determined by discontinuities in interdependence. E. J. Miller determines that these occur at discontinuities in technology, territory, or time.[32]

2. Scheduling

Work groups that are interdependent with other work groups for the production of a complete product can make scheduling decisions over their areas of responsibility, that is, what to produce next, if (a) the products for which these groups are jointly responsible can be produced in a divergent or convergent sequence which is known and similar for similar products, and (b) some minimal storage in space and time exists in the flow of materials and/or information between work groups. These latter two dimensions correspond to E. J. Miller's discontinuities based on territory and time. Reeves and Turner describe a batch production factory where both conditions I2(a) and I2(b) existed.[33] The production manager in this plant needed only to concern himself with flows between work groups, leaving product scheduling decisions to be made within the groups.

3. Directing the Flow of Signal Inputs

Higher organizational levels can aid work groups producing under condition E1 by directing the flow of signal inputs to it. When signal inputs consist of raw materials, this can be accomplished through improved engineering techniques introduced by staff specialists. When the work group produces a complete product or service and signal inputs consist of requisition orders from customers (internal or external to the organization) who can articulate product or service specifications, higher organizational levels can aid the work group by directing customers to the group by use of telephone, advertisement, building directories, and so on. When the customer cannot articulate product or service specifications, the organization can staff specialized boundary spanning groups to perform the function of translating demand into specifications and transmitting them to the group for processing.

4. Self-containment of Maintenance Activities

As autonomous work groups are not "toti-potential," maintenance inputs must be replenished by higher organizational levels as they are used up.[34] Disruption of ongoing conversion activities can be minimized through implementation of any of the following when conditions permit: (a) upgrading workers to perform their own setup and maintenance work; (b) enlarging group boundaries to include members who can perform the necessary group services; (c) improving scheduling by management to supply maintenance inputs as they are required; and (d) making technicians available for consultation as required.

5. Self-containment of Information

Figure 1 shows that a portion of the work group's output, flowing to parallel or suprasystems as products or services, returns to group members as feedback concerning the consequences of their conversion activities for producing acceptable outputs. Feedback is *self-contained* when group members can contribute among themselves sufficient information to assess whether conversion activities result in acceptable outputs. This is almost always the case when conversion activities are manual with or without the assistance of tools. Feedback is *disjunctive* when members cannot contribute among themselves sufficient information to assess whether conversion activities result in acceptable outputs, but must rely on parallel or suprasystems to supplement partial information.

Disjunctive feedback can be converted to self-contained feedback by assigning quality control activities to the work group. This is easiest to accomplish in manual manufacturing processes; it is more difficult when the work group produces services directly for customers or monitors semiautomated or automated equipment. In the former case, R. N. Ford reports the limination of disjunctive feedback for teams of framemen at the American Telephone and Telegraph Company by having team members contact customers directly upon completion of circuits;[35] in the latter case, self-contained feedback may not be possible (with equipment as presently designed). Under present conditions, work group members can maintain steady-state conditions by frequent interaction with supervisory and technical personnel.[36]

NOTES

1. J. Ellul, *The Technological Society* (New York: Vintage Books, 1964).

2. Ozbekhan defines knowledge about means as "information about the rules that optimize the effectiveness of any action and maximize efficiency in the application of any skill" (p. 153). He defines skill as "the physical or intellectual dexterity that a person is able to apply so as to bring about a specific desired outcome in terms of rules that pertain to the attainment of such an outcome" (p. 154). H. Ozbekhan, "Planning and Human Action," in P. A. Weiss, (ed.) *Hierarchically Organized Systems in Theory and Practice* (New York: Hafner, 1971).

3. Arendt distinguishes between tools and machines on the basis of their relationship to the worker. "Unlike the tools of workmanship, which at every given moment in the work process remain the servants of the hand, the machines demand that the laborer serve them, that he adjust the natural rhythm of his body to their mechanical movement . . . even the most refined tool remains a servant, unable to guide or replace the hand, even the most primitive machine guides the body's labor and eventually replaces it altogether" (p. 129). H. Arendt, *The Human Condition* (Chicago: University of Chicago Press, 1958).

4. F. Hertzberg, B. Mausner, and B. Snyderman, *The Motivation to Work* (New York: Wiley, 1959).

5. G. I. Susman, "The Concept of Status Congruence as a Basis to Predict Task Allocations in Autonomous Work Groups," *Administrative Science Quarterly*, 15, no. 2 (June 1970), 164–175.

6. M. Patchen, *Participation, Achievement, and Involvement on the Job* (Englewood Cliffs, N.J.: Prentice-Hall, 1970).

7. F. K. Berrien, *General and Social Systems* (New Brunswick, N.J.: Rutgers University Press, 1968).

8. E. J. Miller and A. K. Rice, *Systems of Organization* (London: Tavistock, 1967).

9. Instead of complete products, the term "products" could refer to components of products assigned to a group which cannot be produced by a single individual. In this case, recommendations for structure which follow for whole groups could apply to subgroups of two or more individuals assigned to components of products.

10. C. I. Barnard, *The Functions of the Executive* (Cambridge: Harvard University Press, 1938), p. 23.

11. M. Meissner, *Technology and the Worker: Technical Demands and Social Processes in Industry* (San Francisco: Chandler, 1969), pp. 26–27, 29.

12. J. D. Thompson, *Organizations in Action* (New York: McGraw-Hill, 1967).

13. T. K. Reeves and B. A. Turner, "A Theory of Organization and Behavior in Batch Production Factories," *Administrative Science Quarterly*, 17 (1972), 81–98.

14. J. D. Thompson, "Organizations and Output Transactions," *American Journal of Sociology*, 68 (1962), 309–324.

15. A. K. Rice, *Productivity and Social Organization* (London: Tavistock, 1958). See also G. I. Susman, "The Impact of Automation on Work Group Autonomy and Task Specialization," *Human Relations*, 23 (1970), 567–577.

16. C. B. Perrow, *Organizational Analysis: A Sociological View* (Belmont, Calif.: Brooks/Cole, 1970).

17. Barnard, *op. cit.*, pp. 29, 30.

18. See n. 12 *supra*.

19. J. G. Miller, "Living Systems: Structure and Process," *Behavioral Science*, 10 (1965), 337–379.

20. J. D. McEwen, "The Cybernetics of Self-Organizing Systems," in C. F. Benello and D. Roussopoucos (eds.), *The Case for Participatory Democracy* (New York: Grossman, 1971).

21. H. Bavelas, "Communication Patterns in Task Oriented Groups," *Journal of the Acoustical Society*, 22 (1950), 725–730.

22. H. Guetzkow and H. A. Simon, "The Impact of Certain Communication Nets upon Organization and Performances in Task Oriented Groups," *Management Science*, 1 (1955), 233–250.

23. P. G. Herbst, *Autonomous Group Functioning* (London: Tavistock, 1962). See also E. L. Trist, G. W. Higgin, H. Murray, and A. B. Pollock, *Organizational Choice* (London: Tavistock, 1963); R. N. Ford, *Motivation Through the Work Itself* (New York: American Management Association, 1969); Rice, *op. cit.*, and Susman, *Impact of Automation, op. cit.*

24. J. G. March and H. A. Simon, *Organizations* (New York: Wiley, 1958).

25. Susman, *Impact of Automation, op. cit.*

26. Thompson, *Organizations in Action, op. cit.*

27. Meissner, *op cit.*, pp. 29–33.

28. Thompson, *Organizations in Action, op. cit.*

29. *Ibid.*, p. 29.

30. Trist et al., *op. cit.* See also Rice, *op. cit.*

31. J. G. Miller, "Living Systems: The Group," *Behavioral Science*, 16 (1971), 302–398.

32. E. J. Miller, "Technology, Territory, and Time: The Internal Differentiation of Complex Production Systems," *Human Relations*, 12 (1959), 243–272.

33. Reeves and Turner, *op. cit.*

34. J. G. Miller, "Living Systems: Basic Concepts," *Behavioral Science*, 10 (1965), 193–237.

35. Ford, *op. cit.*

36. M. Fullan, "Industrial Technology and Worker Integration in the Organization," *American Sociological Review*, 25 (1970), 1028–1039.

Quality of Working Life – The Context of Change

In this part attention is shifted away from the immediate focus on the workplace to look at its context. What is happening in man's relationship to his work is bound up in his relationships to his world. If man today is immensely potent, capable of transforming his planet through his mastery of technology, he feels more impotent than ever because of technology's mastery over him. We have become dominated by our own creation and seek to free ourselves: the idealists of the alternative society by denying technology; the dropouts by accepting its benefits but rejecting its claims; the less radical by seeking to tame it.

The successes of technology were obtained through its congruence with a set of social values, motives, and institutions, whose weakening is the hallmark of our time. There is no social institution unaffected by these changes: the family, the school, the university, the church. Even the military, the police, and the organs of government, charged as they are with maintaining the fabric of society, have been swept up in these changes. At the workplace they are manifest in the difficulty of recruiting people, especially the young, for certain jobs, the challenging of traditional forms of authority and control, the rejection of career values, the preference for mere leisure over more pay.

These changes are neither catastrophic nor totally irreversible; to some extent their consequences can be absorbed by changes at the workplace or within the work organization; to some extent they are the outcome of, and respond to changes in, the work organization itself. Because of the significance of work organizations in society, changes in them have profound effects on all social activities and institutions. But whether we look to changes in society to effect changes at work, or to changes at work to bring social changes, we cannot neglect their interconnection and interdependence.

By work man relates himself to the world in which he lives, to the world of people and things around him, and to his own "self." In the active use of his powers, man fulfills and constantly creates his destiny. His work *is* the man in modern society.

Work has been man's chosen route to achieve his teleology, whatever it is. He worked for the greater glory of God in the age of faith and for greater prosperity in the economic age. When salvation by faith was replaced by salvation through work, industry replaced the church as the dominant social institution. Our political, social, and educational institutions had to be framed so as to enable industry to thrive and grow, because the products of our social institutions, men and women, were needed for this end above all.

Because industrial—and, for that matter, agricultural—work was unpleasant and hard but had to be done, submission to discipline emerged as the prime virtue. And because man creates himself by his work, he must acquire self-discipline in order to grow: he must learn to love his work. This creates the strange paradox that we must love working but, if we love doing it, it is not really "work." Tom Sawyer made the great discovery that "work consists of whatever a body is obliged to do, and play consists of whatever a body is not obliged to do." [1] What happens to a society when technology has eliminated the need for work as we have hitherto understood it? Work in the sense of self-discovery, self-creating, would presumably still be essential; work in the biblical sense would not, nor would man's work be the instrument of man's exploitation by man. Now there are signs, though they have been much exaggerated, that the dominance of industry as the principal form of work organization is passing, at least in those countries sufficiently advanced to be labeled, optimistically, as "postindustrial societies." These are the highly successful industrial societies, whose social institutions have developed to a high degree those characteristics needed for the supply and maintenance of industry. And, just because they were so efficient at instilling and developing the "work ethic," they are now less in need of it.

Social and ethical changes of this kind take time to develop; meanwhile the society's institutions are all predicated on an older morality, one example of the phenomenon described as "culture lag." When society needs change in such a fundamental aspect as its definition of work, upon which all its institutions have been built, it is bound to suffer an intense and prolonged crisis, a condition of anomie which most advanced societies are now experiencing.

As the other social institutions begin to respond to change, the old dominant institution of work is exposed and cries of betrayal are heard: the schools are no longer instilling the will to work; the family has shirked its responsibilities; the church has lost its way; and as for the universities . . . But among these voices of despair others can be heard, and they are saying hopeful things. First, however, we should try to describe the signs of change to which we have referred.

For many years now we have become accustomed to the steady decline of employment in agriculture and in the other "primary," or extractive, industries—mining and quarrying—and to a new phenomenon, the simultaneous growth in production. Beginning with the Industrial Revolution, workers left the land to enter manufacture, and employment in the manufacturing industry grew steadily. It is now declining! In the United States the factory, the paradigm of work organization, now provides employment for little more than one worker in three.

Sign 1: Manufacturing industry ceases to be the principal type of employment. In Britain there is growing reliance on immigrant workers in service occupations and in the least attractive jobs in industry. In continental Western Europe, the phenomenon of the *Gastarbeiter*, or "guest worker," is even stronger; whole sectors of German and French industry keep going by employing workers imported from Greece, Yugoslavia, Turkey, Spain, and North Africa. In the Swedish motor car assembly plants of Volvo and Saab, the assembly lines are manned by people from southern Europe, Turkey, and Finland because young Swedes will not take the jobs offered.* In the United States there coexist for the first time persistent unfilled job vacancies along-side persistent pockets of high unemployment.[2] Sometimes this phenomenon takes another, less visible form: an alternative to importing labor is exporting jobs; that is, some corporations are moving parts of their operations outside the United States because they cannot get people to do certain jobs "regard-less of what they are paid. In less developed countries there are still people anxious and ready to take them." [3]

Sign 2: Young native workers in the developed countries refuse to take certain kinds of jobs. These jobs are not just the hot, dirty, noisy ones; rather, they are jobs which deny personal satisfaction. No doubt, the worst working environments and conditions have improved beyond all recognition over the last fifty years, thanks in large part to unions. The sweatshops are things of the past: work is cleaner and safer; hours of work have steadily declined; the five-day week and the three-week holiday are the norm; unemployment bene-fits, severance pay, personnel and welfare services have all made the physical conditions of work manifestly easier. Yet absenteeism and high labor turnover have increased rather than declined.

In an enlightened society which does not need everybody's contribution to work, an individual can elect not to work if he will also accept the ambig-uous status and living standard of a dropout. Without perceiving signs of an alternative society all round us, we can yet see in Britain symptoms corre-sponding to those described in America:

> growth in the number of communes;
> numerous adolescents panhandling in such meccas as Georgetown, North Beach, and the Sunset Strip;
> various enterprises shifting to 4-day work weeks;
> increasing welfare caseloads;
> retirement occurring at ever earlier ages.[4]

Sign 3: More young people opt out of "work" altogether; more older people retire as soon as they can. More young people are also deferring their entry into the work force. Not only are many more continuing education after the

---

* The recent development of Saab Scania and Volvo Kalman are in part responses to this phenomenon.

statutory school-leaving age; many prefer not to seek a permanent career even after leaving college or university. But, as we noted, if manufacturing industry needs fewer workers, what is there to fuss about? If fewer people want to work in industry, so much the better: industry needs fewer workers.

We have already mentioned that it is not industry, even manufacturing industry as a whole, which cannot find workers; it is *some jobs* in *some industries* that are hard to fill. If the assembly line keeps cropping up in this connection, it is because it is the paradigm of a particular kind of work organization. And it is on the assembly line that the highest rates of absenteeism, the most persistent conflict and even deliberate sabotage are encountered. Indeed, in view of the objective evidence, the often quoted figures of workers who express satisfaction with their jobs can only be an indication of the low expectations people have of what their working lives will be like. But these same figures show that the young are far less satisfied with their jobs than their elders; in the United States, for example, only one third of the young white blue-collar workers are satisfied "most of the time" with their jobs, compared with half of those over age 30 and nearly two thirds of those over age 55.

Sign 4: Dissatisfaction is higher among the young. In the absence of longitudinal data, we can only conjecture whether the middle-aged worker of today was equally radical in his youth. Of course, today's 45-year-old worker entered employment in wartime and his seniors experienced the depression. We do know that in Japan, where social change has been far more rapid, the differences in attitude between young and older workers is even more marked.[5] One big question with the "generation gap" is, of course, whether the young hold their values because they are young or whether they represent a permanent change which will punctuate all of society in the long run. Takezawa believes that some of the changes in basic values are indeed permanent. As we indicated, today's young workers have stayed longer in school and, many of them are better educated than their elders.

As Gardell shows below, the result is that there are now in some countries two labor markets—one for the healthy educated young worker and the other for the rest. The employment policies of organizations allowing "natural attrition" to take care of the redundancies brought about by change of technology exports to the community the problems of the older, less educated.

In selection 21 Takezawa shows that in Japan social changes are apparently creating a three-sector labor market of young, middle-aged, and older workers; significantly, while young operate in a sellers' market, they are concerned with self-realization and more frequently feel their "abilities buried under organization."

Does it matter? If more and more people are employed in white-collar jobs, service industries, scientific and professional services, and public administration, does not this indicate the problem is diminishing of its own accord? Will not automation remove all the repetitive jobs? And if all the necessary work can be done in three or four days a week, will not people accept—indeed be quite happy putting up with—jobs they do not like? As to people retiring earlier, in a world that does not need everyone in the labor force, why worry if some want to opt out of work altogether? Can we already see an alternative society emerging to validate a life devoted to not working?

These are all pertinent questions, and in the long run they may all be answered in the affirmative. They, and many more, are needed to challenge our assumptions about work and about life. We propose here to deal only with their more immediate implications, which is a different matter. First, then, the shift of employment from manufacturing industry and the growth of the white-collar sector. One of the formerly attractive aspects of service, as compared with manufacturing industry, had been its relative freedom from close supervision and the degree of personal control it offered over the way one did a job and the time in which it was done. A further attraction of a white-collar job was its higher status, its closer and more "intimate" relationship with management. "Us" and "them" separated the manual worker from the nonmanual rather than the employee (manual and nonmanual) from the employer. False consciousness, no doubt, but from a psychological viewpoint one cannot tell how false is one's consciousness. Today, however, disaffection is prominent among workers in the service industries and public employment, and white-collar unionism is growing and no less militant than that among manual workers.

What do these manifestations mean? First, there has been a vogue for "efficiency" and "productivity," work study and scientific management in the service sector, and introduction of "systems," electronic data processing and whatnot in white-collar jobs. Independence has gone out with inefficiency and pressure has come in with productivity. And the job of the clerk finds itself on the opposite side of the technology from management. Simultaneously, the advancement to "staff" status of many manual workers has removed some of the more blatant status differentials between them and the clerks. In England, for example, the public service motive in industries such as the railways has been devalued by the recent "cost-saving" cutbacks. What all this means is that parallel with the shift of employment from manufacture to tertiary industry and from manual to nonmanual occupations, tertiary industry has been acquiring more of the characteristics of manufacturing industry and white-collar jobs have been getting less attractive. Salvation does not come automatically with these changes.

And automation? There is no doubt that automation has already removed some of the heavy, hot, unpleasant jobs. But of itself it does not remove dull, uninteresting, uninvolving jobs (though it *can* be designed to do so). It can also provide tedious lonely nerve-wracking jobs—monitoring dials in isolated clinical surroundings. Automation, like any other technological change, provides an opportunity for, and a choice of, job design; it does not necessarily provide good jobs or good working lives, which is not, of course, quite the same thing. The trouble is that the people who design automated plants are trained to have technical rather than human and social considerations in mind.

Some fifteen years ago, ergonomists (human factors psychologists) demonstrated that, to manipulate the controls of certain machine tools comfortably, you needed to be approximately four feet six inches tall and possess a reach of slightly over eight feet. Since then designs have improved a little. Even today few if any designers of automated systems consider the implications of their designs for the working life of their operatives. Thus, it is twenty-five years since the Tavistock Institute's experiments in mechanized coal mines in England demonstrated that advanced technology does not necessarily imply a particular form of work organization. But it is only ten years since they published their results in a book,[6] and even less since any of it was incorporated into the training of industrial engineers. We may hope that in time these considerations will be borne in mind when the choice of technology is made; at present quasi-scientific decisions are taken with only half the evidence considered.

Thus, in the development toward a postindustrial society there are no automatically operating factors which will insure that future jobs are less alienating than today's or that working lives improve. But perhaps work itself will become a thing of the past? After all, working lives are shorter, working hours are fewer, vacations are longer. Surely there may come a point where the investment of time in work is small enough for its discomforts to be a minor matter? This is another seductive argument, and it has some evidence in its favor. It appears that many prefer a shorter work week. Where the 4-day work week has been adopted the pattern of absenteeism has persisted in the face of changes of this kind. It is highest on the first and last days of the work week *of whatever length*. And, the fewer days there are in the work week, the greater is the proportion of the week represented by one day's absence.

The reduction of the work week as an incentive implies and encourages an instrumental orientation to work. Such an orientation generates the pressure to reduce it still further. There is no reason to postulate a point at which this instrumental orientation would be reversed. Nor is there any reason why there should be a particular length of work week which would simultaneously satisfy the need for society's work to be done and the collective wish of people to be at leisure. We might even find that the less work that has to be done, the harder it will be to persuade people to do it.

Discussing shorter work weeks and working lives raises the question of leisure. Like money, leisure is one thing when you do not have much of it, and another altogether when you have a great deal of it. Unlike money, however, it may be less attractive in large quantities than in small. It is true that work is a central life interest for some—not for all—and that the proportion for whom it is may be declining. Furthermore, those for whom it is not a central life interest probably invest less of themselves in their work. They are the instrumentally oriented workers Goldthorpe encountered on the assembly lines of Luton.[7] Faunce and Dubin have argued that if their low self-investment allows them to invest more of themselves in out-of-work activities (a "compensatory" theory), then there is much to be said for not trying to involve them further.[8] If, on the other hand, their low self-investment in work impairs their ability and motivation to invest themselves in other activities, there is reason to be concerned about a purely instrumental orientation toward work.

Faunce and Dubin, on the whole in selection 19, incline to the compensatory view; other studies, however, have shown that increased participation in decision making at work has been accompanied by increased participation in local politics and community activities. While this question remains unsettled, it seems reasonable to believe that both hypotheses are correct, but for different people. For some, emotional withdrawal or dissociation from their work is deliberate, leaving them freer for wholehearted involvement in other matters; for others, this dissociation is imposed by their situation and is emotionally debilitating. Certainly the picture of accommodation presented by Goldthorpe needs careful review in the light of the subsequent protracted industrial unrest among the groups he studied.

Therefore, we are led to conclude that current trends do not seem to be removing or reducing the problem. Indeed, it appears the problem will grow because (1) we are less willing to tolerate the harshness of our society which in the past coerced people into working at the penalty of starvation or pauperism; (2) the supply of immigrants willing to take on the disagreeable jobs is diminishing, and their native progeny are not likely to want them either. Even the first generation is beginning to rebel, as revealed by the recent Renault automobile plant strike in France. The withdrawal of their labor would be quite catastrophic. It has been estimated that there are 6 million foreign workers in the expanded European Economic Community and 1 million in Switzerland.[9] It has also been estimated that there are more Korean nurses in West Germany than in Korea, and that whole districts in Turkey are without able-bodied males.

If the "guest worker" operates as an external proletariat, the role of internal proletariat has long been taken by married women. Cultural as well as economic factors have determined the extent to which they have been used as an employment potential, as Agassi describes in selection 18. Such wide differences within the West European tradition as those between the Netherlands with 7 percent married women employed and Finland with 60 percent indicate this clearly. However, while a society may conceivably reverse its policy on immigration when foreign workers are no longer needed, the cultural changes required to adapt to such changes in employment of married women are irreversible. Moreover, women are not so content to accept the roles hitherto offered them. As Agassi says, any notion that their jobs have some- how been "nicer" than men's is misconceived.*

So, if a benevolent Providence is not solving our problems or washing them away, what then? Then we must set out deliberately to improve working lives, improve jobs. Do we know how? And do we know what makes for good jobs, good working lives? We have neither good a priori experience nor the basis of well-grounded theory on which to base our views of what constitutes a "good" job or a "good" working life. Nor are the empirical data unassailable. For- tunately, we can always hope to amass more and better data, but these cannot be obtained by conventional methods. You can ask people if they are happy in their work, satisfied with their jobs, and so on, and indeed you can obtain consistent "measures" of job satisfaction (see Part II). You can go further and identify those aspects of their jobs that people find satisfying and those they find disagreeable. And, providing that you can find ways of altering jobs so as to include more of the one and less of the other, you can then check again to see whether people are now more satisfied. This kind of procedure is well established and loosely described as "job enrichment."

But beyond this approach there are three traps: The first is that, if the hierarchy of needs is a sound concept, then the enriching of jobs to satisfy needs should and would evoke the emergence of new higher needs leading to new dissatisfactions. The logic of this theory and of job enrichment is a commitment to an ever widening horizon, a continuous process of enrichment. Self-actualization, the "highest need," is itself limitless; men like gods need jobs for gods, and outside the ranks of distinguished emeritus professorships at some universities, there are few jobs of godlike proportions.

The second trap is that of adaptation or habituation. We are most familiar with this in terms of income: a handsome salary increase is very welcome; commitments grow rapidly to absorb it and render our financial position as precarious as before. We are soon no more satisfied with our income than we were before.

The third trap concerns judgment: When asking people about their jobs they can tell you what bothers them, what pleases them, and so on along the dimensions of their actual experience. It is a far more risky matter asking them to evaluate what they have not experienced or have experienced in

---

* Even secretaries are apparently responding with their feet to the lack of stimulus in their jobs. Esso Petroleum, with a turnover of 50 percent per annum, was able to reduce this by nearly half by teaching bosses how to delegate (*London Times*, April 22, 1974).

very small degree only. When people say they would like more "participation," for example, they know they would like to have their views listened to and their ways of doing things adopted. But, in practice, participation does not mean me and my boss talking things over and coming to an agreement; it means Joe, Tom, Bill, Mary, and me working things out together. Until we experience this kind of a relationship, we cannot have valid views about whether we want more or less of it or, indeed, what we would be letting ourselves in for. If, then, we want to explore the advantages and disadvantages of making changes of this kind, we can do it only by the time-honored device of "try it and see."

In summary, we are members of a society which has become largely, although not exclusively, formed around work relationships. The big changes took place when work relationships became more and more distinct from kin or community relationships. When work ceased to be coextensive with the whole of life it became its point and focus, and our social institutions reflect this. Now, progressively, work has become problematic but not completely so. By rejecting work we reject society—not for oblivion, but for what is optimistically called the alternative society. Our institutions still embody the dominant value systems of the past which, of course, is one reason why radical youth reject all present-day organizations and institutions, forgetting that people live a long time. The authority relationships in work, needed when few were educated and the few who made the decisions took the risks, still dominate our work organizations even though the needs have passed: the need for society to order and structure all its institutions to serve industry is passing as industry ceases to be the dominant institution; authority relationships are changing in schools and universities, in hospitals (slowly), even in the armed services. As industry ceases to set the patterns for society and ceases to set the patterns for work organization, industry itself becomes more susceptible to its environment. In short, the balance between work and life is changing.[10]

Taking note of such turbulent environments, some researchers have shown that we can survive and evolve by adhering to values rather than to set goals.[11] Our own response is to seek promotion of human values in work. In doing so we must be responsive to value changes in society. The phrase "human values" has a reassuringly permanent ring to it. But these values are constantly changing and take meaning from the concrete situations to which they have to be applied, and which themselves change with technological, economic, and demographic developments. We do not have to be "progressive" or faddish but, as social scientists concerned with work and better working lives, we must be aware of the changing social definitions of work and changes in the work ethic. When the former president of the United States proclaimed his desire that Americans should rally to the work ethic, he referred to the view of work of particular classes of society, of a sector of Western civilization during a limited historical period associated with certain religious denominations: the so-called Puritan Ethic, variously linked to the emergence of capitalism, early industrialization, and the frontier mentality. For a successful demonstration of his powers, Canute should have studied the tides; the President's studies equipped him no more adequately to reverse historical trends. Values *in* work are closely related to the value *of* work and, as the latter values change, so do the former.

Unfortunately many social scientists, responsive to changes in social values and social ethics, tend to be interested primarily in the poor or the oppressed or those who appropriate the rhetoric of poverty and oppression; they tend to leave the study of industry and other work organizations to those bound by conventional wisdom. The balance between work and life is changing, a process that affects everyone. The consequences for work organizations are profound. We repose much hope in their reorganization from within. But their role in society and their relationships with the other institutions of society are changing as well. They, too, must be managed intelligently; this will require considerably broadened sensitivities calling for the addition to managers' armories of the insights and help that can be provided by the newly evolving field of social science research and application concerned with the quality of working life.

NOTES

1. Mark Twain, *The Adventures of Tom Sawyer.*

2. M. Feldstein, "The Economics of the New Unemployment," *Public Interest,* 33 (1973), 3–42.

3. Hearings before the Committee on Finance, U.S. Senate, 91st Congress. Second session on H.R. 16311 Family Assistance Act of 1970 (Washington, D.C.: Government Printing Office, 1970), Hearings, para. 3, p. 1479.

4. *Work in America,* Report of Special Task Force to Secretary of Health, Education, and Welfare (Cambridge: MIT Press, 1973).

5. S. I. Takezawa, "Changing Workers' Values and Implications of Policy in Japan," selection 21.

6. E. L. Trist, G. W. Higgin, H. Murray, and A. B. Pollock, *Organizational Choice* (London: Tavistock, 1963).

7. J. H. Goldthorpe, D. Lockwood, F. Bechhofer, and J. Platt, *The Affluent Worker: Industrial Attitudes and Behaviour* (Cambridge, Eng.: Cambridge University Press, 1968).

8. W. Faunce and R. Dubin, "Individual Investment in Working and Living," selection 19.

9. *Industrial Relations—Europe*, 1, no. 6 (June 1973).

10. Some changes are visible, such as adoption of "flex-time," nonuniform daily work schedules, permitting men and women to fit together work and other commitments. In Sweden some firms engage in group job filling, leaving who fills which jobs when to groups of women or to married couples. As with other new workplace changes, these arrangements devolve some traditional management prerogatives onto groups of workers.

17

The Quality of Working Life: Challenge to Continuity

John J. McDonough

UNDERSTANDING the challenge to continuity for the individual worker is basic to assessing the impact of the quality of working life movement. Changes it seeks to introduce call for major shifts in orientation of people at all levels of the work structure. The principal danger facing the quality of working life movement lies in underestimating the challenge it represents to continuity as seen by the ongoing organizations whose structural forms are its target. Relevant to this is the concept of "appreciative system" involving the interpretative schema which permits the individual to organize his experience and make sense of the world; it is a network of reality concepts and value concepts. The central integrative function of the appreciative system lies in its ability to reduce the vulnerability of the individual to the demands and conflicts associated with maintaining the network of relationships that define life in his environment. Change efforts which do not take account of their impact on the appreciative system run the serious risk of placing individuals into "binds" leaving no serious option other than resistance to change.

In a sense, the appreciative system is a shield between the individual and his milieu. The main difficulty in understanding the dynamics of continuity is rooted in the very function of appreciative systems, which masks the variety and character of the principal relationships that comprise the milieu.

The quality of working life movement[1] engages structures at their weakest links—the appreciative systems of workers, union officials, middle and top managers. Failure by the movement to reach beyond an incremental definition of its impact may produce structural binds leading to polemic reactions.

The paradox which confronts change efforts in the area of quality of working life is that, in order to move toward a work ethos permitting the individual to derive greater intrinsic satisfaction from his work, he must first abandon the scheme which he now employs to deal with the very discontinuities that the movement is directed at transcending. Unfortunately, widespread skill in understanding the dynamics of system continuity does not presently exist.

An appraisal of the scale and character of the structural change embodied in activities associated with the phrase, *quality of working life*, begins appropriately with an attempt to capture the levels of meaning associated with the phrase itself. The first such level merely poses the general question about the opportunities provided by the workplace to man, whereby he can find greater expression for his innermost needs. The second level moves a step beyond that by introducing a set of values which give direction to the general question. The concept of workplace democracy in its broadest context, however, is the core idea most popularly associated with the phrase. The emphasis on individual choice is symbolized by the related notions of "autonomous work group" and "self-regulation," which together capture both the spirit and direction of the structural change desired in shifting the locus of responsibility and control toward the task level.

The basic objective of this selection is to make an assessment of the impact of the quality of working life movement.[1] We seek to understand the challenge to continuity represented by the movement at the level of the individual worker in terms of its impact on the integrative scheme which he employs to manage the diverse elements making up his work environment. When viewed from this perspective, it becomes evident that the most significant challenge facing the movement lies in the fact that major shifts in orientation of individuals will be required at virtually every level of the work structure—from that of the blue-collar worker to the union official and the top corporate manager. Failure to incorporate an understanding of its impact at this basic psychological level will predictably trigger a struggle of ideological proportions, involving the basic organizing schemes whose boundaries define the limits of continuity for the individuals upon whose cooperation the success of the movement so critically depends.

The Conceptual Perspective

The weak link in existing approaches to planned change lies primarily in the lack of understanding of the dynamics of social system continuity. There are no schemes which permit the analyst to engage simultaneously to forces of continuity and the forces of change. Vickers is searching for precisely such a scheme when he states:

> If I want to intervene in some situation, so as to secure an enduring and predictable change in it, I shall usually be unwise to regard this as merely a problem of changing state A to state B. I must at least *understand the conditions which maintain state A through time* and predict those which will suffice to maintain state B.[2]

The search for the appropriate level of analysis which would provide a common denominator for thinking concurrently about change and continuity leads again to Vickers and his concept of the "appreciative system."

Appreciative Systems

It was principally through this concept that Vickers began to link the processes of continuity and change.[3] As he began to see the role which these "shared systems of interpretation" played in providing the basic "setting" and thrust of social systems, he recognized that appreciative systems were the implicit target of social change efforts and that an understanding of their general function was an essential ingredient of any systematic attempt to comprehend change processes.

There are two basic functions, one primarily psychological and the other social, at the heart of Vickers' concept of the appreciative system. The first function concerns the basic interpretative schema which permits the individual to organize his experience and make sense of the world. Vickers describes the appreciative system as "a net of which weft and warp are reality concepts and value concepts" with reality concepts providing the basic categories of experience. He devotes considerable attention to the role of values when he defines the appreciative system as "a set of readinesses to distinguish some aspect of the situation rather than others and to value these in this way rather than in that." He distinguishes these readinesses from instinct and identifies their limitations:

> These readinesses have to be learned; and like all learning, these are necessarily limiting, as well as enabling. They facilitate further learning consistent with those patterns.[4]

It is the function which Vickers outlines for the appreciative system within social systems, however, that places the psychological set squarely in the center of the change process. As to the overall regulative process within social systems, the appreciative system serves as a basic directional force through the setting it provides to the system. The settings of these shared schemes themselves become the setting of the social system, in terms of its readiness and ability to see and value one way as opposed to another. Vickers draws the analogy between the setting represented by the appreciative system and the setting of a man-made regulator, "as we speak of the setting of a man-made regulator, to describe the governing relations to which it is for the time being set to respond."[5]

The Integrative Function

The power of the concept appreciative system in thinking about continuity does not manifest itself until its integrative function is revealed more clearly. The central integrative function of the appreciative system lies in its ability to reduce the vulnerability of the individual to the demands and conflicts associated with maintaining the *set* of relationships that define life in his environment. It is this function which explains the organizing principle behind the appreciative system and provides the insight necessary to explain the massive levels of resistance that change efforts have elicited during the last decade and that underlie the need for a deeper understanding of the processes of continuity vis-à-vis change.[6]

Simply stated, change efforts which do not take systematic account of their impact on the appreciative system run a great risk of placing individuals into intense "binds," leaving no serious option other than resistance to change. Invariably, change is defined in a way that unwittingly attacks the existing appreciative system, without offering an alternative scheme which would provide a way of integrating the environment in terms of the individual's needs of dealing simultaneously with the *set* of relationships involved. The fact that resistance to change has provided an option which, when pursued collectively, is relatively low in risk (for the individual) does not take away from the fact that the impact of planned change efforts at the psychological level has been grossly underestimated, requiring that individuals abandon the basic organizing schemes which provide a central orientation toward the environment.

An understanding of the integrative function performed by the appreciative system provides a vantage point to the individual of continuity, which permits the linkage of continuity and change. Shirley Jackson's famous short story, "The Lottery," is used here as a more concrete illustration of the integrative function.[7]

The Lottery

The scene is a small modern farming community. It is the day of the annual preharvest lottery in which the entire community participates. The story focuses on the events leading up to the drawing and reaches a climax with the "winner" being *stoned to death* by friends and neighbors. The matter-of-fact, almost casual manner in which the ritual is conducted leaves the viewer unprepared for the "barbaric" outcome; it is most vividly dramatized when, as the crowd closes in for the kill, the victim's small son is handed several rocks with which to participate in the stoning.

The Integrative Function and Continuity

On the surface, the story depicts in classic terms the manner in which traditions outlive their "time." To come to grips with the forces of continuity represented in the perpetuation of the lottery, however, it is necessary first to shift one's focus from the lottery as a ritual to the appreciative system for which the ritual provides periodic reinforcement and which shapes man's basic stance toward life.

At a highly symbolic level, the lottery has become a central integrative mechanism which provides the individual member of the community with a means for dealing with the fundamental uncertainties of life—death and survival. In a subtle but significant way, it helps the individual to steel himself against the forces of fate. The beauty of its design lies in the way in which it makes a *real* winner of everyone; that is, everyone who walks away from the lottery this year and everyone who will participate in it next year do so with an unblemished record. The victim, once identified, becomes a "non-person" in the eyes of both family and community. The victim's fate serves to reinforce the survivors' own sense of invulnerability, giving them a feeling of mastery and control over fate. Annual participation in the lottery provides the individual with a psychological toughness which frees him from momentary (and perhaps paralyzing) concern with matters of death and survival—a stance, it should be added, that was highly consistent with the realities present, at one time, by the environment.

From an interpretative standpoint, the lottery assumes a major role as a "binding" mechanism which ties the community together and symbolizes its members' mutual interdependency. As such, it provides man with a basic way of integrating the major relationships in his life:

1.   man and his natural environment;
2.   man and his social environment;
3.   man and his existential environment;

the main source of uncertainty lying in the connection between man's survival and his ability to control the natural environment (i.e., food, health, shelter). In addition, it helps to provide a sense of community in a setting which is highly conducive to pitting man against man. And, finally, it helps to steel man against momentary concern with the uncertainties associated with death and survival, thus freeing him to focus his energies on more substantive activities associated with survival.

At the level of the individual member of the community, continuity is defined in terms of his ability to engage in all three relationships simultaneously. The distinct integrative function performed is the substitution of an appreciative system which stabilizes the environment and relieves the individual of the burden of monitoring the condition of those relationships individually and taken together, vis-à-vis his own needs. In a sense, then, the appreciative system is a shield between the individual and his milieu,[8] a shield which, when congruent with the situation, enables him to channel his energy into the activities that "make a difference." The price of integration is reduced sensitivity to the field of forces represented by the *set* of spatial and temporal relationships which define the corridors of his existence.

Change and the Structural Bind

Serious pressure to change or abandon the tradition will place the individual community member in a difficult predicament. Abandonment of the ritual is virtually synonymous with abandonment of the basic psychological scheme which provides stability in terms of the primary life relationships (natural, social, existential). In the absence of a new and equally functional integrative scheme, the individual has no recourse but to evaluate any change proposal as to its threat to the stability of his environment and take whatever action is necessary to defend the existing order. To advocate change which ignores this integrative function will predictably place the individual member of the community in a "structural bind." This term refers to a situation which requires abandonment of an existing appreciative system at the integrative level, where all avenues of action short of such a maneuver have dysfunctional consequences associated with them. The essence of the structural bind is the imminent danger of discontinuity defined in terms of managing the relationships which the existing scheme helps to stabilize.

The main difficulty associated with understanding the "forces of continuity" is rooted in the very function of appreciative systems which, by definition, masks the variety and character of the principal relationships that comprise the milieu in question. Lacking a grasp of the nature of the relationships whose interplay defines the integrative function performed by the appreciative system creates considerable danger that change will be defined incrementally. The problem-solving process associated with structural change is short-circuited by the fact that the first real awareness of the underlying structure of a situation and the definition of the structural problem occur simultaneously. It is this trap which gives the approach to problems involving structural change their incremental bias in terms of the manner in which the formulation of the problem shapes and limits the search for alternatives.

Three central ideas flow from this discussion of "The Lottery" which will guide the appraisal of the scale and character of the change represented by the quality of working life movement:

1.   The lottery serves to illustrate the notion that it is necessary to take one's analysis beyond the point where the shortcomings of the existing structures are identified, to the level where the forces which maintain those structures in place through time can be identified and understood. Accordingly, the ultimate prospects for the quality of working life movement lie in the ability to comprehend, at once, the functional and dysfunctional sides of the traditional structures.

2.   The key to this level of analysis is the appreciative systems which permit the individual to manage the set of diverse relationships that comprise his environment. The critical question for the quality of working life movement is: What requirements for change does the movement impose on the set of appreciative systems which exist in relation to the work environment?

3.   The third element concerns the explosive quality of change efforts that require abandonment of appreciative systems at the integrative level. From the standpoint of the quality of working life, then, the question is: What are the requirements for orderly change that necessitate major shifts at the appreciative system level?

The principal danger facing the quality of working life movement lies in underestimating the challenge it represents to continuity as seen by the ongoing institutions and organizations whose structural forms are its principal target.

The meanings attached to the phrase, *quality of working life*, discussed earlier, suggest that the movement is in serious danger of falling into the trap represented by an incremental definition of the structural shifts required. The question is not whether the values represented by "self-regulation" and the "autonomous work group" are desirable but, rather, how do we get there from here?

The Challenge to Continuity

The quality of working life movement will test the existing level of understanding structural phenomena at its weakest link—the appreciative systems of the blue-collar worker, union official, and middle and top managers, all of which will be challenged in the process. Failure to reach beyond an incremental definition of its impact will place those individuals whose basic orientations must shift in structural binds, producing the kind of polemic reactions which predictably accompany ideological conflict.

It is not necessary to go beyond the blue-collar worker in this attempt to understand the nature of the structural bind involving the quality of working life and the individual. It is not known whether all blue-collar workers welcome with open arms efforts to enrich their jobs. Efforts toward more central involvement in the work situation will clash sharply with the basic orientation toward work, as demonstrated by a sizeable segment of the work force who have exhibited an *instrumental* orientation toward the workplace.[9] The term "instrumental" denotes the fact that the central meaning of work for this segment is the provision of the means to pursue "real life interests."

The organizing principle behind the blue-collar worker's instrumental stance toward the work situation can best be characterized as an attempt to minimize the intrusion of the workplace into his total life space. The nature, then, of his structural response to the conditions, risks, and opportunities presented by the work situation has been to take up a highly defensive stance which rests on a basic assumption that in the final analysis the costs of attempting to satisfy his aspirations and needs (the economic, social, and psychological opportunities) through the workplace outweigh the benefits by some margin.

At an integrative level, this stance helps him to regulate the primary relationships in his file. The labor contract permits him to delimit the demands of time and energy which the employer can place on him (physical and psychological). It also provides the collective strength for his basic psychological orientation, which is designed to place equally sharp limits on the exchange of his view of himself as reflected in the workplace and his view of himself as an existential being. He looks beyond the workplace for his fulfillment and identity and views work as the price that he must pay for the freedom to pursue his needs outside its sphere of influence, the top priority being devoted to a stance which controls that sphere of influence.

In the short run, then, efforts to enrich jobs will run counter to the basic structural stance assumed by a sizeable segment of the work force. The blue-collar worker has sought refuge behind a shield which permits him to control the basic relationship between himself and the work situation. The very mechanisms which serve to integrate the basic relationships in his life stand squarely in the way of attempts to elicit his interest in and commitment to the kind of reform represented by the quality of working life movement. Its first requirement is that he step out from behind that shield.

Organized labor reflects, as one would suspect, a comparable orientation. Historically, its function has been to protect the worker from excessive and unreasonable demands at the workplace. Its efforts have been almost exclusively directed at increasing the ratio between such demands, on the one hand, and the economic benefits derived by the worker for his efforts, on the other.[10]

It is at the level of middle management that the structural conflict represented by the autonomous work group movement is most obvious. Middle management's very function is defined in terms of mediating the inherent tension that exists between worker and organization; the middle manager has, in a very real sense, a vested interest in the tension that exists between the top and the bottom of the organization. In this regard the notions of self-regulation and autonomous work group represent a radical shift in orientation for the "man in the middle," whose operating style is usually dictated by the needs of playing off one hierarchical level against another.

At the level of top management, the bind is exacerbated by the fact that organizations are being called upon to make several severe structural shifts in several directions at once. The quality of working life movement is not alone in the field; as a structural mechanism the organization is under enormous pressure from a number of directions:[11]

1. Accelerating but uneven rates of technological change have created an environment of considerable uncertainty for the individual firm. In terms of survival, the market economy represents an unyielding and relentless source of pressure.

2. Immediate pressure exists for the individual firm to accept greater levels of responsibility for its actions as they affect the larger society (i.e., employ hard-core unemployed, prevent air and water pollution, meet higher consumer standards, etc.).

Top management, then, is faced with the prospect of responding to increased tensions represented by the quality of working life and the social responsibility movements, without any relief of the pressures to meet traditional economic profit objectives. It is not likely that top managers will give more than "lip service" to quality of working life measures unless they can be seen as providing him with a way of bringing increased order to his task environment.

The historical and likely response is that, as organizations come under increased strain, top management will attempt to "tighten the screws" in a manner that adds to rather than alleviates the basic set of tensions. Genuine interest in quality of working life activities at that level will be contingent on a perspective which sees the movement toward increased democratization within the workplace in the context of, and congruent with, the need to make the organization more adaptive.

The key to an understanding of the lottery is the recognition that, to the individual community member, changes challenge not merely a ritual but a "way of life." The quality of working life movement represents a similar challenge. The character of the movement makes it necessary to bring the appreciative system into full view as an ingredient of change. It is not suggested that it is a unique movement (among social movements) in regard to the need to conceptualize its impact at the level of the appreciative system. Rather, it is the scale of change embodied in the movement as to the volume and variety of appreciative systems that must shift (and in relation to each other) making this need more intense.

It is recognized that the argument over the need to integrate the concept of the appreciative system into existing approaches to change will elicit mixed emotions, for the principal insight derived in the process is increased sensitivity to the "knot"—which defines the change problem. The knot embraces the fact that change requires the individual to abandon the very stance which has been instrumental in helping him to cope with the discontinuities imposed upon him by his presence in the workplace. The quality of working life movement seeks to provide individuals with the opportunity to develop greater continuity in their lives by deriving more satisfaction from their work. The paradox confronting change efforts in this area is that, in order to move toward a work ethos permitting the individual to derive greater intrinsic satisfaction from his work activities, he must first abandon the scheme which he employs to deal with the very discontinuities that the movement is directed at transcending. As a result, it is not hard to understand how the worker as well as the manager associates continuity with the status quo, and discontinuity with change. The first step, however, in unraveling this knot lies in the development of a conceptual scheme which provides an understanding of its dimensions and permits managers and workers to comprehend the nature of the shift at an abstract level.

Widespread skill in understanding the dynamics of system continuity does not exist. Accordingly, the central issue facing the quality of working life movement is the capacity of the individual work system member, who is imbedded in the existing structure and whose very way of looking at the world is an integral part of that structure, to see and understand the character of his own appreciative system in relation to the circumstances which produced it. The key, then, to both the knot and the level of choice implied by the notion of workplace democracy lies in the ability of the individual system member to reach a sufficient level of awareness of structural dynamics, as it pertains to his own situation to reach informed decisions regarding participation in quality of working life activities. The challenge represented by that movement is to provide the concepts and methods which will permit the individual to extend his understanding of structure to the level where he can begin to make it work for him.

NOTES

1. The term "movement" is used throughout this paper to refer to the broad range of activities directed at increasing the opportunities whereby man can derive greater satisfaction from his work, and which the phrase, quality of working life, helps to link together.

2. Geoffrey Vickers, *Freedom in a Rocking Boat* (New York: Basic Books, 1971), p. 197.

3. The concept of the appreciative system is developed principally in Geoffrey Vickers, *The Art of Judgement* (London: Methuen, 1965).

4. *Ibid.*, p. 68.

5. *Ibid.*, p. 67.

6. Schon's experience with change led him to coin the term "dynamic conservatism" as a descriptor of the intensity and pervasiveness of resistance. See Donald Schon, *Beyond the Stable State* (New York: Random House, 1971), chap. 2.

7. Shirley Jackson, "The Lottery," *New Yorker*, 1948.

8. The notion of the shield is developed by Peter L. Berger and Thomas Luckman, *The Social Construction of Reality* (Garden City, N.Y.: Doubleday Anchor Books, 1967), p. 102.

9. Robert Dubin, *The World of Work: Industrial Society and Human Relations* (Englewood Cliffs, N.J.: Prentice-Hall, 1958), pp. 254–258.

10. For a concise historical review of the principal orientation of the union movement and the thrust of the milestone labor legislation in the United States, see Richard Walton, "Criteria for Quality of Working Life," selection 5.

11. See F. E. Emery and E. L. Trist, "The Causal Texture of Organizational Environments," *Human Relations*, 18 (1965), 21–32.

18

The Quality of Women's Working Life

Judith B. Agassi

THERE is a fundamental difference in female and male work roles and a need for examination of the nature of these socially accepted sex-bound roles. Although no society is without a sex-based division of labor, there is an extraordinary variety of sex typing of occupations across cultures suggesting that the sex typing is not based on unchangeable, genetic, physiological, or psychological differences between the sexes, but is and has been a social construct. Industrialization brought a huge expansion of service occupations which, accompanied by increased education for girls, has created many more work opportunities and brought to the fore problems concerning "women's two roles." In all countries, to varying degrees, women's jobs remain inferior in matters of skill, pay, prestige, and authority. The main vehicle for maintaining this inferiority is the stereotype of femininity, held widely by members of both sexes—a stereotype in sharp conflict with women's actual success in the world of work. It is not only the pressure of norms which weakens women's commitment to work; it is also the inequality and low quality of their jobs. Several societal trends, however, are weakening these latter norms: the rise of the women's movement and concern over population growth. Women at work are not equally distributed within the economy. While some differences in sex distribution are understandable, others are due to prejudice and to the vested interests of the present predominantly male incumbents in many kinds of jobs. There is an erroneous impression in some quarters that most women's jobs are somehow better than men's: less difficult, more refined, and involving more service to others. However, women in industry are now performing the most fragmented and stressful jobs which require high levels of accuracy but offer little intrinsic interest. Most women do not compete in an open labor market; most are shunted into "women's work"—a matter of inequality and discrimination which, until recently, has been both widespread and legal.

New anti-discrimination laws in Western countries have brought some redress, but de facto discrimination is still rampant. Needed are more real choices for women in and out of the home: community support services, career ladders, and development of meaningful rewarding job designs.

It is futile to discuss the quality of women's working life without analyzing the very basic difference between the female and male work role. This requires an examination of the nature of the socially accepted sex roles today as well as an evaluation of the chances for their alteration in the future. At present, both sex roles in general and sex-based work roles in particular are in a considerable state of flux all over the Western world; not only is there intense criticism leveled against the status quo, and increasing experimentation with divergent patterns, but statistical evidence shows that we are now witnessing considerable changes in the work behavior of a large part of the female population.

The Female Work Role: Its History

One feature of the present division of labor of the sexes appears to be basic: women almost universally have the care of the children, especially infants and small children at least up to age 6 or 7. The physical care of small children does not necessarily involve either confinement to a nuclear family home or exclusive pursuit of the domestic chores of food preparation and the making and care of clothes; yet the female work role nearly always involves these services for the children and, with the exception of men who live outside a family-type household, for the male members of the family as well. In agricultural societies women also pursue "productive activities"—ranging from the gathering of food or its cultivation through horticulture, agriculture, and animal husbandry to food processing—not only for their own household but also for exchange or sale.

One thing is clear: As varied and extensive as the work activities outside the domestic sphere may have been in different societies and in various periods in time, it has been taken for granted that a married woman would first fill the domestic and child-care role, either by doing the work herself or by supervising other women doing it.

The Emergence of Women's Two Roles

Industrialization brought far-reaching changes in the world of work. On the one hand, the proportion of small independent self-employed entrepreneurs, farmers, artisans, storekeepers, merchants, and manufacturers in the population declined drastically. On the other hand, the numbers of those working for wages and salaries increased.

One immediate result of the Industrial Revolution was that masses of girls and women went into the new factories, just like men. Thus, the place of economic activity and the home became separated, and the old economic partnership between husband and wife, parents and children, became increasingly rare. Girls and women in great numbers worked in factories and in mines, for long hours under the harsh conditions of the time, often at great detriment to their own health and that of their children.

With time, however, parallel and coeducational schools began to offer formal education for girls, similar to that for boys. In addition, high industrialism brought with it the enormous expansion of the tertiary or service sector of the economy, with jobs for which girls and women often were at least as well qualified as men and which did not involve harsh physical conditions or night work that progressive labor legislation had meanwhile made illegal for women. In the United States unmarried girls streamed into offices, stores, banks, schools, and hospitals. Since World War II they ceased leaving automatically upon getting married, and those who did leave often returned several years later. More and more middle-class women married; the ratio of married women rose considerably and, also, of working married women. The problems of women's two roles—reentry into the labor market, part-time work, sex typing of occupations, widespread inequality and discrimination in hiring, training, promotion, pay, and fringe benefits—have now come to the fore.

Some Statistical Signposts toward Equalization

In industrialized countries today, the most important factor determining the rate of female participation in the labor force is society's attitude toward the employment of married women and especially of mothers: in the Netherlands and rural Norway, the opposition to their employment is still strong and only 7 and 9.5 percent of married women go out to work; the rate of female labor participants is 22.6 and 23.8 percent, respectively. In the United States and Great Britain, where norms have adapted to the "two roles," the figures are 41 percent and 39 percent, respectively. In Sweden and Finland, countries which have openly encouraged and favored their economic activity, 53 percent and 60 percent, respectively, of married women work.[1]

While everywhere more married women enter the labor force, the percentage of young girls in the labor market is declining in all those countries that have recently raised the age of compulsory and free education and increased the number of their student populations. In most Western countries, age curves of female labor participation still show a peak during the ages 15 to 25. Yet there is a change: before World War II there was a continuous decline after the age of 25, and no older age group achieved as high a labor participation; nowadays most countries still show a steep dip in the 25 to 30 age groups, but they also show a steady climb from age 35 upward. Female labor participation remains on a plateau until about age 55 or 60, the difference being largely determined by the official retirement age of women. In some countries this middle-age plateau is now as high and even higher than the peak participation of young women before motherhood.[2]

Though at present there are still many women in Western countries who do not work outside their own households, the percentage of employed married women, including mothers with children of school age, is constantly rising. Even at the present level of labor market participation, nine out of each ten baby girls will be employed during their lifetime. While these statistics point toward an equalization of women's worklife with that of men, it would be wrong to underrate the still existing inequalities and basic differences.

The Norms of Female Roles and Their Effect on Women's Commitment to Nondomestic Work

Statistics point to the increasing participation of women in productive work whose value is included in the GNP. Yet the degree of their participation remains less extensive—51 percent of the population making up 24–43 percent of the labor force in Western countries—and less intensive; many more women than men work part time. In addition, women's position in the world of "productive labor" is inferior in matters of skill, pay, prestige, and authority. It is argued here that the average intrinsic quality of women's jobs is also inferior to that of men's jobs. An obvious explanation of this situation derives from the fact that women are late-comers in the relatively open, competitive labor market; and, as usual, incumbents try to exclude newcomers from the better positions. The main vehicle for keeping them out and down has always been the stereotype of femininity, held widely by members of both sexes. This stereotype is in sharp conflict with women's success in the world of work.

Women's Preparation for Work

Women's education was until recently based on the assumptions that women's major achievement is marriage and children, not work and career; that proper feminine characteristics are supportive, nurturing qualities; that women are or should be noncompetitive, nonaggressive, passive, averse to taking responsibility and authority, concerned with nest-building but unadventurous and devoid of the capacity for abstract thinking. Therefore, the domestic sphere of activity is deemed more appropriate to women than the labor market; and if in the labor market, their proper position is in supportive, service, and routine activities.[3] The education of women results in less aspiration for careers and fewer marketable skills than that of men. Thus, for example, though more than half of the graduates from U.S. high schools are girls, they are considerably less than half of the graduates from college. Similarly, most women with higher education are either not trained for any occupation or trained for one of three major sex-typed occupations: grade-school teaching, office work, or nursing. There are few women in apprenticeships and vocational programs except domestic and secretarial subjects. Parents, counselors, and teachers have long neglected and discouraged the intensive and prolonged preparation of girls for highly skilled occupations and professions on the assumption that (1) these occupations and professions are unsuitable to feminine nature, and (2) the investment and effort are not worthwhile because of the expected short worklives of women. Employers have denied women training for positions of higher skill and responsibility using (1) the femininity argument, (2) the short worklife argument, and (3) the argument that men resent working for a woman. As a result, women are relatively less skilled, especially for positions of responsibility in technical and executive occupations, and in the professions.

Stages in Women's Life Cycle: Marriage

In several Western countries, even until quite recently, public and private employers used to dismiss female employees on marriage.[4] But, even without such drastic action, marriage very often seriously disrupts the worklife of women. Consequently, marriage for women has often meant a comedown from more skilled to less skilled work; it has tended to lessen women's aspirations and commitment to work as a career.

Birth of Children

In Western countries, in recent decades, the birth of the first child marked the stage in most women's life cycle when they left the labor market for a long period or even permanently. At this point, additional strong norms about the proper feminine role come into play, which condemn any desire of the young mother to work outside her home as both unnatural and callous.

In many Western countries a paid maternity leave of several weeks' duration, covering the period when the mother is physically unable to work, is part of accepted health and labor regulations. In the United States this progressive measure has not yet been established by law.

Thus, under present typical conditions in the West, of the nuclear family in its one-family dwelling, the mother of an infant either has to stay at home until the child can attend nursery school, if one is available—when she will barely be able to go out to part-time work or study—or has to find substitute day care by finding somebody to care for her infant in her own home or somebody else's home or an institutional group setting. A publicly supported or subsidized network of crèches (day care centers for infants) is found only in those societies or during those periods where and when the norm condemning the employment of mothers of infants has been breached. The same is true in regard to development and support of nursery school, kindergarten classes, school lunches, afternoon supervision for grade-school children, and even summer day camps.

Reentry

The pressure of the norms against mothers of young children working and the dearth of suitable child care arrangements have been counteracted by the following trends: (1) a reduction of the domestic role, (2) the rising education and expectations of women, and (3) the availability of many more jobs in the service sector. The result is the *reentry* of women at middle age (40–45 years) into employment or refresher study for employment. Since the 1950s labor statistics in many Western countries have pointed to this phenomenon and its growth. However, more and more younger married women, from age 30 upward, are now reentering the labor market, utilizing the gradually expanding child care services as well as family and paid arrangements. Many of these younger reentrants work part time, at least at the beginning.

According to recent evidence, it may be that a growing number of young mothers in the United States have worklives with hardly any interruption; for them the pattern of an early period of work followed by several years of an exclusively domestic role and subsequent reentry into the labor market does not apply at all. The proportion of working married women in the 20 to 24 age group (husband present) with preschool children increased from 13 percent in 1951 to 33 percent in 1970.[5]

Different Groups of Women and Length of Their Work Life

As a result of the pressures of accepted norms, the most numerous group of women, the *typical* group, those getting married and bearing children with a husband present, tend on the average to have a considerably shorter worklife than men. Other groups have longer and more intensive worklives: women with children who have no husband to support them (divorced, deserted, unmarried, or with a handicapped husband) tend to work longer years, in spite of their heavy domestic and child-rearing responsibilities, because they have a strong economic motive and because society's norms are not opposed to their working —or even demand it to prevent their dependence on welfare. Women who are married, remain married, but are childless have even longer worklives, nearly as long as those of men. Finally, the worklives of single and childless women are even longer than those of men. While this group is also heavily concentrated in women's occupations, it nevertheless contains a larger percentage of women in positions of responsibility, authority, and higher incomes than do working women in general.[6] In the past a good number of women with a strong commitment to work—for example, professionals—remained single for the express purpose of pursuing their careers. As long as the norm prescribed firing women teachers and civil servants when they got married, only single women had a chance to advance to positions of authority in these occupations. And, lastly, men considered the confirmed spinster a woman somewhat outside the conventional norm of femininity and, therefore, more suitable for positions of responsibility.

The Female Role, Commitment, and Motivation to Work

As we have seen, the effect of the pressure of accepted norms about the female role as wife and mother has been and still is weakening women's commitment to work careers. It is, of course, not only the pressure of the norms which weakens women's commitment to work; it is also the pressures of inequality and low quality of jobs. A number of societal trends are weakening these norms, such as the rise of the women's movement, the ecology movement's denouncement of population growth, the establishment of effective methods of birth control, the liberalization of sex mores, and the severe criticism of shortcomings of the contemporary nuclear family. As to the inequality and low quality of women's jobs, these aspects are still rather underrated as factors reducing women's commitment to work.

As to motivation, most working women, as most working men, declare income as the major motive for work.[7] Working women's income is of considerable economic importance, even when it is additional to the husband's. In many families, it is a woman's income which makes the difference between poverty and sufficiency or between lower and middle-class living standards. Moreover, many working women are heads of families, and often sex discrimination is the major cause of their poverty. Indeed, the major difference between men and women as far as motivation to work is concerned is not their wish to earn money, but the obstacles that society places in the way of women working at all, working full time, and earning a "living wage."

It would be very useful to know more about the factors which influence women's commitment as well as expectations and attitudes toward work. Yet, to this end it would be necessary to (1) examine meticulously women's family situations, their own and their husbands' views about women's work outside the home, their own work history, and the characteristics of their present jobs; (2) relate all this to women's perception and evaluation of the characteristics of their jobs, both "hygiene" and task characteristics; and finally (3) compare results with those of a male control group.

Present Content and Quality of Women's Work

Many have extolled the virtues of the "homemaker's" work role: the relevance of her work to the well-being of those nearest and dearest to her; the pleasant work conditions; the freedom to organize her own work and take breaks, and the variety of her tasks as cook, maid, baby nurse, educator, chauffeur, gardener, and often also bookkeeper. Yet critics from the women's movement condemn this work outright as subordinate, of low skill, limited and limiting, dirty, and unpaid.[8] Being housebound, women feel lonely and out of the mainstream of modern life. The repetitiveness and noncumulativeness of the housewife's work and the nonpermanence of her product, permit her little sense of achievement. In addition, the modern housewife is frustrated because it is hard for her to evaluate her own work performance and because society rewards her work with neither suitable recognition nor pay.

The Unequal Distribution of Women over the Occupations

Women are not equally distributed in the economy.[9] In the United States, official labor statistics divide all occupational groups into eleven categories: for men the two most populous categories (nearly equal in size) are craftsmen and foremen, and operatives, together occupying about 40 percent of all working men. Yet for women, by far the largest category, over 34 percent, is that of clerical workers (only 6.3 percent of men and the seventh category), followed by service workers except in private households, about 18 percent. The most striking difference between men and women here is that the category of craftsmen and foremen ranks ninth for women, comprising only 1.5 percent of all employed women. For men the category of managers, officials, and proprietors is the third largest, accounting for about 13 percent of the male "productive" population; for women this category ranks sixth, not quite 5 percent. Professional and technical occupations constitute the third category for women, 15.1 percent, and the fourth for men, 14.3 percent; this is the fastest growing among all categories. The fourth category for women is operatives, a category which declined slightly in importance during the sixties but has recently increased again. The fifth category for women comprises sales occupations—eighth for men—employing about 7 percent of working women who make up about 40 percent of this entire group. The seventh occupational category for women, about 4 percent, is that of private household workers, a nearly exclusively female occupation where women account for about 96 percent of the total. Significantly, it is the third—17 percent—for black women; it is also the category with the lowest pay, where work tends to be intermittent, and where workers are neither covered by minimum wage and hour laws nor benefit from unemployment and workmen's compensation.

Which other occupational categories are predominantly female? Women hold 73 percent of all clerical jobs, and 57 percent of all service jobs (except private household). Among professional and technical workers and among sales workers, women exceed slightly the average for all occupations.

From statistical evidence regarding these eleven major occupational categories one cannot learn much about the content, characteristics, and quality of women's jobs. One can see, however, that women are nearly excluded from those manual jobs in manufacturing industry that demand higher skill and training, and from industrial jobs that carry some authority and responsibility. One can see also that women in the United States are severely underrepresented in the category of managers, officials, and proprietors, and in that of farmers and farm managers, whose work role is characterized by a considerable degree of authority and responsibility and often also of initiative and autonomy. In the category which increasingly provides the largest number of jobs demanding considerable specific skills and constant use of knowledge, judgment, and initiative—professional and technical jobs—women now seem to keep pace with men.

In offiical labor statistics the eleven categories are grouped into four large categories: "manual," "white collar," "service," and "farm work." As over 48 percent of all working men (and only 16 percent of women) do "manual" work, as the largest group of working women (nearly 60 percent) perform "white collar" jobs, and as nearly 22 percent of the rest perform "service" jobs, the erroneous impression has been created that most women's jobs are somehow better than men's: less difficult, less dirty, more refined, involving more formal education, and more service to human beings. Yet an examination of the 36 occupations, in each of which more than 100,000 women worked in 1960,[10] reveals that manual jobs amounted to well over 6 million and brainwork jobs to over 4 million, while about 3½ million jobs involved a mixture of both, with the manual part usually predominant. Obviously, all clerical jobs were officially counted as white-collar jobs, whereas in reality some clerical occupations of women are largely manual (typist, file clerk, keypunch operator); most of the female "service" jobs are either semiskilled operatives' jobs—for example, in laundries—or outright unskilled cleaning jobs. Most of the lower—near exclusively female—jobs in education and health services, such as teacher's aide, nurse's aide, and practical nurse, are largely manual. The confusion is enhanced by the fact that the largest male occupational group of "craftsmen and foremen" is traditionally classified as manual, yet nowadays their work often includes a considerable amount of paperwork and even of brainwork. In conclusion, there exists absolutely no evidence for the assumption that the totality of women's jobs is comparatively more stimulating mentally than those of men.

Sex Typing of Occupations and the Dual Labor Market

Women are concentrated in a rather narrow range of occupations; or, in other words, a very large number of working women are employed in occupations stereotyped as female occupations. If we consider not the four or eleven large statistical categories of jobs, but more specific occupations, we shall see that nearly two thirds of working women are concentrated in only 36 out of hundreds of occupations, and one third in only 7 occupations: secretary, saleswoman in retail trade, private household worker, grade-school teacher, bookkeeper, waitress, professional nurse. The first three occupations—secretary, saleswoman, and private household worker—are large groups, each with well over a million workers;[11] the next three, grade-school teacher, bookkeeper, waitress, with over 700,000; the seventh, eighth, and ninth occupations—professional nurse, sewer and stitcher in industry, and typist—each have more than a half million workers. In addition, nearly all the 36 occupations which employ more than 100,000 women are also typical "women's occupations," where women make up over 50 percent of the membership; only 4 have less than 50 percent, and all have more than the 40 percent that would be proportional to the rate of women in the labor force. The sex typing of occupations is extreme: in 19 occupations, women make up 90 percent or more; in 8, from 80–89 percent; and in another 7, from 75–79 percent of the total employed. In 1960 at least 59 percent of the female labor force was in occupations where women comprised 70 percent or more of the workers.[12]

How does an activity or occupation become a female enclave? Much of this development is lost in history, yet we can look at more recent examples whose history we can still trace. A few occupations became women's occupations in times when male labor was short, and female labor was cheaper and sometimes also better qualified. Thus, at the time of the American Civil War, male school-teachers were in short supply and young women took their jobs at a cheaper rate. At the turn of the century when the typewriter appeared on the scene in America, young men who could spell English were scarce; young women who could spell moved into the new occupations of typist and secretary. Once an occupation is sex typed as "women's work," men tend to shy away from it and the differentiation becomes even more pronounced.

How much did physiological differences contribute initially to this occupational differentiation? With the rise of modern industry new traditions evolved. Those branches of industry which originally demanded much muscle power became male preserves, and have remained so even after further mechanization made such power redundant. In addition, a tradition evolved according to which women (and little girls) should be assigned to those industries where smaller and more delicate fingers seemed more useful, as, for example, in the spinning mills. Thus this part of the textile industry became women's work. Yet the hypothesis that female sex-typed occupations are simply extensions of the domestic role—that is, the processing of food and the manufacture of clothes—is false: the entire "apparel" or "needletrades" industry including shirt making and men's suits became a women's industry only after the old craft skills had become less important and the work had turned into low-skilled, routine production. The few remaining skilled jobs in these industries—namely, maintenance, setting up, pattern making, and cutting—remain reserved for men. Likewise, the technologically-advanced production of flour, bread, beer, and sugar are male enclaves.[13]

The following is an important characteristic of sex-typed jobs, yet one systematically overlooked in industry today: women are concentrated in those branches where the characteristics of the material—such as limp cloth and foodstuffs, or the extreme smallness of the parts to be processed and assembled, as in electric bulbs or electronic circuits—pose considerable difficulties for automation. Women in industry are now performing the most fragmented, accurate, and straining jobs. This has been explained by the contention that women have natural qualities of passivity, like routine and repetition, have a penchant for accuracy, a dislike of initiative and responsibility, and also fear mathematics and mechanics. In fact, these are not "natural" qualities; rather, women are still ready to take low quality and dead-end jobs because their commitment to work as a career is weaker than men's. They are ready to work in the poorly paid jobs of declining industries because frequently their income supplements the larger one of a husband.

The common characteristic of typical female occupations (and of women's specializations in otherwise male occupations and professions) is that of low prestige. Whenever a previously high-prestige occupation becomes female sex-typed—for example, medicine in the U.S.S.R.—it declines in prestige as well as in pay, conditions of work, and quality of task characteristics.[14] Even in those professions which have become women's work (e.g., teaching and social work), the higher, more prestigious positions remain reserved for men.

Sex typing in nearly all cases is unjustifiable—at least, no longer justifiable. Yet, the sex typing of jobs divides the labor market, creating a "dual labor market." Women do not compete in an open labor market; most are shunted into "women's work" and there compete with other women. This dual labor market facilitates inequality and discrimination.

Inequality and Discrimination

Until quite recently, outright and open discrimination against working women was widespread and legal. Women were excluded from entire occupations, from branches of industries, and from the higher reaches of other occupations simply by not hiring them or accepting them for training. Separate job advertising was the rule. The assumption, of course, was that these occupations were unsuitable for women. Likewise, open pay differentials for equal work (e.g., for identical positions in the Civil Service) were the practice; here the official justification was that women "needed" less money.

During the last two decades, however, one Western country after another has signed international and national nondiscrimination laws. Gradually, these laws have led to some practical results. Practices such as open exclusion from hiring and training, separate posting, and open pay differentials are gradually disappearing when challenged in the courts. But de facto discrimination and de facto pay differentials are still rampant. Women's income in the United States is only 62 percent of men's after adjustments have been made for level of education, occupational status, and part-time employment—according to the latest study of income differences.[15] Official figures for those Western countries that publish them range from 60 percent in Great Britain to 79 percent in Sweden, and are usually lower than the national average for women operatives in industry and somewhat higher in clerical and professional and technical jobs.

In Great Britain, even recently, many unions still concluded lower pay agreements for their women members.[16] Some cantons in Switzerland still officially maintain lower salaries for their women employees.[17] Yet today the main devices for paying women less are the hiring and segregation of women into special (all female) wage groups or separate all-female job classifications, so as to avoid the situation where women do "equal work" with men in the same firm; starting all male entrants automatically two or three wage levels above that of female entrants; not giving women chances at training and promotion; not appointing women to supervisory or administrative positions—all these devices, together with the social sex typing of occupations, keep women in a separate and inferior labor market.

What Is Needed to Enhance the Quality of Women's Working Life?

The Problem of Enhancement or Reduction of the Domestic Work Role

Is reduction or compensation for the domestic work role necessary for all women? It is quite likely that a certain number of women with strong domestic and especially strong maternal leanings can be largely satisfied and psychologically well adjusted to a prolonged or even a lifetime domestic work role. It is wrong to denigrate these women and press them into career work roles which do not suit them. Women should be neither pressured nor confined into an exclusive domestic or a full-time lifetime labor market role, but should have the choice between them. It is to be assumed that for the foreseeable future most women will aim at some combination of the two roles; day care centers will greatly facilitate this.

Most women today and in the foreseeable future will still have to fill a considerable domestic work role, and most are no longer satisfied by this role alone. Women, like men, seek work for satisfaction of the psychological needs of self-actualization, achievement, recognition, and social contact, in addition to pay; for many, these needs are no longer met by the exclusive domestic work role. Yet most women's jobs, just like most men's jobs, also fail to satisfy these needs and therefore should be redesigned.[18] Many women's jobs have certain characteristics that are especially harmful because they compound the same characteristics existing in the domestic work role: the domestic role demands very little intellectual exercise, so do most women's jobs; domestic work requires a lot of routine and repetition, women's jobs are the most repetitious in the labor market; the housewife's products are without permanence, women are concentrated in the production of nondurables; domestic work consists largely of personal cleaning and feeding services, women are concentrated in cleaning and feeding jobs; housewives suffer from lack of achievement and recognition, most women's jobs lead nowhere. In order to compensate for the domestic work role, women's jobs should be intellectually challenging: women should design, produce, and maintain more durable artifacts; deliver personal services other than just cleaning and feeding; have built-in chances for achievement, advancement, responsibility, and recognition.

What Is Needed to Eliminate Present Inferior Work Roles?

The low quality of so many women's jobs is a direct outcome of the segregation of women into a separate labor market of separate occupations, branches, and departments. A conscious effort should be made to break the sex typing of occupations; male entrants should be welcomed to the female occupations; women should gain training and entrance into previously closed or restricted occupations, especially those technologically advanced and expanding, into government, business, finance, and the professions. It should become illegal to hire women into separate job groups and pay female entrants less than male entrants. Women should demand open posting of jobs within the firm and information about qualifications needed for all jobs. They should not be excluded from any job because of obligatory overtime or night work. Women in part-time work should not be paid less per hour than in full-time work; they should have the right to proportionate fringe benefits, including pension rights. Paid maternity leave should be incorporated into labor laws of all nations. Women workers should have a right to additional optional unpaid maternity leave with job security. They should also be given the right to a period of optional part-time work without loss of pension, training, and seniority rights.

There are those who claim that as long as most women adhere to the pattern of withdrawal and reentry and/or periods of part-time work, they will not be able to overcome their relatively inferior position. In the light of recent changes in male work patterns, this seems no longer inevitable; the rigid, full-time plus overtime, year-round, uninterrupted worklife in one and the same occupation is no longer sacrosanct. Flexible work time, four-day work weeks, optional overtime, training leaves, sabbaticals, mid-career changes, all these are breaking up the conventional male work pattern. Therefore, it should not be too difficult to gain full legitimation for the female work pattern; discrimination justified by the difference between male and female work patterns should not be tolerated.

Viable Career Ladders for Women

Until now, careers for women were not the norm. That women should acquire more experience and skill and progress gradually to positions of greater challenge, responsibility, status, and pay was not considered necessary.

Women's jobs were considered as simply "jobs," not as steps in a career ladder. A young woman is hired for a sales job as a salesclerk, a young man as a "management trainee"; most young women enter business as typists, file clerks, receptionists, switchboard and telephone operators, keypunch operators, cashiers, bookkeepers, and secretaries with little prospect that their work role will ever become much more challenging and responsible. Reform of women's clerical jobs demands the breaking down of the barrier separating them from management or administrative skills.

The rapidly expanding health and education sectors are rigidly stratified, with women occupying the lowest menial and the middle semiprofessional levels while the top professional, administrative, and research positions are nearly exclusively taken by men. Each level is rigidly separated from the other with no chance to rise upward. In the West, until recently, this was considered perfectly in accord with "nature"—as men should be doctors and women, nurses. Men teach in schools of education, draw up curricula, are school principals, and inspect schools; women carry out their plans and follow their instructions as teachers; women from the working classes act as nurses' aides, teachers' aides, practical nurses, and do the cleaning, laundry, and kitchen chores in schools and hospitals.

In order to improve the quality of the numerous women's jobs in the fields of health and education, it is essential to open up career ladders. First attempts in this field resulted from the realization that recruiting welfare mothers into low-status, low-pay health jobs without any prospects was futile. Therefore, attempts were made through teamwork, on-the-job training, and special training to let low-level workers acquire paramedical and social relations skills and thus enhance their jobs; to open up avenues of advancement to nurses through the acquisition of preventive health and administrative skills and take on responsibility for the organization and administration of entire community health teams.[19] Another attempt was to open up a new avenue reaching into the sacred precincts of the physician through the physician-assistant program. Men and especially women with practical health care experience and a minimum of undergraduate-level science courses can, through an 18-month course, become assistant medical practitioners.[20]

Such breaking down of barriers and establishing of career ladders should also be attempted in the fields of education, social work, and librarianship. Even private household work can be improved through the establishment of a skill ladder; the skills needed for it are at present undefined and it is treated as unskilled work. A Belgian experiment has shown that by training and accreditation for such domestic activities as laundry work, cooking and serving meals, baby care, and so on, and assuring the trainees of placement and wage rates in accordance with the number of skills acquired, even these jobs can be greatly improved in competence, dignity, and pay.[21]

The Improvement of the Mass of Existing Women's Jobs

The large majority of women's jobs in manufacturing, laundries, restaurants, typing pools, keypunching, and billing are fragmented, repetitive regimented, and mindless, without room for initiative and judgment. Women have a disproportionate share in assembly work, eye-straining work, basic work cycles of a few seconds only, and pay by piece rate. Their knowledge and skills are greatly underutilized. Factory operatives with a high shool diploma are treated as if they could neither read nor write, much less think. Clerks with a B.A. degree are not permitted to compose a letter or sign it. Telephone operators are made to use set phrases.

Job enrichment experiments of clerical positions in industry, banks, and telephone companies have shown that without major technical changes many clerical service jobs can be greatly improved by letting the individual employee take over a meaningful portion of the service process, such as comprehensive relations with a number of customers, stockholders, or subscribers, and granting her maximum autonomy within this area. Other clerical jobs have been improved by the autonomous or semiautonomous work group method—encouragement of multiple skill acquisition, rotation of activities, scheduling and responsibility for product or service quality within the group—again without major changes in the physical layout of the office.[22]

A much more comprehensive and exciting model of the improvement of clerical jobs is the office team of the General Foods plant in Topeka, Kansas.[23] Here a team of ten persons (seven women and three men) work according to the autonomous work group method: moreover, they have entirely done away with the traditional status barriers between (1) lower-skill office work, such as switchboard, typing, filing, and keypunching; (2) mid-level secretarial work for management, specialized clerical work such as payroll, materials ordering, or billing; and (3) the semiprofessional work involving corporation law and state labor law problems, usually considered managerial. Everybody performs the low-level chores for herself or himself, takes turns at the switchboard, and is encouraged to train even for managerial skills to the limit of her or his wish and capability.

Experience of the redesign of women's industrial and manual service jobs is still very scanty. Even in progressive firms such as Texas Instruments in the United States,[24] Olivetti in Italy,[25] or Philips in the Netherlands, where considerable efforts have been made to enhance the quality of men's jobs, little or nothing has as yet changed in the women's departments, where tiny, often microscopic components are being spot-welded, assembled, and checked. An interesting exception is the Philips experiment, which let groups of women devise a new group method of assembling tiny electrical bulbs.[26] In assembly of larger components, there is the Norwegian electrical heater experiment in which women of rural background successfully cooperated with men in the operation of autonomous work groups, gradually attempting technically more demanding activities as well as approaching positions of responsibility.[27] In the United States there is the experiment of the Corning Glass plant in Medfield, Massachusetts, where women operatives assemble individually entire hot plates and medical instruments or, in the case of large and more complicated instruments, work in semiautonomous groups—in both cases doing away with the traditional fragmentation and lack of initiative of typical women's industrial jobs.[28]

Areas in which there is still lack of or scant experience and which might pose considerable need of changing the technical system are (1) industrial jobs which involve the handling of microscopic components, such as in electric bulbs and electronic circuits, and accurate eye-hand coordination; and (2) jobs in technically backward and often declining industries such as large parts of the needletrades and food-processing industries. Here women perform enormously fragmented and repetitive activities which involve considerable manual dexterity and speed. In both areas basic improvement may hinge on the automation of many processes now performed by hand, using electric hand tools, tending, connecting up, and correcting the work of isolated and often unsatisfactory semiautomated machinery.[29] In both areas, too, competition is keen from Third World countries where both men and women are still ready to perform these low-quality jobs for considerably lower wages than in the West. Therefore, many prosperous United States firms tend to transfer their electronic assembly departments to such countries and declining textile, needletrades, or food industries rely on remaining rural, minority, or immigrant female labor, paying the lowest wages in industry; both groups are reluctant to invest sizeable sums in developing new automated machinery, in spite of the fact that prototypes do exist and that some are already in operation in Japan, Germany, and even Israel.[30] Perhaps some government encouragement such as special tax concessions or, for small firms, the establishment of cooperative modernized facilities, would be necessary to induce management to embark on this needed technological modernization; at this point government tax concessions or other assistance could be made contingent on management's agreement to the redesign and radical improvement of the quality of women operatives' jobs.

Conclusion: Urgent Need for Research and Coordination of Reform Attempts

The reform of women's work life is still in its beginnings; most reformers have not treated it as a specific object with conditions and problems that are different from those of men's work life. Those fighting discrimination against women and struggling to erase women's inequality in the world of work often have not considered sufficiently the wider goal, the enhancement of women's overall working life. Researchers concerned with women's jobs need exchange of experience and coordination among themselves. The efforts of quality of working life reformers need coordination and exchange of experience with fighters for women's rights.

Both groups are in dire need of more reliable information about a wide range of characteristics of women's jobs and women's reactions to them: what characteristics hurt them most; to what extent they are ready to press for changes and train for more responsible jobs; what part of the female population prefers the exclusive domestic role and what are their characteristics; more comparative individual, family, and detailed work histories, in order to better analyze trends of change in women's work behavior; how individual work experience, education, family conditions, national and ethnic background, husband's attitudes, and influence of the views propagated by the women's movement affect women's attitudes toward and expectations from work.

There is still an enormous amount of outright male resistance to the upgrading of women's position in the world of work; but there is also a large amount of simple ignorance and confusion about what different groups of women want and need. And this can and should be overcome.

NOTES

1. International Labor Organization, Organization for Economic Cooperation and Development, country statistical yearbooks, and censuses. Compiled by Marjorie Galenson, *Women and Work* (Ithaca, N.Y.: Cornell University Press, 1973), p. 18.

2. Based on "Labor-Force Participation Rates of Women by Age," in Galenson, *op. cit.*, pp. 17, 20.

3. A recent and comprehensive statement claiming that this stereotype is based on the genetic inferiority of females in aggressiveness and in abstract thinking and that therefore girls should not be socialized to compete with males is in Steven Goldberg, *The Inevitability of Patriarchy* (New York: Morrow, 1973).

4. Thus in the Netherlands only "the legal requirement that women retire on marriage has been removed in government service and in public school teaching" has recently been abolished, "but there are still clauses in private union agreements giving the employer the right to discharge a female employee if she marries. Teachers in Holland's many private schools are among those subject to such provisions. The maternity protection tax on employers, to finance compulsory maternity leaves, encourages employers to fire married women." In "Switzerland which has failed to ratify the ILO's Equal Remuneration Convention . . . marriage may constitute grounds for discharge from federal employment." Galenson, *op. cit.*, pp. 77, 79. In the period of mass unemployment of the thirties, public opinion in most Western countries was in favor of dismissal of women on marriage.

5. Valerie Kincade Oppenheimer, "Demographic Influence on Female Employment and the Status of Women," in Joan Huber (ed.), *Changing Women in a Changing Society* (Chicago: University of Chicago Press, 1973), p. 185.

6. Elizabeth M. Havens, "Women, Work, and Wedlock: A Note on Female Marital Patterns in the United States," in Huber, *op. cit.*, pp. 213–218.

7. Women's Bureau, U.S. Department of Labor, *Handbook* for 1969, p. 8, reports the economic reason as crucial; also, Canada Department of Labor, *Occupational Histories of Married Women*, 1960, p. 64, comes to the same conclusion.

8. An early yet trenchant analysis of the work of the housewife can be found in Charlotte Perkins Gilman, *Women and Economics* (Boston: Small Maynard, 6th ed. 1913), pp. 67–75, 157 (1st ed., 1898).

9. Subsequent statistics are compiled from *Employment and Earnings*, 20, no. 1 (July 1973).

10. Unfortunately, this detailed statistic has not yet been updated; it appears in U.S. Department of Labor, *op. cit.*, p. 96.

11. These are 1960 figures; the absolute number of private household workers has since declined, but it is still among the six largest.

12. Valerie Kincade Oppenheimer, *The Female Labor Force in the United States. Demographic and Economic Factors Governing Its Growth and Changing Composition*, Population Monograph Series No. 5 (Berkeley: University of California Press, 1970), p. 75; according to Oppenheimer, *op. cit.*, 1973, p. 187, there has been no decline in the concentration of women in the traditional female occupations and it may even be greater.

13. For the unequal distribution of women over the food industry and its relation to the state of technological development, see *Employment and Earnings*, 20, no. 2 (August 1973), 63.

14. Excellent illustrations of this process can be found in Alexander Solzhenitsyn, *Cancer Ward*.

15. Larry E. Suter and Herman P. Miller, "Incomes of Men and Career Women," in Huber, *op. cit.*, p. 208.

16. Galenson, *op. cit.*, p. 41.

17. *Ibid.*, p. 77.

18. Until recently it has been claimed that, notwithstanding the low quality of most women's jobs, surveys demonstrated that women were mostly satisfied with their jobs; it was implied that women were satisfied with jobs that men were not. See Galenson, *op. cit.*, p. 42, quoting a 1967 British Ministry of Labour survey of working mothers, 92 percent stating they were either very or fairly satisfied with their jobs; p. 68, quoting a 1966 Helsinki interview study of married couples: although the wives' earnings were only 60 percent of their husbands', they were nevertheless more satisfied with their work. Yet the recent Michigan University Survey Center's national sample work satisfaction survey, reported in Harold L. Sheppard and Neal Q. Herrick, *Where Have All the Robots Gone?*, found higher rates of job dissatisfaction for women than for men in all age groups. Apparently, there exists as yet no survey of work satisfaction/dissatisfaction of women and men in jobs as similar as possible.

19. See Suzzanne B. Greenberg, "Curriculum Development and Training for Community Health Workers," *Comprehensive Health Services, Career Development, Technical Assistance Bulletin*, 1, no. 7 (May 1970), 1–8.

20. See *Bulletin*, Northeastern University, Physician Assistant Program.

21. Personal observation, in Brussels during the 1950s.

22. Frederick Herzberg, "One More Time: How Do You Motivate Employees," *Harvard Business Review*, January-February 1968, pp. 59–60; see also W. J. Paul and K. B. Robertson, *Job Enrichment and Employee Motivation* (London: Gower Press, 1970).

23. Personal observation, August 1973.

24. Personal observation, 1969.

25. Personal observation, March 1972.

26. Described by its initiator, H. P. Vossen, "Experiment in the Miniature Bulb Department of the Terneuzen Works of Philips in the Netherlands," unpublished paper, April 1972.

27. Described by L. A. Ødegaard, "Summary of Third Field Experiment," Industrial Democracy Project, Phase B, unpublished paper.

28. See Michael Beer and Edgar F. Huse, "A Systems Approach to Organization Development," *Journal of Applied Behavioral Science*, 8, no. 1 (1972).

29. These kinds of typical women's industrial jobs are described by Judith Buber Agassi, "Women Who Work in Factories," *Dissent*, Winter 1972, pp. 233–236. See also Ulrike Marie Meinhof, "Frauen sind billiger," *Frankfurter Hefte*, June 6, 1967, and Jean Tepperman, "Two Jobs: Women Who Work in Factories," in Robin Morgan (ed.), *Sisterhood Is Powerful* (New York: Random House, 1970), pp. 115–124.

30. The introduction of much more advanced textile and needletrades machinery than that used currently in most U.S. plants has been reported from these countries.

19

Individual Investment in Working and Living

William A. Faunce and Robert Dubin

Two dimensions are suggested along which people can be classified in their relationship to work and nonwork situations. The "assignment dimension" has to do with the "fit" between the individual's personality and the behavioral requirements of his work situation. In some occupations the fit is crucial, while in others such congruence is not critical and there may be fairly wide zones in indifference in the overlap between individual and job characteristics. The assignment problem becomes more complicated from the point of view of an individual's career. Initial placements may be made with little consideration of career development, thus creating a career assignment problem. Many workers have to conform to behavioral requirements that draw on only limited features of their personalities and capabilities.

The "adjustment dimension" involves the consistency or complementarity of the individual's behavior as he moves from one behavior setting to another.

The interactions between personality and social environment may be conceptualized in terms of either a "spill-over" or a "compensatory" model. If an individual adjusts in much the same way to all his social environments and if work is a central commitment, then there is a spill-over form of adjustment from work to nonwork settings. If there is poor adjustment in one central life area, he may "compensate" for it by better adjustment in others. Spill-over and compensatory forms of adjustment are not necessarily mutually exclusive; for example, a lack of fit along the job assignment dimension may cause some spill-over of the lack of self-esteem which can be adjusted to by some form of compensatory behavior to restore self-esteem. Self-investment refers to the readiness to "risk" one's self-evaluation in a given behavioral setting. A model is presented for analyzing the consequences of various processes by which self-esteem is "tested" and according to which self-investment may be increased or lowered. Neither of these attempted forms of adjustment is likely if initial self-investment is low. Withdrawal of initially high self-investment can manifest itself in changes in occupational aspirations and in changes in interaction networks. Self-investment strategies may be either to maximize gains or minimize costs, and may affect occupational choice in that occupations differ in the risks associated with the maintenance of self-esteem.

This analysis is concerned with aspects of the relationship between work and other areas of life experience; its objective is to propose a conceptual framework for the analysis of this relationship. First, the degree of "fit" is considered between individual needs and job requirements; then, analysis turns to the adjustment process which occurs when this fit is poor. One mode of adjustment to a situation in which important personality needs are not being satisfied through work is the withdrawal of self-investment from the occupational role, a process that will be described in the concluding section.

There are two fundamental dimensions along which people can be classified in relating their personalities to work and nonwork situations: the "assignment dimension" has to do with the fit between the individual's personality and the behavioral requirements of his work situation, and the "adjustment dimension" deals with the consistency or complementarity of the individual's behavior as he moves from one behavioral setting to another. We can assume that the individual is constant in his behavior and will enact his various roles in a way to reveal the underlying consistency of his personality.[1] Alternatively, we can assume that the individual is adjustive in his relation to his environment and that his personality is totally expressed by the sum of his individual behaviors in various social settings.[2] In the second view, the individual may not be fully revealed in any given setting, and may be understood only if the totality of his behaviors are summed across all behavioral settings. These two dimensions and their implications for the individual's working life will now be considered in turn.

The Assignment Dimension

One of the most pervasive general principles of psychology is that of wide individual variability on all measured dimensions of personality and physical behavior. This has been empirically established many times. An examination of the jobs necessary to perform the productive work of a society reveals just as broad a range of variability in human requirements to perform work adequately. Over many dimensions along which jobs are measured, there is a wide range of contrasts among individual job requirements on each of the dimensions of, for example, specialized technical knowledge; physical strength and endurance; variety; responsibility; autonomy; and so on. The combination of the characteristics of jobs that, taken together, define individual jobs reveals a comparable variability.

How does such variability affect a labor force? How is correspondence established between the variability among individuals in their personality and behavioral characteristics, on the one hand, and variability in job characteristics relating to human performance, on the other? How is a fit established between people and jobs so that the personalities and/or performance characteristics of individuals are consistent or at least do not conflict with the human behavior required on jobs?

Attempts to solve the assignment problem of matching individual personalities with job demands have led to technologies for measuring personality, and to more adequate means for describing jobs.[3] In some occupations the degree of congruence is crucial or at least material to the success of the individual fulfilling a job. It is not at all clear that the fit between individual personalities and job demands is critical in many jobs. There may be wide ranges of tolerance for a nonbalance or nonmatch. Indeed, there may be a zone of indifference in the range of individual characteristics as it overlaps with job characteristics so that how good the fit is between the two may have very small consequences for job performance.[4] This zone of indifference may also apply to the perceived quality of work experience from the point of view of the individual worker.

The assignment problem becomes somewhat more complicated from the point of view of an individual's career. Individuals may be selected for initial placement without direct reference to where they may end their career in the organization. The primary exceptions to this practice are executive training programs in which certain technical criteria may be used in choosing young people as potential executives. In European countries, and increasingly in the United States, initial selection is based on prior educational performance, and the individual is "fitted" to the organization with some attention (usually at higher level jobs) to the mid-career or even end-career job requirements that he is predicted to fulfill. The phenomenon of "career anchorage," for example, is a powerful tool in measuring how managerial employees adjust to the fit with their jobs.[5] For the bulk of industrial and commercial workers, however, the fit between personality and behavioral requirements is usually limited to the individual's initial job, thus creating a career assignment problem that personnel policy has not dealt with adequately. For example, what happens to a worker, either on the job or in his general social adjustment, if he gets out of balance in the relationship of his personality to progressive job requirements? This aspect of adjustment will be discussed later on.

Modern criticism of the assignment problem rests on grounds somewhat different from the lack of balance between personality and job requirements, asserting that the job demands are overpowering with respect to the person. An individual hired into an industrial occupation has to conform to behavioral and social interaction requirements that draw upon only limited features of his personality and performance capabilities. Argyris has characterized this development as fostering and maintaining immature attitudes and behavior on the part of the individual because that is all that is required in his job performance.[6] He argues that jobs need to be redefined so that individuals may utilize and develop their personality and performance capabilities. "Job enlargement," "job enrichment," and "self-realization" are code words describing the proposed modifications that will result in a better fit between personality requirements and job demands. A failure to achieve appropriate fit may adversely affect persons' subsequent adjustment in the larger social order, a dimension that is discussed more fully below.

The Adjustment Dimension

The adjustment dimension implies that an individual makes some sort of peace with the requirements of his environments. The nature of this adjustment has several facets: First, he may react to a behavioral setting as though it were the only one in his life, his reaction to his performance being either satisfactory or unsatisfactory or falling somewhere in between. Most studies of job satisfaction reveal that individuals report themselves as being on the positive side of a scale ranging from dissatisfaction to satisfaction.[7] Thus there appears to be some skewness in the response to a single environment such that most people view it as at least mildly satisfying, if not more so. This has led theorists to the curious conclusion that there is a kind of passive adjustment process by which individuals accept an undesirable environment with resignation, reducing their levels of aspiration and levels of performance to meet only the minimum requirements of the setting. Theorists, like Argyris,[8] have concluded that individuals may adjust to an environment at a level of "immaturity" which is just sufficient to perform acceptably in that environment.

This kind of theorizing appears to be wholly inadequate for two reasons. In the first place, the skewness in the response to a satisfaction with work measure toward the positive end of the scale may more simply be interpreted as the plasticity or adaptability of man to his many environments. Man learns to live with the presented environment of work and, even though it may have dulling and monotonous characteristics, can accept it with indifference.[9] Neutrality and indifference rather than active adaptation, such as that proposed by Argyris, are a real response to dull and boring work. A second and quite different criticism of this kind of theorizing lies in the fact that inevitably it reaches broad conclusions about man's psyche and adjustment to the world, on the basis of measuring *only* his working environment and reaction to it, the familiar "alienation" theme.[10] This is a very serious flaw which few researchers have even taken into account. Therefore, the present authors find it unsatisfactory to work with this kind of model in examining man and his social worlds.

The interactions between personality and social environment may be modeled in two alternative ways in which interactions may be conceptualized through a "spill-over" model and a "compensatory" model.[11] Assume a model in which the individual adjusts in approximately the same way to all his social environments. If, from this standpoint, the work organization is considered as a central environment in an industrial society, then this model would predict that the individual has a spill-over form of adjustment from work to nonwork settings. Thus, if the work environment maximizes his opportunities for personality expression, he will operate in the same way in nonwork environments and there will be a spill-over of his work adjustment into other institutional areas of behavior. Essentially, the spill-over model views the individual as having certain constants in his personality structure such that, whatever his adjustment is in a central institutional setting, it will be comparable in other institutional settings.[12]

An alternative to the spill-over model is the compensatory model, in which the individual's adjustment in a central institutional setting, like work, is so salient that it compensates for poor adjustment in other institutional areas.[13] Individuals who find work challenging, satisfying, and rewarding may show a considerably lower investment of self in other settings, simply because the high level of reward achieved in work is sufficient to compensate for less rewarding behaviors outside work. On the other hand, for the individual who finds work unrewarding, there may be very significant compensatory adjustments with a high level of self-investment in nonwork institutional settings.[14] The compensatory model also considers the nature of the adjustment in a given behavioral setting, and relates it to the probable forms of adjustment in other behavioral settings. Thus, rather than seeing the individual as victim of his social environment, he is seen as having considerable control over his destiny with autonomy in ordering his life interests and energy expenditures, and as being able to find opportunity in a complex social environment to compensate in some behavioral settings for inadequacies in others. This is essentially an optimistic view of complex social life, which takes into account the freedoms associated with industrial societies as they relate to choices made for self-investment in the many available behavioral settings.

The spill-over and compensatory models address themselves to the same analytical problem: each tries to relate the individual's adjustment in a given behavioral setting to his probable adjustment in other behavioral settings. They reach very different conclusions, however, as to the nature of this adjustment.

Assignment Plus Adjustment Dimensions

The assignment and adjustment dimensions, put together, suggest a somewhat more complicated model than those represented by each dimension alone. The assignment model suggests that the individual, in a given behavioral setting, may find himself at a point in a range, from good to bad fit, of possible adjustments to his environment. The level of adjustment between personality and situation may change through time as his working career unfolds; adjustment may move from a positive level to a negative one, or vice versa, or it may oscillate between the extremes. There may also be secular trends that are related to his life history. This is diagrammatically represented in Figure 1.

The spill-over model of adjustment views the individual as moving through his life history making a comparable adjustment in all areas of living which may vary as to level in his life history. Thus a high level of satisfaction may characterize an early period of his life, followed by some decline, but climaxing in late maturity in a distinctive withdrawal from life experiences. Across all institutional areas of participation, the individual achieves approximately the same level of adjustment for any particular point in his life history, as shown in Figure 2.

The compensatory model of adjustment suggests that the individual may have a single or at most a few areas in which he invests a great deal of himself and from which he draws high levels of satisfaction, and many areas of life experience where his level of self-investment is much lower and his returns are of lesser consequence. This model encompasses the possibility that the degree of investment and reward from a given behavioral setting or institution of basic interest may vary through his life history; the area of commitment may also change from one point to another. A compensatory adjustment model may be characterized as shown in Figure 3.

Thus far, spill-over and compensation have been treated as alternative models which produce quite different conclusions as to the relationship between work and other areas of life experience. The two processes, however, are not necessarily mutually exclusive. There may be spill-over of habits

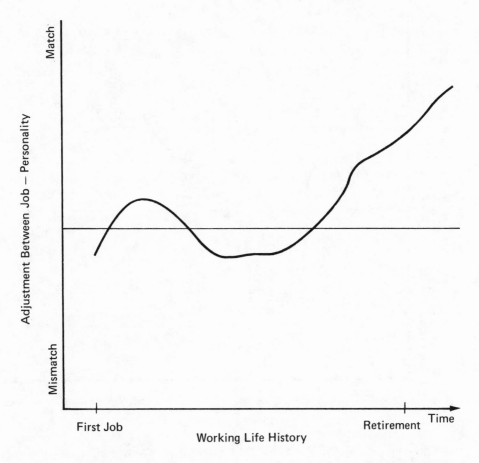

Figure 1. Adjustment between Job Requirements and Personality: An Example.

acquired at the workplace, and at the same time a necessity to compensate in other settings for needs that are not being satisfied in the occupational role. From this perspective it becomes important to specify the conditions under which either spill-over or compensation or both may occur. Among the variety of functions that work can potentially serve, there are some that may be sufficiently important as to require compensatory behavior in other settings if they are not adequately served through work. The maintenance of self-esteem would appear to be an example; the spill-over process would produce a generally low self-assessment for persons who cannot gain self-esteem through work-related achievements. It seems more reasonable, however, to expect that if there is a lack of fit along the assignment dimension between the need for maintenance of self-esteem and the opportunity for achievement on the job, adjustment will involve some form of compensatory behavior.

Given, then, the assignment dimension and the adjustment dimension with their two alternative models of the individual in his relation to his social roles

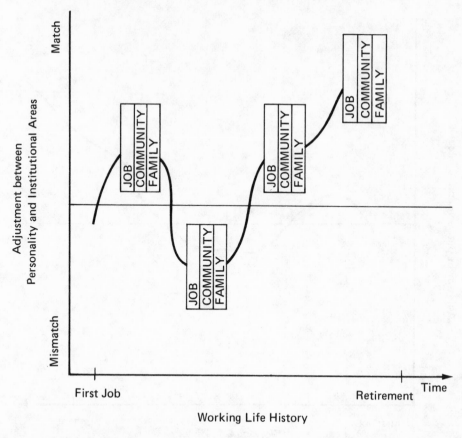

Figure 2. Spill-over Model of Adjustment between Personality and Institutional Areas of Participation: An Example.

in a number of behavioral settings, how can we deal with the problem of motivation for self-investment in a particular setting? This problem is central to the following analysis, which focuses on processes of self-investment in social settings.

Self-investment

Work is one of a variety of activities that are potential competitors for investment of time and energy. The "return" on that investment becomes empirically meaningful only when one can specify what it is one expects to gain from participation in the activity. A. H. Maslow, in his hierarchy of needs, suggests that lower-order needs for food, shelter, or security must be satisfied

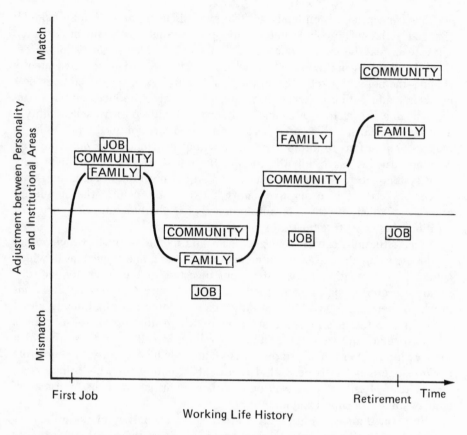

Figure 3. Compensatory Model of Adjustment between Personality and Institutional Areas of Participation: An Example.

at least to some extent before higher-order needs, such as self-esteem and self-actualization become important.[15] The term *self*-investment refers to instances in which these latter needs are at issue; self is invested or "risked" in the sense that an evaluation of self may be confirmed or disconfirmed and one's conception of self may, therefore, be modified. The mechanism that "drives" self-investment is the payoff in self-esteem derived from each behavioral setting.

Self-investment is a process through which the degree of effect of social encounters upon self-esteem becomes differentially distributed among social roles. It seems clear that success or failure in the performance of some social roles has a much greater impact upon self-esteem than success or failure in others. The extent of investment of self in any role is dependent upon the amount of return on such investments in the past and the anticipated amount of return in the future. This is a formulation comparable to what in psychology is called "expectancy theory."[16]

This conceptualization lends itself to analysis using an exchange model.[17] If social exchanges involve some calculation of gains, costs, and profits, then self-esteem may be seen as one payoff in terms of which profit or loss is defined. In social encounters in which self-esteem is invested—and consequently risked—the hoped-for return from the "commodity" exchanged is an enhancement or reaffirmation of social status which, in turn, produces either an increment in self-esteem or a confirmation of an already positive self-identity.[18] The term "social status" is used here to refer to a location in the hierarchy of persons or positions resulting from the unequal distribution of *anything* that is valued. In this usage, identification of the boundaries of the status assignment system—for example, whether it is a friendship group or a nation-state —becomes crucial in order to identify the relevant values, the significant others who constitute the relevant audience of evaluation, and the person or positions that constitute the status hierarchy.

Social situations can be analyzed according to the extent to which values producing occupational status differences are present, and the extent to which actors in the situation have self-esteem invested in the occupational role. Figure 4 presents this categorization. Cell 1 in Figure 4 represents situations in which there is no possibility of either gain or loss in occupationally based self-esteem. Situations in cell 2 are ones in which any loss of self-esteem is minor, specific, and transitory. Situations falling in cell 3 are those in which there is interaction among status equals and in which quality of work role performance is not at issue. Cell 4 represents situations in which there is an actual "test" of self-esteem resulting in either confirmation or discomfirmation of an evaluated occupational identity.

While the dimensions in Figure 4 are dichotomized, they may also be conceived of as continuous, and the relationship between them is therefore more complex than this figure suggests. In Figure 4 it is intended to emphasize (1) that there may be social exchanges to which occupational status is relevant that do not have any significant impact upon self-esteem (cell 2), and (2) that even where there is self-investment in the occupational role, self-esteem is not affected by all work-related social exchanges (cell 3). With regard to this second point, while we assume that an evaluated self-identity requires confirmation by others, this self-esteem "testing" is an episodic rather than a continuous process.

	Relevance of Occupational Status to Social Exchanges	
	Low	High
Self-investment in the Occupational Role Low	1	2
High	3	4

Figure 4. Occupational Status and Self-investment.

A successful test of self-esteem will have the effect of sustaining or increasing the level of self-investment. A failure to confirm an evaluated self-identity, however, does not automatically produce a lowering of self-esteem. In Figure 5 a model for analyzing the consequences of the self-esteem testing process is presented. The left-hand boxes of the diagram represent the range in variation of self-investment in the occupational role. If the starting point in the process represented by the model is entrance into the labor force, then this variation is accounted for almost exclusively by differential exposure to values emphasizing the importance of work. Any stage in a career could be considered a starting point, however, and if, for example, the model is used to analyze the consequences of achieving or not achieving a promotion, the initial variation in level of self-investment would also be a product of prior experience with amount of return on investment in the occupational role.

The person who starts with a high level of self-investment in the occupational role and who subsequently achieves recognition for successful performance of this role will have a favorable self-evaluation confirmed and his level of self-investment will either remain constant or increase. The consequence of occupational success for a person starting with a low level of self-investment in the occupational role may, particularly if this is a recurring experience, be an increase in level of investment in this role. This is not a necessary condition, however. For persons who are maintaining a satisfactory level of self-esteem through investment in nonwork-related roles, occupational success may have little bearing on self-conception.

Thus far only the paths of Figure 5 from high and low levels of self-investment to recognition of occupational achievement have been discussed. Failure to achieve this recognition may have little or no consequence for persons with a low level of investment in the occupational role. For those with a high level of self-investment, however, this experience creates dissonance that requires resolution. Figure 5 suggests two categories of response to this

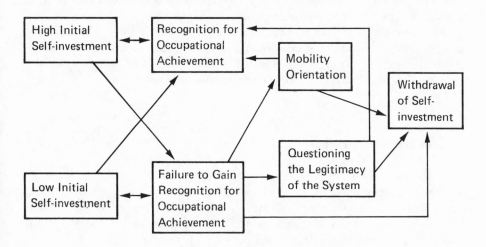

Figure 5. Interactions of Self-investment and Recognition of Achievement.

situation: one involves an attempt to produce change in the actor and the other to produce change in the system. A mobility orientation involves a disposition on the part of the actor to try harder or to make whatever changes in himself are necessary to gain recognition for occupational achievement. The alternative, questioning the legitimacy of the system, would most commonly involve an attempt to change the values on which status assignment is based. Manual workers who actively seek to gain more recognition of the dignity and worth of manual labor would be one example of this orientation. The result of success in terms of either upward occupational mobility or inducing change in the status assignment system would be a return on the self-investment in work in the form of recognition of achievement. Continued failure to achieve either of these objectives would represent disconfirmation of an evaluated self-identity of loss of self-esteem. Since in this instance social exchanges in the occupational role are not profitable for self-esteem maintenance, the probable consequence is that the investment will be withdrawn and the actor will look elsewhere for self-investments on which there is a higher probability of a pay-off. Neither a mobility orientation nor a questioning of the legitimacy of the system are likely to occur where there is an initial low level of self-investment, which accounts for the path in Figure 5 running directly from failure to gain recognition for occupational achievement to withdrawal of self-investment.

One of the consequences of withdrawal of self-investment from the occupational role is a shifting of occupational aspirations. The primary orientation toward work is likely to become a concern for finding a secure position and a steady income.[19] There may also be an attempt to minimize expenditure of time and energy on the job in order to preserve these resources for more important, nonwork-related activities. Another expected consequence is a change in interaction networks. One would expect that withdrawal of self-investment from the occupational role would produce an attempt to avoid social exchanges to which occupationally based status distinctions are relevant. In general, it can be assumed that people seek relationships in which the criteria used in status assignment are the same as those used in self-esteem maintenance, and avoid relationships in which there is inconsistency between status assigning and self-esteem-maintaining criteria. A decrease in the importance of the occupational self-identity for self-esteem maintenance should therefore require some realignment in the network of social relationships.

Self-investment Strategies

Figure 5 represents only the basic structure of the self-investment process. This model could be elaborated by introducing the concept of investment strategies. For example, the choice between attempting to maximize gains and minimize costs reflects different self-investment strategies. To some extent, this choice is determined by the level of self-investment since minimizing costs would be expected to occur with a low level of self-investment whereas, with a high level of self-investment, profit from social exchanges may result from either reducing costs or increasing gains.

Which of these options is selected may affect the process of occupational choice since occupations differ in terms of high or low risk with regard to maintenance of self-esteem. High-risk occupations are characterized by wide intrapositional status distinctions and frequent "tests" of self-esteem so that there is, in effect, more to be gained or lost (e.g., some types of sales positions and positions in the performing arts). Public schoolteaching may be regarded as a relatively low-risk occupation since occupancy of this position guarantees some status payoff; but there is infrequent evaluation of work role performance by peers. In addition to these structural dimensions of the occupational role, the actor pursuing a strategy of maximizing gains may *introduce* occupational status distinctions into social exchanges by frequently asserting status claims and thereby forcing evaluations by others.

The attempt to minimize costs, on the other hand, would dictate a more cautious strategy in which tests of self-esteem resulting from assertion of status claims would be induced only when the probability of a payoff is high.

The preceding discussion suggests a possible relationship between a society's level of economic development and the probability of self-investment in the occupational role. In preindustrial societies (and in most isolated rural areas within industrial societies) there may not even be a differentiated occupational self-identity to serve as the objective of self-investment. The content of the self-image which is related to work may be distributed across a number of identities, including those associated with sex and family status, and may not exist as an independent point of reference for self-attitudes. The emergence of the self, historically, as an object of orientation has been described by Erich Fromm as the process of "individuation." [20] In early industrial societies, in which the institutional structure is oriented primarily toward accelerating economic growth, the value placed upon productive work could be expected to increase, and occupational achievement to become a primary basis for status assignment.[21] There is also at that stage sufficient division of labor to permit the emergence of occupationally based self-identities which become important for self-esteem maintenance. With increasing industrial growth and differentiation, the alternatives to work as a basis for status assignment multiply. The affluence of mature industrial societies could also be expected to decrease the value placed upon occupational achievement. Contemporary American society seems to have a cultural lag between an ideology regarding the virtue of work and the reality of the declining importance of work as a basis for status assignment and self-esteem maintenance.

The Meaning of Work

Research in the sociology of occupations indicates that work has very diverse functions and meanings for the contemporary labor forces of indus-

trialized countries. The concept of selective self-investment that has been developed here may help explain some of this diversity. Changes in the function
and meaning of work that may be expected at various career stages are one
illustration. As noted above, new entrants into the labor force vary considerably in their level of self-investment in the occupational role; almost all
young people beginning work, however, appear to have some self-investment
in it. Exposure to the work ideology of modern industrial production brings on
the anticipation of at least some return on self-investment in this area. Those
starting in lower-level blue- and white-collar jobs find limited opportunities
for occupational mobility and for changing the status assignment system,
particularly in the large bureaucratized work organizations in which most are
employed. Withdrawal of self-investment from the occupational role is likely
to occur early in the career of such workers,[22] not only because their early
work experience involves a limited return on the investment of self, but also
because their initial level of self-investment was probably low. The lack of fit
between job requirements and personality is undoubtedly one of the reasons
why self-investment is low, the assignment dimension accounting for that
effect since many blue-collar as well as clerical jobs make minimal demands
for self-investment.

Young workers with working-class and lower-class backgrounds very likely
begin early to develop self-investments that are alternatives to investment in
work because they do not anticipate a large payoff in this area. Above the age
of 30, most persons in lower-level blue- and white-collar jobs appear to have
a purely instrumental orientation toward work—with a primary emphasis
upon security—and appear to actively avoid social exchanges in which occupational status distinctions are relevant.[23] Since the career stage at which the
withdrawal of self-investment in work occurs is partly dependent upon the
initial level of investment, a decline in the importance of work in American
society could be expected to accelerate the process described in Figure 5
above. Note that this form of adjustment is represented by the compensatory
model of adjustment to social life, as set forth early in this selection.

However, withdrawal of self-investment from the occupational role does
not occur only among lower-level blue- and white-collar workers. In fact, it
occurs to everyone at some point in his career if retirement is included as a
career stage; undoubtedly, a decline in the importance of work for self-esteem
occurs to almost everyone at some point short of retirement. The issue here is
the stage in a career at which the withdrawal of self-investment takes place.
For those who gain initial recognition for occupational achievement and are
able to sustain their self-investment in this role, there is a point in mid-career
at which further return on this investment may become problematic; for
example, there may be active questioning of whether the time and energy
required to sustain a high level of self-investment in work is worthwhile.
Almost everyone reaches this juncture in his career because there is an almost
inevitable decline in the profit from social interchanges involving work-related
values. This may occur when one reaches the apparent upper limit on mobility
in an interpositional hierarchy. It may also occur simply because, beyond

certain levels of recognition for achievement, there are diminishing returns on further success.

The outcome of this process is unlikely to be a complete withdrawal of self-investment, but rather its dispersion into new areas of anticipated greater returns. Thus, there may be a curvilinear relationship between success in occupational role performance and extent of self-investment in that role, in which lower levels of self-investment are found at either end of the success continuum. The stage in a career at which the decline in self-investment occurs is dependent upon level of self-investment in work and also upon structural characteristics of the occupational role, affecting both the possibility of receiving recognition for achievement and the pattern whereby it is accorded. While most people reach this stage prior to retirement, some sustain a high level of self-investment in the occupational role to the end of their work experience.

The Quality of Working Life

The quality of working life is clearly a normative concept and is usually defined in terms of extent of autonomy, opportunity for creativity, and recognition for achievement on the job. There is at least inferential evidence, however, that these attributes may not be highly valued in the absence of self-investment in a job. Victor Vroom, for example, reports that "job satisfaction for persons who are ego-involved in their jobs is significantly more positively related to the amount of their opportunity for self-expression in their jobs than is the case for persons low in ego involvement." [24] There is an overabundance of evidence from industrial research that almost everyone assigns importance to these attributes as *abstract qualities* of a good job. However, the on-the-job behavior of persons in occupations in which low levels of self-investment could be expected does not show active pursuit of autonomy, opportunity for creativity, or recognition for achievement. There is undoubtedly a reciprocally reinforcing relationship between these job attributes and self-investment: where they are present, self-investment in the job is encouraged which, in turn, increases the value assigned to them. Thus, self-investment in work is a necessary condition for improving the quality of work experience.

Looking at the life history of an individual and focusing upon the fit between his personality requirements and the work he performs for a living, we see that the fit may be very close, loose, or discrepant. Where the fit is close there is likely to be a higher level of initial self-investment in work. If he performs reasonably well, the organization will "pay" him with self-esteem-sustaining or -enhancing rewards of money, and recognition and promotion that may have a feedback to increase the level of self-investment.

As the working life history of the individual unfolds, the fit between his personality and the successive jobs or positions in the organization may be modified. Thus, a high level of self-investment in work may be replaced by a declining self-investment if his rewards are lower than he expected. On the other hand, self-investment is enhanced when the rewards are ample and continuous throughout his working life. Thus, he can be viewed as having a shifting adjustment between his personality needs and their satisfaction in his working situation.

From the standpoint of the larger society and the adjustment of the individual to his total social life, two models have been suggested, the spill-over effect and the effect of compensatory adaptation. The evidence for the spill-over model is largely impressionistic and evaluative and can be summarized under the general heading of "alienation." It is assumed that an individual who finds little reward and opportunity for self-investment in work will spill over this orientation into his total social life; he will be similarly situated in his nonwork social relations. From this effect derives the notion that the character of industrial work produces alienated individuals in the society.[25]

The alternative model is designed to show compensatory adaptation to social life. If the work situation demands minimal self-investment, the individual will find other arenas of social life within which to make his major self-investment. There is fairly broad evidence of this kind of adaptation in advanced capitalist and socialist industrial societies. Indeed, modern consumerism in all advanced economic nations, whether capitalist or socialist, strongly suggests that the central life interests of their citizens are rapidly shifting to nonwork areas of life. Work may be a necessary behavior that is socially demanded for limited periods of life, but the affluent society creates opportunities for self-investment in the consumption of the products of affluence, and may even demand that citizens invest themselves in such pursuits as evidence of good citizenship.[26] On balance, the data seems to show that the compensatory model is perhaps more substantially supported empirically than is the spill-over model. This issue, however, needs far more research.

NOTES

1. Although the literature on this issue is broad, the following is the central reference: S. Freud, *The Basic Writings of Sigmund Freud*, translated and edited by A. A. Brill (New York: Modern Library, 1938).

2. Cf. G. H. Mead, *Mind, Self and Society* (Chicago: University of Chicago Press, 1935); and E. Goffman, *The Presentation of Self in Everyday Life* (London: Allen Lane, The Penguin Press, 1969).

3. See, for example, E. F. Borgatta and W. W. Lambert (eds.), *Handbook of Personality Theory and Research* (Chicago: Rand McNally, 1969); and in the realm

of job description, J. K. Hemphill, *Dimensions of Executive Positions*, Ohio Studies in Personnel, Research Monograph no. 98 (Columbus: Bureau of Business Research, Ohio State University, 1960). The problem of fit between personality and jobs has been central in analyzing work careers, approached from both a psychological and sociological standpoint. The Minnesota studies have placed emphasis on the relations of demographic, social, and psychological characteristics of individuals to the successful adaptation to work, while Super has pursued a similar line of inquiry. (R. V. Dawis, L. H. Lofquist, and D. J. Weiss, *A Theory of Work Adjustment* [*A Revision*] [Minneapolis: Industrial Relations Center, University of Minnesota, 1968]; D. E. Super, *The Psychology of Careers* [New York: Harper & Bros., 1957].) Sewell and his students have also attempted to tease out the relationships among demographic, social, and psychological factors and career choice (W. H. Sewell, A. O. Haller, and A. Porles, "The Educational and Early Occupational Attainment Process," *American Sociological Review*, 34 [1969], 82–92, and W. H. Sewell, A. O. Haller, and G. W. Ohlendorf, "The Educational and Early Occupational Attainment Process: Replication and Revision," *American Sociological Review*, 35 [1970], 1014–1027). All of these studies have so far left the field open to considerable development since their results are not conclusive.

4. R. Dubin, *The World of Work* (Englewood Cliffs, N.J.: Prentice-Hall, 1958).

5. Some managers aspire to maximum career achievement and do not consider themselves successful until they get to top jobs; others measure their success by how far they have progressed from starting jobs. C. Tausky and R. Dubin, "Career Anchorage: Managerial Mobility Motivations," *American Sociological Review*, 30 (1965), 725–735. See also D. R. Goldman, "Career Anchorage Points and Central Life Interests of Middle Managers," unpublished Ph.D. dissertation, University of Oregon, 1968; and R. B. Bowin, "Career Anchorage Points and Central Life Interests of Middle Managers," unpublished D.B.A. dissertation, University of Oregon, 1968.

6. C. Argyris, *Personality and Organization* (New York: Harper & Row, 1957); *Integrating the Individual and the Organization* (New York: Wiley, 1964).

7. See, for example, F. Herzberg, B. Mausner, R. Peterson, and D. Capwell, *Job Attributes: Review of Research and Opinion* (Pittsburgh: Psychological Service of Pittsburgh, 1957).

8. C. Argyris, *Integrating the Individual and the Organization* (New York: Wiley, 1964).

9. See R. Dubin, "Industrial Workers' Worlds: The 'Central Life Interests' of Industrial Workers," *Journal of Social Issues*, 3 (January 1956), 131–142, and Dubin, *World of Work, op. cit.*, chap. 14.

10. See R. Blauner, *Alienation and Freedom: The Factory Worker and His Industry* (Chicago: University of Chicago Press, 1964).

11. H. L. Wilensky, "Work, Careers, and Social Integration," *International Social Science Journal*, 12 (Fall 1960), 543–560.

12. M. Meissner ("The Long Arm of the Job: A Study of Work and Leisure," *Industrial Relations*, 10 [October 1971], 239–260) found that among sawmill workers, those who had technologically constraining jobs and opportunities for minimal sociability on the job tended to have restricted sociability in the community. Conversely, those who had ample opportunities for sociability on the job also displayed a greater tendency to be sociable off the job. His conclusions represent exactly the kinds of conclusions that follow from the spill-over model.

13. Dubin, "Industrial Workers' Worlds," *op. cit.*

14. This thesis has been set forth a number of times as both theory and established fact. See, for example: Johan Huizinga, *Homo Ludens: A Study of the Play Element*

in Culture (Boston: Beacon Press, 1955); C. Wright Mills, *White Collar* (New York: Oxford University Press, 1953); Eric Larabee and Rolf Meyersohn, *Mass Leisure* (Glencoe, Ill.: Free Press, 1958); and John H. Goldthorpe et al., *The Affluent Worker in the Class Structure* (Cambridge, Eng.: Cambridge University Press, 1969).

15. A. H. Maslow, *Motivation and Personality* (New York: Harper & Bros., 1954).

16. See L. W. Porter and E. E. Lawler, III, *Managerial Attitudes and Performance* (Homewood, Ill.: Irwin, 1968); and V. H. Vroom, *Work and Motivation* (New York: Wiley, 1964).

17. G. C. Homans, *The Human Group* (New York: Harcourt, Brace, 1950), and P. M. Blau, *Exchange and Power in Social Life* (New York: Wiley, 1964).

18. A convenient summary of various conceptions of self-identity and its reinforcement will be found in the several chapters of Borgatta and Lambert, *op. cit.*, and in B. J. Biddle and E. J. Thomas, *Role Theory: Concepts and Methods* (New York: Wiley, 1966).

19. E. Chinoy, *The Automobile Workers and the American Dream* (Garden City, N.Y.: Doubleday, 1955); and Tausky and Dubin, *op. cit.*

20. E. Fromm, *Escape from Freedom* (New York: Holt, Rinehart, & Winston, 1941).

21. Cf. M. Weber, *The Protestant Ethic and the Spirit of Capitalism* (London: Allen & Unwin, 1930).

22. See, for example, Tausky and Dubin, *op. cit.*

23. See, for example, J. H. Goldthorpe et al., *The Affluent Worker: Industrial Attitudes and Behaviors* (Cambridge, Eng.: Cambridge University Press, 1968), and J. H. Goldthorpe et al., *The Affluent Worker in the Class Structure* (Cambridge, Eng.: Cambridge University Press, 1969).

24. V. H. Vroom, "Ego Involvement, Job Satisfaction, and Job Performance," *Personnel Psychology*, 15 (1962), 159–177.

25. Blauner, *op. cit.* See also Report of Special Task Force to Secretary of HEW, *Work in America* (Cambridge: MIT Press, 1973).

26. The most obvious evidence for this assertion is the notion of a guaranteed annual income that is now being touted in the United States as a substitute for other welfare programs. Obviously, the good citizen can be a consumer only through the medium of his guaranteed income since working, or even seeking work, would no longer enter the eligibility formula. But it is just as clear that we now conceive of consumerism as the engine of the economy, and much of modern governmental fiscal and economic policy is directed at monitoring and stimulating or dampening consumer spending as the economic climate dictates (Cf. John K. Galbraith, *The Affluent Society* [Boston: Houghton Mifflin, 1958]. Even the ecological movement makes consumerism the center of its prescriptive solutions to pollution and resource problems and, in the demand for moderation in consumption, gives a backhand acknowledgment that consumerism has been the dominant, if not the preferred, image of good citizenship.

20

Compatibility-Incompatibility between Organization and Individual Values: A Swedish Point of View

THE debate about worker satisfaction and safety has begun to take on political and economic importance in Sweden. The so-called rational design of work conflicts with the full satisfaction of needs. Two labor markets are created—one for the young, healthy, and well educated, and one for everybody else. Many older, less educated workers fall victim to work rationalization. Managements, unions, and the workers themselves tend to accept these outcomes as legitimate. "Efficiency" within an organization often creates costs elsewhere, and material gains have been seen to outweigh these costs. There is compelling evidence that the socio-technical conditions of fractioned jobs and technocratic control produce alienation and have an impact on the individual's total life situation and health. Although differing mechanisms of perception and adjustment play a major role in reducing conflicts between individual needs and organizational demands, many individuals are dissatisfied with their work.

Some firms have embarked on large-scale experimentation to align work more with workers' needs. They are assisted by the Development Council for Cooperation Questions sponsored by employer and employee confederations and the governmental Industrial Democracy Delegation. Overcoming dissatisfaction with and alienation from work in Sweden are linked to four value areas: (1) *economic*—increased satisfaction should lead to higher performance and lower turnover and absenteeism in a tight labor market; (2) *humanistic* —the individual has a right to a meaningful and interesting job and this is important for its own sake, irrespective of its effect on economic criteria; (3) *health*—especially mental health, which is seen to be adversely affected by alienation; (4) *industrial democracy*—an ideological issue relating not only to greater self-determination at the workplace but to influencing decisions having to do with the general management of the firm.

Most experiments with job design in Sweden today are narrowly based on economic considerations and decided upon by management. Managerial prerogatives in other areas have inhibited more participative decision making; worker influence has at least been advisory. However, the unions are asking for changes in the labor laws so as to make issues of work environment and organization negotiable. A government committee has been appointed for this purpose.

Introduction

The emergence and development of industrialization have made it possible to improve our material standards of living, and few people will doubt the significance of that achievement for the human condition. On the basis of this material progress, moreover, it has been possible to pursue vigorous reform: for instance, in the fields of welfare and education. However, in spite of, or owing to, all material advances the conditions bound up with the efficient performance of work are beginning to receive growing attention. Apart from wages and hours of work, we have begun to pay attention to the content of jobs, organization of work, and environment in which work occurs. Questions are being asked about whether these can be regarded as compatible with human health and work satisfaction. Although not new, the debate about industrial safety and worker satisfaction has recently begun to take on political and economic importance.

Physical Work Environment

For many decades, unspectacular but often intensive day-to-day efforts have been devoted to combating accidents and physical ill health at the workplace. But when these meant consideration for man rather than for production, industrial safety has had to sell itself to corporate management by invoking economic arguments, such as "accident prevention pays off." The worker also had to be sold since safety regulations and environmental protection have often been uncomfortable and sometimes meant lowered piecework earnings.

In Sweden these problems are now duly noted and forces have been set in motion which seem firmly resolved to reduce these problems and risks to the smallest possible dimensions, although not solved once and for all. However, after all is said and done, these problems of physical work environment generate relatively little controversy.[1]

Individual Needs

Turning to psychological and sociological aspects of work, the job world abounds in examples of man as a physiological/psychological component of the production system. Given this kind of outlook, man will continue to remain a thing, an object to be cared for and adjusted by different means; man will still be asked what he *knows* and what he can endure—not what he *wants*.

In recent years, however, a research philosophy has begun to emerge which views the individual as a subject: that is, one proceeds from analyses of the individual's own experiences and manifestations of needs and tries to relate these to production determinants, organizations, and job content. The basic assumption here is that people are basically more alike than unlike, and that all of us share certain fundamental needs: survival, security, bearing responsibility, and personal self-realization. All of us are gregarious creatures who like to partake of human fellowship, and one means toward this end is to be of service. If anything tells us apart, it is the economic and sociotechnical prerequisites to meeting these needs, which vary strongly with education, position in the occupational hierarchy, and the nature and content of the job.

Large groups of people are not enabled to enjoy economic and social resources to the same extent as others, and that state of affairs is obviously
mirrored in their subjective experiences and manifestations of will. Thus
some people desire radical changes in the societal and occupational spheres;
others—perhaps the majority—are more resigned, having given up all job
expectations except for economic rewards and given up aspirations to power
and participation in the production system.

Consequences of Rationalization

This emerging philosophy does not square with the prevailing notions
of efficiency and profitability. If anything, the existing so-called rational design of our workplaces conflicts with demands for a more deep-going satisfaction of needs: first, there is a tendency for two labor markets to be created—
one for the young, healthy, and well educated, and one for everybody else;
and, second, workplaces are created which alienate people and wear them out.
These propositions are developed more fully below.

Today, many people—no longer "good enough" and no longer "profitable"—
are displaced from the labor market. News of production rationalizations and
plant shutdowns are legion in Sweden today. These events affect not only
manual workers, but also white-collar and managerial personnel. What fate
awaits these persons? Many investigations reveal that, whenever a firm goes
out of business, one of every five who lose their jobs remains permanently
unemployed. The principal victims are those over 50 years of age or those who
suffer from some disability and have low educational attainments; they find
it hard to obtain new employment once they have become "redundant." [2]

In highly mechanized workplaces, firms impose job requirements of a kind
with which only an elite group can cope. Here firms prefer to reduce their
manpower by letting "nature take its course," the so-called attrition process,
which usually means that persons who fall short of the mark are separated
or reassigned. As a rule this is not considered to present any social problem,
but is felt to be quite legitimate by managements and trade unions, and sometimes even by employees themselves. This development splits the labor
market into the two submarkets mentioned earlier.

These practices illustrate that the present-day criteria of efficiency and
profitability are pushing firms to adopt methods of rationalization incompatible with human striving; they certainly do not square with the interests of
those people who are adversely affected by these methods. Efficiency for the
firm entails costs transferred to the public sector under labels such as labor
market policy, occupational welfare, social services, and the like, which casts
some doubts as to the economic and social soundness of productivity measures
used today. But even where structural change is concerned, the trade unions
and the politicians must be made to share the responsibility. All have had the

same interest in seeing that the productive apparatus runs effectively and stays competitive, and there has been a consensus that gains in material standards outweigh the individual and social costs involved. As shown in the selections by Berglind and Meidner, there are signs today that increased knowledge about the price for welfare and the unequal distribution of affluence makes for some doubts as to the continuation of this policy.

Fractionated Jobs

With respect to conditions *inside* firms, the quest for greater efficiency has promoted mechanization and a division of labor resulting in meaningless work and circumscribed jobs with one-sided and low educational requirements. The content of these jobs creates conflict between a person's self-esteem and his opportunities to influence and achieve self-realization. Corporate management generally assumes that people do not really care to have responsibility and that the only reason they work is because they must. This makes it necessary—so the argument runs—to have a system which produces high-level performance irrespective of whether the individual is interested in his work. A cardinal principle, therefore, has been to distinguish between the execution of work operations, on the one hand, and planning and control, on the other. Further, successive efforts have been made to break down job tasks into the smallest possible components and keep training and learning times to a minimum. Compulsory rules for the performance of work have also been thought necessary. Here one can identify: first, systems used by technicians to control elements of working speed and methods—for example, assembly-line production, work measurement, and the like; second, comprehensive systems of rules and administrative procedures for maintaining order and discipline. And piece rates or similar incentive pay schemes are used to link the individual's interest in good earnings with the firm's interest in good performance, with the result that the individual pledges his allegiance to the goals of the economic system.

To all appearances, tasks characterized by serious restrictions on the exercise of discretion and skill are considered boring and uninteresting by the vast majority of people, and often are also associated with feelings of coercion and mental strain. Such tasks seem widely diffused in the industrial society even if it is important to stress that great variations in these respects occur in mass production as well as in process production industry. The recurring correlations between work's sociotechnical conditions and feelings of alienation in different industries and firms, as well as in different age, sex, and income groups, reinforces the impression that those differences of discretionary and skill levels afforded by the production technique describe central psychological factors in the work environment, whose impact also seems to extend to the individual's total life situation and health. The result of our studies suggest that the organization and content of work essentially identify real determinants of human satisfaction from and participation in the production system.

Naturally, this does not mean that production technology alone decides whether an individual will find his work interesting and meaningful. Obviously, people differ greatly from one another in how they perceive work owing to differences in level of aspirations and differences in conditions in and outside the workplace. Different mechanisms of selection and adjustment also play a major role in reducing conflicts in the individual case. But the fact remains that many individuals are dissatisfied with their work—and their numbers increase the more their tasks are objectively rated as fragmented, repetitive, and circumscribed. Hence the current efforts, both by individuals and the labor market, to realize the principle of "the right man in the right job" do not appear to have been especially successful, at least if these efforts are to be consistent with upholding everybody's right to interesting and "meaningful" work. Even with improved techniques of job placement to accommodate individual wishes among the old, the disabled, and other disadvantaged groups, this approach would offer no more than a marginal solution to the greater problem of an increasing gap between demand and supply of interesting and challenging jobs in most industrial societies.

Coming to grips with problems of monotony and stress in industrial work requires a work environment that widens the scope for self-determination, decision-making influence, and the exercise of occupational skill. This approach is essential in view of the rising expectations that accompany a higher standard of living and a growing educational attainment.

Our investigations show a mounting criticism of repetitive and constrained tasks by the younger working generation, as well as a more widespread desire for greater responsibility and more skilled work. This may be taken to reflect a higher level of aspiration. Other investigations show higher rates of turnover and absence among young employees, as well as greater difficulties of recruiting youth for jobs in factories. These empirical findings seem to indicate that young workers find the industrial environment less and less acceptable on physical, psychological, and social grounds.

Democratization of Workplace

Parallel with these developments in the labor market and in the job world is a development in the surrounding society characterized by political striving for greater equality and more freedom of decision and choice. Demands for greater self-determination and participatory management spring from various sources, among them insights gained by a longer period of formal education. Higher levels of aspiration in regard to job content and participatory management are the main theme of all studies concerned with generational differences in attitudes to work. It is in this conflict between aspiration and industrial reality that we shall look for the deeper, underlying causes of the unrest that sometimes flares up in the labor market, of the refusal of many young people to work in factories, of the high rate of turnover and absenteeism. These conditions argue that democracy cannot come to a halt at the factory gates, for it is the workplace and the production system which must be adapted to human aspirations, not the other way round. We cannot make do with solutions which imply that groups with less freedom of choice—for example, aliens and women—would fill those jobs which the male domestic labor force does not want. Nor can we go on accepting a state of affairs which bars so many elderly people, the handicapped, and other disadvantaged persons from gainful employment.

It is reasonable to assume that longer range solutions will have to aim at work environments which look satisfactory to the labor force as a whole. Among other things, this means that jobs must be organized to provide scope for a higher degree of self-determination and greater potentials for making use of all the facets of human ability. This kind of thinking is in conflict with time-honored principles of industrial work organization, and for some firms may well imply lowered productivity and difficulties in continuing production within this country. However, a number of firms have embarked on large-scale programs of experimentation involving broader definitions of job responsibilities, delegation of decision-making processes, alternatives to assembly-line methods of production, and so on. Similar efforts are being made under the auspices of the Development Council for Collaborative Questions, a body jointly sponsored by employer and employee confederations, and the Industrial Democracy Delegation, which is run by the Swedish government. There are also ambitious experiments to replace straight piece rates with mixed rates of payment or straight hourly rates; the trade unions have made demands for the adoption of monthly salaries.

While it is too early to make any definite judgment of progress, a great deal of evidence suggests that the measures taken have led to greater work satisfaction—and in many cases to increased productivity and lower absenteeism as well; yet it is also obvious that gains in work satisfaction and health will be achievable in many cases only at the cost of losses in productivity as conventionally measured. The question of whether the latter development can be considered acceptable will probably become a central issue of collective bargaining and public policy during the 1970s.

Recognition of Alienation

The fact that dissatisfaction with and alienation from work are now widely regarded in Sweden as important social phenomena may be linked to at least four different value areas. First, under a set of *economic* motives, work satisfaction and work involvement are supposed to be conducive to higher performance levels and/or lower labor turnover and absenteeism. The shortage of manpower, turnover, and absenteeism are especially difficult for large, highly rationalized firms with a high proportion of repetitive and circumscribed jobs; obviously, this causes many firms to take an interest in quality of working life issues.

Second, there is a *humanistic* motive which stresses the intrinsic value of work satisfaction. Democratically governed societies have generally accepted values to the effect that an individual has the right to a meaningful and interesting job, the right to influence decisions involving his own working situation, the right to freedom from arbitrary rules, coercion, physical and mental attrition, and so on. Therefore, the individual's reaction to work becomes essential for its own sake, irrespective of whether any direct connection can be demonstrated with productivity or some other economic measure.

Third, there is a motive which derives from the value area of *health*, building upon notions of a relationship between health and alienation. It seems reasonable to assume that the potentials of work to satisfy ego-related needs bear not only upon work satisfaction, but also upon general life adjustment or mental health. Working conditions that afford limited opportunities for influencing decisions, perceived meaningfulness, and self-realization tend not only to reduce work satisfaction, but also to instill feelings of inferior ability and lower prestige in the larger society and to diminish general life satisfaction and well-being.

Fourth, there is an ideological set of motives that links the issue of how jobs are organized to the issue of *industrial democracy*.

This is based on the realization that providing greater influence for employees at the workplace presupposes a greater degree of self-determination and responsibility in their daily work assignments. Unless these preconditions are met, reforms of the economic/political structure will not really affect the ability of individuals to influence decisions, and as such will not affect their work satisfaction either. Conversely, it is assumed that greater self-determination and responsibility at the workplace will create a more active orientation to work and thereby intensify demands for influence over decisions, including those which have to do with the general management of the firm. These notions seem to have had some influence on experiments extending industrial democracy that are now under way in Sweden in both the private and public sectors.

It should be noted, however, that most experimental work on job design and work organization in Sweden today is based on economic considerations. Firms are interested in social and environmental issues because they have to cope with manpower problems, unavailability, turnover, and absenteeism. Also obvious is that management decides what might or might not be done. The workers' possibilities to demand change are to a great extent circumscribed by the fact that union-management agreements in Sweden give management the right to "hire and fire" and to "distribute and manage jobs." These rights or prerogatives have for decades inhibited more participative democratic decision making in working life: worker influence through different forms of representative democracy has always been of an advisory kind only. Recently, however, the Confederations of Labor (blue collar LO and white collar TCO), decided to ask for such changes in Swedish labor laws that in practice will make issues of work environment and work organization negotiable. A government committee has also been appointed to effectuate this change in power relations in the workplace. When this change has been accomplished, a new situation will have emerged in which the workers can demand conditions and solutions that today may be approached only through slow and careful research and development controlled by management.

Issues for Social Scientists

Of course, there will always be some conflict between the demands of the workplace and individual needs, but the trend discussed above presents a much greater possibility for humanizing working life than would otherwise be feasible. Social science will probably find itself in increased demand, and it is of strategic importance for social scientists interested in enhancing the quality of working life to concern themselves with trade union problems and undertake research which might be used by the workers in their effort to create a sounder work environment.

There is no doubt that workers and worker organizations are much more inclined than are managements to have the future development of production systems be controlled not merely by economic values, but by social values as well. Thus, programs aiming at "enhancing the qualities of working life" must be anchored in those power structures which most likely will endorse broader sets of values—not only values of economic progress in the traditional sense. The problems involved concern all citizens, including politicians, labor leaders, managers, and other opinion leaders. The duty of social scientists interested in quality of working life is much broader than serving economic interests; this means that there must be an open debate about compromises that will be required between economic and social goals and that social scientists must be prepared to share their research and experience in open discussion among different interest groups and power centers in order to contribute to the changes in ideas and values which are necessary prerequisites for important and lasting improvements in the quality of working life.

NOTES

1. First, no one's interests are served by people falling ill or sustaining injury on account of conditions at the workplace. Preventive measures against accidents and ill health in the traditional medical sense are easily reconciled with the prevailing philosophy and values of business economics.

Second, commitments to occupational health programs and ergonomics do not require a break with the prevailing scientific management philosophy. Physiology, the medical sciences, and traditional industrial psychology are already in wide use, and their application will expand to adjust the environment to the reaction modes and tolerance limits of individuals, as well as for purposes of employee selection and placement. All this is necessary and first-rate—with the reservation that, if we stick to the dominant scientific management philosophy, we continue to reinforce the mechanistic view of man which science contains and which today controls the development of virtually all walks of life. The purport of this mechanistic view of man is to dehumanize not only the job world but also other aspects of the human condition.

2. In an ongoing study on the social and psychological consequences of plant shutdown, statistics indicate that no more than about 60 percent of displaced workers have gained lasting new employment 1½ years after the demise of the former employing firm. The increase over time is extremely modest. Included in this figure are 15 percent who transferred to affiliates of the same corporate group, having made the transfer immediately after shutdown. None was added to this group during the 18 months for which we have compiled statistics to date. As a rule, those transferred by the parent company are persons of good educational background: salaried employees, supervisors, or skilled production workers. The uneducated and the elderly are dumped on the community to look after. Of those who become jobless more or less permanently, a large proportion are afflicted with some illness or injury. The proportion of unemployed on the sick list increased somewhat during the 18-month period under investigation, which may be interpreted either as unemployment contributing to sickness or people on the sick list as an alternative, perhaps more legitimate, way for society to distribute its economic subsidies to the unemployed. We are still investigating whether illnesses are also more common among the long-term unemployed, by comparison with corresponding age groups in an equivalent, still-operating firm. (S. Berger, *Plant Shut Down—Consequences for Man and Society, Geogiafiska Regionstudier* no. 9, University of Upsala, 1973.)

21

Changing Workers' Values and Implications of Policy in Japan

Shin-ichi Takezawa

WITHIN only three decades since World War II, Japan has experienced four major stages in relation to work which, in their historical order, have developed within the last 100 years in the industrialized Western nations: (1) conditions of subsistence; (2) material advancement; (3) social recognition; (4) self-realization. This rapid transformation of Japanese society in less than thirty years has produced diverse and conflicting values among different generations that can be summarized as follows: young workers desire more opportunity for self-realization; the middle generation, feeling "betrayed" by economic growth in view of a narrowing of age differentials in compensation, is more concerned with earnings than are the other age groups; older workers are deeply concerned with employment security and subsistence, partly because of forced early retirement in a population with increasing life expectancy.

The work force is divided into three age groups: the young, up to the mid-twenties; the middle, up to the late forties; and the old workers in their fifties and sixties, just before and after compulsory retirement at age 55. The young workers are in a sellers' market and beginning salaries have increased much more than those of older workers. Interfirm mobility no longer results in disadvantages in compensation for young workers. Their values are changing strongly toward endorsing "Don't think about money or fame, just live a life that suits your tastes." Automation is seen as a threat to the younger factory workers' concern for self-realization at work, which they consider very important. However, despite recent increases in autonomy and small work group work design, many managers see practical limitations to such innovations.

The diverging interests of the young and middle generations require careful balancing of personnel policies and union activities. A serious problem faced by the middle generation involves differing growth rates in industry; inflexible employment systems prevent them from moving smoothly into the growing sector. The early retirement age for a population of increasing longevity results in many problems for older workers, many of whom have to return to work after "retirement" in order to maintain previous subsistence levels. Exacerbating the problem is the fact that the family system no longer provides protection for the aged. Some union leaders protest against quality of working life programs because they see as premature the allocation of resources to these programs before more basic needs are satisfied.

The rapid transformation of Japan from a near-subsistence economy to a postindustrial society in less than thirty-years, since World War II, has not taken place without consequences. This condensed experience has inevitably produced diverse and conflicting values among different generations. It has also been primarily responsible for the vast discrepancies in the socioeconomic conditions that affect the quality of working life of each worker generation: for example, old workers are still deeply concerned with basic employment security, whereas young workers sincerely desire an opportunity for self-realization. A proper policy mix for the betterment of working life in Japan must incorporate such diverse needs of different generations.

Changes in Values: Condensation and Diffusion

Several years after the end of World War II, an implicit consensus emerged among labor, management, and government leaders about the nation's goal—to reach the standards of living of the advanced Western nations—and the means to achieve it. Management would assume the primary responsibility to improve productivity, labor would share the productivity gain through collective bargaining, and the government would pave the way for other parties to play their respective roles.

Within twenty years the goal has almost been achieved. The per capita GNP surpassed 2,000 U.S. dollars in 1971 (computed at the 1971 year-end exchange rate: 308 yen = 1 dollar), showing an almost triple net increase within 11 years. The employment ratio of primary industry workers declined from 32.6 percent in 1960 to 19.3 percent in 1970. Average cash compensation for manufacturing male workers rose to the levels of those of Italy and France around 1970. For city workers' households, the Engel's coefficient (percentage of food items in family budgets) fell from 38.8 percent in 1960 to 31.6 percent in 1971, while their saving propensity rose from 14.9 percent to 19.6 percent during that period. Compensation disparities also narrowed substantially between wage and salary earners. As a result, the nation as a whole became increasingly middle class, as shown in Table 1; the percentage of the three "middle" categories rose from 73 percent in 1958 to 89.4 in 1971.[1]

Changes in values had come to the attention of managers much earlier, however, in the late 1950s, when generation gaps developed among workers on the production floor. The *dorai** or "dry" young workers' declining interest in work, little identification with the company, and growing mobility were puzzling to many managers. At this time the concept of human relations, the personalized approach, gained sudden and popular support among many managers as a means to deal with these problems. The youth unrest of that

TABLE 1.

Perceived Standards of Living

(in percent)

Perceived Standards	1958	1960	1965	1968	1970	1971
Upper	0	0	0.6	0.6	0.6	0.6
Upper-middle	4	4	6.7	7.6	7.8	6.8
Middle-middle	37	41	49.7	51.4	56.8	56.3
Lower-middle	32	32	30.3	28.0	24.9	26.3
Lower	17	13	8.9	7.6	6.6	6.4
Unidentified	10	10	3.9	4.8	3.3	3.6
TOTAL	100	100	100.0	100.0	100.0	100.0

Source: Public Information Office, Cabinet Secretariat, *Public Opinion Survey on National Life,* 1972 (in Japanese).

---

* The Japanese word *dorai* was coined as an antonym of *wetto,* both becoming fashionable around 1960. *Dorai* meant calculating, self-centered, heartless, rationalistic, etc. *Wetto* (←wet) meant devoted, unselfish, other-oriented, sentimental, etc.

time, partly a product of the 1960 political turmoil, seemingly came to a halt around 1963, but management's concern with changes in values was further accelerated; every year young workers, fresh out of school, looked somewhat different from the previous year's crop, so much so that finally a well-known professor of business advised industrial managers to "treat the youngsters like foreigners."

In addition to the influence of accelerated social change, another peculiarly Japanese factor plays a role in generation gap issues—the social status of the young workers. Despite the sharp rise in earnings, the young generation still belongs to the lowest status group in Japan in every aspect of their working lives, a status they are "scheduled" to outgrow because of almost universal upward mobility as they gain age and seniority. Indeed, Professor Tominaga refers to that generation as a "quasi-class" [2] and, for all practical purposes, it has been a popular subject during the last fifteen years both in management courses and business literature.

Even though generation gaps had already appalled many elders in Japanese industry, Japanese workers were found to identify strongly with their workplace in crosscultural comparisons. Table 2 reveals two interesting facts: first, Japanese production workers showed marked signs of generation gaps as early as 1960; second, they nevertheless assigned greater importance to the role of the workplace in their lives than did American workers.[3] Although comparative data are not available for more recent years, the data in Table 3 suggest the continuing prevalence of somewhat serious work attitudes among Japanese workers of today.[4]

TABLE 2.

Identity with Workplace

(in percent)

I think of my company as	USA (1961)			Japan (1960)		
	TOTAL	YOUNG	OLD	TOTAL	YOUNG	OLD
1. the central concern in my life and of greater importance than my personal life;	1	2	1	9	7	16
2. a part of life at least equal in importance to my personal life;	22	30	24	57	62	45
3. a place for me to work with management, during work hours, to accomplish mutual goals;	54	49	55	26	20	34
4. strictly a place to work and entirely separate from my personal life.	23	19	20	8	11	5
TOTAL	100	100	100	100	100	100

Source: Arthur M. Whitehill, Jr., and Shin-ichi Takezawa, The Other Worker: A Comparative Study of Industrial Relations in the United States and Japan (Honolulu: East-West Center Press, 1968).

A new holistic approach to the problem of changing values gained strength toward the end of the 1960s with the popularization of a somewhat nebulous term called *ikigai*. One author defines *ikigai* as the satisfaction of psychological needs, such as

1. need for existence-fulfillment;
2. need for change and variety;
3. need for future anticipation;
4. need for human interaction;
5. need for freedom;
6. need for self-actualization;
7. need for meaning and valuation.[5]

The role of work in *ikigai* is a debatable question among philosophers as well as among personnel managers. Sensible managers limit their approach to *hatarakigai* (work-related *ikigai*), on the ground that *ikigai* is a private sanctuary inviolate to business. The whole argument has served—as has the broad concept of alienation—to clarify the limitation of such conventional concepts as job satisfaction and morale, opening the eyes of the materialist to the existence of nonmonetary values. As a result, the present trend in the analysis of quality of working life issues in Japan emphasizes an integrated approach, in which neither psychological variables nor material conditions must be omitted; job situations and off-the-job conditions have to be reconsidered, and the time span or the career perspective must not be forgotten. In Japan such a global approach is believed essential to the balanced allocation of resources and responsibilities for the betterment of working life.

TABLE 3.

Concepts of Work—1970

(in percent)

Items	Age groups				
	16–19	20–24	25–29	30–39	40–49
1. Work is only natural to man; devotion to work is admirable.	54	54	61	67	72
2. Work is an important opportunity to demonstrate one's ability.	19	25	18	16	12
3. Work is just a means to earn income.	23	17	18	15	14
4. Unidentified.	4	4	3	2	2
TOTAL	100	100	100	100	100

Source: Public Information Office, Cabinet Secretariat, *Values of Working People* (in Japanese), 1971.

The following sections deal with three different age groups: the young, middle, and older generations. The term "young generation" refers largely to workers in their teens and early twenties. The middle generation are mostly workers with families, in their late twenties to forties. The older workers are in their fifties and sixties and, thus, just before or after compulsory retirement at age 55.

The Young Generation: Meaning of Life and Work

The present-day young generation of Japan grew up with the advancement of the nation's economy; that is, their present environment probably shows little resemblance even to what it was only ten years ago. Some of the major changes in the socioeconomic environment may be summarized as follows:

1. In the rich growing economy, the labor market has become a sellers' market so far as young workers are concerned. This is not true of older workers.
2. The starting pay of the production worker has climbed twice as fast, within ten years, as that of the worker in his fifties.
3. Compensation of the young generation today shows little difference among firms and industries. For the young generation the "dual" economy no longer exists.
4. Interfirm mobility no longer results in discriminatory compensation disadvantages to the young generation, while older workers must still expect such disadvantages.
5. Most consumer goods and leisure activities are designed for the youth market.

One consequence of these improvements is the removal of external strains from the young generation. The first column in Table 4 represents the responses of army conscripts in 1930. By comparison, the postwar data from four successive nationwide studies (1953, 1958, 1963, and 1968) show a marked and systematic difference. Both the stoical "Red Guard" posture and the "get ahead," N-achievement characteristic of the 1930 respondents have declined considerably with the possible exception of a reviving emphasis on money. Furthermore, the relaxed attitude represented by the "live a life that suits your own tastes" choice increased steadily during the 15-year period. The study also suggests an interesting possibility: this value change is likely to persist over the years, regardless of age. A chronological analysis based on the birth year of the respondents, presented in Figure 1, shows that each birth-year group, though not of the same sample, adhered to an almost identical preference pattern irrespective of the year of actual study.[6] In all likelihood, the proportion of tense, self-sacrificing workers will eventually decline in Japanese industry.

The increasingly relaxed attitudes of the new generation upset not a few managers around 1965, when the economy was undergoing a recession. These managers looked upon *mōretsu-shugi* (hardboiled work-centeredness) and *mai-hōmu-shugi* (family-centeredness) as a useful dichotomy boldly to categorize their subordinates. A recent factorial study of worker values suggests, however, that these values are not polarized in the psychological framework of Japanese workers. In fact, work-centeredness and family-centeredness are similar probably because they share the same dimension of "serving others." On the other hand, leisure-centeredness, which is essentially personal in nature, may or may not conflict with work-centeredness or family-centeredness.[7]

With respect to alienation from work, automation and mechanization are a real threat to Japanese factory workers; and young workers in particular are increasingly concerned with the limited opportunity for self-realization at the workplace. A study conducted by the Ministry of Labor in 1970 disclosed that 63.9 percent of the large plants (1,000 or more workers) reported an increase in monotonous work for the preceding 5-year period; only 6.4 percent reported a decrease.[8] The pace of factory work has also been accelerated; PAC (Performance Analysis and Control), a measured day work system, for example, normally doubles factory performance levels within a year without monetary

TABLE 4.

Ways of Life

(in percent)

Question: There are all sorts of attitudes toward life; of those listed here, which ones would you say come closest to your feeling?

Items	1930	1953	1958	1963	1968
1. Work hard and get rich	17	9	12	12	13
2. Study earnestly and make a name for yourself	8	5	2	2	2
3. Don't think about money or fame; just live a life that suits your own tastes	11	34	38	45	51
4. Live each day as it comes, cheerfully and without worrying	3	9	12	15	16
5. Resist all evils in the world and live a pure and just life	30	28	26	16	10
6. Never think of yourself, give everything in service of society	23	11	8	3	5
Others and D.K.	7	4	2	7	3
TOTAL	100	100	100	100	100

Source: 1930 data quoted in Cabinet Secretariat, *Opinion Survey on Social Trends* (in Japanese), 1965. The postwar data from The Institute of Statistical Mathematics, *A Study of Japanese National Character*, vol. II (in Japanese), 1970.

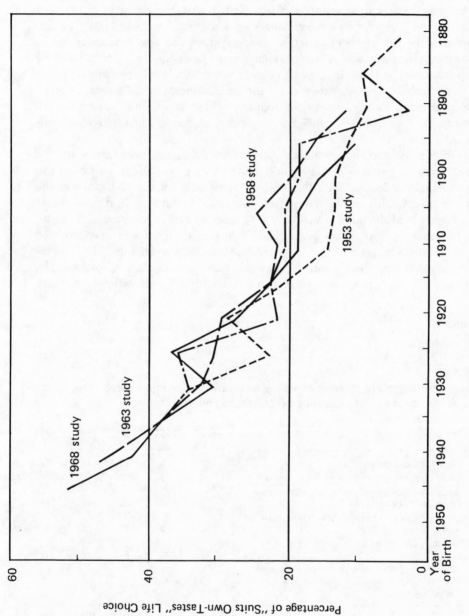

Figure 1. Persistence of Values. *Source:* Institute of Statistical Mathematics, *A Study of Japanese National Character*, vol. II (in Japanese), 1970.

incentives. In the context of the Japanese employment system, it may be recalled that the young generation is the most effected by such changes on the production floor.

A trend which may have a far-reaching effect on the economy in the long run is the loss of appeal of big businesses to the young generation. For larger manufacturing firms (500 or more workers), the separation rate rose from 17.1 percent in 1958 to 21.7 percent in 1971, while among smaller firms (5 to 29 workers) it fell from 34.5 percent in 1958 to 26.9 percent in 1971. It seems clear that this loss of appeal is primarily due to the blocked satisfaction of higher needs such as self-actualization (see Table 5).[9]

Thus, the quality of work problems experienced in Japan may be considered quite similar to those faced by older industrial nations, with possibly two qualifications: first, older workers are not necessarily interested in, and may even resent, management allocation of resources to quality of work measures; second, human relations seem to be an active "motivator" as well as a "hygiene factor" to most Japanese workers. Nonetheless, it seems true that self-realization is increasingly a very important need of the young generation of Japanese workers.

An attempt was made in a study conducted by the Japan Committee for Economic Development to identify the job features most appealing to young workers employed in twenty-five large firms.[10] The data in Table 6 show that

TABLE 5.

Images of the "Big Company"—1970

(percentages representing ratio of choices made to total number of respondents, asked to make up to 3 choices)

Items	Male Below Age 22	Female Below Age 22	Male Above Age 35	Total
1. Assurance of materially comfortable life	17.2	22.0	36.3	26.1
2. Monotonous and uninteresting jobs	49.0	26.5	21.2	31.6
3. High social prestige and reputation	9.0	32.6	17.9	10.3
4. Cutthroat competition among employees	6.9	18.2	7.3	10.3
5. Good employee benefits and services	55.2	66.7	57.0	59.2
6. Good education and training opportunities	26.2	22.7	41.3	31.3
7. Too much pressure through rationalization	16.2	13.6	1.7	9.9
8. Good care of former employees after retirement	13.1	14.4	28.0	19.3
9. Abilities buried under organization	52.4	29.5	18.4	32.5
10. Others	8.3	10.6	6.1	8.1
11. No answer	3.4	5.3	6.1	5.0
N:	(291)	(264)	(358)	(913)

Source: Labor-Management Council for Productivity, *Attitudes and Behaviors of Younger and Older Workers* (in Japanese), 1970.

work autonomy and new experience were the two job aspects most appealing to all worker groups. It is also shown that a substantial number of production workers viewed contact with people, clearly a human relations concept, as an important feature.

At the practical level, management in Japan usually participates in quality of work programs on the job and in sponsored recreational activities designed to counteract alienation. There is a growing trend to introduce autonomy and small group work under the leadership of rank-and-file representatives, as well as innovations in industrial engineering to improve the quality of work life; but many managers see practical limitations to such innovations. Perhaps the most well-known technique popularly applied in Japan is the small group movement, often called Quality Control Circles.

TABLE 6.

Desirable Job Features—1971

(percentages representing ratio of choices made to number of respondents)

Question: Which job features do you wish to find in your work at the company?
You may indicate up to three choices.

Items	*Production Male (High School)*	*Clerical Female (High School & Jr. College)*	*Clerical & Technical Male (University)*
1. Opportunity to contact different people on the job	10.6	16.8	9.8
2. Autonomy to handle work at your own responsibility	18.0	16.8	18.8
3. Opportunity to meet people of the other sex	5.7	3.4	0.7
4. Opportunity to participate in individual competition	4.5	1.4	1.7
5. Group-based work where individual achievement is buried	3.3	1.5	1.3
6. Close working with manager and senior colleagues	4.2	4.4	4.3
7. Little supervision from manager or senior colleagues	11.1	7.7	6.5
8. Manufacturing feature products of the company	2.8	0.9	3.6
9. Challenging work trying the limit of your ability	7.1	5.1	11.0
10. Easy work well within your capacity	3.9	5.8	1.1
11. New work with no previous experience	11.0	14.6	12.4
12. Corporate planning, research, and development	7.4	3.4	16.4
13. Others (Specify)	0.8	1.3	0.8
No answer	9.6	16.9	11.6
N:	(1,429)	(1,163)	(651)

Source: Japan Committee for Economic Development, *Problems in Leading the Youth* (in Japanese), 1972.

The present proliferation of small groups on the production floor seems logical in view of the country's collectivistic cultural background, representing, at least in part, a natural extension of the traditional practice of interactive decision making. Although formerly a prerogative of executives and staff workers, and denied to most production workers, the leveling process in society has helped to integrate that feature into the regular work patterns on the floor.

In view of the preceding analysis, the following policy considerations seem relevant to the quality of working life issues of the young generation:

1. Transformation of values, a necessary consequence of development, first takes place among the young generation. Some of the changed basic values will be carried throughout their career, gradually affecting all of society in the long run.

2. The young generation already show signs of activated needs for recognition and self-realization; the quality of working life program must meet such needs.

3. The concept of management must be redefined for first-line supervision to include the creation of an environment conducive to responsible individual and group autonomy.

4. Management participation in off-job aspects of working life still seems important, but must be redefined as assistance rather than interference.

5. Shorter work hours help man cope with the monotony of present-day work. Early introduction of a shorter work week seems to be a necessary step forward.

The Middle Generation: Compensation and Career

The middle generation experienced, at least in part, both the postwar poverty and the beginning of prosperity in their adolescence. They take pride in Japan's economic achievement, but tend to view their share in it as not too gratifying. Major changes in the economic environment that have affected them may be summarized as follows:

1. Their earnings advantage over junior colleagues has declined substantially in recent years.

2. They are the most hardpressed age group economically, prohibitive housing costs being the worst problem of all.

3. Frequent transfers and job changes resulting from new technology, tend to nullify the value of accumulated skills of this generation.

Around 1960 a beginning production worker, at age 18, probably expected to triple his earnings within ten years, hoping for a fivefold increase after twenty years of service; at least that was what he saw among his senior workers. Now a production worker, at age 38, earns only three times as much as a beginner, and the difference is more than likely to narrow still further. In other words, a worker now in the middle generation, who in his youth was the least privileged under the strict seniority rule, will never be able to recover the difference in earnings during his work life. As a result, his generation tends to be dissatisfied with compensation more than any other age group, and studies show that job content, human relations problems, and long hours are a relatively minor source of irritation. Their concern with "money" rather than "time" emerges clearly from the data obtained from male workers in various age groups and summarized in Table 7.[11]

The diverging interests of the young and middle generations require careful balancing of personnel policies and union activities. If the majority of the work force is young, as is often the case in fast-growing firms, both union and management may choose to concentrate their efforts on quality of work and recreational activities. If the average worker is older, as in declining industries, remuneration issues must take precedence. In recent years, some labor unions submitted demands to management asking for minimum compensation guarantees for different age groups. This was an apparent effort to prevent a further narrowing of age-based compensation differentials.

The Japanese system of compensation seems to be moving further into a system primarily based on cost of living. The narrowing of age-based differentials, though quite substantial, may look even smaller when compared with the squeeze taking place among groups with different education. For the

TABLE 7.

Acceptance of Overtime Work—1970

(in percent)

Statements	Age Groups			
	TWENTIES	THIRTIES	FORTIES	TOTAL
I would not work overtime; my time is too precious to spare	20.0	10.3	8.2	12.6
Overtime premium should be raised to match the sacrifice of personal time	37.1	46.2	24.3	36.0
I would work overtime whenever possible to earn more money	11.4	20.5	29.7	20.8
We should work overtime regardless of pay if it is necessary for production	20.0	10.3	27.0	18.9
Others	8.6	5.0	5.4	6.3
No answer	2.0	7.7	5.4	5.4
TOTAL	100.0	100.0	100.0	100.0
N:	(70)	(78)	(74)	(222)

Source: Japan Productivity Center, *The Practice of Hours, Holidays, and Vacations* (in Japanese), 1970.

following comparisons, the income statistics of the particular year were used as the basis of career income computations: In 1961 the career income of a middle school graduate was 58.0 percent of that of a college graduate, and that of a high-school graduate 64.1 percent. By 1969 these figures rose to 67.3 and 74.3 percent, respectively. Within another ten years they may even climb to 87.0 and 90.0 percent. (Comparative percentages for the United States are 46 and 63 for 1956, 42 and 61 for 1958, and 46 and 63 for 1966).[12]

The small correspondence between compensation and work contributes, at least in part, to the freedom of action in organizational redesign and personnel transfers. In 1971, 29.8 percent of the firms studied by the Ministry of Labor reported that transfer with work content change had affected 5 to 10 percent of their production workers during the previous year. In 16.5 percent of the firms studied, such transfers had affected the working life of 10 to 20 percent of the employed work force.[13]

One difficulty in frequent organizational change and personnel transfer involves the coordination of individual plans and organizational needs. Career white-collar workers, who used to view compulsory transfer as part of the game, today resist transfer orders not infrequently. A decade ago, management introduced annual, self-assessment reports, in which each employee assessed his present performance, suitability of his current job, preference regarding another assignment, and readiness for job rotation. Some firms also have optional training programs to prepare applicants for assignments of their own choice; however, participation in career planning needs considerable developmental effort in the future, particularly for production workers.

The most serious problem faced by the present-day middle generation involves differing growth rates in Japanese industry. Although almost every Japanese organization has an inherent drive for growth, not every firm grows at the same rate. Inflexible employment systems then prevent the middle generation from moving smoothly into the growing sector, while the declining sector will find internal cost pressures prohibitive—and rising—as the age structure of its work force continues upward. Union-management relations are certain to decline in such enterprises, the middle generation finding itself trapped in this vicious circle. There are already signs of mounting unrest in some public services, such as railroad transportation and utilities.

Finally, two problems will be considered briefly that involve working women, who now comprise a sizeable portion of the middle generation work force: one is the shortage of adequate child care facilities for working mothers, who point out that it is the greatest bottleneck in their working life; public investment in nurseries and child care centers must be increased for the protection of both children and mothers. The other problem is management's overall lack of interest in creating opportunities for self-realization of women workers in private industry. Today many women continue to work after marriage, but have few opportunities for creative work. Research indicates that many women value "responsible jobs" more than "high compensation," and they are often the most receptive toward job enrichment and the small group movement.

Some of the important policy considerations emerging from the analysis of the middle generation may be summarized as follows:

1. Even though the leveling process in society deserves due recognition, today's middle generation feels "betrayed" by the process of economic growth. The narrowing of earnings levels seems primarily responsible for this dissatisfaction.
2. The middle generation shows a greater concern with earnings than do the other age groups. This is probably a composite result of their stage in life, their basic value structure, and external factors.
3. The compensation scheme may continue to be need-based; the principle should be "payment on the basis of need, and contribution on the basis of ability."
4. Participation of individual workers in career planning, transfer, and re-training should be invited through institutional arrangements.
5. Women in private industry seem to need special provisions for self-actualization.

The Older Generation: Employment and Social Security

The older generation, now in their fifties and sixties, spent most of their youth during World War II. Their basic needs seem restricted and modest, activated mostly at subsistence levels. The problems of this generation, by far the most neglected group in industry in present-day Japan, have arisen as a consequence of several interrelated socioeconomic conditions:

1. During the last twenty-five years the average life expectancy of the Japanese has increased by 20 years.
2. Compulsory retirement at age 55, however, has remained almost un-changed in industry during the same period.
3. Employment opportunities for this group have not expanded as fast as for the young generation.
4. The traditional family system has ceased to provide protection in old age.
5. The development of social security, particularly provisions for old age, has lagged behind economic growth and is totally inadequate.

Special legislation was enacted in 1971 to promote the employment of older workers. The law redefined the term *chūnen* (literally translated as "middle age") as the age between 45 and 55; previously, *chūnen* was officially defined to begin at age 35.

In 1947 life expectancy at birth was 50.06 years for men and 53.96 years for women; compulsory retirement at age 55, then, was not considered too early for most people, particularly since they received a lump sum retirement allowance of some 30 months' pay. The most recent life expectancy figures, released in 1972, showed 70.17 years for men and 75.58 years for women, but compulsory retirement age for regular employees in large firms has remained almost unchanged, at age 55. Some collective agreements have provided for extension of two or three years, but further extension is rare except in small industries. From management's point of view, extension means additional complexity in managerial appointment and higher per capita labor costs due to length-of-service increases, and labor unions have chosen to concentrate on general pay increases, bypassing the minority issues of old-age workers.

Japan has also experienced a phenomenal growth in nuclear households in recent years; between 1965 and 1970, for example, the number increased by 2,488,000. Married children living separately from parents usually means that the parents continue to work after compulsory retirement. Increasingly, parents cannot depend on their children in old age. The chronological trend of this development is shown in Table 8.[14]

Most retirees continue to work because they need the income; one national study of 4,400 "retired" employees showed that 74.8 percent continued as employed workers, 12.1 percent were self-employed, and 13.1 percent were totally unemployed. Among those gainfully employed or in search of work, 77.6 percent mentioned "sheer necessity" as their reason for working. Only 27.9 percent of working retirees earned as much or more income after retirement, while 38.3 percent earned less than 70 percent of their former income.[15]

Although the Japanese employment system is often referred to as "career employment," employers do not necessarily assume responsibility for the placement of workers forced into retirement. Practices vary from firm to firm, but more than half of the retiring employees are estimated to seek their "second" jobs through friends, newspaper advertisements, or public employment agencies, the remainder depending on the employer for placement. As to

TABLE 8.

Expected Dependence on Children in Old Age

(in percent)

Items	1950	1952	1955	1957	1959	1961	1963	1965	1967	1969
Expects no dependence on children	21.3	19.3	22.0	24.7	27.7	27.6	48.0	47.3	48.8	50.5
Counts on support from children	54.8	51.0	45.0	43.5	39.4	35.1	33.4	35.3	31.9	28.6
Help desired, but seems impossible	3.9	8.1	8.5	8.4	7.8	8.3	—	—	—	—
Never thought about; No answer	20.0	21.6	24.5	23.4	25.1	29.0	18.6	17.4	19.3	20.9
TOTAL	100.0	100.0	100.0	100.0	100.0	100.0	100.0	100.0	100.0	100.0

Source: Mainichi Shinbun, Public Opinion Poll on Population Problems, 1969 (sampling methods have been altered since 1963).

public expenditure in social security, it has grown by 3,000 percent over the last twenty years, yet social security was only 6.7 percent of GNP in 1971. Even though comprehensive efforts are under way, most areas need much improvement, the only possible exception being medical programs. Among the least advanced is old age pension, both in terms of coverage and benefits.

The older generation is not a vocal group, on the job or otherwise, but various studies point out clearly that immediate needs of this generation are primarily for basic security and subsistence. Some union leaders protest against quality of work programs because they realize that it is premature to allocate resources to these programs before more basic needs for certain groups of workers are satisfied. The primary concerns of the older generation involve the following:

1. Security and subsistence needs require attention. Even though this may be true of any society, the prevailing socioeconomic conditions in Japan emphasize the urgency of such needs.

2. Extension of compulsory retirement to age 65 should receive serious consideration, with as little change as possible in work content and workplace.

3. Minimum compensation for workers between ages 55 and 65 may also be based on living costs, as is done for the middle generation. At least minimum guarantees should be established.

4. Inducements should be provided by government to promote employment of older workers in industry.

5. Improvements in old-age pension and other social security programs are vital to the quality of life of this generation.

The Quality of Working Life in Transition

The foregoing analysis deliberately covered issues beyond those normally discussed in connection with the quality of working life; a narrower treatment would have lacked proper perspective in the Japanese context. This has been an epistemological choice.

Work is a complex phenomenon with many facets. Man has uncovered one facet after another from different perspectives and different disciplines. The focal framework for analysis and action in each industrial nation, however, is remarkably closely related to the society's stage of economic development. This is to be expected since the adoption or rejection of a framework is a function of human values which are, in turn, largely conditioned by economic development. At the risk of obvious oversimplification, four major focal concerns are identified which seem to have developed, one after another, in the cumulative process of industrialization.

1. *Concern with conditions of subsistence.* Marxism, labor policies, factory social policy; minimum wages, employment security, accident prevention, militant unionism, and so on; from the mid-nineteenth century; war may reduce a society to this stage.

2. *Concern with material achievement.* Taylorism, Fayolism, industrial engineering, productivity movements, business unionism; efficiency, organization, management, wage incentives, profit sharing, merit rating, and so on; beginning at about 1890 (USA).

3. *Concern with social recognition.* Human relations, industrial democracy, group dynamics; democratic leadership, supervisory training, participation, morale surveys, and so on; beginning about 1930 (USA).

4. *Concern with self-realization.* Behavioral sciences, quality of working life; creativity, small group, self-management, flexible work times, and so on; beginning about 1960.

Within only three decades since World War II, Japan has experienced all four stages in rapid succession, moving from postwar poverty to affluence. The violent labor disputes of the late 1940s signified the stage when the nation was concerned with subsistence. The productivity movement around 1955 marked the emergence of the second stage; at that time, also, the concept of business unionism began to attract labor's attention. Around 1960 a sudden outburst of interest in human relations signaled the arrival of the third stage. And, no doubt, the new interest in *ikigai* issues in more recent years marks the beginning of the fourth stage.

This condensed experience probably accounts, more than anything else, for the systematic differences in values among the generations in Japan. At the same time the surrounding socioeconomic conditions as well as the life stage of each generation seem to reinforce its specific value structure. Our expectation that the present age groups' respective attitudes toward work are consistently related to the historical development of man's concern with work is strongly supported by the data and analyses in the preceding sections.

Table 9 also seems to confirm this hypothesis. A study conducted by the Ministry of Labor in 1971 asked 17,251 male workers what they valued as improvements for the future.[16] Highly valued items included, regardless of age, compensations, shorter hours, social security, housing assistance, and tax reductions. These statements suggest that Japanese workers are still interested mostly in material achievements, the second stage in the history of industrial development, and that it is unlikely they will slow their present pace of work suddenly in the near future.

A closer look at the table reveals, however, some systematic differences among the age groups: the younger groups are more concerned with shorter hours, jobs compatible with ability and personality, and with general, public environmental concerns. The young generation is also concerned with human relations. The middle generation is more interested in material acquisitions, such as earnings, property, and home ownership. This group also shows greater interest in career education and training. In contrast, the higher age

TABLE 9.

Improvement Preferences—1971

(in percent)

On the Job	LESS THAN 19	20–24	25–29	30–34	35–39	40–44	45–54	55–64	65 AND OVER	TOTAL
General compensation increases	32.7	32.4	33.8	34.5	35.1	34.2	31.4	27.1	22.7	33.2
5-day week, shorter work hours	25.2	21.8	19.1	17.9	16.7	15.4	12.7	15.1	16.3	18.1
Assistance to property and house ownership	6.2	9.0	12.2	14.4	14.3	13.7	11.8	10.6	8.2	12.0
Jobs compatible with ability and personality	10.2	12.5	12.2	8.9	9.0	7.6	7.4	7.8	5.6	9.9
Provisions for career training and education	6.5	8.4	8.0	7.7	6.2	5.4	5.1	3.3	3.9	6.9
Improved employee benefits and services	7.2	7.9	6.2	6.5	5.6	5.2	4.9	9.5	18.0	6.5
Extension of compulsory retirement age	1.6	1.5	2.3	3.8	5.8	9.4	17.0	15.8	14.6	5.9
Improved safety, work environment	6.7	4.6	4.1	4.3	5.5	7.0	7.6	7.4	6.9	5.4
Others	3.7	2.0	2.0	2.0	1.8	2.3	2.1	3.4	3.9	2.2
TOTAL	100.0	100.0	100.0	100.0	100.0	100.0	100.0	100.0	100.0	100.0

Off the Job										
Improved social security schemes	23.9	26.9	27.8	29.8	30.8	31.7	32.3	32.9	33.5	29.4
Solution of housing problems	19.2	26.1	30.7	29.5	24.0	21.3	20.0	16.9	15.5	25.4
Tax reductions	14.9	17.8	16.9	16.5	18.3	21.9	25.0	25.0	24.5	18.9
Improved traffic schemes	10.8	6.7	6.4	7.5	9.5	9.5	8.0	9.0	10.3	7.9
Prevention of industrial pollution	11.2	7.6	6.4	7.0	8.1	7.5	7.3	7.9	8.6	7.5
Increased leisure hours	13.9	10.6	7.2	5.7	5.3	4.4	4.4	4.9	6.4	6.9
Improved public parks, water systems, etc.	6.2	4.3	4.4	4.0	4.0	3.8	3.0	3.3	1.3	4.1
TOTAL	100.0	100.0	100.0	100.0	100.0	100.0	100.0	100.0	100.0	100.0

Source: Ministry of Labor, *Study of Worker Attitudes* (in Japanese), 1972.

groups tend to place more importance on basic subsistence items. To older workers, extension of retirement age, employee benefits and services, accident prevention, social security, and tax reductions seem to have a real appeal.

The question to what extent such value differences reflect the present conditions encompassing each generation and life stage, and to what extent they stem from the differences in the basic value structure of each age group are certainly debatable. It appears true, however, that socioeconomic conditions, life stage, and value structures operate in the same direction, and hence tend to enforce rather than cancel each other's effects.

With a view to long-range policy considerations, the following conclusions may be offered to labor, management, and government leaders.

1. The quality of working life problems seem to cover a wider range of human needs in Japan than in already advanced, slower moving industrial nations. Activated needs of Japanese workers as a whole range from subsistence to material to social and self-realization needs. Neglect of any area could lead to unbalanced policies for action.

2. The central concern of Japanese workers still seems to involve material acquisition. This is probably the result of, as well as the driving force toward, accelerated economic growth. Weakening this may be hard to achieve, particularly for the middle generation. If it becomes a national goal, it may best be achieved by capitalizing on the values of the young generation.

3. At the practical level, the parties concerned must consider, in their policy decisions, the generational characteristics of the work force. Self-realization and social needs are more important to the young generation; earnings are more meaningful to the middle generation; and security and subsistence are the concern of the older generation.

4. Continuing value changes will necessitate a shifting emphasis in the policy mix in future years. The trend seems to point to less emphasis on subsistence and more emphasis on *ikigai* and *hatarakigai* issues, although much depends on the improvement of socioeconomic conditions.

NOTES

1. Committee on Manpower, Economic Council, *Human Development and Worker Welfare for the New Era* (in Japanese) (Tokyo: Shiseido, 1972), p. 159. The author served as a member of the committee in preparation of the report.

2. Kenichi Tominaga, *The Status and Role of the Young Generation in Contemporary Society* (in Japanese), unpublished paper, 1971, p. 7.

3. Arthur M. Whitehill, Jr., and Shin-ichi Takezawa, *The Other Worker: A Comparative Study of Industrial Relations in the United States and Japan* (Honolulu: East-West Center Press, 1968), p. 111.

4. Committee on Manpower, Economic Council, *op. cit.*, p. 165.

5. Mieko Kamiya, *On the Subject of Ikigai* (in Japanese) (Tokyo: Misuzu Shobo, 1966), pp. 43–58.

6. Institute of Statistical Mathematics, *A Study of Japanese National Character*, vol. II (in Japanese with an English résumé) (Tokyo: Shiseido, 1970). The wording of the question is taken from the translation provided by the original authors.

7. Committee on Manpower, Economic Council, *op. cit.*, p. 168.

8. *Ibid.*, p. 92.

9. *Ibid.*, p. 165.

10. Japan Committee for Economic Development, *Problems in Leading the Youth* (in Japanese) (Tokyo: Japan Committee for Economic Development, 1972), Appendix, p. 15.

11. Committee on Manpower, Economic Council, *op. cit.*, p. 276.

12. Ministry of Labor, *The Analysis of Labor Economics, 1969* (in Japanese) (Tokyo: Government Printing Office, 1970). Reference Materials, pp. 46–49.

13. Committee on Manpower, Economic Council, *op. cit.*, p. 94.

14. *Ibid.*, p. 243.

15. Ministry of Labor, "Study of Retired Workers," *Labor Data Report* (in Japanese), no. 31 (1971), 1–8.

16. Ministry of Labor, "Study of Worker Attitudes" (in Japanese), unpublished data, 1972.

PART
VI

Quality of
Working Life –
The Context
of Bargaining

IN Part V, Gardell (selection 20) drew attention to those who might be displaced by those very factors which make for improvement of the lot of the better placed workers. Piore analyzes the forces which make for a "dual labor market." This same theme is discussed in different ways by the other contributors Meidner, Ginzberg, and Berglind.

Piore attributes to the policies of labor unions the development of a dual labor market in the United States—one for those who can and want to hold down a secure, moderately progressive job, and one for those who cannot or do no want to make the grade in the first. Their pursuit of security for their members hinders the initiatives of employers who are therefore brought also to seek stability by exporting the variances they encounter from the market onto a weaker sector of employment where layoffs, bankruptcies, short runs, and so on are the norm rather than the exception. And it is the weaker, the disadvantaged, who gravitate to this sector. Furthermore, Piore argues, managements in the privileged sector are hindered—by the rules of seniority, job allocation and its derivatives, job evaluation, and work study, into which they are pushed by union demands for security—from experimenting with new forms of organization which would enhance quality of working life by means of more flexible manning policies.

His suggested remedies, which include government pressure and legislation, are aimed at reducing the number of jobs in his "secondary" sector to those which could be filled by people to whom, for one reason or another, temporary employment is an advantage or at any rate no hindrance. One possible remedy he suggests is the kind of employment guarantee provided by Japanese firms. It is perhaps ironic that Takezawa (selection 21) suggests that today these policies are proving less attractive to the young in Japan. The social changes in Japan are apparently creating a three-sector labor market of young, middle-aged, and older workers. The young operate in a sellers' market. Under the old Japanese system workers' pay increases with age; older people find it hard to move to the expanding growth industries and are left as a very expensive tenured factor in the declining industries which can least afford it. The middle age group is simultaneously squeezed by the narrowing of age-based differentials, outbid by the young in new industries and unable to displace the old in the declining ones.

It is also somewhat ironical that the two Swedish selections describe very similar phenomena, but in the context of quite different union policies and in a context where government intervention in the labor market has been far greater than in the United States. Meidner describes the development in Sweden of a dual labor market as a consequence of increasing technological sophistication, growing search for efficiency to meet international competition, and structural factors such as the discrepancies between industrial regions and those dependent upon primary production, low mobility of married women, and so on. Changes in outlook and education play their part. In this highly successful egalitarian society two clear sectors have separated out—the privileged with good jobs and secure employment, and the rest. Drawing upon the comparison with environmental policies elaborated by Cherns and Davis (selection 1), Meidner advocates acceptance by Swedish industry of greater social responsibility. This is not the only illustration of the relationship between the growth in concern with quality of working life and that with social responsibility on a wider scale. Berglind, too, offers us a rider on Piore's theorem of the dual market. He poses the dilemma: poorer quality of working life or fewer employed but having high quality of working life. As Berglind indicates: "There is no simple solution to this dilemma. If we want to maintain work as a human right we need not only improve working conditions for a highly efficient majority. We must also create working conditions that give a chance to the less efficient to be a part of productive society."

Is the case made that a higher quality of working life is likely to be for the elite only? A danger exists but should not be overstated; it is clear that we cannot afford to neglect labor market issues. And this is the theme of Ginzberg's selection. He musters the trends in social and economic development which make for and against quality of working life. Where Piore sees trade union demands for security as a hindrance, Ginzberg sees their demand for equality of treatment of wage and salary earners as a motive for management to restructure work. He points out that governments tend to support weak enterprises whereas only the stronger can afford to experiment. Because, again, it is the stronger firms with low labor costs relative to capital employed which can afford to experiment, these experiments do not reach large numbers.

However, if trade unions can change their priorities and if government uses its initiative to punish bad employers (which it is loath to do fearing that their failure will increase unemployment) and reward good ones, the forces restraining advance in quality of working life could become supportive of it.

In the light of Ginzberg's detailed analysis the description of a two-class labor market appears oversimple. But the possibility that much effort may be directed into improving the quality of working life of the few to the neglect of the many needs to be faced. The quality of working life in the vast government bureaucracies is low for many. We need new approaches to support the advances in other sectors beyond the strong firms in the private sector.

22

Job Monotony, Employment Security, and Upward Mobility in the Labor Market Structure

Michael J. Piore

AMERICAN workers' complaints about the availability and equality of available jobs is related to the dual structure of the industrial labor market. The secondary sector of this market is made up of marginal jobs with a tendency to offer low wages, poor conditions, little chance of advancement, lack of security, and capricious supervision unrestrained by a cohesive set of work rules or formal grievance procedures. The discontent of lower-class workers stems from their confinement to the secondary sector and a resultant lack of upward social mobility, and from the perceived precariousness of their situation. Other sources of discontent are job monotony and inadequate industrial health and safety conditions. The underlying cause of continuing job anxiety of the working class is seen in terms of the structural adjustments in the organization of work, attributable to the pursuit of employment security by industrial unions.

A similar version of this selection has appeared as Chapter 3 in James O'Toole, ed., *Work and the Quality of Life: Resource Papers for "Work In America"* (Cambridge: M.I.T. Press, 1974); and *Social Policy*, Volume 4, No. 2 (July–August 1973).

Anxiety about security stems from the way in which the unions have been forced to settle not for guarantees, but for arrangements distributing scarce employment and income among the labor force. These arrangements make it costly for the employer to lay off and rehire, thus leading to a stabilization of employment in the unionized sector but also to the development of insecure secondary employment. The conflict between job security and work variety has been aggravated by trends in industrial engineering, which have biased the design of jobs toward narrowing the range of tasks in each work assignment. Paradoxically, the challenge is creating more job security. Freedom of job assignment allows for greater experimentation with job enrichment. Trends which could assist American unions to accept freedom of job assignment include supplementary unemployment insurance, more union power to bargain for security of employment, and a government commitment to full employment. An alternative to efforts to develop guarantees through collective bargaining is to impose such guarantees by law.

Essentially, this selection represents an attempt to understand the complaints of American workers in terms of a number of hypotheses about the structure of the American labor market. The term "hypothesis" is used advisedly. The theory of discontent developed here is logically consistent; it is also broadly consistent with American labor history in the twentieth century, and more or less consistent with the conventional wisdom about what workers are complaining of. But neither the believed facts nor the implications have been subject to rigorous empirical examination.

Diagnosis of the Problem

The theory attempts to deal with complaints from low-income minority groups, on the one hand, and from higher income blue-collar and middle-income white-collar workers, on the other. These groups correspond more or less closely to those referred to in sociology as the lower and the working classes, although the inclusion of white-collar workers stretches the conventional usage of the latter term.[1] The discontent of these groups of workers seems real enough; among the lower class, it has made itself felt in urban riots and lesser forms of unorganized unrest, as well as in increased political awareness and support for organized campaigns and protests. Symptomatic of the discontent among the working class have been political support for protest candidates and the relatively high incidence of rejection of collective bargaining contracts by union rank and file. For reasons that will become apparent, the concerns about technological change and automation, which predominated in the late 1950s and early 1960s, also have to be included here.

Although the discontent of the two groups of workers seems obvious, it is less clear precisely what that discontent is about. The basic discontent of the lower class was thought to be unemployment—the unemployment rates for statistical categories dominated by lower-class workers (Negroes and Spanish-surnamed persons) are indeed high. But research conducted among these groups in the mid-1960s suggests that their discontent centered upon the *quality* of available jobs, and that the high rates of unemployment derived from either the character of the jobs themselves, which had high rates of layoff and discharge, or from the workers' attitudes toward the jobs.[2] This is probably not true in the current recession labor markets, since even poor jobs are now scarce. But, presuming the economy is brought back to what has been considered full employment in the past, the research suggests that the discontent of lower-class workers should be considered as relating to the quality of employment opportunities.

This problem is best defined in terms of a dual labor market with a primary and a secondary sector. The secondary sector is made up of marginal jobs distinguished, relative to jobs in the primary sector, by a tendency to offer low wages, poor work conditions, and little chance of advancement; by harsh, often capricious supervision, unrestrained by a cohesive set of work rules or a formal grievance procedure; and by great instability and little employment security.[3] The discontent, then, of lower-class workers stems from their confinement to the secondary sector of the labor market.[4] It should also be noted that the discontent has been concentrated in urban areas among second-generation inmigrants from rural areas (in the United States and from abroad) although, in terms of the characteristics defining secondary jobs, those born and raised in the rural South or abroad probably have the worst jobs.[5]

Putting these two facets of lower-class discontent together suggests that perhaps the causes might best be diagnosed as a lack of upward social mobility. The process of migration to the city has given a sense of mobility to those who have moved; the possibility of moving has given a sense of opportunity to those who have remained behind. Discouragement and discontent are felt by the children of those who originally moved, who now find themselves trapped in jobs that, if not precisely those of their parents, closely resemble them in their debilitating aspects and fall miserably short of the jobs to which they aspire and to which their parents have aspired for them.[6]

However, the discontent of the working class does not seem to be associated with social mobility in this sense. Rather, it seems to center on the precariousness of what has been achieved, and on the fear of falling behind their present positions. Thus, in the early 1960s, the working class was preoccupied by the thrust of technological change; in the late 1960s it was preoccupied by the threat to their life style and employment security posed by black and other groups applying pressure from below.

The other source of discontent among the working class is the quality of the work which they perform, particularly job monotony; the revolt of the rank-and-file union members, especially the young, suggests that monotony is a problem. At the point in the life cycle when the adjustment to monotony must be made, there is increasing resistance to it.[7] And to this list of working-class complaints has lately been added a new concern: industrial health and safety.

The Underlying Causes

The continuing job anxiety of the working class, their concerns about monotony and standards of health and safety, and the complaints of the lower class about the quality of their jobs and limited employment opportunities may be viewed as joint products of a single phenomenon: structural adjustments in the organization of work, attributable to the pursuit of employment security by industrial unions. In this sense, the root of their problems can be traced to the labor legislation of the 1930s which permitted unions to organize, and which placed them in a position to negotiate arrangements that stressed employment security.

Two aspects of these arrangements are critical: First, they are negotiated on a decentralized basis between individual employers and representatives of their own employees. Thus there is considerable variation in the amount of security achieved and, more importantly, a large sector of the economy, which under existing labor legislation has never been under any real threat of unionization, has no employment security at all. Second, in very few cases is the employment security which has been achieved absolute, and a good deal of attention in agreements has focused upon sets of rules for distributing scarce jobs and income among the labor force.

The decentralized nature of employment security arrangements and the incompleteness of unionization to which it is related act to aggravate the dichotomy between the sectors of the dual labor market. If the unions have succeeded in stabilizing employment in the primary sector, they have essentially done so by shifting the cost—or part of it—from their constituents to the employer. The employer has in turn looked for ways in which he can shift these costs to other parts of the economy, and the existence of an unorganized sector with no deterrent to varying employment levels to fit demand has provided a means of doing so.

Primary employers avoid hiring new workers for fear of unsustainable increases in demand, and seek instead to transfer these peaks to employers in the secondary labor market. And this is not simply a question of variation in demand over the business cycle, but also one of normal fluctuations in demand in the course of a year, from season to season, or randomly from time to time, due to a myriad of factors which may be peculiar to an industry or an enterprise. Thus, employers under pressure from unions to stabilize jobs would be looking periodically to transfer demand, even in a full-employment economy.[8]

Many of the other characteristics distinguishing primary and secondary sector jobs indicated earlier can be seen as derivative of the process of employment stabilization in the primary sector,[9] and to the weakness of trade unions in the secondary sector today. Thus, lack of training and chance for advancement can be traced to the temporary nature of employment opportunities in the secondary sector which, in turn, provides no incentive to the employer to invest in his work force (or, for that matter, for the worker to invest in himself).[10]

The aspects of primary work which seem to underlie the complaints of the working class—job monotony and industrial safety—may also be seen as the by-product of employment stabilization. The variety and complexity of work required to hold the interest of an employee in a job is a lot greater when the job is more or less permanent than when it is temporary. Thus, work is probably a good deal more monotonous for permanent workers in the primary sector than it was in earlier periods of history, when job tenure was shorter and less secure. Similarly, a number of the industrial health problems which have become matters of concern in recent years are the result of prolonged, continued exposure to materials, air, or noise, unlikely to affect in any important way a person who holds the job temporarily, or intermittently over a prolonged period.

But probably a more important factor than concern over monotony and health, and certainly the basic explanation for the continuing anxiety about security among the working class, is the particular manner in which the issue of employment security has been resolved in American industry. As a rule, unions have been forced to settle not for guarantees, but for arrangements distributing scarce employment and income among the labor force. These arrangements make it more costly for the employer to lay off and rehire, thus acting to deter layoffs and, indirectly, tending to stabilize employment. It is these indirect effects which constitute the basis for the argument that the management of fluctuations in labor demand in the unionized sector fosters the development of secondary employment.

The procedures which have developed rely heavily upon a system of job assignment by seniority. The details vary substantially among plants, but the basic idea is that a worker's seniority is defined by his date of hire, and the employer is obligated to permit senior workers whose jobs are temporarily or permanently eliminated to displace ("bump") more junior employees from their jobs so that the most junior employee goes out the door. Seniority is also used to allocate promotion opportunities, although competence is frequently considered in combination with seniority. In most American industry the wage is linked to the job, and thus the rules for job allocation determine pay and income as well.[11]

Through the seniority system, therefore, both the worker's employment security and his pay have come to be uniquely bound to a specific job assignment. Thus, not only has movement between enterprises been reduced, but movement among work assignments within an enterprise has also become narrowly restricted. In a sense, then, reliance upon seniority has generated a conflict between job security and work variety.

Finally, this conflict has been aggravated further by trends in industrial engineering which have biased the design of jobs toward narrowing and routinizing the range of tasks connected with each work assignment. There is no clear scientific basis for this trend; experiments suggesting that productivity is enhanced by job enrichment are sufficient to warrant at least a careful examination of the issue, but industrial engineering practice has been virtually unaffected by this possibility and has not shown much interest in the issue.[12]

The attitude of trade unions toward industrial engineering has come to be one of cooperation. Time and motion studies, job evaluation, and the like, if they do not actually appear in collective bargaining contracts, have at least become the language of industrial relations. In a number of situations the unions have actively cooperated with management and even initiated the introduction and application of such engineering tools;[13] or they have acquiesced generally in management-initiated applications of industrial engineering precepts, training their own people to review management decisions in this context.[14]

To explain union acceptance of industrial engineering, one must, again, look to the role of seniority and the reasons for union reliance upon it. Although seniority is not the only basis upon which jobs and income could be distributed —alternatives include ability, qualifications, need, or work sharing—it is the most prevalent. Without seniority rules, the distribution of jobs and income presents union leaders with the task of choosing among the members of their organizations in a situation in which the gains of one group inevitably result in losses of the *most serious* kind to another group. Such a choice is a threat to the political position of union leaders and could possibly destroy the union itself. The importance of this last point cannot be overestimated; it presents the nightmare of an anxious work force fighting among itself for limited jobs, a fact which historically has been the major deterrent to the stability of American trade union organization. Seniority resolves this issue once and for all; it is an objective criterion, easily defined, leaving no room for interpretation and, hence, barring manipulation by the union leader, the employer, or one group of workers or another. However, the ability to use seniority in this way as an unambiguous standard for the distribution of pay and security depends upon a system of unambiguous job assignments. And this, in turn, creates union interest in the kind of rationalization, even simplification, of the job structure which industrial engineering has introduced—an interest which, it may be noted, is as strong as the unions' interest in the principle of seniority itself. The use of seniority in this way also requires that differences among workers with respect to job performance are sufficiently small that virtually any worker can move into a vacant job leading to narrow jobs that make workers vulnerable to technical change.

In sum, it is argued that the fact that security was limited and unions were forced to worry about its distribution worked to further enhance monotony in the primary sector of the labor market. The distributional rules which developed have linked security to specific job assignments, encouraging union acquiescence in the further narrowing of these assignments through industrial engineering and job simplification. Paradoxically, in so doing the unions may have heightened the very insecurity with which they were attempting to deal, for the definition of a job in terms of a limited number of narrow carefully defined tasks certainly enhanced the possibility that it could be mechanized out of existence. In any case, the fact that unions have been unable to achieve complete employment guarantees has left the working class with continuing job anxiety, rendering it extremely sensitive to pressure from below in the social structure.

Some Possible Solutions

The argument of the preceding section, that the root causes of discontent with quality of jobs lies in the job security arrangements negotiated by the industrial unions in the 1930s, suggests that the cure is to be found in changes in those arrangements. One possible direction of change is a weakening of the unions' power, which would permit the degeneration of existing security arrangements. Such a solution would reduce the barriers between the primary and secondary markets and the practices that maintain security at cost of job quality. It would do so, however, at a substantial cost in terms of the job security and anxiety of workers now in the organized sector, and at great sacrifice to the procedures that insure equity and due process, which unions have painfully built up at the workplace over the last thirty years.

The real challenge, then, is to look for more job security rather than for less. In particular, if current difficulties of blue-collar workers are caused by efforts to ration scarce jobs among the firms' work forces, this could be remedied by imposing a complete guarantee—by insuring, in other words, that there will always be employment for workers who have already been hired. The Japanese economy provides a model of such guaranteed employment in much of its modern manufacturing industry, and there is reportedly considerably greater freedom in job assignment than in similar American enterprises. In Japan, as well, the employment guarantee has produced a pay system in which the wage is based upon seniority and is largely divorced from a particular job.[15] The limited experience with employment guarantees in this country also points to greater freedom in job assignments. Indeed, in the organized sector such guarantees have generally arisen because of an effort by management to obtain precisely that freedom to vary work assignments.

Freedom of job assignment is not, of course, the same thing as job enrichment, but it allows far greater experimentation with this and other means of reducing the monotony of the work experience. If the earlier arguments proposed in this selection are correct, moreover, employment guarantees will free union leaders to press for changes in this direction. It is possible that collective bargaining is already evolving, if slowly, in the direction of providing employment guarantees. The logic of the supplementary unemployment insurance in the automobile industry and similar arrangements negotiated in allied industries is to make labor costs independent of layoffs. If the general trend points in that direction, then, indeed, any of the proposals designed to increase union bargaining power—repeal of Section 14(b) of the Taft-Hartley Act, the mandatory provision of unemployment benefits to striking workers, for example—should hasten the introduction of such guarantees. Similarly, policies designed to reduce the cost of employment fluctuating to the employer and make him more willing to provide employment guarantees will have this effect. Of such policies, a renewed commitment by the government to full employment is probably one of the most important steps. Another alternative would be a government insurance system protecting the employer when employment guarantees would otherwise prove an intolerable burden.

It seems unrealistic, however, to expect that *extensive* employment guarantees would develop through private collective bargaining. Existing labor legislation produces very great variation in union power across the economy. There is great reluctance to tailor the laws to the realities of individual industries and, so long as a single code is applied more or less uniformly, it is very difficult for unions to secure the power to obtain guarantees in sectors where they are weak without creating intolerable concentration of power in sectors where they are already strong.

The alternative to efforts to develop guarantees through collective bargaining is simply to impose such guarantees by law. This might be done either by direct prohibition of layoff or by a system of fines (or enforced severance pay). Fines are, in principle, preferable to prohibition since they can be tailored to different situations permitting flexibility and avoiding perverse incentives. To a certain extent, fines are already inherent in the experience-rating provisions of the unemployment insurance system.

The cost of all these efforts to further stabilize employment in the primary sector will increase pressure to transfer variation in demand to the secondary sector—and they must be seen in that light. This requires a much more elaborate review of the dual-labor-market distinction than can be developed here. A brief sketch of the critical elements, however, involves two points in addition to those developed thus far.

First, lower-class workers seeking upward mobility, with which this selection is concerned, are not the only people in the secondary market. There are also youths whose intermittent work patterns are connected with school and leisure time activities, and who are flexible in their income needs and in the timing of their work activities. A number of working women whose first commitment is to family responsibilities are also found in the secondary market, as are first-generation immigrants working to accumulate a fixed sum of money and planning to return to their place of origin. For such people, the kind of short-duration jobs generated as a consequence of the efforts of primary employers to evade permanent commitments during temporary peaks in demand are not a major problem, particularly if there is full employment so that new jobs are appearing as older ones run their course. If it were possible to free disadvantaged workers from secondary jobs which are not a part of a socially acceptable life pattern, the existence of a secondary sector, *per se*, need not constitute a social problem.

Second, employment in the secondary sector is not composed solely of the temporary employment peaks transferred from the primary market. A number of secondary jobs are inherently of short duration: seasonal jobs in some parts as construction, agriculture, recreation, vacation, and so on. Other secondary jobs are relatively permanent, but may be adjusted to a transient labor force such as in hotels and hospitals, for example. It is also possible to stabilize many of these employment opportunities; a number of the inherently short-duration jobs can be built into some continuous employment experiences through hiring hall arrangements of the kind used by the construction and maritime unions to give continuity of employment to their members. Although existing labor legislation tends to penalize such arrangements, special governmental arrangements could be developed, as has occurred on the New York waterfront, or there could be changes in labor law.

What these considerations suggest, in sum, is that both the composition of the work force in the secondary sector and the composition of jobs are susceptible to rearrangement through public policy. It may be possible now to reduce the number of jobs in that sector, not simply to a level where disadvantaged workers are no longer required to fill them, but to a level where the remaining work force, for whom a short-term job carries no social stigma, is large enough to handle the increased spill-over of temporary work which more stringent employment guarantees in the primary sector would create.

NOTES

1. See, for example, the definitions in Herbert Gans, *The Urban Villagers* (New York: Free Press, 1962), pp. 242–254.

2. Peter B. Doeringer et al., *Low Income Labor Markets and Urban Manpower Programs*, Research and Development Findings no. 12, Manpower Administration (Washington, D.C.: U.S. Department of Labor, 1972).

3. Pressing for such changes will undoubtedly have to await a new generation of union leaders, however. An acceptance of industrial engineering and its bias toward rigid and confining job assignments has been built into the ideology of American business unionism, and leaders who reject it are generally viewed by the movement's elder statesmen as immature, radical, or demagogues. It will certainly also take a new generation of industrial engineers to respond to such pressure.

4. Michael J. Piore, "On-the-Job Training in the Dual Labor Market," in Arnold Weber et al., *Public-Private Manpower Policies* (Madison, Wis.: Industrial Relations

Research Association, 1969), and "Jobs and Training," in Samuel Beer et al., *The State and the Poor* (Boston: Winthrop, 1970), pp. 53–83.

5. See, for example, *Report of the National Advisory Commission on Civil Disorders* (New York: Bantam Books, 1968), pp. 109–218.

6. For an explicit treatment of this theme, see Claude Brown's autobiography, *Manchild in the Promised Land* (New York: Macmillan, 1965).

7. Cf. among the many recent articles on this, Barbara Garson, "Luddites in Lordstown," *Harpers*, June 1972, pp. 68–73.

8. There are a variety of institutional arrangements through which demand transfer is accomplished. The most prominent are probably subcontracting and temporary help services. Employers can also maintain a secondary sector within their own establishments, although often this requires the acquiescence of trade unions. Another common way of handling peak demand "in house" is to cycle people through the union probationary period, discharging workers and hiring replacements just before the probation is completed when they would become subject to the protection of the collective agreements.

9. See Peter B. Doeringer and Michael J. Piore, *Internal Labor Markets and Manpower Analysis*, pp. 13–40, 163–183. See also Michael J. Piore, "On-the-Job Training in a Dual Labor Market," *op. cit.*, Part II, pp. 113–122.

10. In fact, the employer's strategy in transferring peak demand to the secondary sector is generally to preserve the skilled aspects of the job in house and to transfer out unskilled tasks. When demand slacks off, the unskilled tasks are brought back to the primary establishment and assigned to skilled employees in order to provide enough work to meet employment obligations. Even the harsh working conditions that characterize the secondary sector are sometimes the by-product of the temporary nature of the work and the short time horizon of the employer which deters investment in physical plant.

Training on the job generally represents an investment either by the employer in his work force or by the worker in himself; when employment is temporary, the employer has no such incentive. If the worker had an incentive, the employer might find it worthwhile to structure his work environment so that workers could train themselves; but in secondary work not only is employer attachment temporary, but occupational and industrial attachment is, as well.

11. See Doeringer and Piore, *op. cit.*

12. Eaton H. Conant and Maurice D. Kilbridge, "An Interdisciplinary Analysis of Job Enlargement: Technology, Costs, and Behavioral Implications," *Industrial and Labor Relations Review*, 18, no. 3 (April 1965); Louis E. Davis and Ralph R. Canter, "Job Design," *Journal of Industrial Engineering*, 6, no. 1 (January 1955), and Louis E. Davis, Ralph R. Canter, and John F. Hoffman, "Current Job Design Criteria," *Journal of Industrial Engineering*, 6, no. 2 (April-May 1955).

13. Jack Stieber, *The Steel Industry Wage Structure* (Cambridge: Harvard University Press, 1959).

14. William Gompers, "Trade Unions and Industrial Engineering," in W. Grant Ireson and Eugene L. Grant (ed.), *Handbook of Industrial Engineering and Management* (Englewood Cliffs, N.J. Prentice-Hall, 1957).

15. Cf. Robert E. Cole, *Japanese Blue Collar* (Berkeley: University of California Press, 1971); Robert Evans, *The Labor Economics of Japan and the United States* (New York: Praeger, 1971).

23

The Obligations of Industry and Society in the Swedish Labor Market of the Future

Rudolf Meidner

THE Swedish labor market is strongly affected by economic conditions outside Sweden, the growing debate in Sweden as to the merit of measuring progress only in terms of increased material welfare, and the uncertainties concerning the economic future that are shared by companies, individuals, and unions. Recent changes in technology and in markets have shut down some enterprises, and there has been both increased temporary unemployment and particular problems for the less able workers to gain or regain employment. There are imbalances in employment as many companies are experiencing manpower shortages, especially of young, well-educated people unwilling to seek Industrial employment. The Swedish labor market of the future will have to reckon with even faster structural changes, including increasing business failures resulting in the elimination of "weak" groups of workers. The solution calls for joint efforts with the *one* common denominator: to humanize

With modifications and abbreviations this selection is an address to the congress of the Association of Swedish Metal Manufacturers, Stockholm, September 28, 1971.

working life, that is, to carry over the self-evident aims of societal life to working life.

Swedish unions, unlike those in some other countries, favor rationalization, through national policy of employment. There is a need for the formulation of a long-term economic policy for industrial expansion to replace the present fire-fighting actions. The Swedish labor exchange, now better equipped than ever before, still cannot provide for industry's manpower unless the industrial environment itself is improved. There is also an urgent need to increase public awareness about pervasive problems of the work environment. The Swedish unions have moved away from the idea that extending industrial democracy would be a threat to productivity, feeling that without such an extension the development of productivity might be in danger. However, vigorous attempts by individual companies to improve the working environment could weaken their competitive ability. While some such costs should be shared by the public, the most critical problem is how industry can be persuaded to undertake the necessary expenditure.

In order to examine the obligations, it is necessary to analyze the experiences of the Swedish labor market of today and attempt to sketch a few developmental trends. Certain conditions are essential and will remain so during the period under consideration here: First of all, our economy and, consequently, our labor market are determined to a great extent by economic conditions outside of Sweden. It is an illusion to believe that a small country with minimum trade barriers, strongly dependent on export, can shape its economy according to its own design.

Further, there is a growing debate in Sweden on the merit of measuring progress solely in terms of increased material welfare; factors such as the external and internal environment, satisfaction with life, cultural activities, and similar objectives should also be considered in assessing the whole development of welfare. "Earning power" and "efficiency" are no longer nondebatable words, but nevertheless they are the basis for the country's industrial success in the world.

Swedish trade, which is wide open to the world, will in the future be subjected to constant structural reform, probably at an increasing rate. This implies, in plain terms, the growth of companies and trade which are economically sound and capable of competing, and the elimination of those which are economically weak. For example, mergers increased strongly during the 1960s and so, too, did the number of shutdowns; industry is being forced into specialization on such products where Sweden is a step ahead of other countries. Therefore, the future labor market will have to reorganize and adapt, which creates an atmosphere of increasing uncertainty—for companies, for individuals, and for trades. Capital equipment will become economically obsolete at an ever increasing rate, training may lose its value for the individual, and the occupational experience of a lifetime may suddenly cease to be an asset and become a burden instead. Statistics show that an increasing number of companies are closing down and, consequently, a growing number of people are being forced out of work.[1]

For decades, Sweden has lived with the idea of having successfully created an economy of full employment in the literal meaning of the word; that is, all who are willing to work can obtain employment. This belief has been confirmed by the low unemployment figures, by official forecasts, indicating a shortage of labor rather than unemployment, and, too, by industry's own experiences of difficulties in recruiting skilled manpower. By international comparison, Sweden still has a high degree of employment, but the manpower studies conducted regularly since the beginning of the 1960s and the figures reported by the so-called Low Income Committee make it necessary to reassess this view. Only about half of the adult population has a full annual income; the so-called latent jobseekers number a few hundred thousand; those who cannot seek gainful employment because they have no one to care for their children number several hundred thousand; and those obviously unemployed during some part of the year number about 300,000; all this out of a work force of about 4 million. Moreover, the signs are that the difficulties for these groups are increasing because the nature of industrial work is changing with demands on physical ability decreasing, and demands for speed, attentiveness, and ability to endure mental strain increasing.

However, there is no doubt that many companies are experiencing recruiting difficulties and manpower shortages. Young, well-educated workers are often unwilling to seek industrial employment. The present and, probably to a still higher degree, the future labor market shows a strong imbalance: within the same locations there is simultaneously a lack and an abundance of manpower, and there is regional imbalance with a good supply of labor in certain parts of the country and a shortage in the areas of expansion. Maldistributed employment in Sweden, which is believed to have full employment, is a painful reality and the disparity is becoming more severe as the country's ambitions rise. On the one hand, the Long Term Planning Committee has found that expanding industrial firms are short of manpower and many signs indicate that this shortage could become permanent. On the other hand, the Low Income Committee's survey shows poor utilization of manpower. In Sweden there are hundreds of thousands of people willing to work—women, the older and/or handicapped, and those from sparsely populated areas; their demand for work grows proportionately with the rhetoric about everyone's right to work, rhetoric which acknowledges the welfare society's most important promise to its citizens.

To recapitulate, the Swedish labor market of the future will have to reckon with even faster structural changes, with increasing trends toward concentration, a strengthening of the trend toward internationalization, increasing business failures resulting in the elimination of "weak" groups of workers, and growing recruitment problems for industry accompanied by even greater demands from new, previously neglected groups of workers for entry into productive employment. These problems can be solved only by joint well-coordinated efforts that have *one* common denominator: to humanize working life—that is, to carry the aims which have become self-evident in political life over into the domain of working life. There is strong agreement on the social goal to make a welfare society in which individuals have social security, good opportunities for education, and possibilities for influencing political development in a democratic way.

National labor market policy is, and will remain, the principal instrument for making structural transformation socially acceptable to individuals; it constitutes the basis for the positive view on rationalization and increased efficiency, which the Swedish trade union movement has expressed for decades—in direct contrast to trade unions' views in many other countries. Compared to other countries, Sweden has a well-organized labor market policy, yet it is clearly unsatisfactory in many respects. Only 25 percent of all employment is handled through government labor agencies; measures to encourage mobility are few, compared to the efforts undertaken to assist immobile labor in the underdeveloped regions; and, while there are long lines of applicants for vocational guidance and rehabilitation, only a fraction of them are accommodated by special workshops.

A serious handicap is insufficient research funds, which hampers the evaluation of measures and steps already taken, as well as further development of products and services. Although today large companies set aside a certain, often significant, share of their income for research and development, frequently the most important source of innovation and growth, the Labor Market Board, which can be viewed as a group of companies with an annual turnover of several billion *kronor*, has no resources to analyze its activities scientifically in order to improve them. However, continued expansion of labor market policy is of vital importance; the present policy is responsible for 1½ percent of GNP and about 5 percent of the national budget. If the previous assessment of the Swedish labor market of the future is realistic, these results must be increased in the not-too-distant future.

But the expanding role of labor market policy, an essential requirement for increasing material and social welfare, is changing to an even greater extent into one of formulating a long-term *economic policy* for industrial expansion. Selective efforts are increasing and becoming more widespread; improvisations, fire-fighting actions, temporary arrangements, and emergency solutions must be replaced by deliberate long-range planning. One of the founders of modern labor market policy expressed the opinion that its role is principally to remove the obstacles that prevent the labor market from working properly. But that role will be inadequate in the economy of the future which, to a much greater extent, will be concerned with demands for readjustment and structural reorganization.

There is no intention here to discuss industrial development policy; it is merely emphasized that an expanding labor market policy will gradually include more and more elements of such a policy. But the fact that society is taking upon itself a greater part of the responsibility for the *direction* of both industrial and geographic economic development will make industrial policy more controversial than labor market policy.[2] However, a national labor market policy, in all its aspects, can have no impact without the active cooperation on the part of public and private firms in matters such as manpower planning, training, and so on. Only a few problem areas can be mentioned here which will, in the future, be of even greater importance. The *first* problem concerns the working environment. Our labor exchange, although it has never been so well equipped or effective as it is now, cannot manage to provide for industry's manpower unless the industrial environment itself is decidedly improved. The *second* problem concerns putting to work the large, growing numbers of people whom the private and public companies find unattractive: principally the older, handicapped, or poorly trained workers. If these so-called marginal groups cannot be integrated into working life, the Swedish welfare society will become disabled and remain incomplete.

These two closely related problems deserve greater analysis. The general public's interest in environmental problems has come to be focused primarily on the external environment. Knowledge and consciousness of the threat to our environment is sweeping across industrial countries like a religious awakening. By comparison, the interest in matters dealing with the working environment is still very limited. A manifestation of this discrepancy, for example, is the fact that the important 1971 United Nations conference in Stockholm on environmental problems would have paid no attention to the working environment had a special report not been prepared by Sweden. Even in this country, however, the amount of attention given to nature conservation when compared to that given to the working environment is absurd; there may be storms of agitation about a few square kilometers of national parkland in Lapland but silence about obvious deficiencies in the working environment. Certain features of nature, which in Sweden can be enjoyed by just a few people during the short summer, attract public opinion to a far greater extent than do problems concerning the environment in which millions of people have to spend the principal part of their productive lives.

And there is overwhelming evidence of deficiencies in the working environment. Numerous studies, carried out by the trade unions as well as researchers, paint the same picture time and again: A very large number of manual workers see their working situation as unsatisfactory, and their health threatened by noise, heat, dampness, chemical substances, or mental pressures. These subjective opinions cannot be dismissed as unsubstantiated; the Low Income Committee, for instance, has found a definite relationship between these opinions and the actual physical conditions of those consulted. But, in addition to deficiencies in mental and physical health, there is also concern over contentment at work and over the work environment in the widest sense.

Unlike the labor market and labor market policy, substantial research has been done in Sweden on people at work. Industrial sociological and psychological research has shown that people are not satisfied with working conditions over which they have no influence, with working procedures that they cannot control, or with duties which are tedious and give no sense of responsibility. The performance of simple tasks under strong pressure of time and, furthermore, often in isolation from fellow workers creates alienation which, intensified, can lead to a totally negative work attitude; work is then seen solely as a necessary sacrifice for earning a livelihood. It is obvious that young people with a higher education begin working life with greater demands and expectations than have previous generations. But they are often confronted with a working environment which—though in certain respects better than in the past—is worse given the growing demand for meaning in work.[3] In Sweden today, workers lacking satisfaction in their working environment or in their own contribution react by suddenly changing jobs, often aimlessly; there is a high incidence of absenteeism and increased ill health. And experience tells us that high labor turnover and absenteeism rates vary considerably with the fluctuations of the economy. The idea that these so-called disorganization phenomena are symptoms of an over-full employment economy is not helpful. What must be learned now is that behind the somewhat technocratic expression "disorganization phenomena" are human reactions which can be stifled in a weak economy with a lower demand for manpower, but tend to become stronger with improved education and rising expectations.

The question of the working environment is closely connected and may be seen as a part of the question of industrial democracy, which is aiming, among other things, to give the individual influence in the shaping of the workplace and the organization of work. This was one of the main subjects very seriously discussed at the 1971 congress of the Swedish Confederation of Trade Unions (LO). At the congress people got away from the idea that extending industrial democracy would be a threat to productivity. One could go a step further and say that without such expansion the development of productivity is in danger.

Although democratization of working life does not increase costs, but rather provides dividends in the form of more efficient work contribution (some research findings indicate that this is more than an idle expectation), it cannot be denied that vigorous efforts to improve the working environment may result in quite heavy expenses for the individual company, which may weaken its competitive ability. This situation is analogous to that which arises when growing demands are made on industry for natural conservation. The principle that every company ought to bear its own environmental costs is in itself unexceptionable, but it cannot be carried further than to the point where competition from companies in countries with lesser ambitions involving environmental policy becomes overwhelming. If, in the final analysis, all citizens must—directly or indirectly—bear responsibility for the consequences of deficiencies in our working environment, then it is also reasonable to expect that all citizens are responsible for part of the cleanup costs (estimated at more than a billion *kronor* per year in the report, presented at the UN conference mentioned above). The most critical problem is, however, how industry can be persuaded to make these financially demanding investments.[4]

Now to the second and final matter, which should also fall under the heading "humanization of working life," and which is concerned with the integration of weak or disadvantaged groups into our working life. There are tendencies in our changing, structurally unstable economy, threatened with competition and pressed toward increasingly rigorous rationalization, to treat unfavorably large groups of people who are "inadequate" physically, mentally, socially, or lack training. Sociomedical and rehabilitation experts speak about a nationwide elimination of these groups from the labor market; educators and sociologists believe they can show a growing split between those who are well equipped as to training, age, and health and those who are not; the Low Income Committee has shown great disparities in welfare which cannot be tolerated. This trend is Sweden's most serious social problem, which can destroy Swedish society from inside. A new segregated society is threatening to appear, which could be more difficult to overcome than the old feudal society. One of the most important factors behind this problem is inequality in employment, which can be solved by new recruitment and employment policies. It is poor consolation that unemployed persons receive allowances on which they must live, that older, work-exhausted people receive early retirement pensions, that married women compelled to leave working life are totally dependent on their husbands' income, that handicapped people receive income from working in special workshops. As long as this society has a philosophy which puts work highest among all human activities and which allows man's worth to be decided by his productive contributions, everyone ought to have the possibility to make such contributions. The final responsibility for this philosophy, then, belongs to society which, by means of laws, mandatory regulations, and allocation of quotas, can require employment of workers which, in fact, companies do not want.

But this is not a good solution. A great deal of social responsibility lies with the companies to solve these problems to the best of their abilities, without compulsion from society. This requires manpower planning with these groups in mind, ingenuity in finding suitable work, greater tolerance and flexibility, and elimination of prejudice against people with weaknesses—weaknesses which often do not affect their contributions in the workplace.

Where lies the fault? Have the labor market authorities lacked resources for carrying social justice over into industry? Has society's support been inadequate to counterbalance the real or suspected deficiency in the working capacity of manpower made available?

Questions like these will become increasingly critical in the labor market of the future. Neither society, the trade unions, nor industry, and least of all the workers, most closely affected, are interested in continually expanding special work arrangements. Rather, investments for the direct placement of people into working life must be intensified, and the shape of these investments will certainly be one of the greatest problems of the future labor market.

NOTES

1. The Labour Market Board's statistics underestimate the true scope of the frequency of shutdowns and reductions in production, but they probably provide a measure for the development: in 1969, 10,000 people were affected; in 1970, about 20,000; and the figures for 1971 were close to 40,000. Fortunately, the need to reorganize does not result in difficulties for all these people, probably not even for the majority. But numerous studies have clearly shown that, in spite of great efforts by labor market authorities, about 10 to 15 percent of those discharged cannot find new employment. Of these the older, handicapped, and poorly trained people predominate.

2. One of Sweden's foremost economists has warned that, because of constantly increasing use of selective measures, the country is on the way to becoming a neomercantilistic society, which is somewhat more refined wording for a controlled economy. For my part, it is very difficult to see how we, faced with future problems for our economy and with our aims set for employment and welfare, can avoid expanding our labor market policy and, consequently, accepting a more active role for society as far as the development of our economy is concerned.

3. Many years ago, in a huge American machine shop, I saw a formerly skilled worker listlessly sweeping the floor in front of a machine which was operated by numerical control. His only duty was a few simple manipulations every sixth hour. Technical developments had made his work easy but his working day long and empty.

4. One way, unacceptable from a narrow budgeting point of view, but reasonable from an economic point of view, is to grant tax relief for clearly environmentally motivated investments. (Measures in this direction have been taken by the Swedish government in 1974.) Another way would be a leasing arrangement for certain machines which are beneficial to the environment. No such method is without its opponents or free of problems, but the time has come for new public initiative.

24

Work Structuring and Manpower Realities

Eli Ginzberg

EUROPEAN employers who have entered upon experiments into the redesign of jobs—aimed at higher worker satisfaction and performance—have done so largely because of problems in recruiting and retaining sufficient blue-collar workers. However, the relatively small number of experiments with work restructuring suggests that most managers prefer conventional solutions—for example, tapping new sources of labor supply—to engaging in experiments, the consequences of which cannot be foreseen. In most industrial societies the distribution of the incremental surplus that is to go to the work force is strongly influenced by the trade unions, which tend to press for better pay and material conditions rather than an enhanced experience of work as such. However, it is the unions' support of quality of working life that will be decisive. Without union support, the employer's scope for initiating new programs is limited.

Modern governments have played a key role in strategic areas of improving work life: minimum wages, hours of work, health, safety, and unemployment insurance. But further reduction of the work week will be approached cautiously because of the punitive loss of output which could jeopardize a country's international competitive position. The ongoing changes in manpower taking place in major industrial nations have already affected quality of working life and promise to continue to do so. Seven trends are described: the shift from a goods-producing to a service-producing economy; the need of modern economies for an even larger number of educated and trained personnel; the increasing employment of women and the fact that women, for reasons of either biology or pervasive social roles, do not fit the prototype of the male worker; the later entrance of people into work and their earlier exit from full-time employment; the "second career," facilitated by earlier vesting of pensions, increased expenditure on adult education, and higher personal incomes; the decline in the total number of hours worked; and the accelerated growth of large organizations with more decision making at the top, more bureaucratization, more rationalization of work, and more rigidity and impersonality.

As to the impact of these trends on quality of working life, there is little evidence that large organizations have found a way to provide highly trained workers with the autonomy the latter desire without running larger risks than they are willing to take. Employers have a long way to go in providing genuine equality of opportunity for women. Reduced hours of work allow for greater compensations elsewhere, but do not add to enhancing quality of working life. Finally, there are dysfunctional aspects to the size of organizations, perhaps for all members and certainly for most.

In this selection the interface is explored between work structuring and manpower realities from the following vantage points: an overview of the principal experiments in selected European countries—France, Italy, the Netherlands, Norway, and Sweden—whose efforts involving work structuring were reviewed in the spring of 1972; a theoretical assessment of the influence of manpower and economic parameters upon changing the quality of working life; an explicit analysis of major manpower and labor market transformations affecting industrialized societies and their impact upon the quality of working life. The concluding selection summarizes the impact of the labor market on restructuring and notes, without elaboration, the further impact of selective societal trends on altering the quality of working life.

European Labor Markets and Work Structuring

When pressed to explain why they entered upon experiments in work structuring—efforts directed to design and redesign of jobs or "structure of work" in order to elicit higher worker satisfaction and performance—most employers called attention to the serious problems they had faced or anticipated in recruiting and retaining an adequate supply of blue-collar workers for manufacturing operations. They had sought relief by hiring foreign workers and expanding the number and proportion of women workers, but the former had led to some serious community and national tensions and the latter had turned out to be a rather shallow labor pool; there are severe limits on the numbers of women who can be enticed into industrial employment, especially if it involves heavy, noisy, dirty work.

Some industrialists were sufficiently unsettled by their experiences that they began to question whether a decade hence they would still be able to manufacture at home, or would be forced to relocate to less developed countries, with looser labor markets, where men would welcome the opportunity of earning $1.50 to $2.00 an hour even if they had to work noisy presses on crowded floors. Some employers questioned whether successful experiments that had led to major improvements in the workplace could redirect the flow of young men into the factories. In their view, difficulties with labor supply went beyond improving the immediate work environment. Even if there were adjustments in wages and benefits, resistance to blue-collar work would probably remain because, from Scandinavia to Italy, the dominant value systems assign blue-collar workers the lowest place on the social totem pole.

However, while the recruitment of native young male workers into industrial employment seems to be the single most direct impingement of labor market realities on work structuring efforts, brief reference should be made to other dimensions, present and potential. The trade unions in several of these countries were pressing employers to put blue-collar workers on an hourly basis or a monthly payroll instead of using wage structures based on piecework, and to provide upgrading opportunities for semiskilled workers in the hope of improving their pay. The rapid growth of manufacturing operations in developing countries, with their much lower wage rates, threatened the competitive advantages long held by more advanced European firms. Unless the latter could increase productivity, they would lose out in the industrial competition among labor-intensive firms, from clothing to radios. As a result, management had to explore new ways of operation, hoping that the incremental surplus would cover labor's new demands.

In this perspective, the experiments with work structuring were forced responses by management. The relatively small number of such experiments in the countries characterized by tight labor markets underscores management's preference for conventional solutions—tapping new sources of labor supply—rather than engaging in major structural innovations, the consequences of which cannot be foreseen. If the recent European experience tells us anything, it is that management will explore a great many alternative ways of meeting its manpower requirements before entering upon large-scale organizational experiments. Apparently, management still prefers to search for solutions in the market.

Some Basic Theorems

The following theorems suggest both the potentialities and limitations of actions initiated by individual employers, the labor movement, and national governments to improve the conditions of working life.

The individual employer is disinclined to enter into any large-scale investment in the absence of a clear perception of the amount and time of payouts. Significant improvements in plant conditions frequently call for sizeable investments with no guarantee, or even likelihood, of a proportionate increase in productivity. But, since employers compete with each other for labor, to the extent that workers favor employment in a better designed and better managed plant, management may invest in improving the conditions of working life. However, the higher the proportion of wages to total costs, the more cautious the employer in experimenting with programs that might increase his wage bill. The fact that a new program may lead to a reduction in his labor costs weighs less heavily than the probability of an increase in his wage bill. But, *pari passu*, the employer whose wage costs account for less than a quarter of his total costs—as in large process industries—may be more inclined to take a chance. He has less to lose, and if the new program works he may have bought himself another period of relative industrial peace.

While the employer's role is critical in acting to improve the quality of working life, one must not overlook the fact that in most industrial societies, when it comes to distributing the incemental surplus that goes to his work force, he takes his cue—directly or indirectly—from the trade unions. The union leadership, surely in the United States, has the first and final word on whether the surplus is to be paid out in higher wages, better fringes, lower hours, and more vacations, or in improving the health, safety, and work conditions in the plant. To date, most unions have opted for shorter hours and higher wages and benefits and for restricting the employer's managerial rights with respect to unilateral determinations of working conditions and work. Most labor leaders are convinced they have had a major influence on improving the conditions of working life even though they have been only peripherally concerned with the structure of production and styles of management. But even here they have brought about changes moderating the speed of assembly lines, setting limits on weights that men and women are required to lift, insisting on rest periods, restricting the powers of foremen, determining the procedures for layoffs and callbacks. One thing is certain: If trade union members decide that improving life in the workplace is to be moved to or close to the top of their demands, that is where the future action will be. But until the unions move the employer's scope for initiating new programs is limited.

These considerations point to major constraints from the competitive market, the protection of managerial prerogatives, and the priority demands of trade unions on the speed with which the individual company will act to improve the conditions of working life. But the same forces that constrain experimentation can, under governmental initiative, encourage it.

Modern governments have played a key role in strategic areas such as health, safety, amenities, hours of work, minimum wages, compensation systems, and unemployment insurance—all of which have been broadly directed to improving the conditions of working life. But governments have not always had a free hand: strict enforcement of existing legislation and administrative policies can put the marginal employer out of business—and his workers out of jobs. Thus it requires not only courage but judgment to know how far to enforce the law. Governments must also balance the potential costs its citizens must bear and the benefits they are likely to enjoy from major alterations in the existing patterns of work. Governments have been loath to introduce legislation reducing the work week from 40 to 35 hours, for example, because of the putative loss of output that such a step would entail. Politicians believe, and probably correctly, that most of their constituents prefer higher income to less work. Another constraint on government action derives from international aspects of competition. Although countries differ in their dependence on international trade, no major country can be indifferent to the competitive implications of domestic legislation that threatens to raise its product costs, particularly of export goods.

Thus government efforts are conditioned by protecting weak enterprises that provide large numbers of workers with a livelihood; by avoiding changes that may prove costly in terms of reduced output; and by introducing innovations slowly so as not to jeopardize the international competitive position of its export sectors.

These several theorems derived from the experience of modern industrialized societies point to the existence of margins for innovation to improve the conditions of working life, even though they stress that the margins are limited because the increased costs are definite while the gains in productivity remain uncertain. Companies and countries alike tend to be cautious and opt for the unsatisfactory present in which they have learned to survive, rather than for the uncertain future that promises much but may spell failure.

Manpower Trends

A number of major trends in the labor market have a direct bearing on the quality of working life. It has often been observed that the most potent influences on societal change are not policies and programs specifically designed to check a danger or respond to an opportunity, but consequences of those forces, singularly and in combination acting once or twice removed, that alter the shape of things to come. The thrust of this section can be summed thus: The ongoing changes in the manpower arena which are taking place in the principal industrial nations of the world have already materially affected the quality of working life and give every promise of continuing to do so. Therefore, let us focus attention on some of these more important trends.

The first refers to the shift from a goods-producing to a service-producing economy. The extent to which this shift has occurred is suggested by data showing that only one out of every three workers in the United States is still in the goods-producing sector—that is, in agriculture, mining, manufacturing, or construction. Even this ratio overstates the case, however, for included in the goods-producing sector are the considerable number of white-collar workers who have nothing directly to do with physical output.

What is the significance of this occupational shift from goods to services in the context of quality of working life? To begin with, it warns against the use of manufacturing prototype for analytical purposes; and it warns especially against the assembly-line prototype, which probably describes the working environment of less than 5 percent of all employed persons. Moreover, a high proportion of all workers engaged in the service sector work in small organizations, though the banking, telephone, and insurance industries tend to be large-scale enterprises with many of the characteristics found in manufacturing. Nevertheless, with each passing year, a smaller number of workers remain in a working environment in which their output is strictly controlled and their work patterns determined by machines to which they are tied. If it is indeed dysfunctional for a human being to be an appendage of a machine and if the exigencies of the production-profit system have led employers to set exhausting work norms, it must also be acknowledged that fewer and fewer workers are caught in such work environments. An increasing proportion of all workers earn their livelihoods under conditions where the employer has difficulty setting norms, establishing the pace, and exercising close supervision.

A second major trend of modern economies is their need for an ever larger number of educated and trained personnel. In the United States the growth of scientific, professional, and kindred workers has outpaced that of every other occupational grouping. While many professionals are self-employed and others, such as university professors, work under their own guidance, still others are employed by large organizations, profit and nonprofit alike. They may be members of teams where their work goals are set by their team leader, or they may even punch time clocks, as in the case of physicians who work in clinics that seek third-party reimbursement. Their assignments are often narrow and become routine, but for all that their conditions of work differ markedly from those of the production-line worker; inevitably, professionals gain considerable freedom in terms of how they work, when they work, and the quality of their output. While all manpower projections represent an exercise in legerdemain, the odds still favor a continuing absolute and relative growth in professional manpower.

A third critical trend relates to women, whose participation in the labor force is steadily increasing in advanced industrial societies. Although the majority of women in past and present paid employment have tended to be less than full-time full-year workers, the career orientation of many of the fully employed seems to differ from that of the male prototype. Many women need and want the extra income they can earn, but the tradeoff between income and time is critical for the married woman with homemaking responsibilities, as is the tradeoff between commitment to her job and commitment to her family. Employers have long acted on the belief that women are more suited to routine work involving finger dexterity, assuming this to be a sex-linked aptitude. It may be, but then again it may be even more deeply rooted in their social roles and different adjustments to and expectations about work. The important point is that females account for an ever increasing proportion of the total labor force, and that women do not fit the prototype of the male worker.

The later entrance of people into the labor force and their earlier exit from full-time employment is a fourth potential trend whose influence and impact have not been given proper attention. Little is known about the consequences of starting full-time work at age 24 instead of at age 14, but it is not difficult to speculate that a longer period of occupational exploration should lead to a better outcome than when choice is practically absent. Similarly, with retirement benefits increasingly available after 20 to 30 years of work, many men in their early and middle fifties can look forward to changing their lives, including the amount and type of work they will pursue. To the extent that this trend continues and accelerates—and for the United States at least an acceleration appears likely—it is also necessary to deal with the quality of working life from a longitudinal perspective.

The trend of later entrance and earlier withdrawal from full-time employment is reinforced by another that goes under the name of "second career." While still relatively small in terms of the total labor force, many men are finding it possible and desirable to change their occupations in midstream. Having taken what they could from their first career, they look around for new, perhaps more stimulating fields of activity and return to school or make other serious efforts to prepare themselves. Earlier vesting of pensions, larger governmental expenditures for adult education and training, and higher personal incomes and savings will unquestionably accelerate this trend.

A sixth trend which also must be taken into account relates to the steady reduction in the hours worked per year, even though in the United States there has been no large-scale reduction in the average working week. But in both Europe and the United States the total hours keep declining, with more holidays and longer vacations as well as paid days off for workers to attend to their personal affairs. The data suggest that the long-term trend points toward a further reduction in the hours worked per year.

Finally, post–World War II developments on both sides of the Atlantic point to the accelerated growth of large organizations in business as well as in nonprofit and government sectors. Universities with 50,000 registered students or hospitals with 2,000 bed patients are no longer exceptional. The recent merger movement in the United States saw the disappearance of a large number of small, well-managed, successful firms that could not withstand the lure of an attractive purchase offer. Although new firms are constantly being formed, the trend points to the continual growth of large companies, where the decision-making process tends to be concentrated at the top, among other reasons because that is the only place where critical determinations can be made about the long-term interests of the organization. Such large organizations tend to be more bureaucratic, subscribe to rationalization of work, and are more rigid and less personal.

This list of major trends affecting the work environment could easily be extended beyond the seven that have been briefly reviewed. For example, the growth of white-collar unionism will undoubtedly provide additional leverage for many white-collar workers; the steadily rising levels of educational achievement and the expectational consequences thereof will unquestionably result in new and different orientations to work on the part of young workers; and rising levels of family income together with improved social welfare benefits will introduce new degrees of freedom in the decisions people make with respect to work, jobs, and careers.

The critical thrust of work restructuring, however, is to bring about a better *fit* between the individual and technology and organization, with an aim of jointly optimizing the goals of the worker *and* his employer. To this end, the experiments have aimed at enlarging the scope of the worker with respect to planning, self-control, and self-regulation—that is, autonomy and a broadening of options—in the belief that in exchange for more satisfying work and conditions of work the individual will become more committed to the organization.

What can be said, then, about the impact of each of these seven trends on the quality of working life? The shift from goods to services suggests that in advanced industrial societies the rigid, highly subdivided, tightly controlled production lines will provide the work setting for an ever smaller proportion of the total work force, but it tells little about the potentials for autonomy among brokerage clerks, salesgirls, telephone operators, sanitation workers, and so on.

The absolute as well as relative increase in scientific, professional, and technical workers suggests the need for more sophisticated measurements of output, and for less reliance on tight controls through time clocks if the potential contributions of these workers are to be optimized. But there is little evidence that large organizations have found a way to provide these brainworkers with the autonomy they desire without running larger risks than they are willing to take. A sophisticated company, in dealing with its professional staff, will adopt personnel policies that more closely resemble an academic than a factory environment.

The agitation on the part of many educated women against discrimination in jobs and careers is indicative of the long way that employers still have to go to improve the opportunity structures for those who are work-oriented, even while they face rising discontent among those who look upon their work primarily as a source of income. With only a small proportion of women reporting that they were dissatisfied with their work, one can deduce that lack of autonomy can be a negative factor for only a very few women workers.*

The later entrance into and potentially earlier departure from the labor force represents a marked increase in the freedom which men and women now enjoy to plan their lives and work, but it is a freedom that cuts both ways: the more young people invest in preparing for work and careers, the higher their expectations and the greater their potential source of dissatisfaction if their goals are not fulfilled. Similarly, if men have the option to retire early, employers often have the option to retire them early. Another broadening of options can be seen in the trend toward a second career, which is enabling increasing numbers of men to move out of fields that no longer command their interest or engage their talents. But here, again, it does not follow that the choice of a second career will prove fully satisfactory.

The reduction in working time can also be seen as a broadening of options. If workers find their jobs oppressive or uninteresting, the fact that they have to spend fewer hours on the job permits them to seek alternative satisfactions elsewhere. But, whatever its merits, this alternative does not add to enhancing the quality of life in the workplace.

Even the trend to larger organizations is equivocal with respect to the subject at hand. For those who reach the top, or even come close to the top, their work is probably more interesting the larger and more complex the organization. On the other hand, for the many down the line—in middle management—the environment is not attractive. If managers look forward to the opportunity to manage, and if their work satisfaction is related to the scope they have to put their ideas into practice, then the trend to ever larger organizations must be viewed as militating against the quality of their working life. And of course the dysfunctional aspects of size are not restricted to those on the managerial level: White- and blue-collar workers are locked into personnel systems and held prisoner by company policies which leave them and their supervisor little room for maneuvers to alter their working environment.

Conclusion

If work structuring represents managerial initiatives to make more imaginative use of technology and organizational arrangements to provide greater autonomy and broaden options for workers with an eye to their improved

---

*Ninety-two percent of all women workers in the U.K. indicate that they are "very satisfied" or "fairly satisfied" with their work, reported in The Economist (London), January 14, 1973.

performance, such efforts must be considered within the labor market forces that are continuously transforming the work environment. Our review suggests that these manpower trends have implications for the success of work restructuring efforts. At a minimum, these manpower considerations point up the need for a broadened framework for considering improvements in the quality of working life. First, it is essential to recognize that the adjustment of people to the world of work changes as they change; hence there is need for a longitudinal perspective that allows for such changes. Second, it is an error to neglect the differences in approaches of men and women to jobs and careers, while recognizing that many women have strong career drives. Next, the implications of the vastly extended period of education and training prior to labor market entry upon the skills workers have to offer, their expectations about work, and their value orientations must also be part of a comprehensive approach to studying the quality of working life. And, finally, a broadened framework must allow for the interplay of the work and nonwork aspects of a man's life, specifically the major alterations under way in such basic areas as authority, legitimacy, equity, and status. Unless these findings in the work arena are studied within their enlarged societal context, we will continue to fly blind not knowing whether changes in the workplace are or are not responsive to the aspirations and expectations of the working man. The need for broadening the framework is the major conclusion to be drawn from this manpower approach.

25

Working Conditions, Employment, and Labor Market Policy

Hans Berglind

AN organization is affected by and influences its environment. The degree of mechanization of the workplace may be largely determined by the supply and price of suitable manpower. Structural rationalization of work causes changes in jobs and in worker qualifications and recruitment, and may cause redundancies, especially of "hard-to-employ" workers who will find it difficult to gain employment elsewhere. It is left to what in Sweden is called "labor market policy" to deal with unemployment.

With continuing economic growth and high employment in Sweden after World War II, the unions were asked to restrain wage demands so as to constrain inflation. A "compromise" formula was devised allowing the unions to use labor market policy to attain higher levels of employment without commensurate increases in inflation while the government was to regulate company profits as a further control on inflation. Swedish labor market policy has resulted in levels of employment higher than those in other Western countries. Nevertheless, there are particular social adjustment problems for older single men displaced from rural jobs, and the number of people seeking vocational rehabilitation has trebled. Labor market policy is considered from the perspective of the society, the company, and the individual. These perspectives are not easy to align. There is also conflict inherent in attempts to maintain full employment and for companies to increase efficiency. Strong efforts are being made to improve working environments while at least maintaining standards of efficiency. The group most difficult to accommodate in this is the "hard-to-employ."

External Influences on Working Conditions

Almost every work organization is affected by its environment and it, in turn, influences the latter. At the present time, this simple ecological proposition provides the usual basis for describing companies and other organizations as "open systems." Thus, when working conditions for members of a work organization are discussed on this basis, it is advisable not to separate what happens within the organization from what occurs within its environment.

The degree of mechanization of the work process and a number of other characteristics are determined, to a considerable extent, by the supply and price of suitable manpower over which management has very little control. Increased mechanization or structural rationalization affects manpower needs in various ways. Not infrequently, employees have to be dismissed because the need for manpower declines or the organization cannot use a portion of its previous manpower in the present, modified production system. In the interest of profits, organizations separate those who are difficult to retrain for new duties—usually in Sweden the older and badly trained workers, the "hard-to-employ." These workers are dumped on the labor market, and whether they can be retrained for other employment, depends on a number of circumstances such as the supply of vacant jobs and their location, the nature of such jobs, and the existence and quality of available manpower.

Organizational attempts to rationalize the total work process, often necessitated by external circumstances, thus lead to a series of human consequences:

1. The work is transformed making different demands on those who shall perform it.

2. The latter leads to internal or external recruiting of workers with different qualifications.

3. To the extent that those already employed cannot be transferred, and that the number of job openings does not increase simultaneously, by "negative selection," workers become available in the labor market.

4. Not infrequently these workers have difficulty obtaining reemployment in the open labor market.

Labor market policy and operations are left to solve the problems of the displaced workers.

The fate of workers who are "left over," rather than what happens to the working conditions of those who remain employed, is the crucial question about the extent to which technological development results in better or worse working conditions. The answer will vary substantially, depending upon the technological level at which changes take place. If a manual type of production changes to that of a conveyor belt, then usually both the level of qualification drops and workers become more alienated.[1] If the change is to a more advanced technological level—for example, to process control—the change may have the opposite effect: less restricting and more interesting working conditions. But, and this is essential for the premise considered here, the work situation may also become more demanding; fewer people than before can meet these demands, and the more expensive machinery stimulates a more careful selection of staff. Thus employees with acceptable qualifications can have their conditions of work improved while a growing number of workers become redundant and hard-to-employ.

Market Economy and Growth of Society

The process described in the preceding section presupposes the existence of a number of market mechanisms: work organizations which compete with one another or, in any case, cannot set wages and prices wholly according to their own choice; they endeavor to optimize profit and pay their employees fair market wages. Thus, there exists a labor *market* in which the price is in part determined by supply and demand for manpower as a commodity.

The development of a labor market probably does not differ between privately owned and public operations. State and other public authorities usually compete for manpower in the same market, and the concept of profit or earning power considered characteristic of privately owned companies has gained a firm foothold (in any case, in Sweden) even within public enterprise and administration.[2]

C. B. Macpherson has pointed out two underlying features in our "possessive market society": the great importance of market relations and the handling of "labor as an alienable possession."[3] "Since the market is continually competitive,' those who would be content with the level of satisfaction they have, are compelled to fresh exertions by every attempt of the others to increase theirs." [4] One must run to keep up.

The negative aspects of the market system are emphasized for there are risks of more and more human relations becoming market relations assessed in terms of money, of people becoming more alienated on account of routine tasks, and of duties becoming difficult so that more people will be unable to sell their labor. On the positive side, there is increased prosperity which has characterized the development in many highly industrialized countries. Although many people have indeed sold their labor, they still have gained considerably in the exchange, a contention that seems supported by some Swedish data discussed below.

The Changing Swedish Society

In 1968 the Swedish Low Income Committee carried out a field survey on a sample of about 6,000 people to shed light on the social and economic circumstances of the country from several points of view.[5] In one report, based on the committee's material, Robert Erikson has mapped out patterns of social mobility in Sweden.[6] In interviews a series of questions were asked about circumstances during adolescence (up to age 16). Since a representative sample included those with ages ranging from 15 to 75, the responses can be used to illustrate the social changes that have occurred during the previous sixty years. Figure 1, based on Erikson's report, shows some of the results.

As is often the case in sociological surveys, the results must be approached with reservations. The questions asked here for retrospective information are perhaps subject to faulty memories of a distant adolescence. The changes appear evident from Figure 1, namely, it is becoming increasingly less common to have

1. a mother whose only role is that of housewife
2. lived in the same place throughout adolescence
3. grown up in the rural region of the country
4. more than three brothers or sisters
5. had economic difficulty during adolescence.

The last response is more subjective, making for difficulties of interpretation. The actual circumstances leading to perceived better economic circumstances by the younger generation are not known; that is, how much the mother's gainful employment and the smaller number of children contributed to this, and how much depended on increased geographical mobility and thus better occupational possibilities.

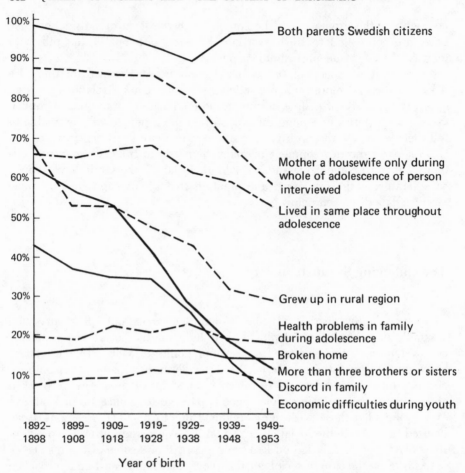

Figure 1. Characteristics of Youth by Present Age. *Source:* S. Johansson, *Statistisk Tidskrift*, 2 (1972). See specifically "Summary: Conceptualizing and Measuring Welfare."

These data reflect developments prior to the 1950s. Important changes in Swedish society are continuing and it is against a background of rapid changes, especially since the mid-1960s, that some of the acute present social problems must be seen. Of primary interest here is the rapid structural transformation which has taken place within the Swedish economy, leading to concentration in certain branches of the economy—both *economically* and *geographically*.[7] On the whole, the transformation over the period 1950–1970 has meant a substantial decline in agriculture and a strong growth in the service sector, above all, "public services." During this 20-year period, employment in agriculture declined from 17.8 percent to 6 percent while public services increased from 8.0 percent to 17.6 percent. During the same period industry proper declined just a few percent.[8] The geographic changes have seen population growth in the cities and absolute reduction in small municipalities in the forest counties.[9] This trend is expected to continue. Moreover, the average income of city residents has become very much higher. Thus in the Stockholm area the average income a few years ago was 48 percent higher than the average income in northern Sweden.[10] As may be expected, there is greater availability of employment in the cities, not to mention more doctors, dentists, colleges, and other services.

In view of these developments, there is growing concern with the negative aspects of dismissals associated with mergers and the consequent difficulties of finding new employment. To an even greater extent, there is growing doubt whether the differences in wages and productivity, which appear to characterize the various regions, are a true picture of the economic advantages of the workers who have moved. Presumably, a fairly large number of regional differences in wages are due to such factors as differences in training, overtime, allocation of working hours per day, and so on.[11] Additionally, men who move not infrequently lose a number of social welfare benefits which sometimes cannot be compensated in terms of money.

Labor Market Policy

Briefly, the present Swedish labor market policy was initiated following the end of World War II, when the Swedish trade unions were faced with a dilemma: the anticipated postwar economic crisis did not occur; instead, there was continued economic growth marked by a high level of employment with a risk of inflation. The trade unions were asked to restrain their demands for higher wages as a means of fighting inflation.[12] The confederation of manual workers unions (LO) sought a formula for compromise, in which full employment could be coupled with monetary stability without forcing the trade union movement to give up its autonomous role in the wage-setting process.[13] The policy recommended by the trade unions was to use selective labor market policy to attain a higher level of employment without equally high inflation and the government to firmly apply fiscal policy to regulate company profits, dampening a cause of inflationary competition for manpower.

This led to the development of the "solidarity wage policy" which aims at reducing wage differentials in a given industry and between industries. This wage policy puts great pressure on weak companies to rationalize production and when unsuccessful, the companies are forced to shut down. Active labor market policy—with retraining programs, moving allowances, and other measures—seeks to ease local problems of adjustment and assist the transfer of labor to more viable enterprises or sectors of the economy.

Four widely held concepts are central to the practical shaping of current Swedish labor market policy. First, labor market policy is seen as the mechanism for overcoming supply and demand frictions in an imperfectly functioning labor market.[14] Second labor supply is taken to be insensitive to wage differences. If people need to be moved from a less productive area of the economy to a more developed one, no "pull" is needed in the form of wage differences. "Pushes," in the form of shutting down inefficient companies, are seen to be more effective. This concept has not been shared by employers. Third is the assumption that rapid structural transformation is inevitable for economic development. Swedish industry is heavily dependent on its ability to export. Thus, like it or not, rigorous rationalization must be carried out if prosperity is to be maintained, and preferably increased. Indeed, this is a prerequisite for Swedish social welfare policies. Finally, there is the distinctive optimism as to man's ability to readjust, given training, retraining, or rehabilitation. It is assumed that it is comparatively easy to move people between different kinds of work and locations. Only very recently has the validity of this assumption begun to be seriously questioned, which is discussed in more detail below.

Changes in Employment and in Society's Values

Swedish labor market policy has succeeded in maintaining a high level of employment, well ahead of other Western countries.[15] Sweden has a high rate of employment for women. During the 1960s married women began to work in increasing numbers, particularly in the 35–44 age group. The trend for men, however, is a declining rate partially related to increasing length of schooling and growing redundancy among older men.[16] This is particularly true in forest areas and can be seen in the data in labor force studies. The level of employment is lower for the age group 55–64 and, above all, for the unmarried. Presumably, older single men form a group of which an especially large number are seen to be ineffective and not profitably usable. They are probably more often labeled as "not in the labor force (LF)" rather than as being unemployed.

It is not known to what extent older single men in the sparsely populated areas are disadvantaged, particularly because of rationalization of forestry operations. There are, nevertheless, many indications that this age group has difficulties in the cities. Single men receiving public assistance, for example, have increased very greatly in urban areas.[17]

During the 1960s the Labor Market Board increased help to workers in difficulties.[18] Those in some form of sheltered employment increased during the 1960s from about 4,000 to about 27,000; more than 100,000 are seeking vocational rehabilitation, roughly three times as many as ten years ago. Despite rehabilitation, an increasingly small portion of these persons can obtain employment in the open labor market (now only about 11%).[19]

TABLE 1.

Unemployed and not in the Labor Force (LF) among Married and Unmarried
Men, Age Group 45–64 (Per Cent)

Age	Marital Status	Category	1965	1966	1967	1968	1969	1970	1971	1972
45–54	Married	Unemployed	0.5	0.5	1.1	1.3	0.6	0.6	1.1	1.3
		not in LF	2.0	1.3	2.2	2.3	2.5	2.4	2.5	2.6
		Total	2.5	1.8	3.3	3.6	3.1	3.0	3.6	3.9
	Unmarried	Unemployed	1.2	3.2	1.3	2.4	2.4	2.1	2.6	2.3
		not in LF	11.5	13.5	14.9	16.1	18.2	16.7	15.1	17.3
		Total	12.7	16.7	16.2	18.5	20.6	18.8	17.7	19.6
55–64	Married	Unemployed	0.8	0.8	1.5	2.1	1.7	1.2	1.7	1.8
		not in LF	8.4	8.4	8.4	8.2	9.2	10.0	11.4	12.5
		Total	9.2	9.2	9.9	10.3	10.9	11.2	13.1	14.3
	Unmarried	Unemployed	0.9	2.9	3.8	3.2	2.8	1.8	2.7	2.5
		not in LF	23.2	23.3	20.4	20.5	27.7	30.7	29.2	30.0
		Total	24.1	26.2	24.2	23.7	30.5	32.5	31.9	32.5

Source: H. Berglind and A. L. Lindquist, *Elimination from Labor Market*, Chap. 3 (Lund: 1972).

Can the Aims Be United?

The aim of Swedish labor market policy is to bring about "full, productive and freely chosen employment." This goal is to be attained by eliminating deficiencies in the labor market's mechanisms to make it more efficient. But in recent years these goals have not been attained since it has been increasingly difficult to find employment for particular groups of people.

The aims or goals of labor market policy must be considered from three perspectives: that of society, of the labor-using organization (the enterprise), and of the individual. Some aims of each are presented below. Perspective:

National Economy	Enterprise	Individual
Full employment	Maximum profits	Acceptable livelihood
Stable value of money	High efficiency	Suitable job
Rapid economic growth	Continued independent existence	Good work environment
More equal distribution of income		

Even if the goals listed here are not precisely defined, it seems fairly apparent that they are difficult to reconcile. This is true both within the perspectives and among them. If we take the perspective of the national economy, it has already been noted that it may be difficult to reconcile full employment and a stable value of money. In fact, the conflict between these two goals constitutes the basis for the "new labor market policy" which was directed at minimizing this conflict as far as possible.

The aims of companies or work organizations, on the other hand, are more consistent. Continued independent existence is a prerequisite for increased efficiency, which is a prerequisite for setting the limits of profits. Conflicts between goals may arise when maximizing short-term profits that can threaten a company's continued existence.

From the individual's perspective, he may have to tolerate a poor working environment in order to attain an acceptable level of income.

There are obvious conflicts between the three perspectives. Increased efficiency may lead to deterioration of the working environment, depending, among other things, on which technological level the increase in efficiency takes place.

The most significant underlying conflict, however, is of a different kind. The difficulties of reconciling increased efficiency for the company with full employment for society and suitable work for the individual have been indicated. The more the concept of efficiency extends to the whole of the labor market, the greater is the risk that the less effective workers will be removed from the labor market, making in effect for two markets. For the time being, great efforts are under way to improve the working environment while maintaining at least the present high efficiency. At the same time, there is an obvious risk that ever more people will be excluded from the improved working environment—the less productive ones.

There is no simple solution to this dilemma. If we want to maintain work as a human right we need not only improve working conditions for a highly efficient majority. We must also create working conditions that provide the opportunity to the less efficient to be a part of productive society.

NOTES

1. R. Blauner, *Alienation and Freedom* (Chicago, 1964). See also B. Gardell, *Produktionsteknik och arbetsglädje* [Summary: Production technology, alienation, and mental health] (Stockholm, 1971).

2. This state of affairs is worth noting, especially when development in highly industrialized countries means that the industrial sector shrinks at the same time as the service sector and public administration increase in size. In Sweden, in 1970, the latter area was responsible for 49 percent of the total volume of labor, as opposed to 36 percent in 1950.

3. Tom Burns, (ed.), *Industrial Man* (Harmondsworth: Penguin Books, 1969).

4. *Ibid.*, p. 34.

5. S. Johansson, "Välfärdsbegrepp och välfärdmätning" [Summary: Conceptualizing and measuring welfare] *Statistisk Tidskrift*, no. 2 (1972).

6. R. Erikson, *Uppväxtförhållanden och social rorlighet* [Summary: Conditions of childhood and adolescence and social mobility] (Stockholm, 1971).

7. B. Ryden, *Fusioner i svensk industri* (Stockholm, 1971). This study of mergers showed 3,576 took place in 1946–1969 with half occurring in 1965–1969.

8. 1970s Long Term Planning Committee, *Svensk ekonomi 1971–1975 med utblick mot 1990* [The Swedish economy 1971–1975 looking toward 1990], SOU 1970: 71 (Stockholm: 1970).

9. *Balanserad regional utveckling* [Balanced regional development], SOU 1970: 3 (Stockholm: 1970).

10. A. Dahlberg and L. Holmström, *Arbetsmarknads-och lokaliseringspolitik* [Labor market and location policies] (Stockholm, 1971). Cf. particularly chap. 3.

11. *Ibid.*, p. 54ff.

12. *Tio ekonomer om arbetsmarknadspolitiken* [Ten economists on labor market policy], SOU 1968: 62 (Stockholm, 1968). Cf. especially Meidner, Öhman et al.

13. *Ibid.*, pp. 7, 185.

14. *Arbetsmarknadsverket och arbetsmarknadspolitiken* [The Labor Market Board and labor market policy] (government official report), SOU 1968: 60 (Stockholm: 1968).

15. B. Elmgren, *Arbete at alla* [Work for all] (Stockholm: 1972).

16. H. Berglind and A. L. Lindquist, *Utslagningen på arbetsmarknaden: omfattning och utvecklingstendenser* [Summary: Elimination from the labor market] (Lund, 1972), cf. chap. 3.

17. W. Korpi, *Fattigdom i valfarden* [Poverty in welfare] (Stockholm: 1971).

18. B. G. Reubens, *The Hard-To-Employ: European Programs* (New York and London: 1970).

19. See n. 16 *supra*.

PART
VII

Quality of
Working Life –
A Central Issue
in Industrial
Relations

THE industrial relations context of enhancing quality of working life is extremely complex. The history of the trade union movement and its experience has been different in each country. The traditional issues differ and so do the myths which are so potent in determining attitudes. Many trade unionists are powerfully influenced by the martyrdoms, the battles, and the horrors of the past, identifying their managerial negotiating opponents of today with the villainous enemies of the struggles of the day before yesterday. The attitudes, like their folk memories, are the product of culture-specific experiences. Unions, like other organizations, draw their strength from, but are limited by, their history.

For historical reasons some union movements are strongly ideological, others pragmatic. There is a world of difference between the anticapitalist stance of the French CGT, for example, and that of the typical American union whose members and leaders feel they have done none too badly with capitalism.

To history and ideology we must add structure. Some countries have one, some many union movements, which may be split along political and confessional lines. In many countries unions are predominantly industrywide—one industry, one union. In others unions may be industrial or craft, with competition between them for organizing groups of workers—the industrial relations manager of the Ford Motor Company's works in Dagenham used to describe the difficulties created for him by the need to negotiate with twenty-two different unions.

Traditions of bargaining differ. In some countries—France, for example—virtually all bargaining is conducted at the industry level, in others, as in Britain, plant bargaining is highly developed.

With all these and other differences too numerouse to mention, it is inevitable that trade union attitudes to any issues at all will cover a wide range. All have in common, however, an attitude of cautious suspicion toward any new development sponsored by management. The first assumption is that whatever it may be it is a device to obtain more productivity without paying for it. And there is no question that the motives for many "improvements" have been economic. Even if the motive is partly humanitarian, many managements would hesitate to admit it, preferring to justify their good works by the claim that it pays rather than to cloak their economic motives in the hypocrisy of good works. It is easy for the unions to perceive any such change as a new

way of continuing the old exploitation. Nor have all attempts at "job enrichment," for example, been totally free from economic motives.

Unions have a greater fear than that measures to enhance quality of
working life will increase exploitation. They fear a weakening of their position
on two counts: first, that management, by offering benefits to those workers
which have not been demanded by the union on their behalf, undermines
their claim to be the sole protectors of workers' rights and interests; second,
that as workers learn to work more closely with management they may
question the need of the union, that participation is a means of weaning the
worker from his union.

Managements, then, have often approached unions to share in experiments
aimed at enhancing quality of working life. Outside Scandinavia, unions have
tended, at best, to maintain a neutral posture. Strongly ideological unions
have opposed such measures. Even where they are not ideologically
opposed, unions face special problems in cooperating in this field. Where
there is no tradition of workplace bargaining, issues of work allocation and
organization have remained outside the unions' purview; they have neither
the knowledge nor the machinery to engage in it. And, even where workplace bargaining is common, the union is not set up to deal with matters which
fall outside its normal range. The union can demand safeguards such as a
guarantee against redundancies or can, as in the case of the Italian unions,
demand that jobs be upgraded while leaving management to work out how.

Clearly, unions are likely to be in a far stronger position if they choose to
demand enhanced quality of working life for their members and persuade
managements to comply. But if this is in the context of bargaining, this would
allow management to obtain a *quid pro quo*. Not surprisingly, unions prefer
to be in a position to exact their own quid.

Confusing and muddying the waters are the relationships of "humanization
of the workplace," "industrial democracy," "worker participation in management," "co-determination," and "quality of working life." Not only do these
mean different things to different people, they have different degrees of
ideological depth, and are rallying cries for different interests. While they need
in no way conflict with one another, concentration on one can be to the exclusion of all others and may even lead to the others being perceived as
antagonistic to the true faith.

These issues are described and analyzed in some detail in the selections
which follow. They give accounts of trade union attitudes and approaches
and the historical and structural reasons for them in many European countries
including Yugoslavia, Sweden, Norway, Austria, and Switzerland, as well as
the six original members of the European Economic Community.

Since these selections were written, the United Automobile Workers'

Union in the United States has negotiated contracts with General Motors, Ford, and Chrysler in which, at the instance of the union, clauses have been included establishing joint management-union committees to improve quality of working life and to encourage and monitor experiments in job redesign. Whether these are the first swallows of summer remains to be seen.

26

Union-Management Conflicts over Quality of Working Life Issues

Henry Douard and Jean-Daniel Reynaud

ORGANIZATIONAL structures are seen as resulting from power struggles at different hierarchical levels under the guise of technological constraints and efficient coordination. Decisions to centralize or to disperse control affect job design. Two examples are given from French industry: (1) A tool-making plant had difficulties with its foremen who were victims of a very complicated role structure devised by management to enhance its rights of intervention. In the long chain of command, the foreman felt isolated from all decision centers, but they had few conflicts with their men. The entire organizational structure allowed no one (except the plant manager) to have a full grasp of the situation. The organization worked as a system of mutual controls (e.g., planning and production) with the engineer and the manager exercising control which was reinforced by the conflicts arising from any incident. A new plant manager tried to bring about change not by working on attitudes but on the organization structure itself: by rotating jobs between foremen and time study people, shortening the chain of command, and bringing foremen and inspectors together. Management was no longer totally occupied with resolving minor conflicts. (2) In a large electrical appliance firm, semiskilled operators voiced many grievances about working conditions. Management called in a group of ergonomists whose findings were so palatable to the unions that the latter put out a pamphlet calling for organized action in this area of industrial relations. Cases were cited of operators having to use their knowledge and initiative in order to get the work done. The principal results were demands for improving the status of semiskilled jobs and that operators should have some power in bargaining with management.

French unions have had a rather weak hold on work practices and thus emphasize the more easily controllable aspects. In the French system of industrial relations, working conditions are not a negotiable issue, and bargaining is generally conducted on an industry-wide basis, not at the plant level. The consultative but nonbargaining (by law) role of the work's committee is not satisfying to the unions. The practical solutions to enhance quality of working life as an industrial relations issue in France still have to be found although some advances have been made since 1968. Management's freedom of action has led, at the plant level, to a piecemeal approach rather than a systemic treatment. The current problem in France involving quality of working life is not its stake in industrial conflict, but in the difficult institutionalization of conflict.

It is increasingly assumed that conflict is a built-in aspect of organizational life. The relationships which take place among the various levels of the organizational hierarchy are power relationships, involving pressures and attempts to enlarge spheres of influence. The coordination of tasks, for example, in a specific production process, cannot be considered to take place in perfect harmony. Although management is usually a party to conflict, it can act as arbitrator, making the final decision. In this context, the content of jobs would seem to be in part the result of an interplay of these power relationships.

If these assumptions are correct, the organizational structure of a plant is the result of the power struggle that goes on at the different hierarchical levels under the guise of technological constraints and efficient coordination. The creators of this structure may have a rather large range of choices: for example, between various mechanisms of control which are more or less centralized or participative. Their decisions may mean different criteria for job design and control methods at the various levels of the organization; any dysfunction, therefore, could be considered to reflect the nature and purpose of these decisions.

In the first part of this selection, a case study conducted in a French tool-making plant is described, placing the effects of a system of power relations into perspective. The analysis of the problem involved has led to some changes in the organization of the plant that affect such relationships.

The second part describes the way in which the power relationships are articulated between management and labor, and institutionalized in the French system of industrial relations.

A Case Study in Power Relationships

The general management of the firm was faced with a foremen problem in a tool-making plant. In a recent work stoppage over a minor matter (a disagreement over the assignment of parking places), the foremen had sided with the workers, taking part in the stoppage, a very unusual step for men who are considered the lowest level of management.

At first, management thought this action merely reflected some general underlying discontent. It asked for a study to learn more about the opinions and attitudes of the first-line foremen, expecting that the findings would recommend some kind of human relations training or improvement of the communication and information network. However, the study took a different direction. It became clear at the outset that the foremen were the victims of a very complicated distribution—or, better, stratification—of roles, and that dysfunctions were built into the system. Management had created a complicated network of power relationships to enhance its right of intervention, and this was largely the reason why conditions of work were felt as deteriorating in the plant and why the situation was in some respects a stalemate.

The plant produced tools for making out bodies on a unit production basis, performing all the processes from casting to finishing. On the average, 1,500 hours of work were required to make a tool, each with its own characteristics, having different specifications and sequence of operations, the opposite of an assembly-line production.

The plant employed about 350 very highly skilled tool makers with long experience. Such men were very hard to find in the labor market and were highly unionized. In view of the nature of the work and the experience and skill of the workers, one would assume that a minimum of supervision and coordination was needed, that is, the men had a very large degree of autonomy. In practice, however, the opposite situation obtained: the organization put very tight controls on these workers.

The plant situation was as follows: customers' orders arrived irregularly with very strict deadlines for completion. Planning was very difficult and it was practically impossible to have a steady flow of work. The planning department staff were not too familiar with the problems of production and always sought to satisfy delivery requirements of customers, backed by pressure from general management. Many conflicts arose between them and the shop, which management had constantly to resolve.

A time study office defined the sequence of operations required and allocated work times to each, distributing the workload among gangs. As may be inferred, conflicts at this point were at their worst. The time study people were confronted by powerful opponents—foremen and highly skilled workers; their decisions encroached directly on the autonomy of both. It might be worth noting here that the time study office was next to the manager's (with glass windows). Quite clearly, their work was guided by a technological rationality, but it also had a strategic purpose—to force upon the workers management's view of the best technical method, time needed, and so on, to do the job. And these were the points of greatest discontent in the plant, the place where most disputes arose. The times allocated—always considered too long or too short—were the focus of controversy. The choice of the machines was criticized, too, by the workers, who believed they were the only ones who knew which were best.

A small group of inspectors, reporting to another plant doing later processes, checked the different parts of tools before assembly. The organizational gap between inspection and production made the settlement of disagreements very difficult (e.g., tolerances not kept). The disagreements were often appealed to the top. All daily technical problems were referred to the technical engineer, who had a monopoly over technical knowledge.

As to the foremen, their situation can be summarized as follows: When workloads were not too heavy and rather steady, they could get along with their job. But when there were difficulties the weakness of their status became apparent. First, their responsibility consisted exclusively of distributing work and inspecting performance. They took no part in its execution (though they were former workers) or in the decisions, which were left to the time study office. They felt their tasks were routine, promoting lack of interest and isolation. Like the workers themselves, they felt they were losing their skills. The decision-making power seemed to them widely disseminated between noncommunicating groups—shop superintendent, plant management, general management, inspection, planning department, time study—and when a problem arose they did not know where to report. On the other hand, foremen had very few authority problems and very few conflicts with their men. They had common interests, similar training and work backgrounds. The chain of command was very long. At plant level there are six levels in the hierarchy going down from plant manager to technical engineer to shop superintendent to foreman to gang boss to worker. Above the plant were those levels from general manager through manager to assistant to manager. Additionally, inspection and planning reported to the manager at firm level and time study reported to the plant manager.

An Interpretation of the Problem in Terms of Power Relationships

At first glance, the difficulties of the plant would seem simple to understand. The firm's organizational structure shows an effort toward rational use of capacities along the accepted lines of planning: time study, inspection, with technical testing control at the level of the engineer. Although very complicated and with an excess of hierarchical levels, this clockworks organization faithfully follows the principles of scientific management. Following the efficiency dogma has led to some dysfunctional consequences. Part of the current discontent could even be explained by the nostalgia for craftsman-type methods of production.

However, even the overview just given makes this interpretation quite untenable. The foremen were in a situation in which they could not get a clear idea of the total process. They could not settle minor conflicts, having to search for the appropriate decision maker, because of the rules of the functional departments or the complications of the hierarchy.

The entire organizational structure seemed to deny a full grasp of the process: the planning department, sensitive to customers' demands, did not know much about production problems; the time study staff (incidentally, staffed by people of the same training as the foremen) decided the details of execution but was kept away from the machines; the inspectors could reject the finished work, but could not specify in advance what was desired. The many conflicts that arose seemed embedded in the definition of the tasks. This rigid hierarchy favored the centralization of all decision making and adjudication centralization, which makes possible the ascent of all decisions, differences, and disagreements to the top.

The organization works as a system of mutual controls (planning and production, time study and production, inspection and production), with the engineer and the manager exercising control which is reinforced by the very high number of conflicts that arise from any incident. The firm's manager explained, for instance, that the old craftsman system was uncontrollable because the absence of a worker halted all work on his tool. Though superficially sound, this argument seems more a rationalization than an explanation, given the difficulty of delivering orders on time in the present system. In fact, however, the ongoing conflicts are not unforeseen consequences of a rational organization: they are the basis of a strategy of extreme centralization of power.

The foremen's situation emerges significantly as a result of this strategy: leading to their feelings of powerlessness, of encroachment from different groups, of loss of interest in their jobs all point to the same fact—the conscious strategy of management to retain all controls in its own hands.

Conflicts, consequently, would not disappear with the introduction of human relations training; although temporarily useful, it would not change the constant recourse to arbitration at the top. However, a new plant manager tried to change the direction by working not on behaviors and attitudes, but on the organizational structure itself and on the very definition of the work roles. For instance, he decided to rotate jobs between foremen and time study people; he made various changes to shorten the chain of command; he organized study groups on product quality, bringing together foremen and inspectors, and in some cases representatives of customers' plants. He held regular consultation and orientation meetings on organizational structure. While rather modest in themselves, these steps—which should be followed by others—tended to enrich the jobs of the workers, build a bridge between the functions of foremen, time study, and inspectors, and enrich the jobs of the foremen by widening their responsibility. At the same time, management was no longer totally occupied with resolving minor conflicts and had more time to attend to customers' demands, technological innovation, and personnel administration. Without changes in technology and product and in the general context of the firm, there is the prospect of a gradual change in the work roles which results in a different distribution of power.

Initially, the organization defined each function with very restricted responsibilities. This was not the result of a rational division of work, but was designed to insure dependence on higher management. The conflicts arising out of the incapacity of each member to grasp the total process were built into the structure in favor of continuous arbitration and control from the top. The new changes, in contrast, attempt to enrich the functions of the workers and the foremen, and to facilitate direct coordination among planning, time study, and inspection. This changes the locus of operative decisions; their enhanced autonomy is closely linked to a new different distribution of power.

A Case Study in Institutionalization of Power Relationships

In this section, the manner will be described in which the power relationships outlined in the preceding section affect labor-management relations in France.

The power relations analyzed thus far are largely implicit; they provide a perspective for organizational solutions and are useful as a hypothesis to explain them; but they are only implicitly involved. A case of conflict at the shop-floor level reveals a more explicit relationship.

In the provincial plant of a large electrical appliance firm, the semiskilled operators voiced many grievances involving working conditions. Management decided to seek a study of this from a group of academic researchers in ergonomics or work physiology. It should be noted that the request was made by the works committee, through its chairman the plant manager. Thus the initiative for the study was a joint one, coming from a conflict situation.

The study was completed after one-and-a-half years and the results made available to all members of the plant. The unions found them so palatable that the CFDT local (Confederation Française Democratique du Travail) used them very extensively in a pamphlet calling for organized action.[1] Though the initial problem had been mainly nuisance and discomfort on the job, the rationale of the pamphlet has a much larger significance which will serve as an example.

Relying heavily on the study by the ergonomists, the pamphlet makes a general attack on poor working conditions, badly designed jobs requiring heavy physical effort that could be avoided, excessive mental pressure because of strict work pace, inequity of workload and effort among jobs, and so on. The critics were not just denouncing the planning department. They were questioning the so-called scientific basis of "rationality" of the planning department—not only because it does not recognize individual differences in capacity and skill among the operators and combines in the same job heavy physical effort and precision operations, but also because the accurate determination in advance of all operator movements is deemed an impossible task.[2] Criticized is the so-called scientific management of work[3] which disguised arbitrary decisions as "technical reasons." This is reinforced by the fact that the planning technicians under scientific management have no training in adapting jobs to people. At stake are not only the criteria of the decisions, but the distribution of power to make them.

What follows are logical conclusions. The pamphlet cites all the cases where operators have to take the initiative and change the prescribed ways of working so as to make for effective production, where they have to improvise because of variances or material defects, where they help one another to solve problems, and where they themselves train newcomers. The conclusion is that the semi-skilled operators are really responsible for effective production and that management has to draw upon their "knowledge" and "work skills" to ensure that jobs are well done.

The criticism is interesting on two accounts: First, it sheds light on what is left of initiative and responsibility in jobs which seem very poor in content and strictly determined from above. In itself, this notion should come as no great surprise for time and motion study technicians, at least those who are conscious of the limits of their planning. But it is used here to demand "an improvement of the status of semiskilled jobs." The context makes it quite clear that the demand is for a higher classification and higher wages, but not only for that; it is, too, for job enrichment, using as a point of departure the daily working practices, and it is articulated as a grievance.[4]

Second and more important, what is left of initiative and responsibility is used to argue that the semiskilled operators have some power in bargaining with management. The pamphlet considers the possibility, among others, of using "working to rule": "If we did the work exactly as it is prescribed," it reads, "that would stop production." In other words, the operators already have some autonomy in their work, unskilled as it is, and this autonomy could be a source of power in case of open conflict.

This rather detailed account of the pamphlet is an example of how the analysis of work can be used in a conflict situation. But it provides few details on how these grievances can be resolved and states the objectives in very general terms. The reason is a basic one: There are difficulties in translating the gripes and feelings at the shop-floor level into union strategy.

Work Conditions and Unions: The Case of the Confederation Générale du Travail[5]

The problem of working conditions came to the forefront in the major strikes of 1968 and in several minor ones in the following months when it was articulated, but often not in its full implications (work pace, workload, work week, shift work). The left-wing groups of the unions tried for some time to identify the problem with their cause.[6] What was new, in fact, was not the topic itself, but its very strong expression and the radical aspect of some grievances.

The problem has been a traditional concern of the unions, and they integrated it very easily into their programs. Each federation did it in its own style (and this style was influenced by their respective relations with their left-wing groups). Some conclusions may be drawn from the case of the CGT.

The confederation's paper printed the report of a study in February 1972, calling "for working conditions in keeping with the human needs of our time" and concluding with a list of demands.[7] The main conclusions are stated in the "action program," called for by the Federal Congress of April 1972.[8] At that congress, a shortened version was given in the report of the Federal Executive Council, presented by its secretary-general, Georges Séguy.[9]

These reports develop the confederation's position on the problem of working conditions. And this time the term has a more inclusive meaning, incorporating work pace and schedules, as well as interesting work and opportunity for advancement. Some elements of this union strategy are outlined below:

1. At the outset, the CGT launches a very strong attack against employers' initiatives. Job enrichment, improvement of work on assembly lines (and, it adds, participative management)[10] are accused of being "a wide maneuver in ideological demagoguery." The employers, "faced with well-grounded demands by their workers, try to deceive and trap them into class collaboration." Their purpose "remains the same: to go on with and strengthen capitalist exploitation."

This sweeping attack does not imply that no problem exists. On the contrary, the union's program states as an objective that it is necessary to "improve the quality and variety of the tasks for everyone" and to "give the workers a better share in initiative and responsibility"—a formula that could serve as a rather sound definition of job enrichment. The purpose of this attack is, then, to discredit the initiatives, as exclusively the employers', under the assumption that, in any case, they just look for more profit. And, in this way, the trade unions are the only ones entitled to take initiatives for real improvement. Moreover, having proved to its own satisfaction that nothing is new in this problem except "technical and economic conditions," the CGT is not faced with any basic reappraisal. The problem of working conditions has been brought back to the classical conflict situation between labor and management.

2. To make quite clear that the basic problem is an old one, though the economic and social context makes it more acute and pressing, a good part of the discussion is spent on classical topics like the pace of work or the deskilling process as logical consequences of capitalist exploitation. The current issues, though they deserve to be studied for their own sake and are granted a special chapter in the action program, are the natural result of previous conflicts, articulated in a language congenial to the activists.

3. The main difficulty, however, is to make operative these general demands, that is, to articulate objectives which are controlled by union delegates or elected representatives of the employees. It should be recalled that French unions have a rather weak hold on work practices, and that their powers have to be extended if they are to control them. This is the reason why the list of demands stresses, within the work situation, the more easily controllable aspects. For instance, the CGT asks that work pace, manning, and workloads be posted in the shop; it asks for rest periods and rest rooms; and it demands that employees, worker representatives, and union delegates should be notified in advance of any change in the work procedure. Concerning training and promotion, it asks for "guaranteed cereer development," and for the right for all semiskilled operators to be placed in a new job after one year's experience.[11] In this effort to make demands operative, interest in the variety of work, in responsibility and initiative, is no longer mentioned for very obvious reasons.

4. Lastly, care has been taken to give these demands as broad a formulation as possible, in order to involve the largest number of union members and nonmembers. A striking example is the report of the Executive Council which, after giving a systematic view of the problem of working conditions, returns to a very simplified statement insisting only on the shortening of the work week and earlier retirement.[12] Step by step, the complex content of the report is "simplified" in the action program, and from the action program to the Executive Council's report, and not without reason. This process is indicative of the difficulty surrounding the problem in the traditional context of industrial relations.

Is There a Management Strategy?

This question is better understood in the light of some statements from the employers' side. The National Employers' Association did not take a stand as such, but it printed the conclusions of a study group which, while not acting on behalf of the association, speaks in an official capacity.[13] The study group consulted several experts and made a very broad analysis of the "problem of semiskilled workers," discussing wages, classification, status in collective agreements, and time and motion study.

The main purpose of the report was to remind the employers of their responsibilities and to invite them to action. But it cannot be said that in so doing it would close the door to collective bargaining and ignore the trade unions. For instance, when discussing the possibilities for training and advancement, it makes explicit reference to the interindustry agreement on training of July 1970. Moreover, it considers the opportunity to negotiate some of its proposals; promoting a better classification of semiskilled workers, it mentions the current negotiations in several industries on classification. In the same spirit, it stresses the value of the "monthly salary" agreements, which have been signed in different industries since 1970, and proposes several provisions directly inspired by the intent of these agreements. It is fair to say that the stand taken implies no aggression toward unions and no systematic avoidance of bargaining.

In other respects, however, there is a different attitude. Wages are a good example. The employers' committee intends to improve the relative level of compensation for semiskilled workers and concludes: "It would be a very good thing if the law of supply and demand could operate more freely in our country." Limiting the effect of the market is public regulation, the example of the public sector and "a tendency to follow the pattern of civil servants." The committee plans, as a first step, to distinguish between the scale of take-home wages and the scale of minimum rates,[14] and to provide "complementary compensation" for less attractive jobs—no innovation since such a practice is currently in force. But it must be remembered that the difference between effective wages and minimum rates, and even more between the scale of both, is one of the matters unions complain about.[15]

More generally, the employers' association's report sees in agreements already concluded or in prospect an opportunity for more managerial initiative. The national agreement on training could be used as a basis to promote semiskilled workers. However, such promotion is not guaranteed by the agreement and is not a negotiable matter. Likewise, changes in time and motion study methods for the purpose of improving comfort and interest on the job rest on "a steady effort of higher management to change the attitudes of shop management."

In other words, if progress is possible in this field, it must depend on managerial initiative and, while this would not disrupt the pattern of collective bargaining, it would not broaden it. Although "workers' grievances" about working conditions are mentioned, this area is defined as a managerial prerogative, a natural attitude in a system of industrial relations in which the work practices are not a legitimate object for bargaining; it would be surprising indeed if the employers offered to include them in negotiation. In this context, then, it becomes clear why the CGT, before discussing substantive issues, starts with a massive attack on possible initiatives of the "enemy."

Working Conditions and the System of Industrial Relations

The basic stumbling block is rather easy to define: In the French system of industrial relations, working conditions, in its inclusive context, is not a negotiable issue. Only in very exceptional cases does bargaining, properly speaking, take place at the plant level, it is generally industrywide (for a region or for the whole country). It can easily accommodate the work week or special compensation for shift work, but it can hardly concern itself with problems of job content.

The works committee, by law, has a consultative role with respect to working conditions that does not include bargaining. Moreover, the unions feel reluctance toward the increasing role employers have been willing to give them during the last few years (it is very significant that this is not even mentioned in the above CGT reports).

The grievance procedure, handled by employee-elected representatives, would be a more appropriate framework, but is not adequate; it is in most cases strongly centralized because the representatives are elected at the plant and not at the shop-floor level and because it is generally not a step-by-step procedure (most issues go directly to personnel managers). With final and binding arbitration not available, the outcome of a grievance rests largely on workers' action and the procedure tends to discriminate in favor of those grievances which can be most easily generalized.

This overview does not mean that there are no solutions, but that the practical solutions have yet to be found. Industrial relations in France in the last four years have left much room for innovation. But the current uncertainty explains the cautiousness of the unions, as well as the very unobtrusive way in which employers experiment along this line. Results are few, but they exist; however, in most cases management avoids publicizing what it is doing.

In a paradoxical way this situation, which seems to leave total freedom of action to management, is a real hindrance to the development of enhanced quality of working life. At the plant level, it favors a piecemeal approach instead of systemic treatment; prudence suggests seizing local opportunities rather than facing the general problem. Moreover, the diffusion and public discussion of experiments are very limited, and successful attempts have had little influence.

Improving the quality of working life implies a change in the principles of job design, that is, eventually a change in the value system of management. In the conflict context of industrial relations, however, a value system does not arise out of faith, but out of compromise. Changes are possible when they are needed and when institutions are available to develop such compromise. The current problem in France (and perhaps in other European countries too) involving conditions of work and the quality of working life is not their stake in industrial conflict; rather, it lies in the difficult institutionalization of conflict.

NOTES

1. Under the title "special cadences" (special issue: work pace); bulletin of the CFDT local addressed to all its members. February 1972, 12 pp.

2. The conclusion is underscored in the text; "In our judgment, the efforts of the technical people at the top, who decide with the utmost precision the tasks to perform, the way they are to be perfomed, and the time they need in very fragmented work are doomed to failure."

3. The pamphlet says further: "It is a joke . . . that has already lasted too long"!

4. For instance, ". . . very fragmented jobs are really a waste of human capacities and a step-by-step destruction of technical and intellectual wealth. . . . We should fight harder against the constraint of work pace and against fragmented work."

5. It is not attempted to give a general presentation of union attitudes; cf. Y. Delamotte, "Union Attitudes toward Quality of Working Life," Selection 27.

6. Cf. Serge Mallet, "L'Après-mai 1968, grèves pour le contrôle ouvrier," *Sociologie du Travail*, 3 (1970), 309–327.

7. *Le Peuple*, no. 887, February 17–19, 1972.

8. *Ibid.*, no. 893–894, May 1–31, 1972.

9. *Ibid.*

10. This addition is meaningful in view of the CGT's attempt for several years to organize engineers, technical personnel, and administrative staff.

11. This is not a complete list of demands as they are stated in the action program. It should be noted that these demands are rather moderate ones (particularly when compared, for instance, with the privileges of the German works committee, as enlarged by the 1971 law). The last demand is evidently inspired by the FIAT agreement.

12. ". . . our demands are for improvement of working conditions, shortening of the work week so as to reach as soon as possible the forty-hour week with no wage cut, and for earlier retirement with full and adequate pension at age 55 for women and age 60 for men" (G. Séguy report).

13. *Les O. S. Rapport du groupe d'études patronal* (January 1972, 25 p.) (semi-skilled workers, report of the employers' study group).

14. In most collective agreements bargaining is only about minimum rates.

15. It may be argued, with some reason, that this is the only realistic way to achieve results. It is merely attempted here to stress the significance of this procedure for industrial relations. On this matter unions would not object to relative improvement of "low wages" and would even welcome it.

27

Union Attitudes toward Quality of Working Life

Yves P. Delamotte

UNION responses to quality of working life are shaped by their values, goals, and practices. For example, the difference in attitude between Scandinavian unions involved in industrial democracy programs and the Marxist-oriented French Confederation Générale du Travail (CGT) shows the impact of ideologies and values in shaping union reaction. However, the Italian Confederazione Generale del Lavoro, which is equally Marxist, has not taken the negative view of the CGT toward enhanced quality of working life. The CGT's long-term goal is collective ownership of the means of production—a goal to be achieved through class conflict and class consciousness. Its short-term goals involve concrete gains imposed upon employers through union pressure; any agreement can be questioned, otherwise it may be an "adherence" to capitalistic society. Changes toward greater job satisfaction are acceptable as long as they are initiated by the unions.

The Marxist-oriented Italian unions see job redesign and semiautonomous work groups as viable alternatives to traditional job design as long as the initiative comes from the workers. This new power of workers' representatives at the plant level means that organizational changes are no longer seen as a form of exploitation.

Collective bargaining patterns, too, can influence the enhancement of quality of working life. In Holland the unions are highly centralized and there is little or no representation within the plant and little union involvement in work structuring experiments at the plant level. The situation would be quite different in a British plant, for changes in the organization of work there might directly affect union goals and values; management will have to engage in bargaining in order to bring about changes, that is, productivity agreements in which both management and workers stand to gain. Thus British unions will accept change when they can control its content and consequences. Some unions in the United States view job changes aimed at increasing quality of working life as a threat to their goals and practices built into collective bargaining. The strategic value of collective agreements relating to such issues as job security and seniority is seen to be dependent on the stability of the content of jobs. Thus economic group solidarity is seen as more basic than individual job enrichment.

Union attitudes toward the quality of working life may differ from one country to another, within a country from one enterprise to another, and even within an enterprise from one plant to another. Within a workers' federation, positions taken at the top toward the idea may not be reflected in positions taken by a local union, confronted with practical changes. We shall not try in this selection, which is based upon a fragmentary view of the situation, to reconstruct this variety of possible answers. Our purpose is more limited: By way of a few selected examples, we shall endeavor to show the relation which may exist between union response to quality of working life and union values, goals, and practices. The example of Norway and Sweden,* where experiments in this direction are widespread, reflects the existing consensus between employers' and workers' organizations as to the value of industrial democracy and the common belief that it can be implemented in the existing capitalistic system. For the French Confederation Générale du Travail (CGT),* the most influential workers' federation, and Marxist-oriented, the fact that these initiatives emanate from within the capitalistic system conveys their "true meaning" and they should therefore be opposed as a new device for the same old exploitation of workers.

---

* Reviewed in following sections.

This difference of attitude between the Scandinavian trade unions, which believe that there can be some identity of interests between management and the worker, and the French CGT, whose action rests upon the Marxist view of class conflict, shows clearly the impact of ideologies and values in shaping union reaction. It does not follow, however, that Marxist views lead necessarily and automatically to a negative appraisal like that of the CGT. The example of the Italian Confederazione Generale del Lavoro (CGIL),* equally Marxist, demonstrates that some other analyses are possible which lead to integrating the quality of working life into a global and active union strategy. It is suggested in this selection that the difference in attitude between the two Marxist organizations, the French and the Italian, is also due to some achievements of the latter through collective bargaining at the branch and, even more recently, at the enterprise level. The last part of this selection contains some general comments on the impact of collective bargaining patterns upon union attitudes toward the quality of working life.

The Scandinavian Experiments: A Consensus upon Industrial Democracy

Much has already been said about the Swedish and Norwegian experiments and the social context in which they take place. Both the employers' and the workers' organizations agree upon the value of industrial democracy, that is, on the worker exerting a greater influence over his work; both believe that this can be achieved without any collective appropriation of the means of work, and that these experiments can serve the interests of the enterprise as well as those of the workers. Most of these experiments have taken place under the sponsorship of joint committees of representatives of management and of the workers. In Sweden trial experiments have been organized[1] by a number of development councils, which aid, stimulate, and study collaboration as well as to try to increase efficiency within that sphere. One of the most important is the Development Council for Collaborative Questions, which is active in the private sector and has formed a special work group for research (URAF). This council was created as a result of the conclusion, a few years ago, of a national agreement between SAF, LO, and TCO upon questions of cooperation. In Norway, too, the experiments have taken place under the sponsorship of a National Joint Committee, which helped the researchers to select industries and enterprises in which the experiments could be carried on. In the enterprise the experiments were conducted with the support of local unions.

Thus, in both countries workers' unions not only are not opposed to the experiments but take part in promoting them. While they may be very hard bargainers at the national or branch level, they accept the idea of cooperation when they think workers' interests can be served by this means. They know these experiments can help management solve problems of absenteeism and turnover and raise productivity, but they do not consider these goals to be incompatible with their own interests. There is a consensus upon values and the need for efficiency, and that presumes a certain kind of relationship between employers and unions which is not compatible with the Marxist view of class conflict. In Norway the employers insist upon a condition for the success of these experiments: mutual trust between managers and union leaders, who know each other well and often share wartime memories.

The Impact of Ideology upon Union Attitudes: The French Confederation Général du Travail

The CGT, a Marxist organization, has both long- and short-term goals. The long-term goal is to pave the way for a new society with collective ownership of the means of production, a goal shared by the Communist party which is active at the political level. They maintain that progress in this direction can be made only through class conflict and class consciousness. Not only the industrial workers, but the white-collar workers, the technicians, and the engineers as well should be class conscious; that is, they should realize they are exploited and that this exploitation can be brought to an end only with the destruction of the capitalistic society. The CGT presents itself as a "mass organization" and tries to formulate its claims in terms which will attract and mobilize the largest number of people. Its short-term goals involve concrete gains which may be imposed upon employers through union pressure and action. Collective agreements are signed by the CGT if it considers that their content will support its aims; even the fact of signing such an agreement (usually at the industry level in France) does not prevent the union from making new claims if the power relationship with employers becomes more favorable: any agreement can be questioned at any moment. And, most important, it should not be interpreted as an "adherence" (guarantee) to the capitalistic society.[2]

According to the CGT, employers are now discovering that traditional methods of organization of work are less efficient and that some changes are required in order to meet increased absenteeism and the young people's reluctance toward taking industrial jobs. But new methods can only be new devices to attain the same former goals inherent in the capitalistic system. "As long as the capitalistic system exists, organization of work, whatever forms it takes, will remain subordinate to the goal of maximum profit; through it, the employers will go on ever increasing the intensification of work."[3] For the CGT this is the true meaning of these new methods, and it observes that most of the experiments which receive any publicity are accompanied by an increase in labor productivity.[4]

This approach to the problem does not prevent the CGT from acknowledging that industrial jobs are often dull and repetitive, that workers lack autonomy and responsibility, and that something should be done to change this. In the words of one of its leaders: "A change in the organization which will make jobs less repetitive, more responsible, more skilled, is of course a union claim." [5] And an official document issued in February 1972, entitled *Pour des conditions de travail plus humaines en rapport avec notre temps*, states: "The CGT demands that steps be taken within the enterprises to remedy the extreme division of tasks and the trend towards more unskilled jobs. It should aim to increase the quality and the diversity of the tasks assigned to every individual and to enlarge the workers' share of initiative. The semiskilled workers who would be willing to comply should have the possibility, after a year's service, of being assigned to new jobs in order to acquire wider experience leading to higher classification and wages." This indicates that the CGT's view of the quality of working life is a matter of perspective. If changes in this direction result from management's initiatives, they will mean an intensification of work, an increase of labor's productivity, a threat to workers' solidarity and class consciousness: "*Le capitalisme pervertit tout ce qu'il touche.*"

If, on the other hand, the quality of working life is imposed upon the employers by union action, it can convey its true positive meaning. It will then include not only devices to increase variety, autonomy, and responsibility at work, but even measures to alleviate the individual workload, and more generally to neutralize the capitalistic trend toward intensifying work. Indeed, the CGT's platform includes some items such as: limitation of the number of machines which can be served by one man; more rest breaks; reduction of the speed of assembly lines (with more people to replace the workers who want to get away from the line for a while); elimination of shift work whenever it is not a technical necessity; reduction of working hours, and so on. All these changes which do not usually make for increased labor productivity must be imposed upon the employers and can result only from collective action. The quality of working life issue, which is only a "subterfuge" when it stems from the initiative of the employers, becomes worthwhile when it is part of a more comprehensive action and inserted into the perspectives of class conflict.[6] Of course, being a union, the CGT cannot deny the value of more interesting and more autonomous work, although it is not ready to accept willingly that such changes can be achieved in the present system. According priority to changes in this direction implies a different analysis and strategy, as is shown by the example of another Marxist organization, the Federation of Metal Workers of the Confederazione Generale del Lavoro (FIOM-CGIL).

Quality of Work as a Primary Goal: The Strategy of the Italian Federation of Metal Workers (FIOM-CGIL)

The leaders of the FIOM share the views of the leaders of the CGT on capitalistic society and class conflict. But their analysis of the present situation led them to assign to changes in the organization of work an explicit priority among union objectives.

Their position can be summarized as follows:[7]

Work structuring, job enrichment, semiautonomous work groups are all experiments which clearly demonstrate that alternative solutions can be found in lieu of the traditional technical division of work. If the employers are allowed to take the initiative in this direction, these new devices will only make for a greater integration and subordination of the workers. However, if, on the other hand, the initiative comes from the workers, they will have increased opportunities of learning the production processes, of appropriating them instead of being subject to them. This will be a first step toward the "social control" by workers over production processes and will further deepen changes.

However, this drive toward new patterns of organization requires that the old classification systems which perpetuate a technical division of work should also be eliminated. The first step in this direction should be the elimination of job evaluation which, when applied to repetitive and fragmentary tasks, taking into account such aspects of the work as physical strain, heat, and risk of accidents, provides a monetary compensation for unchanged working conditions. Generally speaking, all the systems which allow for a wide differentiation of classifications and wages are arbitrary; the workers should impose simpler systems, defined by themselves, having a very limited number of categories. The promotion from a category to a higher one should mean not only more money, but also more interesting and skilled work.

This program was partly fulfilled during the fall of 1970 after a violent strike, when these methods were adopted for the 40,000 workers of Italsider (that part of the Italian steel industry which is controlled by the government): the job evaluation system was abandoned and the number of worker categories considerably reduced. However, the most impressive achievements were obtained in large companies, such as Olivetti and Fiat. The collective agreements concluded there in 1971 show clearly the relationship in the unions' strategy between changes in job content and changes in classification and promotion patterns.[8]

In these two agreements the number of worker categories was reduced to four. Workers are not supposed to remain in the lowest (4th) category; at Olivetti, according to the agreement, they will normally reach the third category before the expiration of a period of 18 months following ratification of the agreement. Similar items are included in the Fiat agreement, which reads, "Workers classified in the 4th category will be progressively assigned to tasks with a larger operative content (de maggior contenuto operativo) and will be transferred to the 3rd category after at most 18 months spent in the 4th."

Promotion from the third to the second category is also regulated in both agreements, mentioning the number of workers who will be promoted and the time allowed for such promotion. The Olivetti agreement lists the method used to make sure that this promotion does not mean only more money, but changes in work—job enlargement, job enrichment, successive assignments to different tasks, and so on. Attached to the agreement by way of an example is a short description of a new method for assembling a calculator based upon the repartition using small groups of workers. The Fiat agreement includes similar terms and, moreover, provides for the creation of a joint management-union committee to study the problems involved in establishing new assembly lines or reorganizing existing ones. These two agreements show the relationship deliberately pursued by the union with respect to changes in work content, classifications, and promotion (and training) opportunities. They constitute a concerted policy of such changes in the tasks which will justify the reduction of worker categories and collective upgrading within them.

The differences in approach chosen by the Marxist CGIL and the Marxist CGT suggest that even within an identical frame of reference (class conflict), the meaning of organizational changes can also be part of a global and offensive union strategy that go with new training and promotion opportunities, changes in classification and wages, new rules concerning hygiene and safety, new committees to represent workers at the shop level and to exert control upon work loads, and so on. All of these changes did take place. In such a context, reflecting the new power of the unions and of the workers' representatives at the plant level, organizational changes can no longer be presented as a new way of exploiting the workers.

Collective Bargaining Patterns and Quality of Working Life

Another way to approach the unions' attitudes is to try answering the question: What is at stake when the unions are confronted with management's initiatives toward improving the quality of working life? As will be shown with the help of some examples from different countries,[9] the answer varies according to the unions' usual pattern of action. Therefore, the structure of collective bargaining seems especially relevant.

It may look as if the Dutch unions had nothing at stake for they have not tried to interfere with the experiments in work structuring conducted by Philips at Eindhoven, which are taking place in a kind of vacuum as far as industrial relations are concerned. For the small groups of operators assembling a whole TV set, the work is apparently more complex than on the traditional assembly line. However, the workers have not benefited from any change in their classification, nor have they asked for it. They were told when they volunteered for the experiments that they would not get any wage increase and accepted this. In management's view this change in their work does not imply a change of their qualification, according to the criteria of job evaluation, and apparently the union shares this view. It should be noted here that in the Netherlands the focus of union action is at the national level. As John P. Windmuller puts it: "Below the industry level, however, the influence of unions declines rapidly. . . . The contribution of unions to the personnel policies of individual enterprises is either remote or derivative or nonexistent. . . . Most unions have no shop-level or worksite structure through which they could attempt to exert direct influence on working conditions." [10] As long as the national agreement is not violated, the employer seems relatively free to introduce changes in the organization of work, especially if these changes concern only a limited number of workers and are presented as "experiments."

The situation would be quite different in a British plant. Changes in the organization of work there might directly affect union goals and values, and management would have to take into account all the informal rules regulating work and employment, which are covered under the term "custom and practice." In Allan Flanders' words: "These informal rules which management has no say in making but tacitly has to accept range over many subjects. In earlier times they were mainly the trade practices of craftsmen who protected their job territory from invasion by limiting entry and upholding demarcation. Today they are the means by which many workers who are not craftsmen protect their earnings and their bargaining power, but equally their security, their status and their values. Direct regulation of output or stint, the allocation of overtime, of manning scales, of work sharing, of job demarcations of all kinds are well known examples. . . . . Some of them may be officially upheld by trade unions but most are enforced on the shop floor by work or union groups. Shop stewards, not full-time officials, are the principal guardians of C. and P. in British Industry." [11] William Brown observes that "the C. and P. status of some practices only arises when they are challenged, questioned or broken." [12]

In such a context, management wishing to introduce changes in the organization of work will not have full freedom of action, even if it is officially argued that such changes are part of management's prerogatives. It will have to consider all the informal rules which have developed at the plant level and to convince not only the union officials but the numerous stewards as well that some changes have become necessary. The importance of productivity agreements, in the history of British industrial relations, rests upon the fact that managers for the first time realistically accepted bargaining about these practices in order to change them, instead of taking the view that such changes lay within their prerogatives and could not be a matter for discussion (a position which led to no change at all). In a productivity agreement the changes are accepted by the workers' side because of some reciprocity made possible through increased productivity in matters of basic wages and length of working hours.

However, the changes which can be introduced through such bargaining may, of course, improve the quality of working life. In their book, *The Nylon Spinners*, Cotgrove, Dunham, and Vampleur describe changes in the organization of spinning work at one Imperial Chemical Industries plant when more responsibility and autonomy were given to groups of workers.[13] This was the consequence of a productivity agreement, signed in 1968, and covering all the plants of ICI. This national agreement laid down new conditions of wages for all the workers covered and listed the plants where changes in methods should be worked out (trial sites); but the precise changes had to be defined in these plants through special procedures involving work study specialists, shop stewards, and the workers themselves. New job descriptions were thus achieved in each trial site which were later confirmed at the company level by the management and the unions.

In Britain the emergence of productivity agreements concluded at the enterprise or plant level appeared as a new development in an industrial relations system previously based largely upon industrywide agreement; this development acknowledged the power of stewards and workers' groups at the plant level; it created a pattern according to which changes have to be paid for even if they mean more motivating and meaningful work. In the Netherlands, where no such power developed at the plant level, changes seem to be introduced more easily and without a price tag attached to them; the traditional system of centralized bargaining remains unchanged and mobilizes the whole energy of the union.

The kind of reciprocity associated with productivity bargaining makes it more likely that the unions will accept some changes in organization since they can control the content and the consequences of these changes. Quality of working life would fit into the new bargaining pattern. If this hypothesis is sound, however, the rapid decline of productivity agreements in Britain would mean more union reluctance in accepting such changes.

It might be suggested, too, that the reluctance shown by some unions in the United States is due partly to the fact that changes in the jobs could appear as a threat to the unions' goals and practices built into collective bargaining. Collective bargaining is not much concerned with the nature of the tasks and the organization of work. To put the emphasis upon the nature of work—not upon wages—amounts to saying that the focus of union action is not directed to what is really important. The "hygiene-motivation" theory, as put forward by Frederick Herzberg,[14] may be resented by union leaders who have been traditionally active in the area defined by Herzberg as "hygiene." In Mitchell Sviridoff's own words: "Union representatives are clearly suspicious of an analysis that challenges the fundamental precepts of the trade union movement. . . . When you suggest that the basic problem has to do with the nature of the job and the way the plant is structured, rather than wages, fringes, and other things basic to the bargaining process, then union representatives understandably get nervous." [15]

It might also be argued that the strategic value of collective agreements (and of grievance procedures) is dependent upon a certain stability of the content of the jobs. Clauses related to seniority, transfers, promotions, work assignments, and layoffs aim at regulating access to a job or exit from it. The bargaining unit appears in this respect as an internal labor market, functioning under the rules set in the agreement. The strategy of the union, the action of the stewards filing grievances, implies a stability in the structure of the internal labor market and in the content of the jobs. Perhaps this is why union leaders may feel allergic to the idea of changes in jobs: it would mean that the firm ground upon which their action rests during the life of the contract has changed into quicksand.

The notion of "job ownership" is very illuminating, as well as the classical analysis of Selig Perlman in his *Theory of the Labor Movement*. He states that unions' reactions have to be explained by a feeling of scarcity. "If . . . opportunity is believed to be limited, it then becomes the duty of the group to prevent the individual from appropriating more than his rightful share, while at the same time protecting him against oppressive bargains. The group then asserts its collective ownership over the whole amount of opportunity." [16] Analyzing the chapter "The Philosophy of Organic Labor," on the working rules of some unions, he sees the purest expression of "labor's own home grown ideology." Perlman shows that these unions have succeeded in achieving an absolute control of jobs. Working rules are "rules of occupancy and tenure"; they organize the property of common economic opportunity. If these notions still permeate the American unions, this implies that jobs are perceived not as *tasks* which should fulfill the individual needs (for self-realization and so on), but as a *share* in a common economic property which can be protected only through group solidarity; the group solidarity might require that some jobs be deliberately maintained. To consider that some of these jobs are meaningless from the point of view of individual psychological needs is to forget that they have a meaning from the point of view of economic group solidarity.

Conclusions

The foregoing observations show that power considerations may be decisive in determining union attitudes. In some cases unions might fear a loss of power: for example, in the case of craft unions when some job enrichment measures might threaten their jurisdiction over an occupational territory, or if they think that their influence upon the membership might be reduced through "participative" management. In other cases, the unions will hesitate to raise claims to the quality of working life and will shift to more traditional quantitative demands because in their view such demands will mobilize the whole membership more easily and make them stronger vis-à-vis management.

Finally, the most important point is to ascertain under what conditions it is possible to bring about a change of perspective which would make the quality of working life not only a goal of management but a union claim, too. Such a change could take place when unions realize they might lose influence and ground if they adhere to their former patterns. Indeed, the attitudes of the workers themselves might be relevant at this point.

NOTES

1. M. Hedberg, *Summary of Trial Activities at Present Being Conducted Concerning Changes in Work Organization* (Stockholm: Swedish Council for Personnel Administration, 1972) (ron.).

2. In this perspective, gains obtained over a short term should never make the union lose sight of long-term goals and forget that these gains have been reached in a system destined to perish, because it rests upon the exploitation of workers. The essence of capitalism is to push this exploitation farther and farther. Profit seeking leads employers to intensify human work and increase dead work (capital) at the expense of living work.

3. *Pour des conditions de travail plus humaines en rapport avec notre temps: positions et propositions de la C.G.T.* (p. 6).

4. Such is the CGT's view. There is also strong reluctance regarding all new techniques of personnel management, aimed at building small groups of "motivated" employees, who will integrate with the production goals of the enterprise and compete with each other to the detriment of workers' solidarity. The only way for the workers to solve their problems is through class consciousness and class conflict. All such devices—be it management by objectives or semiautonomous work groups —smack of cooperation and participation; their aim is to integrate the employees into the enterprise and, beyond it, into the capitalistic system; therefore, they should be strongly opposed.

5. *op. cit.*, p. 12.

6. In fact, this attitude suggests that the CGT is not committed to changes in the organization of work as one of its primary goals. The main goals are still to reduce working time, to get better classifications and wages, and to improve promotion opportunities; such objectives are more palatable to the majority of workers in industry and better suited to the mobilizing strategy of a "mass organization." As to the working life, the emphasis is laid upon all its aspects which reflect the true nature of capitalism: increased working loads, *"cadences infernales,"* etc. To denounce such exertions is to denounce the evils of capitalistic society, and in this the CGT is on home ground.

7. Cf. A. Litteri, "L'usine et l'ecole," *Les Temps Modernes*, nos. 301–302 (August-September 1971), pp. 181–197.

8. It should be mentioned at this point that these agreements were also signed by the CISC, and the UIL.

9. A more detailed account of the Italian and Dutch experiments will be found in Y. Delamotte, *Recherches en vue d'une organisation plus humaine du travail* (Paris: La Documentation française, 1972).

10. J. P. Windmuller, *Labor Relations in the Netherlands* (Ithaca, N.Y.: Cornell University Press, 1969), p. 399.

11. A. Flanders, *Collective Bargaining: Prescription for Change* (London: Faber & Faber, 1967), p. 69.

12. W. Brown, "A Consideration of Custom and Practice," *British Journal of Industrial Relations*, 10, no. 1 (March 1972), 42–61.

13. S. Cotgrove, J. Dunham, and C. Vampleur, *The Nylon Spinners* (London: Allen & Unwin, 1971).

14. F. Herzberg, *Work and the Nature of Man* (Cleveland: World, 1966).

15. C. R. Price, *New Directions in the World of Work. A Conference Report*, W. E. Upjohn Institute, March 1972.

16. S. Perlman, *The Theory of the Labor Movement* (New York: Kelley, 1970), p. 242.

28

Trade Unions and Worker Participation in Management

Joseph Mire

UNIONS in seven European countries (Austria, Belgium, Denmark, Norway, Sweden, West Germany, and Yugoslavia) argue that their collective bargaining and sponsoring of legislation have had an impact on job satisfaction. Recently, however, they have been baffled by worker unrest despite material improvements. As a result of personal interviews and examination of the literature, the author arrived at six general conclusions involving conditions of transfer of decision-making powers to workers in the seven countries: (1) Transfer of decision-making power must not adversely affect efficiency and, therefore, workers' income; it would then be opposed by both management and workers. Establishment of semiautonomous work groups, committees of cooperation, agreements on rationalization, and systems of self-management have led to increased wages, profits, and production. (2) A pervasive concern in several countries is to avoid having "worker participation" threaten or impinge upon established rights of stewards and/or unions. (3) It has been demonstrated in Scandinavian countries and in particular companies in other countries that enterprises with an established history of constructive employer-employee relations offer the best prospects for pilot projects to improve quality of life in the workplace. (4) A broad program of education and skill training for all workers has to be an integral part of all efforts of humanizing work. (5) Commitment and implementation of a full-employment economy may be a necessary condition to ease fears that improved efficiency will not result in unemployment. (6) More research is required on alternative modes of production, alternative work methods and work requirements.

Unions argue—not without justification—that all their activities, most notably collective bargaining at the shop and industry-wide level and/or their legislative efforts in the political arena have a significant impact on job satisfaction. They have been skeptical and suspicious of management efforts to increase job satisfaction, and they object to the manipulative character of so much of what has passed under the heading of "human relations." Even more importantly, they pointed to the failure of management to assure workers a share in resulting increases of productivity. And, finally, trade unions have a very realistic fear that improved productivity and job satisfaction, no matter how it is brought about, may result in a reduction of the number of available jobs.

In recent years, however, there has been growing recognition that the improvement of the worker's economic, social, and political status of workers has left largely unchanged their jobs at the workplace. Yet it is precisely the situation at the workplace which most fundamentally affects their well-being, both physical and mental. Workers continue to do monotonous and uninteresting work. They have little or no control over their jobs and few, if any, opportunities for initiative, independent thinking, personal growth, and maintaining their human dignity. The growth of industry has meant segmentation and depersonalization.

Worker participation in management in the past has meant primarily indirect participation through elected or appointed union representatives or shop stewards, involving relatively few people. Spokesmen for *direct* worker participation even claim that the institutionalized forms of indirect worker participation have, in fact, become barriers to direct participation, blocking efforts for the transfer of decision-making power to rank-and-file workers.

Trade unions in Western Europe have been baffled by workers' unrest in the face of rising standards of living and material well-being. There has been a notable increase in number of wildcat strikes and rejections of collective agreements negotiated by union leadership, and an additional factor has entered the picture: with rising levels of education, it becomes increasingly difficult to find enough "dumb people to do the dumb jobs." In many countries, critical shortages of labor can presently be met only by drawing on imported labor.

Thus the search is on for ways and means to improve communications, humanize work, democratize the workplace, and seek a wider distribution of decision making in order to enhance dignity and assure a better quality of life.

This survey was conducted to learn what trade unions in some Western European countries*—and in Yugoslavia—are doing to improve job satisfaction through worker participation in management, emphasizing the transfer of some decision-making power directly to workers rather than to elected or appointed representatives such as shop stewards or unions.

Austria[1]

The Austrian Federation of Trade Unions, for several years now, has been engaged in an intensive discussion of worker participation in management. Its study committee on economic policy and humanization of the workplace reported to the federation's 1971 convention as follows:

> The introduction of automated processes means, in many instances, a loss in status and alienation of the worker who turns more and more into an exchangeable and replaceable cog in the wheel of an overpowering economic system. Everything has been planned for him: the machines; the tools; the organization of work; the work process; the work pace and work norms. At the same time it must be recognized that modern technology might free the worker from monotonous work and free him for creative work.
>   This possibility opens new tasks for the trade union movement. *It is not enough to merely assure the worker* a more just division of the fruits of labor. The modern *trade unions must assist workers in finding more satisfaction in their work experience.*

A second study committee, dealing specifically with "Worker participation at the National and Plant Level," recommended legislation providing for more—and more timely—information to the worker on all questions concerning his job; the right to be heard and informed on upgrading and other promotional opportunities, including training programs; the right to see his personnel file; and as much control as possible on how to perform his job.

These recommendations were adopted without dissent at the convention, but the emphasis of the debate was more on the expansion of rights for shop

---

* Austria, Belgium, Denmark, West Germany, Norway, Sweden, and Switzerland.

stewards and union representatives than on the rights of workers at the shop level. However, in his final address, the president of the federation noted: *"We are no longer merely interested in who gets what but also in who decides what. The division of decision making in the plant must concern us as much as the division of the fruits of production. And, next to achieving material benefits for the workers, we must also search for ways to improve the quality of life."*

To attack the problem of physical hardships, the federation has developed a *workplace simulator*, designed to measure the impact of heavy work, assembly-line work, and monotonous work, as well as of noise, heat, light, and draft on the heart and blood circulation. The simulator also demonstrates "model chairs" and other equipment for sedentary and nonsedentary occupations.

The Chamber of Labor[2] has a more skeptical view of the possibilities of direct worker participation in management. There is fear that the transfer of decision making to the workers may threaten the position of shop stewards or that employers, under the pretext of increasing job satisfaction, would in fact drive a wedge between workers and the union and that job satisfaction could be manipulated to the point where workers would find their unions dispensable.[3]

In short, the Chamber of Labor views worker participation in management essentially as a responsibility of shop stewards or union representatives, but not as one of workers at the shop level, a view shared by the majority of the Austrian union leadership.

A visit to a paper factory demonstrated the other side of the coin. The chairman of the shop stewards' committee complained bitterly about the lack of interest on the part of the workers, who leave everything to the shop stewards and refuse to assume responsibility though several such offers had been made by management. To deal with this inertia, the union and the company agreed in their last contract negotiations that in the future *all agreements on piece rates* will have to be negotiated and signed directly between the workers and the personnel office rather than, as previously, between the shop stewards and the personnel office. The new agreement for the metal industry (negotiated in the summer of 1972) contains a similar provision which will result in more active worker participation in wage determination.

A very large sector of Austria's industry (some 70 percent) is nationalized. Contrary to expectations, these enterprises are not in the forefront of experimentation to improve worker participation in management. They seem to be permanently up against the twin problems of underinvestment and overstaffing. Political difficulties are another factor: to stay alive and survive, the nationalized industries have to lean constantly and heavily on the political power of the shop stewards and trade unions. Therefore, "any experimentation to promote direct worker participation at the risk of antagonizing the shop stewards is out of the question."[4]

The Austrian Department of Labor has thus far paid little attention to the problem of job satisfaction and ways of dealing with it. Neither monotony nor assembly-line work is considered as yet to be of serious proportions since the number of workers involved is probably still very small. Nor does it have records or information on any work done in this field by private companies. It is believed, however, that in many places the workers may have a lot more to say about how to do their jobs than is generally assumed, the exact extent depending more often on the individual worker than on management.

Of a total of four plants visited, only two were engaged in serious efforts to promote democracy at the workplace: a bank and a metal-working plant. Both enterprises are strongly unionized, yet the bank employees and metal workers unions, respectively, have kept aloof from the experiments leaving cooperation completely to the shop stewards in both places.

The Bank fur Arbeit und Wirtschaft (Bawag for short) is wholly owned by the trade union federation, but has its own board of directors with independent powers. Its president[5] has long been a student of the problems of worker participation; prompted by a theoretical interest in the subject as well as a concern for the very high turnover rate in the bank, he established (with approval of the shop stewards' committee, but not of the union) a separate economic council whose members are elected directly by the employees. The council is entrusted with assuring the dignity of all employees at the workplace and advising management on the planning of work flow, technology, improvement of productivity, pace of work, and other economic matters.

There was, at the beginning, much skepticism and suspicion on the part of the shop stewards who feared dilution of their powers. A clear line of demarcation had to be drawn between their rights and those of the members of the economic council. The chairman of the shop stewards freely admitted that they had neither the time nor the expertise to take care of the problems which come before the economic council. Some minor jurisdictional conflicts between shop stewards and the economic council occurred, but they were settled by agreement.

The economic council has now been in operation for over two years and the results have been most pleasing to management as well as to employees. Morale has improved measurably. Many significant recommendations for increased efficiency have been realized and a continual dialogue between management and employees on shop problems has been set in motion.

Gebauer and Lehrner, metal-working plant, has gone further than any other enterprise in Austria to try democracy at the workplace. The company has established semiautonomous work groups for every department, composed of the department head, shop steward, foreman, and group spokesmen, the latter being representatives of small units within the department.[6] The work groups have full discretion to determine the flow of work and relative pay for various skills, as well as the hiring and firing of foremen and department heads. They are briefed on production schedules and other production problems and on the financial status of the company.

The company expects worker participation to be realized in five steps:

1. *encouragement* to think about the company, its production, goals, and needs;

2. *consultation* on a variety of problems;
3. *co-determination,* that is, equal say on a variety of matters;
4. *co-responsibility;*
5. *co-partnership.*

As of Spring 1972 Gebauer and Lehrner estimated that about 35 percent of its work force had completed the five stages and were now full participatory members of the company. Also, strenuous efforts are being made to eliminate monotony through further automation. Where this is not possible, the company tries job rotation. All employees are encouraged to be proficient in at least three different jobs. There is resistance to this plan, mostly from female employees, some of whom prefer monotonous work to accepting additional responsibility. Equalization in working conditions and benefits between white- and blue-collar workers has also been largely accomplished.

Company representatives as well as the shop stewards are enthusiastic about the experiment. In addition to rising wages, profits, and production, there have been no serious labor disputes, such as a strike. In fact, workers seem so eager to raise production standards that both company and shop stewards agreed to take steps curtailing some of the excessive zeal in order not to jeopardize margins for health and safety.

It was admitted by management that, practically speaking, department heads do have a great deal of discretion in deciding on the specific agenda for the meeting of the various working groups. Experience and further education and training would in due time, however, bring about a better balance so that workers themselves could play a larger part.

As noted earlier, the union in question is keeping a hands-off attitude, neither supporting nor opposing the program which, incidentally, is shared by the employers' federation.[7]

Belgium[8]

Belgium is an example of successful multiunionism in labor relations inasmuch as strong federations of Christian, socialist and liberal-conservative persuasions exist side by side, cooperating fairly harmoniously in daily operations. Yet they do have different views on worker participation in management.

The Christian Trade Union Federation is strongly occupied with the problem of humanizing the workplace. Several committees at the local and national level have prepared detailed reports and recommendations containing the following proposals:

define the rights of workers at the workplace;
establish objective rules for hiring and firing of workers;
experiment with the establishment of semiautonomous work groups along the Scandinavian model;

equalize blue- and white-collar workers in respect to all social legislation and insurance;

improve the law on shop stewards to give them more information and decision-making power.

The federation is also studying Scandinavian and Yugoslav models, but so far is not participating in actual experiments.

The Socialist Trade Union Federation is interested only in indirect workers' participation, opposing co-determination as practiced in the German coal and steel industry where representatives of workers have equal representation with full rights and responsibilities at the board of directors. The socialist federation believes union representatives cannot sit on both sides of the bargaining table. It is also against more decision-making power for rank-and-file workers because it fears the development of plant egoism and that workers would have to spend too much time in meetings, only "legitimate" unions can represent the workers' interests effectively. However, the federation is in favor of "workers' control," exercised through shop stewards or union representatives, the final goal being the self-management of workers.

Esperance-Longdoz a steel company, has redesigned machines to eliminate monotony and started a program of putting some blue-collar workers into white-collar categories in efforts to achieve democracy at the workplace. Though the plant is 100 percent organized, the unions are not involved in the program and are, in fact, critical of the "selectivity," meaning favoritism, which characterized such transfer into white-collar status.

The Belgian Department of Labor has established a "General Office for Work Improvement," which tries to serve as a clearinghouse on information for programs directed at "democracy at the workplace." None of the trade union officials interviewed so far had any contacts with this office or, in fact, even heard about it. Hardly a conference of unions passes today without some call for democracy at the workplace. Still, there is no consensus on what to do about it and as yet there are no programs in which unions are actively engaged.

Denmark[9]

In 1967 the Danish Federation of Labor adopted a resolution calling for a study of the problems of democracy at the workplace. The study produced two major recommendations: (1) promote in industry the establishment of joint committees of cooperation, and (2) seek legislation to provide workers with a fair share of the economic growth through establishment of a "profit and investment fund for wage-earners."

The first recommendation was realized in 1970, when the Trade Union Federation and the Employers Federation signed an agreement setting up in all enterprises with at least fifty employees "committees of cooperation." Their dual purpose was to promote efficiency and increase job satisfaction. The committees are composed of an equal number of representatives from management and labor. The forms of cooperation vary from plant to plant, but in the summer of 1971 metal worker unions were participating in at least seven experimental programs in the iron and metal industry. The companies had been selected in an effort to provide a variety of experiences, that is, different-sized firms and different types of production, composition of work force, and geographic location. Also, in view of the risks involved, only companies with an established solid base for cooperation were included.[10]

On the whole, the programs are moving forward very well; there have already been some very substantial improvements in productivity at some companies and, consequently, increases in pay, more liberal vacations with pay, and other benefits. Yet foremen have been reluctant to cooperate and there has been occasional friction among the workers: for instance, between male and female, skilled and unskilled, foreign and native.

West Germany[11]

Democracy at the workplace has been a matter of furious debate for a number of years now and a rich literature is available covering every feasible aspect of the problem. Thus far the discussion has produced few positive and practical attempts to come to grips with the issue.

Supporters of direct worker participation come from a variety of positions and directions. For example, social psychologists and industrial engineers are interested in better efficiency and productivity; religious and social reformers are concerned about a more ethical and just society; trade union and political leaders fear that "Germany might slip again into a totalitarian society unless the worker is integrated, into both society and the economy," critics of indirect worker participation seek more direct participation as a counterweight to the presumed conservatism of union bureaucracy. There are some "weak" enterprises which turn to worker participation as a way to save their plants from bankruptcy; there is the league of young employers which has developed a model constitution for plant democracy; and, finally, there are forces on the extreme left who view worker participation at the grassroots as a means to undermine capitalism.

The very strong support given to the demands for democracy at the workplace by the "New Left" may well explain the slowness and hesitancy which has marked the attitude of German trade unions toward the implementation of such demands. Initially, there was much sympathy for the idea both within the German Federation of Trade Unions (DGB) as well as among some of its affiliates, notably the Metal Workers Union, the Postal Workers, and the Public Employees Union. Today, however, this support has largely evaporated.

The DGB continues to pay lip service to the demands for direct representation at the workplace, but only as part of its broader demand for worker participation at the top; that is, representation on the boards of directors of companies, as practiced in the steel and coal industries. Most efforts of the trade unions are directed at this aspect of their legislative program rather than at bringing about worker participation at the plant level.

An important exception is the very serious interest in this subject taken by a top official of the Wirtschaft and Sozialwissenschaftliches Institut in Düsseldorf (an independent research arm of the federation), who sees the problem largely as one of engineering: creating new instrumentalities for worker participation is less important than changing the organization of work. And since there is a shortage of literature on such questions as work requirements, work methods, modes of production, and so on, "progress can be achieved only piecemeal and empirically." Every job should demand some ability, *decision making, opportunity to advance*, and *social contacts*. Job design and job enlargement as well as job rotation are some tools available to accomplish these objectives.[12]

The German Metal Workers Union, a few years ago, was the most outspoken proponent of the demand to give workers more decision-making powers at the shop level. Staff members critical of the institutionalization of the shop steward system drafted an amendment to the German Works Council Law, which would provide for the election of "group spokesmen": to give smaller units in the plant an opportunity to participate in the decision-making process along with the elected shop stewards. The initial reaction of the union leadership to this proposal was quite favorable, but it has since changed to absolute hostility, so much so that the matter can no longer even be discussed at union meetings or in union publications. They fear a weakening of the steward system or of the union, intergroup rivalries in the plant, and that management might use the system of "group spokesmen" to weaken union efforts to secure co-determination at the top.

The Postal Workers Union, too, at first embraced the idea of direct worker participation at the floor level, including the recommendation for group spokesmen, but later turned against the plan; a "model for democracy at the workplace," developed a few years ago by the union, has been abandoned and no copies are available. By contrast, the postal workers are now making a strong effort to strengthen the position of the shop stewards as well as of trade union representatives in the plant. Ironically, the union considers the plan for direct worker participation too supportive of "class harmony" whereas, of course, many supporters of the idea view it as an antagonistic instrumentality.

In sum, the German trade union movement is currently more interested in influencing national policies and achieving worker participation at the top rather than at the plant level. It has shown only sporadic interest in job satisfaction and done nothing to propose ideas which would give workers more power at the workplace, except efforts to improve political and technical training of the workers. Nor do any of the affiliated unions, it seems, currently participate in any of the several management programs which are being undertaken to experiment with various forms of direct worker participation, though shop stewards apparently cooperate in several such efforts.

The twin problems of assembly-line work and monotony are not considered too serious at the moment. The Metal Workers Union estimates that perhaps half of its membership is working on the assembly line, but the percentage is declining. As for monotony, the union believes that management is doing a great deal in view of the tight labor market which makes it difficult to attract labor for boring jobs. It should be noted, however, that the recent amendment to the *German shop steward law*, in force since January 1972, provides for the first time for some modest form of direct worker participation in management. The law gives *individual workers* a right to present complaints and make suggestions on how to perform their jobs. It also requires employers and shop stewards to consider the need for work humanization in planning new production or administrative procedures, methods of production, or jobs. Finally, the law specifically provides for plant assembly meetings of small units of workers and their participation in the negotiation of collective agreements.

Norway[13]

Norway is *the* country where worker participation at the grassroots is being tried in earnest, led by social scientists with the full support of management and the trade unions. Constructive employee-employer relations have been a mark of that country's industrial relations system for some time. Now an attempt is being made to go beyond consultation and negotiation between organizations of employers and workers to find ways and means for the transfer of some decision-making power to the workers themselves. Polls taken among workers convinced the union leadership, first, that the workers could handle more responsibility on their jobs and, second, that a large majority does want to assume such responsibility.

Since the matter of direct worker participation is new territory, it was agreed to embark on a slow step-by-step approach. A Joint Committee for Research and Development for Industrial Democracy was established which reviewed traditional approaches to worker participation in management. This was followed by an examination of additional areas to be covered by collective bargaining, such as providing more information on job problems to stewards and unions. Then the committee turned its attention to a number of enterprises, especially those with problems such as monotony, assembly-line work, and high turnover rates. If the companies were willing to participate in the experimental program, the committee commissioned a detailed examination of production processes and pay procedures. Action committees, composed equally of company and worker representatives, assisted in the examination.

Next, the committee developed several strategies to promote direct worker participation in job design, job enlargement and enrichment, job rotation, and semiautonomous work groups. Finally, the committee arranged for sensitivity training of foremen as well as for permanent self-perpetuating programs of upgrading workers, overcoming in the process occasional serious opposition from skilled workers.

The committee set itself the following goals for a "satisfactory organization of the workplace": each worker should have a minimum of diversity on his job assignment; an *opportunity to learn* and continue to learn; a minimum of decision-making power; a *minimum of recognition*; and an *opportunity to relate* to what he does or produces.

Although the trade unions are fully committed to this program, they are not directly involved because the experiments are confined essentially to production problems and do not yet affect an appreciable number of workers. Union interest in the program, however, is genuine, especially among such unions as metal workers, chemical workers, and paper workers. Some resistance has come from the ranks of skilled workers, expressing concern about the threatened breakdown of demarcation lines between skilled, semiskilled, and unskilled occupations. Similarly, there has been opposition to the shift in the mode of wage payments, that is, away from piece rates for work performed to a system of rewarding knowledge and experience regardless of actual work rendered. As elsewhere, there has also been some resistance from the foremen, since the semiautonomous work groups have assumed much of the responsibility which was formerly theirs.[14]

Norway seems to present the most conspicuous effort to enhance direct worker participation in management. It is an *article of faith that the more the worker is enabled to control his work, the more will he be willing to accept a positive commitment.* The results so far bear out this expectation. Progress in productivity has been substantial and so has been the growth in income of workers.

As in other countries, the nationalized industries and communal enterprises have done no better than enterprises in the private sector in decentralizing decision making. Because of this, the Department of Labor has recently established a special committee to look into the now ongoing experimental programs in the private sector, with a view of adopting some of the experiences for the public sector.

Sweden[15]

Interest in promoting worker participation in management arose almost simultaneously in government, labor, and management circles. In a speech of December 1970, the Swedish prime minister noted that while standards of living for workers had been much improved with respect to housing, nutrition, and education, the plant, where the worker spends some 2,000 hours annually, has changed little, and work may be as dissatisfying as ever. "The task of the 70s," he said, "must be to give workers a better surrounding and more say over his work at the workplace." [16]

The Swedish Federation of Labor then suggested an action program to "democratize enterprises," in response to which the government established three commissions dealing with job security, work environment, and the right to allocate work, respectively.

Management, plagued by serious labor shortages, high absentee rates (10 to 11 percent in the metal industry), job dissatisfaction, and, consequently, rising personnel costs, was more than receptive. To come to grips with these problems, one company, LKAB, experimented with job rotation, job enlargement, allocation and wider distribution of decision making, election of spokesmen for smaller units of workers, and, finally, a promise to put workers willing to work for better productivity on monthly salary.

As in Norway, labor-management relations in Sweden at the top level have been excellent for many years, but there has been little concern for the human problems of the workers at the workplace. This is now being changed; the Swedish Federation of Trade Unions is actively participating in a number of models designed to improve job satisfaction. A joint labor-management development council on cooperation has been established to provide a framework for the initiation of programs and dissemination of information. In 1969 the government set up a similar committee to sponsor experiments in the public sector. In May 1972 labor and management signed an "Agreement on Rationalization" which concerns productivity, job satisfaction, work environment, and job security.[17]

However, Swedish experimentation with democracy at the workplace has not been going on long enough to permit valid conclusions as to its effectiveness at this time. This was emphasized by both the trade union and the employers' federation. According to the latter, the problem of involving workers in decision making proved more difficult than expected for a number of reasons: because of strong, divergent views within the work force on the issue; because union cooperation, though assured on paper, was not always forthcoming to the desired extent; because of opposition from various levels of management, mostly foremen; and because of insufficient knowledge and skills of workers, which in some instances has meant that the foremen had to be brought back.[18]

An interesting model of worker participation in management is Scania's Automotive Plant's (SAAB) job design experiment in connection with establishing a new plant. In consultation with the works council, a development committee was established composed of a job analyst, job designer, and workers from the production section. This group discussed all tool and machine designs before construction began. Further, all quality control as well as care and maintenance of machines was now to be the responsibility of each worker. All technological changes are to be discussed with the workers affected and workers are to be encouraged to learn several jobs. Finally, opportunities for further training are to be provided in such fields as work simplification, product knowledge, technology, and economics.

As a result of their intensive consultations and preparation, the new plant, to be ready in early 1973, will have no assembly lines; instead, there will be seven so-called assembly groups which will be located along an automatic conveyor belt. Every fitter will have a chance to assemble the entire machine from beginning to end, an operation of about 45 minutes.

Switzerland[19]

Early in 1971 the Socialist Swiss Trade Union Federation adopted a program for worker participation in management, which was subsequently endorsed by the Christian as well as the Protestant Trade Union Federation. Apparently, this was the first time that all three federations agreed on a joint political initiative. They are seeking a nationwide referendum to the effect that the parliament legislate participation of workers and/or their representatives in management. The president of the socialist federation defined the purpose of their initiative as an effort "to secure workers participation at the workplace, in the plant, and at the board of directors of large enterprises." He denied any ideological motivation, stating that their concern was solely for a more balanced power position of labor and management at all levels. The spokesman for the Christian Trade Union Federation emphasized concern for the maintenance of harmony in industry which, he thought, was threatened because of the "changing character of control."

The spokesmen for the protestant federation stressed the "unsatisfactory hierarchic character of industry." Ownership of the means of production should not also entail unlimited control over those who work and some form of partnership should be substituted for the present authoritarian system.

Discussions with union representatives reveal a distinct preference for indirect worker participation and grave doubts about how the transfer of decision making to workers could be realized; the seriousness of the need for this was also emphasized. Small and middle-size enterprises predominate in Switzerland and neither antagonism nor alienation are considered of serious proportions. Also, unions have been quite successful in achieving unification in working conditions and social insurance of blue- and white-collar workers.

Yugoslavia[20]

The Yugoslav system of self-management has four functional components:

1.   The workers' collective, the plant meeting of all employees.

2. The workers' council, elected by the workers' collectives for 2 years, which approves all decisions involving planning, research, production, hiring and firing, investments, worker welfare, allocation of profits, and budget matters.

3. The management board, composed of technicians and also elected by the workers' collective for 2-year terms, decides on day-by-day plant operations.

4. The plant director, elected by the workers' council for a 4-year period, manages the plant and develops plans for production, sales, and investment. Formerly, he was responsible to the government, but now he is responsible to the three instrumentalities discussed above. He is elected on the basis of proposals submitted by a commission in which management and workers are equally represented.

One important fact should be noted. The system of self-management evolved primarily in order to get the government and the Communist party out of the economy, so as to eliminate political interference and bureaucratic excesses. By general consent, the major concern of the reform was not so much the expansion of workers' democracy as the promotion of economic and organizational efficiency.

This four-tier model of self-management is seen by some observers as proof that direct worker participation in management has its severe limits. By any measure, it is the members of the workers' council rather than the workers themselves who share, with the management board and the plant director, in the decision making. Tests conducted in various plants bear this out inasmuch as job satisfaction is substantially greater among members of the workers' council than among rank-and-file workers. The required rotation of membership on the council and management board helps in providing more workers with opportunities to participate in the decision-making process. It also guards against institutionalization and bureaucratization of the system except, of course, for the position of the plant director, who does not have to rotate and is thus in an advantageous position.[21]

It would seem fair to say that the system of self-management is superior to the former economy directed by a centralized bureaucracy. There have been over the past few years significant improvements in efficiency and productivity; the growth rate has been high and constant. Much less clear, however, is the impact of the reform on the decision-making power of rank-and-file workers, that is, on democracy at the workplace. At least one trade union official felt that the alienation of workers is worse now than before, because social values are changing and expectations are higher than they were under the former system.

Direct worker participation seems to fall short of expectations. For example, the plant director, although dependent on the workers' council for appointment and reappointment as well as for approval of all matters of significance, has considerable power. As a rule, he has superior knowledge and skills which members of the workers' council cannot hope to match since educational levels are still low in comparison with Western Europe, and more than 50 percent of the work force is said to have less than eight years of schooling.[22] Nevertheless, the opportunity for workers to share in the decision making is there, though it is sometimes not used or used to a very modest degree. Confronted by a choice of more say on how to do the job or more efficiency and subsequently more income, most workers presumably choose the latter, wherever they are—East or West.

Workers' councils vary greatly in effectiveness. They may be rubber stamps in some plants, and in others they do not exist at all. Nor, for that matter, are the government or the Communist party, now effectively deprived of all influence on the economy.

The government can intervene at any time if it finds that decisions of the workers' councils are contrary to the interest of the total economy; for example, if a plant charges what are considered inflationary prices or fails to set aside sufficient funds for investment or resorts to excessive borrowing for investment purposes. These are instances in which the government has intervened. Likewise, the government may choose not to intervene and have the enterprise suffer the consequence of irrational decisions such as, for instance, underinvestment. Moreover, the government, through its power of taxation and credit policies, can decisively affect the amount of income available for distribution to all employees of a plant. And finally it could, of course, also change the system of self-management or abandon it altogether.

The role of the trade unions under the system of self-management is apparently undergoing some changes. Formerly their responsibility was merely to support the concept of self-management and provide educational training opportunities for workers as well as members of the workers' council and of the management board. Unions were assigned a supportive role, but no direct voice in the management of the plant. The practice is somewhat different now. The workers' councils call on them not infrequently for assistance in evaluating proposals submitted to them by the plant director, especially those concerned with the distribution of income. Unions have also been called upon to mediate conflicts within the labor force; for instance, in disputes involving shares going to employees.

Trade unions expect to play an even bigger role in the emerging pattern of annual meetings of several enterprises in the same industry, designed to arrive at some uniformity on standards of pay and other working conditions. These meetings are attended by plant directors and representatives of the Chamber of Commerce, trade unions, and workers' councils. Understandings reached are called *social compacts*, which have to be approved by the workers' collectives of at least two thirds of all enterprises involved. These meetings resemble collective bargaining and it remains to be seen whether social compacts will spread and what they will do to the principle of self-management.

The system of self-management has not been embraced everywhere in Yugoslavia and has not meant complete industrial peace; in fact, *strikes* have increased rather than decreased. There have been more than 1,000 wildcat strikes during 1970 and 1971 over misconceptions and misunderstandings about the system of self-management, while others resulted from the disparity between expectation and fulfillment of self-management goals.[23]

These comments on the Yugoslav system cannot be concluded without noting the openness with which union officials are willing to discuss their system and to expose it to critical evaluation. Praise is restrained and there is no attempt to portray the system as a final answer in economic and social progress. The work "concept" comes up repeatedly, as does the suggestion that its realization will take a long time.

Fundamental factors to be considered in Yugoslavia are the backwardness of some parts of the country with respect to resources, technological equipment, skill, and education of the labor force, and comparatively low standards of living. It is the relative "underdevelopment" of the country which presents the most serious obstacle to its transition to a modern industrial state, and it remains to be seen whether the self-management system is the optimal answer to overcome this obstacle.

International Organizations of Labor[24]

Thus far only peripheral interest in workers' participation at the lower level has been expressed and discussed by international organizations of labor.

The International Confederation of Free Trade Unions (ICFTU,) in February 1972, published the results of an inquiry on "Some Aspects of Workers Participation." However, the survey dealt only with works councils, worker representation on boards of management, and profit-sharing systems. It seems obvious that workers' participation in management as seen by the ICFTU means indirect participation rather than the direct transfer of decision making to workers at the shop level. Nor has the Trade Union Committee on the Common Market, as far as could be ascertained, taken any specific interest or action in regard to rank-and-file democracy at the workplace.

The International Metal Workers Federation, at its meeting in September 1969, proposed the creation of an ad hoc committee to study the problem of democratization in industry. The committee, which includes one member each from Germany, Scandinavia, Italy, Belgium, and Great Britain, and two representatives from the United States, submitted a working paper on democratization composed of five parts: (1) a review of the historic development of society; (2) a summation of ideas and principles, that is, the different forms of democratization in the plants, the company, and society; (3) analysis of different national experiences such as co-determination, control by workers, self-management, and works councils; (4) problems of national and supranational concentration; and (5) conclusions.

The conclusions and recommendations argue for an expansion of worker participation through worker representatives, that is, shop stewards and unions. Only one short paragraph refers to direct worker participation, stating that "the development of human capabilities, information, communication and human contacts, liberation from exploitation, suppression and alienation in work and in leisure time are vital factors in democracy in the plant and in society."

A more specific resolution was adopted at the congress of the International Metal Workers Federation, held in October 1971. It reads as follows:

Democracy at the Workplace

A fundamental demand is for *more humanised organisation of work*, entailing shorter working hours, safety and health protection at work, a radical improvement of work environment. The mental constitution of the human being, his inclinations and his creativity must determine the work process, in contrast to the present trend, which degrades man to being a mere part of the machine. This can be achieved only through true democratisation at the work place.

Democratisation of the plant demands the elimination of all arbitrary managerial authority and privileges. There must be respect for personality and the free expression of opinion at all levels and workers must have an effective voice in all matters affecting their work. This requires *expanded rights in the plant for workers and trade unions, as well as guaranteed full grievance rights under the terms of collective contracts.*

In sum, "democracy at the workplace" and "humanization of work" have become regular and popular items on the agenda of trade union meetings throughout Western Europe, though there is no agreement on their precise meaning or specific strategies to accomplish these goals. Some favor them as a means of "destroying" the system, others as a bridge to "save" the system. In between, a growing number of trade union leaders are less concerned about either ideology, but convinced that unions' responsibilities and obligations must extend to the worker's need for human dignity and respect as well as to his material needs.

From the discussions this author had with unions and management, and from reading their literature, the following conclusions emerge as a *tentative* consensus on the conditions for the successful transfer of decision-making power to workers:

1. It must not adversely affect efficiency—and, therefore, workers' income— or both management *and* workers will oppose it.

2. It must not threaten or impinge upon established rights of stewards and/ or union—or there will be strenuous opposition from these sources.

3. Enterprises with an established history of constructive employer-employee relations offer the best prospects for pilot projects.

4. A broad program of education and skill training for all workers has to be an integral part of all programs for humanizing work.

5. The context of a full-employment economy may be a necessary condition to ease fears that improved efficiency will result in unemployment.

6. More research is required on alternative modes of production, alternative methods of working and work requirements.

NOTES

1. *Austria*
Interviews

Anton Benya	President, Austrian Federation of Trade Unions
Bank für Arbeit & Wirtschaft	President Fritz Klenner Com. Rat Garcis, Chairman of Economic Council Josef Dunkel, Chairman, Shop Stewards
Friedrich Fuerstenberg	Prof. Linz
Gebauer & Lehrner	Dr. Richard Lehrner, President Alfred Erner, Director, Personnel Kurt Gramauf, Chief Shop Steward
Rudolf Ing. Hauser	Minister for Social Affairs
W. Ing. Hrdlitschka	President, Chamber of Labor
Dr. Gerhard Weissenberg	Chamber of Labor
Sepp Wille	Metal Workers Union
Prof. Ernst Winkler	Institute for Arts & Sciences
Dr. Robert Zimmerman	Nationalized Industries

Literature

Arbeit und Wirtschaft	Issues of May and September 1971
Friedrich Fuerstenberg	*Mitwirkung der Arbeitnehmer im Betrieb* (1970)
Institut für Gesellschaftspolitik	*Arbeiter und Augestellte im Technischen Wandel* (1971)
Fritz Klenner	*Chance oder Illusion* (1970)
Osterr. Gewerkschaftsbund	*Wirtschaftspolitik und Vermenschlichung des Arbeitsplatzes* (1971)

2. A semipublic institution separate from, but controlled by, the Federation of Trade Unions.

3. Subjective job satisfaction is not necessarily a sign of progress since expectations of workers can be reduced through manipulations in order to achieve satisfaction. Also, not all workers dislike monotony or desire more responsibility on their jobs. A

survey sponsored by the trade union federation in April 1969 in ten large plants found more than two thirds of white-collar workers and more than half of blue-collar workers well satisfied with their jobs. "There was altogether not enough information available on the subject matter to risk experimenting with new instrumentalities which may impinge on the well established position of the shop stewards."

4. Personal communication to the author by an official long associated with the Personnel Administration of the nationalized industry.

5. Professor Fritz Klenner, who is also the author of a book on the subject, *Chance oder Illusion*, published in 1970.

6. These work groups meet every four weeks and discuss all problems concerning the work assignments. To insure success, the company also established a sensitivity program for department heads and foremen, as well as training programs for representatives of workers.

7. The preference of union leadership for indirect rather than direct worker participation in management was clearly evident at a one-week international trade union seminar, held in June 1972 and sponsored by the trade union federation. The program at Gebauer and Lehrner was explained and debated; fears of creating competing instrumentalities, of plant egoism, of alienating workers from their unions, and of creating new hierarchies took precedence over concern for the transfer of more decision-making power to the workers themselves.

8. *Belgium*
Interviews

George Anderson	U.S. Labor Attaché
George Debunne	President, Federation du Travail Belique (Socialist)
N. Jaraux	Christian Metalworkers Federation

9. *Denmark*
Interviews

Danish Metal Workers Federation	C. Rasmussen, President Charles Hansen, Vice President M. Sheffin, Economist

Literature

Aake Anker-Ording	*Industrielle Demokratie in Scandinavian* (Oslo. 1972)
Association of the Iron & Steel Industries	*Experimental Collaboration in the Ironindustry* (1972)

10. Danfoss A/S, Nordborg; A/S N. Foss Electric, Hillcrd; A/S Haustrup's Fabriker, Odense; Hjbjerg Maskinfabrik A/S, Hjkjerg; A/S Nordiske Kabel—og Traadfabriker, Glostrup; Philips Radio A/S, Copenhagen; Scandinavian Airlines System, Kastrup.

11. *West Germany*
Interviews

Dr. G. Grunwald	Ebertstiftung, Bad Godesberg
Freidrich W. Kaltenborn	Deutscher Gewerkschaftsbund, Düsseldorf

Dr. Rudolf Kuda   I. G. Metal, Frankfurt

Dr. G. Leminsky   Wirtschafts und Sozialwissenschaftliches Institut, Deutscher Gewerkschaftsbund

Hans Matthoefer   I. G. Metal, Frankfurt

Gerhard Scherhorn   Prof. Hochschule fur Wissenschaft & Politik, Hamburg

Fritz Vilmar   Carl Backhaus Stiftung, Hamburg

Ewald Wehner   Postgewerkschaft, Frankfurt

Literature

Ahrensburger Modell   *Soziologische Aspekte der innerbetrieblichen Mitbestimmung* (1971)

Bundesministerium für Arbeit & Soziale Ordnung   *Reform der Betriebsverfassung* (1972)

Richard Hoffmann   *Erweiterung der innerbetrieblichen Mitbestimmung, Gewerkschaftliche Monatshefte* (December 1968)

Karl Otto Hendrich   *Demokratisierung und Leistungsgesellschaft* (1972)

Institute of Labor Studies (Geneva)   *Workers Participation in Germany* (1969)

G. Leminsky   *The Future Role of Trade Unions in the Welfare State* (1972)

Erhard Lenk   *Mitbestimmung* (1970)

Hans Matthoefer   *Mitbestimmung am Arbeitsplatz* (1968)

Ernst Piehl   *Mitbestimmung aus der Sicht der Neuen Linken* (1970)

Helmut Pinther   *Demokratie am Arbeitsplatz* (1970)

Fritz Vilmar   *Mitbestimmung am Arbeitsplatz* (1971) *Menschenwurde im Betrieb* (1969)

12. In a recent speech, Dr. Leminsky also argued that management, which is always developing very careful plans for investment, production, and work organization, must begin to think about the impact of such decisions on the labor force in order to avoid hardships, monotony, lack of creativity, early aging, and so on. Professor Gerhardt Scherhorn, of the University of Economics and Politics in Hamburg, notes that economic theory has concerned itself solely with problems of production and distribution while ignoring job satisfaction. He favors substitution of a polyarchic system for the present hierarchic system of decision making; reduction of levels of hierarchy in the plant; a requirement that all jobs be made meaningful; and, finally, that workers be given an opportunity to participate in the formulation of goals for the company.

13. *Norway*

Interviews

Anker-Ording Aake   Author, Oslo

Norwegian Federation of Labor

Einar Thorsrud

Literature

Anker-Ording Aake

Einar Thorsrud

———

Tor Halverson, Second Secretary
Miriam Nordahl, Staff

Work Research Institute, Oslo

Betriebsotemokratie (Oslo: 1972)

A *Strategy for Research and Social Change in Industry* (Oslo: Work Research Institute, 1969)

Democratization of Work Organizations (Oslo: Work Research Institute, 1972)

14. At another level, the Central Trade Union Federation is making a strong effort to secure in the upcoming collective bargaining negotiations with management an equalization of all working conditions for blue- and white-collar workers.

15. *Sweden*
Interviews

Lennart Granstroem

Ted Lidbom, Labor Relations Specialist

Erik Karlson
Birger Viklund

Swedish Employers Federation

Swedish Federation of Labor

Swedish Metal Workers Federation

Literature

Arne Geijer (President, Swedish Trade Union Federation)

David Jenkins

Bert Lindquist (Manager, LKAB Co.)

Alva Myrdal

Swedish Employers Federation

Saab-Scania

Report on "Industrial Democracy in the Seventies" (1971)

The New Face of Swedish Labor (1971)

Aspects of Employee Participation (1971)

Ungleichheit im Wohlfahrtsstant (1971)

The Changing Work Environment (December 1970)

Scania's Automotive Plant's Job Design Experiment (1971)

16. Arne Geijer, president of the Swedish Federation of Labor, in a brochure published in 1971, called for an integration of the production processes with decision-making and control functions in order to "*increase personal responsibility and with it job satisfaction within the enterprise.*"

17. Ted Lidbom, the labor federation specialist on industrial relations, in an article, "Industrial Democracy," outlined four conditions which would determine the success or failure of efforts to promote democracy at the workplace: (1) the gap between the worker's needs for job satisfaction and his material gains must be narrowed; (2) *all* workers must be given the opportunity to share in the decision making; (3) participation of workers must be based on current skill and knowledge and must be conditional on further training; and (4) direct worker participation in management must not impair or impinge upon the rights and status of union representatives in the plant.

18. The spokesman for the employers' federation held, as a preliminary opinion, that job enlargement, rotation, and reconstruction would hold more promise than semiautonomous work groups; also that experience gained in one enterprise could not easily be transferred to another. A leaflet, published by the Swedish Employers Federation in December 1970, gives a good description of the goals of semi-autonomous groups and the changes they have brought about.

19. *Switzerland*
Interview

Roland Roost

Secretary, Building & Woodworkers Union (Zurich)

20. *Yugoslavia*
Interviews

Bogdan Jerkovic

Belgrade

Bogdan D. Kovcic

Sociologist, Slovenian Federation of Labor, Lenbljana

Neca Jovanov

Director of Research, Yugoslav Federation of Labor, Belgrade (CTUY)

Milos Marinovic

Press Officer (CTUY)

Literature

Administrative Science Quarterly (March 1971)

"Control, Participation, and Effectiveness in Yugoslav Industrial Organization"

Heinz Duerr

Die Realität der Arbeiterselbstverwaltung in Yugoslavien (1972)

Human Relations (1970)

"Workers Councils in Yugoslavia"

Fritz Klenner

Chance oder Illusion (1970)

Peter van Oertzen

Erfahrungen und Moeglichkeiten der Betrieblichen Mitbestimmung (1971)

Berwig Roggemann

Das Modell der Arbeiterselbstverwaltung in Yugoslavien (1970)

21. One important fact should be noted. The system of self-management evolved primarily in order to remove the influence of the government and the Communist party from the economy so as to eliminate political interference and bureaucratic excesses. The major concern of the reform, by general consent, was not so much the expansion of democracy at the workplace as the promotion of economic and organizational efficiency.

22. Many plant directors openly boast about the extent of their discretionary powers; in the Western industrial countries such powers are severely restrained by the strength of the trade unions, whereas in the Eastern socialist countries they are restrained by the state. As one Yugoslav plant director put it: "If I have the support of the workers' council, I can do almost anything and if I do all right by the workers, that is, raise their wages or improve other working conditions, I don't have to worry about the workers' council either."

23. See Heinz Duerr, *Die Realität der Arbeiterselbstverwaltung in Yugoslavien* (1972). Some strikes were apparently successful as, for instance, a strike in March 1971 of more than 600 workers at a railroad equipment company, protesting a

reduction of wages of some 20 percent. The measure was rescinded by the plant director after the company, on intervention of the Communist party (!), was enabled to get a much needed credit from the bank to meet its payroll.

24. *International Organizations of Labor*

Interviews

Ralph Bergman	Automation Branch, International Labour Organization (Geneva)
N. Colerick	International Confederation of Free Trade Unions (Brussels)
Ivar Noren	General Secretary, International Metalworkers Federation (Geneva)
Harry Pollak	Labor Specialist, U.S. Mission to the Common Market (Brussels)
Ken Walker	Acting Director, Institute of Labor Studies (Geneva)

Literature (General)

Daniel Bell	*Work and Its Discontents* (Boston: Beacon, 1956)
Paul Blumberg	*Industrial Democracy* (New York: Schocken, 1968)
S. Fine	"Role of Job Design in Workers Participation in Management" (Paper presented at World Congress of Industrial Relations Research Association, July 1970)
ICFTU	"Some Aspects of Workers Participation" (February 1972)
———	*Conference on Technological Change and Human Development* (1969)
International Industrial Relations Association	*Social Innovations in Industrial Relations,* by Friedrich Furstenberg (1970)

Epilogue
The Product of Work Is People

Phillip G. Herbst

> The assertion that the product of work is people is
> evidently either false or a gross oversimplification.
> For one cannot entirely disregard that, as a result of
> work, we also produce automobiles, color television
> sets, and baby diapers, not to speak of papers for
> conferences, all of which may have some value as
> well.

The significance of what we do is not always evident while we are doing
it. As children, most of us were absorbed in various games either by ourselves
or with others. At the time this was something which involved us intensely
and we took it to be an aim in itself. In retrospect, we are able to recognize
that we were then developing qualities needed to help us make the passage into adulthood. The same holds for the tasks in which we engage in the adult
phase of our lives. At that time our concern is almost entirely with our

relations with the outside world and we become almost oblivious of ourselves. What absorbs us then are our careers, our family, and whatever we do in the way of changing the nature of our environment. The nature of the outer world is seen as the source of the various forms of sensuous enjoyments, of our happiness and our distress. Our intellectual, social, and physical skills are developed and become centered on understanding and finding ways for controlling our environment. At this stage our success or failure appears almost objectively measurable by ourselves and also by others in terms of how much we have achieved. However, it is not a time during which one is able to develop one's wisdom so one does not as yet really know what is of value and what is not and one cannot be sure what is success or failure.

As we begin to enter the postadult period something like a figureground reversal may take place in our values and perceptions. What appeared to be the product begins to stand out as almost a by-product. Then we may become aware that it was not after all how much or how little we achieved that matters but how we went about achieving it. What we have achieved is always in the past and, as soon as achieved, it is no longer truly related to us. However, what we become, our qualities as human beings and our potential for future development, is always in the here and now. This is the product that remains, after everything else is gone, whether we recognize this or not.

The product of our adult life is like a shell, which protects the growth of the fruit inside. As soon as we realize that the shell is not of essential value, we may make use of what we find in ourselves. However, it is possible that one uses work and inner strength to produce no more than an outer shell of success, possessions, and pretensions, and then toward the end of one's career, suddenly, one may quite literally experience oneself as an empty, burnt-out, and rigid shell, and find that one has gained little of value.

During the early part of adult life the choice of what we set out to achieve appears the critical decision, whether it be accumulating a sizeable amount of money or just enough to buy a motorcycle, winning the Nobel Prize, or becoming a university professor. We may feel that we have made a superior choice in seeking to help others or to create a better kind of society. However, it is possible to be just as selfish or obtuse in one's desire to help or save others as in any other kind of pursuit. The significant but less obvious choices at any point in our career lie in the means which we adopt to achieve our aims. It is these which at any time express our human qualities and determine those qualities which we create and develop in ourselves. These are choices which we may make consciously, sometimes intuitively, and often without realizing that we have made them at all or what are their implications. Thus, if we are scientists, we may be able to develop qualities such as nonattachment to theories and beliefs, the capacity to accept that one does not know (or what De Cusa* called "learned ignorance"), the capacity for sustained concentration

---

* G. Heron, *Of Learned Ignorance* (A translation of De Cusa's *De Docta Ignorantia*) (London: Routledge & Kegan Paul, 1954).

on a problem, and that for not biasing facts in favor of a view which one likes or against a view which one dislikes.

It is qualities such as these in whatever kind of work undertaken which become essential during the postadult period when, having developed ourselves in relation to the environment, we turn back to gain understanding and self-control. However, qualities of this kind also enable us to work more effectively during the course of our careers. Whatever success is achieved becomes a source of satisfaction insofar as it confirms that we have developed qualities which we did not have before. When this is not the case, the success achieved will not provide the feeling that we have achieved something of value.

The relevance of human qualities to the society in which we live is easier to see if we go back in time. Europe's distinctive achievement of the past was not simply the development of industrial organizations and science, but the human qualities and values of the Protestant Ethic which, from the time of the Reformation, were built into the institutions we have inherited and which in both the Western world and in the Eastern European countries continue to make these developments possible.

Institutions and organizational forms surviving over many centuries may become objects of veneration; they enshrine people's values, although what they are about may no longer be known. Institutional ideals, however, may remain visible and more or less unchanged even when the value base has shifted or reversed itself. For example, people may retain their criteria for what they consider is a good civil servant or good work, although they may not be clear why some qualities are good and others not.

Thus, while the Protestant Ethic justified itself by achievements in industrial, economic, and scientific development, scarcely anybody today knows what these were. At the same time recognition existed during the initiating phase that what were initially the elite values of an emerging middle class would come to apply to the working class as well. Even at the end of the nineteenth century, however, it was not yet predictable that this would occur.

As the value base reversed itself, industrial, economic, social, and scientific progress either became aims in themselves or it was taken for granted that these would more or less automatically assure human contentment and happiness. For some time the ideal society seemed just around the corner. A gulf does not necessarily exist here between the older and younger generations as far as these expectations are concerned; there is more a feeling of mutual frustration because of an out-of-phase development.

The rising standard of living has led to an increased level of satisfaction— and also to increasing discontent and human unhappiness. If, however, the increased level of satisfaction is canceled out by increased expectations, only discontent and unhappiness remain. And also, to the extent that experienced satisfaction is canceled out, it can no longer be used to compensate for the experience of distress. For the older generation, the progress achieved since the end of World War II has gone so much beyond what was thought possible at the time that distress tends to be well compensated for by the experience of satisfaction with what has been achieved. But for the younger middle-class generation, the group which at present is most exposed to distress, no achievable satisfaction provides sufficient compensation. The gain achieved by adding more cars or swimming pools to the family property is little more than marginal at best, and there is a feeling of surfeit.

Thus, while one generation is predominantly concerned with increasing the level of satisfaction, the other is concerned with decreasing distress. Because these are two quite different concerns, the out-of-phase phenomena of the two generations result. It has been argued that there is always a gulf between generations. However, this overlooks that the two generations were in phase at the time of the German National Socialist revolution in their search for a way of overcoming distress, nor was there any basic generational conflict in Western Europe immediately before World War I.

There is no question that economic, industrial, scientific, and technological developments are eminently worthwhile goals, aims which can be achieved by societal change and which can and do increase human satisfaction and comfort. The first walk on the moon created a considerable amount of enthusiasm, the motorcar may be a more convenient form of transportation, and the modern supermarket may be a better place for shopping than the old corner grocery store (or maybe not) but in any case none of these achievements have an enduring effect on people's experience of either distress or happiness. If there is something of enduring value which resulted, then this lies in the exploration and development of previously unknown modes of human potentialities and in the conditions provided for the development of human qualities, intellectual, social, and moral which was the now almost forgotten initial purpose of the reformers.

In developed Western societies, then, we find at present a high development of whatever provides satisfaction, but not in the understanding of how to overcome distress. Satisfaction derives from whatever can be obtained from the environment, and this is something society is geared to provide. However, the achievement of contentment, peace of mind, happiness, and the development of wisdom, is not obtainable from the environment in the same way, but is found in ourselves, and to achieve them involves a different form of work. These are not based on what we can get from the environment, but they determine how we relate ourselves to our environment.

Whenever we encounter what appears to be an either/or situation, we need to investigate whether we have not constructed for ourselves a false dilemma. The production of food, shelter, and the basic necessities of life is essential for human existence. However, if this becomes an all absorbing and single-minded social pursuit, we run the risk of losing our capacity for determining the direction of our lives and can no longer find what is worthwhile living for. Conversely, societies which become totally committed to aims beyond the satisfaction of material needs may not survive long enough for people to achieve anything worthwhile.

A dilemma emerges when it is assumed that a choice has to be made.

INDEX